Computer Science in Social and Behavioral Science Education

COMPUTER SCIENCE IN SOCIAL AND BEHAVIORAL SCIENCE EDUCATION

DANIEL E. BAILEY
University of Colorado

Editor

EDUCATIONAL TECHNOLOGY PUBLICATIONS
ENGLEWOOD CLIFFS, NEW JERSEY 07632

Library of Congress Cataloging in Publication Data

Main entry under title:

Computer science in social and behavioral science
    education.

        Includes bibliographies.
        1. Social sciences--Study and teaching (Higher)
--United States--Addresses, essays, lectures.
2. Psychology--Study and teaching (Higher)--United
States--Addresses, essays, lectures. 3. Computer-
assisted instruction--United States--Addresses,
essays, lectures. I. Bailey, Daniel Edgar,
1930-
H62.C58483   300'.7'1173   77-25087
ISBN 0-87778-101-X

Printed in the United States of America.

Library of Congress Catalog Card Number:
77-25087.

International Standard Book Number:
0-87778-101-X.

First Printing: February, 1978.

PREFACE

This volume contains papers developed over three successive summer workshops with National Science Foundation support. The first two workshops were part of College Teacher Summer Institutes of the NSF College Teacher Program. The final session was held in 1974 as a College Faculty Workshop of the National Science Foundation Division of Higher Education in Science. The papers in this volume are the product of writing projects initiated during that workshop. The general outline of this collection was apparent in 1974, but really did not jell with tangible, polished papers until the summer of 1976. Over the intervening period, many papers were written and re-written, with eventual survival of about 40 percent of the initial efforts.

On behalf of the contributors to this volume, and on my own part, I wish to express gratitude for the fine job done in managing the business and secretarial aspects of the workshop and in production of the manuscript. Three people in particular stand out in this regard, Loretta Ramsey, Robbie Toney, and Susan Tokarz. Other people too numerous to list here have made valuable contributions to this collection and I hope that individual authors of papers will express to these people my gratitude for a job well done.

Portions of the work reported here, and portions of the development of the papers included in this volume, were supported by NSF grants GY-9379, GY-10506, and GZ-3431. The support of the Foundation is gratefully acknowledged by the editor and each contributor to this volume.

INTRODUCTION

Daniel E. Bailey
University of Colorado

This volume includes a wide variety of materials relevant to the use of computers as instructional tools in the social and behavioral sciences. It does not cover the entire field, however, for to do so with a reasonable degree of depth and accuracy would require a collection of volumes. The coverage of this volume, on the other hand, is representative of the main stream of current developments.

Two general areas are not represented in this volume. One of these is computer-assisted instruction systems, such as TICCIT and PLATO. The other omission is in the use of mini-computers in the instructional laboratory. These areas are missing because of a conscious decision by the editor. It seemed that these two topics required a volume of their own. On the side of computer-assisted instruction systems, we are beginning to see the emergence of large-scale systems. I believe that much of what is discussed in the papers of this collection will find a place in the large-scale computer-assisted instruction systems with improvements, increased sophistication, and highly enhanced human interfaces.

On the other hand, the use of mini-computers in the instructional setting is very much like the use of other computer systems in the same setting, or it involves a development of still another topic, real-time computing. Again, the editorial decision was consciously made to exclude topics paying explicit attention to mini-computers *as such*. A number of references to mini-computer based educational applications are made in the papers in this collection. However, such references make it clear that the mini-computer connection is incidental to the more general issues being discussed.

There are two issues that I feel necessary to discuss briefly in this introduction. The first is the issue of responsibility of the social and behavioral scientist to become technically competent. The second issue has led me to include the final two-paper section, "The Bottom Line," namely the issue of intellectual and factual honesty in computing. In a way, the second issue is a simple reflection of the first. We would not need to have a mathematician and computer scientist like Professor Andree tell us simple things like "computers can produce answers that are wrong," if we were responsible members of the scientific community.

In a number of the papers included in this collection there are pleas for special treatment by computer centers for the social and behavioral sciences. In some of the papers there are appeals for special courses, special processors, etc., motivated by a description of students who are fleeing from "hard subjects." Although these pleas and appeals are honest and sincere, they reflect a state of development that must be overcome before the social and behavioral sciences can expect to have their needs met, either by those fields themselves or by others.

As for pleas for special treatment in computer centers, I must object that such pleas come from inadequate preparation and experience in the computer field. It may appear that the physical scientists, engineers, and mathematicians get all of the "goodies" offered up by the computing center. Indeed, this may be true, and in specific instances it is probably safe to conclude that there is special bias in that direction by computer center operations staff and administration and in the funding of computer activities. However, in the vast majority of institutions, the fact of unequal distribution can be attributed to the productivity of the physical and mathematical sciences and the technological fields. Mathematical software was not provided by the center simply because the center favored mathematicians. The engineering bent of some centers was not somehow provided by the center because of bias in favor of engineering. Physicists do not get better service because the administration likes physicists better than they like psychologists. What is operating, on the other hand, is the fact that mathematicians have developed mathematical software, engineers have developed engineering software and hardware, physicists have developed sophisticated software and systems for their problem solving needs, etc. But social and behavioral scientists have often only asked "where is mine?" When complaints are aired that large files and memory allocations are necessary for social science computing, and that the charging algorithms penalize such use, it often means that the complainer is unaware of basic facts of computer life. The physical scientist brought money and technical expertise with him when he demanded high-speed, high-accuracy computer processors. The social and behavioral scientists must also look out for their own best interests—a task for which they have unfortunately shown little talent. Complaining creates few friends and no resources!

I could continue for many pages in the discussion of topics like those in the above paragraph. However, I will simply move on to a related topic with a caveat for social and behavioral scientists: put your own house in order instead of envying or complaining about someone else's orderly house.

The second issue I wish to bring up here is that of awareness on the part of the social and behavioral scientist about the possibilities of being misled by computer results. It often comes as a shock to the unsophisticated computer user that the numbers that come pouring out of a computer do not necessarily have any meaning. The numerical consequences of a computation are deterministic, but they are not what they may seem to be! The two papers at the end of this book, in the section titled "The Bottom Line," are perhaps the most important papers in the book.

In 1970 there was a paper published in the *Journal of the American Statistical Association* that called into question at least a decade of research in subject areas where computer use of statistical packages was involved—including a very major portion of the social and behavioral sciences, biology, medicine, etc. This paper demonstrated that results obtained from widely used statistical packages were, with high probability, thoroughly without accuracy under conditions normally encountered by social and behavioral scientists. Even today, more than a half decade later, and after many more such studies have appeared, only a very small number of social and behavioral scientists are aware of these startling results. Fortunately, writers of statistical packages seem to be aware of the problem and we can hope that higher standards of accuracy accrue to the unaware social and behavioral scientist.

I have one more critical comment to make to my colleagues. I am amazed at the willingness of the social and behavioral science disciplines to permit undergraduate students to dictate the content and legitimacy of concerns in the disciplines. I have often heard the declarative: "We cannot require mathematics or computer science of our students because they do not want to work in those areas." Why should anyone permit uninformed individuals fleeing from something (i.e., not genuinely attracted) dictate the standards in the social and behavioral science disciplines? Until the social and behavioral science faculties are willing to say to their students that it is required that they be prepared in technical disciplines, the social and behavioral sciences will remain unprepared to cope with the modern world of technology.

It is my hope that by making this book available, we will have added one small additional element to the development of technical competence in the social and behavioral sciences.

Editor's Comments on the Papers

Part I: The Place of Computer Science
in Social and Behavioral Science

This section addresses general issues concerning the place of computer science in social and behavioral science education. As such, this section is at a relatively high level of generality, saving until later sections papers discussing development of details, and practical implementation. It is particularly fitting that Ronald E. Anderson has provided the lead-off paper. He has been a leader in the field of computer applications development in the social sciences over the last several years.

The Anderson paper begins with the assumption that we are going to have computer science in social and behavioral science education. It seems appropriate that this assumption should be leavened immediately with the question of "how much?" Thus, Forrest H. Armstrong's work was selected as the second paper. The degree that computer technology, or any technology for that matter, intrudes into the "soft sciences" is a serious issue. Those of us who were involved in writing this project are computer buffs, and thus we are suspect. Or, at least, our recommendations to do this or that with computers should be suspect, and put to the test of practical benefit, cost-effectiveness, student effects, and the like. Armstrong's paper is a thrust in that direction by a computer buff.

If we are going to have computer science for the social and behavioral sciences, what do we have to do with the computer facilities that are available, and what new facilities are needed, to make the enterprise viable? The paper by Richard A. Wiste and Norman E. Sondak addresses these issues. Early drafts of this paper were stronger statements by orders of magnitude! However, I exercised my editorial prerogatives and pressed the authors into a comparatively sedate point of view. Computer center directors (and that includes myself) will find this paper provocative, if not outright infuriating. The authors place themselves in a position much like the "radicals" of the 1960's, on the outside. They will find a few sympathetic ears of computer center directors and administrative officials in charge of allocating resources, but not very many. The best advice that can be given here, in my opinion, is: "join the establishment and enjoy success." If we social and behavioral scientists become diligent in attempts to require competency of our colleagues, then we will achieve the laudable goals outlined by Wiste and Sondak, and not before.

Only two disciplines are addressed in this section, with regard to general issues of implementation of computer related curricula in the social and behavioral sciences. These two disciplines are psychology and political science. Among the social and behavioral sciences, these disciplines perhaps represent the poles of development, with psychology being by far the most extensively developed in computer science. The other social sciences, such as sociology, anthropology, economics, etc., are probably in the intermediate regions of development. Thus, it is fitting that the two papers (i.e., those by B. James Starr and by Kendall L. Baker, James W. Hottois, and Stuart H. Rakoff) that deal with general curriculum issues in computer science aspects of social and behavioral science education come from these two disciplines.

The final paper of this section, by Ronald L. Koteskey, Fred S.

Halley, James M. Swanson, and Robert J. Tracy, addresses some general issues not discussed elsewhere in this volume. Their section on assumptions and goals is of particular interest. Then, their discussion of applications areas serves as a high-level precursor to the material that follows in the rest of the volume, particularly in Parts II, IV, and V.

Part II: Statistics and Methodology

For many years I was engaged in teaching statistics to psychology students, both at the graduate and the undergraduate level. I even wrote a text that was highly praised in the review literature, but failed to pay enough royalties to compensate me for the paper used in drafting the book! Now, I am liberated! I no longer teach statistics. However, if I did, this second section of this volume would be the most important section of the book. Very practical and useful points of view, specific references, and some very pregnant ideas are presented in this section. The papers are germinal, but not complete in their coverage. However, that is what attracts me to these papers—the thoughtful teacher of statistics and methodology will find these papers provocative, and the innovative teacher will build on that provocation!

For the novice, the lead-off paper of this section, by James M. Sakoda, Ronald E. Anderson, Francis Sim, and Richard A. Wiste, provides a sound overview of the relevant topics and issues. The specificity and practicality is immediately brought to a high level in the paper by Richard S. Lehman, B. James Starr, and Kenneth C. Young. Here, the reader will find the general ideas and overview in the first paper developed to the point that they can be implemented with reasonable amounts of work. The extensive bibliography of this paper should be especially helpful.

The last three papers of this section address specific problems in teaching statistics and methodology in the social and behavioral sciences. The paper by Antanas Suziedelis addresses the computer-generation of data for use by students in statistical exercises. This paper brings the reader into direct contact with a specific example of the issues and methodological principles discussed in the first two papers of this section. A second example, illustrating another topic area in statistics and methodology commonly taught in the social and behavioral sciences, is presented in the paper by

Francis Campos. These two papers illustrate complementary subjects and approaches. The Suziedelis paper represents general concerns with computer generated data for a wide variety of applications in social and behavioral science statistics instruction. On the other hand, the paper by Campos deals with a narrower issue in terms of the statistical subject, but develops the methods and interaction between machine and student in sufficient detail to permit the reader readily to imagine similar developments in his own area of teaching interest.

The final paper of this section, by Michael A. Baer and Nona A. Newman, addresses a problem that has been experienced by all persons who have attempted to introduce computer technology into the large-scale lower-division methodology and statistics courses in the social and behavioral sciences. One's colleagues share the burden of teaching these courses, and often there is a very uneven distribution of background and training among these teachers. As a consequence, the individual with the interest and background to teach computer processing to the students is faced with the problems addressed by Baer and Newman. The solution proposed is interesting, workable, and effective.

Part III: Social Impact

This section is perhaps not adequately described by the section title. "Social impact" seems to cover a much wider area than the three papers of this section appear to cover. However, the title is a compromise to cover the contributions of these three papers. These are legitimate issues in the social and behavioral sciences— but they are not the content often referred to in books with similar titles. Rather, these papers provide an outlook for the social and behavioral scientist in his preparation to teach a course in the social impact of computers.

The initial paper, by James R. Bohland and Ronald E. Anderson, is a simple, direct statement of some basic truths that we tend to overlook in our search for methods, procedures, and exciting subjects in our teaching. We are reminded of the basics of what it is all about—a valuable reminder!

The paper by Roberta Ash, Robert Ogden, and Larry Gluck, on the other hand, gets down to the details of what a course on the impact of computers might encompass. This complements the

Bohland and Anderson paper by offering concrete curriculum details for such a course.

There is growing literature on the social impact of computers and computing. A serious inspection of this literature reveals that there is a great deal of speculation, not founded on fact, in the published books and articles. The paper by Francis Sim and Ronald E. Anderson points out that if the field of study called "social impact of computers" is to be sound, there must be developed scientific methods and a focusing of scientific attention on that field. Each of the social sciences has a contribution to make in such a study. The curricula of the social and behavioral sciences are the places to begin in the development of a social science of computing. In service of this enterprise, Anderson and Sim propose an outline of a course that would launch the formal sociological scientific training for studying computing as a sociological phenomenon.

Part IV: Computer Based Enhancement
in Social and Behavioral Science Education

This section and the next comprise the meat of the book, in the sense that there is the "flesh," as compared with "heart" and the "mind" found in other sections. If it is possible to have a limited but representative sample of applications of computer science in the social and behavioral sciences, these sections would be it. However, I am sure that certain readers will not find here their own choice for computer enhancement in social and behavioral science education. The selection is only representative, not totally comprehensive.

The papers in this section range widely in application of computers, and in discipline. The difference from the papers in the following section is that they describe enhancements to courses and curricula that are otherwise not about computers and computing.

Putting the paper by Dana B. Main in this section was not the only possible choice, because it involves statistics, methodology, and computer simulation, as well as enhancement. On balance, however, I felt that this section really reflected the intent and content of the paper more than the other, narrower sections did.

All of the papers in this section pivot on a unifying theme: how to make a course richer, more rewarding to the student, by using digital computers. Computers and computing are not the subjects of any of these papers, from the perspectives that the student has. Students might learn something about computers and computing by taking a course enhanced in a manner described by any one of these papers. However, such an outcome would be incidental to the course, and the computer enhancement in the course.

The papers cover a number of substantive areas in the social and behavioral sciences: geography (James R. Bohland), psychology of learning (B. James Starr and Sally A. Flanik), political science (James W. Hottois and Stuart H. Rakoff, and Steven Parker), sociology (Fred S. Halley), economics (James Ciecka), and cognitive psychology (William Bewley). They cover a range from batch computing production of materials used in education (e.g., papers by Phillip L. Emerson and Ronald L. Koteskey) to highly interactive on-line work involving man and machine interaction (e.g., papers by Starr and Flanik, and by Bewley).

An instructor in any of the fields of social and behavioral science education will find papers outside of his field of content specialization a potential source of ideas for development of computer augmentation materials and methods in his own field. Although the projects described are specific to the authors, and most are specific to a given discipline as described, they are general in concept and can be applied to virtually any substantive discipline.

Part V: Simulation and Modeling

Separating the papers of this section into a distinct group, apart from the papers of the previous section, is based on the consistency of one theme of the papers—computing simulation of substantive content. In a very real sense, these papers share with the papers of the previous section the theme of enhancing instruction. However, the character of these enhancements is to a certain degree different. Here, the focus is not on method and techniques, but on the substance of subject matter.

The social and behavioral sciences have developed in complexity of theory over the last two decades to a significant degree. This development appears to be concomitant with the development of computer simulation models of social and behavioral phenomena.

One is tempted to state that this increasing complexity is due to the development of simulation models. With such models it is possible to state very complex theories and to let them "operate" in the "make believe world" of computer programs. Whereas such complex theories are impossible to follow with ordinary human memory and logical power, and equally impossible to state mathematically, they are relatively easy to expresss in computer programs. Is it the availability of such tools that has made such complex theories "thinkable," or have the requirements of the sciences to have such complex theories made the computer models acceptable ways of stating the theories? From this near perspective it is impossible to have any confidence in either an affirmative or a negative answer.

The models, or simulations, described in this section are from three disciplines only: psychology, economics, and sociology. The bias is not intentional, but perhaps it reflects the state of modeling in the social sciences. Political science and geography are not as well (perhaps the best word would be extensively) developed as the three fields represented, although I am aware of several elegant simulations in political science, particularly of voter behavior and election prediction. Some of these developments are touched on in papers in other sections of the book.

The reader will find in this section, as in the previous section, many ideas about how to make teaching with complex theoretical subject matter more alive and meaningful to students. Although the ideas range from simulations to discrete state processes, to the complex mathematical models of continuous processes, almost every discipline in the social and behavioral sciences can find fertile suggestions for development.

Part VI: Bibliographies

Two bibliographies are presented in this section. The first presented, "Computers in Science Fiction," by Norman and Vernon Sondak, may at first glance seem to be whimsical. However, the computers of science fiction are more "real" to the common citizen than are the unglamorous computers of computer centers and computer laboratories. Thus, in a very real sense, the computers of science fiction are the computers that some courses in the social and behavioral sciences must deal with! Unless we understand the mad computer called HAL, or all about the humanoid computers with positronic logic, we cannot begin to understand the sociology, psychology, political science, etc., of computers and computing as it affects "the people."

A second reason for including this paper is more personal. I have a wish one day to teach a computer science course formed around the computer in science fiction. It would be a real computer science course, and not a course in science fiction. We would discuss how one might go about producing the fantastic computer systems behind the super-powerful behavior of the entities in the science fiction works. What would computer scientists, and scientists in social and behavioral fields, have to know and do to produce these machines, and to guard against their catastrophic faults? Would the efforts be largely technical or would they be social and behavioral?

The second bibliography is that by Ronald E. Anderson, bringing up to date a bibliography published earlier in the Association for Computing Machinery Special Interest Group's publication.

This is an important bibliography and will serve as a reference source for social and behavioral scientists who are embarking on or continuing the task of using, and teaching, computer science in social and behavioral science education.

Part VII: The Bottom Line

As one computer scientist might have said to another: "Congratulations, we have just discovered the secret of proliferating wrong answers at the rate of 196,732 per second!" So might the entire enterprise be folly and calamity if it is all in error.

This section, containing contributions from one person, Richard V. Andree, is included because of the supreme importance of being correct.

The last paper of this section also deals with the problem of being correct in an economical way.

The section title is not flip. It is expressive of the fact that all the pretty software, fancy printouts, interaction between man and machine, and so on, are all worthwhile only if it is all true. Unfortunately, social and behavioral scientists are generally not trained in judging conditions that must be met before their use of a modern technology, like computers and computing, meets the test of truth. The first of these two papers presents some scary examples of what disasters one can encounter in things that the social and behavioral scientists are likely to do with computers. It is important that these issues be discussed in a book like this! Not only are research results likely to be garbage unless we know what we are doing with computers, but we will also be teaching our students how to produce garbage. Just think of that—a factory to produce garbage producers!

It is my hope that by including this section, education in computer science in the social and behavioral sciences will be moved toward a more solid foundation.

The second paper of the section contains some very valuable lessons in how to produce effective and efficient program code. This is included for two reasons. First, it is important in the social and behavioral sciences that professors, or teachers, be able to meet certain standards of excellence and competence in the technology involved. If any of the readers of this book are inspired to engage in the development of computer science in social and behavioral science education, then this chapter will be important in assisting that person to get started on an appropriate track. However, there is an even more important reason for including this, as well as the other paper of this section, and that is the effect on students. Unless the professor or teacher is aware of the types of issues raised and discussed in these two papers, the student being instructed will be the worse for the ignorance and bad habits of the teacher.

TABLE OF CONTENTS

Part II. Statistics and Methodology.

Part III. Social Impact.

Part IV. Computer Based Enhancement in Social and Behavioral Science Education

Part V. Simulation and Modeling.

Part VI. Bibliographies

Part VII. The Bottom Line.

Computer Science in Social and Behavioral Science Education

PART I
The Place of Computer Science
in Social and Behavioral Science

1.
Social Science Computing Curricula: Guidelines for Development

Ronald E. Anderson
University of Minnesota

Several decades ago a new body of techniques sprouted from the field of mathematics. This new technology, which came to be called statistics, grew into an autonomous academic field despite confining pressures. Although the invention of computer techniques historically lagged behind statistics, its entry into the academic world is strikingly similar. Both fields face issues of disciplinary autonomy and both are undergoing similar struggles between applied and theoretical interests. One outcome of these tensions in statistics has been the establishment of separate programs for applied statistics. While we do not dare make rigid predictions for computer science, we would anticipate similar structures, e.g., *applied* computer science curricula, to emerge.

In evaluating the educational needs of non-computer scientists, we are necessarily focusing upon the applied aspects of computer science. Our discussion will not, however, pursue the obvious question of which discipline or academic department should provide the education. The necessary courses can be built into curricula in either computer science or social and behavioral science. A teaching program can be organized either in terms of individual courses or as an entire curriculum. Actual needs and alternative solutions should be delineated more fully before such decisions are confronted.

A useful stepping-off point is to ask: What should the social scientist know about computer science? Note that this question implies an ideal-type social scientist. We do not presume to answer the question for every student, but it is possible to offer an answer for a hypothetical entity: an "educated," "well-rounded," or "adequately trained" social scientist. To be an educated social scientist requires a wide variety of basic skills and knowledge as equipment to make research decisions. To be an educated social scientist means knowing enough to maintain a scholarly approach to problems and freedom to consider any new idea or method.

Many books have been written on "What the manager needs to know about computers," and "Computers for everyone," but no one has ventured to author a book on "What every social scientist should know about computers." The lack of such books or articles is probably a consequence, in large part, of the difficulty of the task. It is not at all obvious to anticipate useful training for students who will work in emerging fields involving computing. Another major factor inhibiting consensus among social scientists on computer science education is the current mode of adaptation to computer technology. Social science departments are currently dominated by those who completed their graduate education prior to the large scale adoption of computer technology. While most recognize the utility of computerized data analysis and other applications, personal involvement is usually resisted. The typical solution to the dilemma is to rely upon students whenever computer use cannot be avoided. This tendency for social scientists to overdelegate computer work to assistants tends to leave the impression that computer work is low status, uninteresting, and unprofessional. These typical patterns also perpetuate a situation of poor communication between the computer specialist and senior scholar/researcher.

Richardson *et al.* (1971) conducted a survey of sociology departments in the western United States, which showed that most department chairpersons are favorable toward computing requirements for majors. Most chairpersons agreed that computing should be required for graduate students and that the opportunity for relevant courses should be available for undergraduate students. But the study also found that very few departments had actually implemented such computing courses, even when they were not available in other departments. Thus it would appear that the actual level of commitment to computing curricula is rather low. A few even take adamant positions against the support of computer curricula for social science students. Still, recent

CONDUIT surveys (see Anderson, 1975; Boynton, 1975; and Castellan, 1975), of college instructors using computers in their teaching, demonstrate that a sizeable number of social scientists use computer-based instructional techniques. These surveys also found that approximately 10 percent to 15 percent of the psychology and sociology departments offer computer courses, indicating that at least a footnote has been made. Such courses tend to be very heterogeneous with some focusing upon laboratory automation, others upon programming, and others upon "computer methods for data analysis." There is good evidence that the use of, if not the curricula for, computers has become institutionalized in most academic social science environments.

Types of Instructional Requirements
in Social Science Computing

Any recommendations of courses for specific students or curricular programs must necessarily take learning objectives into consideration. The adequacy of an educational experience cannot be defined apart from the goals of the learning process, and these goals cannot be defined apart from the social context within which the learner expects to function. Specifically, curricular recommendations for the computer education of the social scientist cannot be made without consideration of students' career goals. A typology of student career goals is presented in Figure 1, with computer-related learning needs listed for each career goal. The career goals are listed in order of increasingly greater knowledge and skill.

1. *Liberal Arts Education.*

Students desiring only a liberal arts education, with an emphasis in social or behavioral science, need to be generally literate about computers, attaining what is sometimes called "computeracy." At the present time there is little consensus on the definition of computer literacy nor is there agreement on what should be included in such courses. It is clear, however, that even a general understanding of society now necessitates some knowledge about computerization.

2. *Research Analyst in Social Science.*

Some students major in the social sciences anticipating a

Figure 1

*A Typology of Curricular Needs
Pertinent to Social Science Computing*

STUDENT CAREER GOAL	LEARNING NEEDS IN COMPUTER SCIENCE
Liberal Arts Education (BA degree)	General computer literacy
Research analyst in areas of social science (BA or MA degree level)	Computer applications in social research Computer programming Data base management
Research/Teacher in social sciences (PhD degree)	Computer applications in research Computer programming Data base management
Social science computing	Computer applications in research Computer programming Data base management Statistical computing Real-time computing systems Text processing systems Other optional specializations

research position in a human service agency, government, or industry. Training for these jobs has not become well institution-alized yet, although an MA program in behavioral sciences for the "Survey Data Analyst" was recently started at the University of Chicago. A good understanding of elementary computer science principles is important for effective computer utilization in middle-range research roles.

3. Researcher-Teacher.
While the senior researcher may primarily supervise research analysts, he still must have a basic understanding of the capabilities of computing and computer data processing. This understanding must be more extensive than a superficial knowledge of a particular analysis package. A beginning knowledge of program-

ming and data management is critical for making adequate decisions regarding the execution of research procedures.

4. *Social Science Computing Specialist.*

Specialists are needed for the development of social information systems and computer-based research techniques. Such roles are largely undefined in the current occupational sector, but it is clear that the necessary training includes selected courses in both computer science and social science.

These four career goals should not be taken as comprehensive, especially since new roles may rapidly emerge with the evolution of computer information systems. For instance, paraprofessional persons may be needed for assisting scholars in the use of on-line retrieval systems. The complexity of computerized systems makes it impossible to predict fully what the opportunities will be and what training will be necessary.

A First Course in Social Science Computing

Any of the learning needs discussed thus far requires or could benefit from a beginning course in computer application for the social/behavioral sciences. Consequently a suggested course description has been outlined here.

INTRODUCTION TO SOCIAL SCIENCE COMPUTING

OBJECTIVES: This course is designed as a first course in computing and computer applications for social science students. Its aim is to provide a general and accurate understanding of what computing is and how it can be applied to social science. Included in the course are training in the skills of using several computer systems, a programming language and statistical packages.

OUTLINE
(1) Introduction to computer environments: elementary computer science, nature of computer systems; programming concepts; operating systems; data processing techniques, and interactive and batch systems.
(2) Principles of computer programming: introduction to algorithms; elementary FORTRAN programming; input/output techniques.
(3) Data processing and data management: data base organization; file management; merging, sorting, editing; special data base problems.
(4) Introduction to statistical processing systems: intermediate and

advanced SPSS usage; review of various statistical systems such as ISIS, OMNITAB, BMD, SNAP, MISS, etc.; use of special purpose programs, e.g., Small Space Analysis, cluster analysis.

(5) Introduction to computer simulation: review of types of simulation models in social science research.

(6) Introduction to text processing: content analysis using canned programs, problems in text processing with various programming languages.

(7) Review of miscellaneous applications: for example, laboratory automation, computer graphics, human-machine dialogues, and network structure analysis.

ILLUSTRATIVE TEXTS:

Meyers, D., Jr. *Time Sharing Computation in the Social Sciences.* Englewood Cliffs, New Jersey: Prentice-Hall, 1973.

Nie, N. *et al., Statistical Package for the Social Sciences.* New York: McGraw-Hill, 1975.

Rattenbury, J., and P. Pelletier. *Data Processing in the Social Sciences with OSIRIS.* Ann Arbor, Michigan: Institute for Social Research, 1974.

The problem in implementing such a course is not in finding literature; the Anderson (1974) bibliography on social science computing cites 600 books and articles. Likewise, there are hundreds of programming languages and applications packages that can be used and taught. The serious problem or dilemma is having to select the best references and techniques from the vast array of materials, tailoring them to one's particular computering and instructional environment. This selection process includes the decisions concerning programming language, and instruction on analysis and data management systems.

Perhaps the most difficult and challenging dimension of implementing this introductory course is student motivation. Not only do social science students typically share an anxiety about complex technology, but they also tend to dread confrontation with mechanical techniques. In this regard computer science may have an advantage over statistics because it is possible to transmit a sense of intrigue and enjoyment in the process of computer programming. The "secret" seems to be for both the instructor and students to assault and surmount the alienation from computer science that can often be found in social science departments.

Advanced Aspects of a Social Science
Computing Curriculum

Branching from the first course in social science computing to more specialized topics can take any number of directions. The structural organization of the literature as given in the Anderson (1974) bibliography suggests courses in each of the following areas:

(1) Statistics, Data Analysis, and Management;
(2) Simulation Modeling;
(3) Text Processing (including content analysis); and
(4) Laboratory Automation and Real-time Systems.

In addition, social scientists should explore issues in computerization generating courses such as:

(5) Social Aspects of the Computer World, and
(6) Philosophical and Psychological Aspects of Computing.

Perhaps the most compelling undeveloped area of social science computing curricula is that of social information systems (SIS): information processing systems designed to support the operation, management, and decision functions of social research and public administration support organizations that collect and maintain social information, i.e., data on attributes of individuals and collectivities. Although information systems designed for public administration are often very different from those designed for social science research, they have many elements and techniques in common.

Conclusion

The design of curricula in social science computing should not be viewed as simply a way of providing a needed educational service. In a broader, long-term perspective it is another step toward attending to important new problems. The introduction of new courses and training of students in social applications of computing will ultimately build the structure within which research on socio-computer issues can flourish.

References

Anderson, R.E. Bibliography of Social Science Computing. *Computing Reviews*, 1974, *15* (7), pp. 247ff.

Anderson, R.E. Diffusion of Computer Utilization Among Sociology Instructors. Paper presented at the annual meeting of the Association for Computing Machinery, 1975.

Boynton, G.F. Political Scientists' Use of the Computer in Undergraduate Education. Paper presented at the annual meeting of the Association for Computing Machinery, 1975.

Castellan, N.J., Jr., The Instructional Use of Computers in the Teaching of Psychology. Paper presented at the annual meeting of the Association for Computing Machinery, 1975.

Richardson, J.T. *et al.* Computers in the Social and Behavioral Sciences. *The American Sociologist,* 1971, *6* (2), pp. 143-152.

2.
Computer Science and the Undergraduate: How Much of a Good Thing Is Enough?

Forrest H. Armstrong
University of Wisconsin—Green Bay

Among those pieces of intellectual baggage carried by a good many of us in the social and behavioral sciences today is the idea that computer science is a Good Thing. Given the myriad ways in which computers have enabled us to expand our ken and deal with questions and data sources not feasible with the previous technologies, such an attitude is altogether understandable. Even those of us who might demur, saying, for example, that "computers are dehumanizing," would be hard pressed to argue that computers have not become fixtures in modern life that affect us all, regardless of profession. It is easy to point to the abundant evidence that all of us, citizens and scholars alike, may find it necessary to know something about computers. Another point may be more difficult to resolve: how much of a Good Thing is Enough?

To answer such a question definitively is, of course, impossible. The factors involved are many and complex: the nature of students, curricula, faculty, machine technology, and societal needs. All are, of course, in constant flux: the advent of the mini-computer is but one example of a development that quickly made much writing on computer science instruction obsolete. But other factors may change more slowly and, as a result, present a set of constraints within which we must work but to which we may not pay sufficient attention.

My thesis is simply this: we should make certain that our computer science requirements are appropriate given the nature of our students and the educational opportunities they enjoy.

I have a particular interest in the student with whom we all have the greatest amount of contact, the "average" undergraduate major who will not seek an advanced degree in the field. Examination of the context in which such students will be working suggests to me that computer science is likely to be a "tool subject" for them, relevant in relationship to their substantive field rather than for itself. Moreover, many faculty and curricula cannot cope with students wishing to undertake behavioral research. Under these conditions, I think we often overtrain our students in computer science. As I will outline below, I think that these students will be well prepared to meet their educational opportunities if they take a package of computer science, statistics, and research methodology totalling no more than six semester credits.

I do *not* suggest that this is the ideal situation; I do, however, suggest that in light of present realities we may be doing the student a disservice when we recommend or require that he spend more time than this on such matters. If we wish to remedy the situation, our path is clear: we must seek to change other aspects of the educational environment.

Computer Appreciation

Given the pervasiveness of computer utilization in modern life, it seems reasonable that the general undergraduate have some *brief* introduction to "computer appreciation." Of prime importance here is the debunking of myths about computers that students may well bring as part of their intellectual baggage. One would probably be able to introduce students to the basic I/O devices and CPU functioning as well as the role of the programmer and programming language within one or two class hours. If the student leaves with nothing more than the idea that the computer is basically a slave-like device and that one ought usually to blame "computer problems" on the human programmer rather than on the machine, he will have spent his time well. Within another hour or so the student might be given a survey, again in very general terms, of the range of applications for computers in modern life, especially incorporating examples of non-mathematical uses. While there is ample material to allow development of semester-long computer appreciation courses, I doubt it would be educationally justifiable.

Expectations and Opportunities

Computer appreciation materials such as those mentioned above could and probably should be utilized at any institution of higher education in the country, even those that do not have access to a computer, and with any student regardless of field or prior preparation. Beyond such a minimal level, though, consideration of what the average undergraduate in social and behavioral sciences needs to know about computer science is inescapably linked to the expectations the institution has of him and the opportunities it provides him for the utilization of such skills.

In some situations it is unwarranted for students to be required to take tool subjects such as computer science and statistics. If the institution must work with such a disastrous student-faculty ratio as to make anything save large lecture classes and multiple choice testing unfeasible, and/or if the expectations the institution holds for its undergraduate students are so minimal that it does not assume they will be trying to do original investigation or even read scholarly journals, then it is clearly inappropriate to require the student to master tools of research and investigation. If the institution is basically committed to achieving a regurgitation of facts from its students, it is absurd to require that they master a tool for questioning. Such institutions are still more numerous than one would like, though hopefully declining in number and significance.

A second institutional context also presents problems; while less dramatic than the first, it is also probably more prevalent, and one to which most of us are likely to be party in some degree. In such institutions, students are expected to achieve some degree of sophistication in research tools, yet are frustrated in their attempts to make use of them. Whether because many professors still resist behavioral research or because those of us who do see its virtues fail to take the effort to provide alternatives to the traditional library paper, student research skills all too often atrophy from disuse. Ought our students learn research tools because we want them to be able to investigate hitherto unreachable areas of scholarly inquiry, or have we merely made certain that we have provided them with the accoutrements of the scientist in the accepted fashion of the day?

Computer Science for the Undergraduate
(What, Where, Why, How?)

Assuming that both expectations and opportunities in the local context are appropriate, we can proceed to an examination of what the average social and behavioral sciences undergraduate needs to know about computer science and what we might do to facilitate his learning it. Note that I have used the term "needs" consistently in this paper. By doing so, I mean to focus upon the utilitarian dimension of computer science as a tool, an aid to the undergraduate in his investigation of scholarly topics. There are other dimensions, such as the aesthetic, which individuals may wish to explore, but I suspect that among contemporary social and behavioral scientists in general and certainly among such undergraduates the most common usage of the computer is as a computational device for counting, arranging, displaying, and calculating statistical analyses.

There is no necessary reason for performing any of those things with the aid of the computer; previous generations of scholars have used the hand calculator, the slide rule, or paper and pencil. But with computer facilities increasingly available to the scientist and with widespread availability of software to perform standard tasks, the instances in which the computer is not the logical device to use are rapidly decreasing. In addition, computers have opened up to the social scientist the possibility of working with large scale data bases that now have become the basis for much of the current research in the field. Given the great cost and difficulty of collecting social science data, students in particular are likely to undertake secondary analysis of commonly available data. Thus they are almost forced to use the computer for their work.

Because of the close connection for the undergraduate between the computer and statistical analysis, it makes sense to consider the integration of instruction in the two fields. In this way, the student is helped to make the linkage between the what—statistical analysis—with the how—operating the computational device, which today is a computer rather than a desk calculator. If we do no more than this, however, we run the risk of training students to use tools without knowing when or why to use them or how to interpret aspects of research methodology—the where, when, and why—with computer science and statistics, so that the student becomes truly educated in the area rather than just trained. By integrating these three aspects of subject matter, the student is able to work simultaneously with all five elements of investigation—the what, where, when, why, and how. If education has to do with the raising and answering of questions, how better might we help students grasp the process than by assisting them to deal in a holistic fashion with the structuring of questions, the generation or location of data, the testing of hypotheses through the use of appropriate statistical techniques, and the means for doing so in an effective and efficient manner?

A significant amount of time can also be saved by such an integration—one can, for example, explain the scientific method once rather than three times and then progress to other topics. For this reason, all the necessary material in the three areas might be covered within no more than six semester credits at a level sufficient to carry the general social and behavioral science undergraduate through to his baccalaureate. With the luxury of nine credits one could go into significant depth on topics of special local interest, but the additional three credits are not necessary in my view to prepare the undergraduate to undertake meaningful investigation.

Implementation

How might such a program look? Any institution considering attempts to implement a course sequence such as the one mentioned above would do well to consider the characteristics of its students as well as the nature of its own resources—faculty expertise, computing center facilities, and financial implications of undergraduate computer use. One of the central facts to remember is that secondary schools have been quite slow in making it possible for a student to gain the same kind of exposure to social and behavioral science that they long provided in areas like science, mathematics, language, and history. It is my experience that, as a result, many students have already committed themselves to a major based on their secondary school experience without ever having had the opportunity to sample what social science has to offer. It is unfortunate that the social science major often ends up in the field less from the positive choice associated with a strong motivation intrinsic to the subject matter than as a last resort: he has decided that he does not like the memorization of dates and battles which often characterize history pedagogy, and either in high school or early in college he has typically had a bad experience with mathematics or physical science. Because social science curricula have commonly required less of a lockstep progression through the sequence of courses in the field, it is common that students wait until late in their college careers to come to social and behavioral science. The attendant problems for instruction in research tools described for political science (see Baker, Hottois, and Rakoff, Chapter 5 in this volume) are probably common to the whole social and behavioral science field.

In my experience, another important factor has been the strongly negative perception so many students hold of their own mathematical (or even arithmetic) abilities. Such students may tend to resist instruction from the mathematics department, which is often the sole purveyor of courses in statistics and computer science. We may decry the "reasonableness" of such feelings, but the fact remains that negative affect impedes learning and makes the transfer of knowledge to later classes less effective than it might otherwise be.

One solution to this situation is for the institution to provide alternative opportunities for students to learn such subject matter. There are three possible problems with this approach: the first is that proliferation of such courses may cause difficulties in institutions that have mandatory ceilings on the number of different classes that may be mounted at any time; the second is that the cost of instruction may rise in all such courses with the addition of another distinct course in the area; and the third is that, whether due to the ignorance of the faculty member teaching the course or the lack of rigor thought to characterize the "soft" sciences, such courses will be seen as necessarily inferior to courses taught by "real" mathematicians. That we can all think of instances when each of those charges would have merit, though, is not to suggest that we ought to reject the concept. Rather, we should consider the effects of the tradeoff in output terms—how well are the students in each environment internalizing the subject matter and able to utilize it?

Doing no more than changing the name of the course from

mathematics to something relatively non-threatening is likely to have a significant impact on the affective dimension of the student's reaction to the course. Given that there are numerous social scientists who are well trained in relevant aspects of mathematics, there is no necessary reason why they should be less competent as instructors of such material, nor that they will necessarily be less rigorous in their approach than the mathematician. (They may well embrace a different set of priorities, wherein little or no emphasis is placed on theorem proving or the utilization of calculus in their classes, but for the social science undergraduate these may well not be necessary or appropriate.) The somewhat increased costs of instruction and the opportunity cost associated with assigning social and behavioral science faculty to teach such courses may be the price we will have to pay if we want the general social and behavioral science undergraduate to tool up effectively in research skills.

Course Content

Ideally, the subject matter of the three areas—computer science, statistics, and research methodology—can be blended in such a fashion that students see the ways in which the various components of the research environment interact. If done well, the student will be motivated to progress from one level of analysis to another by his innate intellectual curiosity. I am unaware of a sure-fire means for achieving uniformly high student interest. The instructor who artfully integrates his subject matter, though, may find that by facilitating student understanding he has also engendered a greater level of interest than would otherwise be the case.

Probably the greatest difficulty with such a course sequence is in knowing where to begin. It always seems that there is an infinite regression of topics that ultimately become circular, yet one must break into the loop somewhere. Harboring a strong preference for working deductively, I think a case can be made for beginning with a discussion of the scientific method. Keeping in mind that students probably have never seen a researcher at work across the entire span of a project, I strongly recommend bringing in an example within the first few class periods which would demonstrate the various stages of a research project and provide an overview of the process the students will be studying and implementing for the subsequent two terms. I suspect there is an advantage to borrowing the researcher with the "hottest" research on campus to capture the student's interest, but the instructor could substitute his own research if he chose. In either case, the enthusiasm demonstrated by a researcher seeking answers to significant questions is likely to do as much to get the course off to a good start as anything one could provide.

Another thing that should be dealt with very early in the course is introducing the student to the computer. The way this is done will vary with the nature of the facilities and the amount of computer science to be included in the courses, but in some way the student should be assisted in making a successful run, even if he does nothing more than log on and receive a page of output. The essential thing here is to help the student gain a sense of mastery over a potentially formidable machine.

I am hard-pressed to argue that we ought to expect the general undergraduate in the social and behavioral sciences to become at all sophisticated in a programming language, for I cannot see that he will have much use for it. He clearly needs to know I/O procedures, though one might consider substituting instruction in the idiosyncrasies of one or more of the better statistical packages that the student will be using; SPSS, BMD, OSIRIS, OMITAB, and CROSSTAB come immediately to mind as being widely available.

He might be able to profit from some knowledge of arithmetic operations, particularly as they are not terribly demanding to learn, and flow charting might prove to be a reasonable substitute for instruction in logic. Social scientists may find attention to data handling particularly useful, including file building, coding, and storage. On the other hand, it is probably unreasonable to do anything more than introduce concepts like looping and branching, but they do need to get a feel for some of the common programming devices which they might study in more depth *if* they should someday come to need to write their own programs. Assuming the system will accept it, I would suggest that language instruction be done in BASIC, due to its similarity to English, its use of defaults, and its general simplicity.

Most of these topics within computer science can be linked to other statistical or methodological problems, thus helping the student grasp the utility of the various concepts he is being presented. The student might, for example, find flow charting and hypothesis building and testing a good pairing, and he might write his first (only?) "original" program in conjunction with learning to calculate the mean.

The choice of precisely which statistical analyses to teach and in what order will be strongly affected by local considerations. Students pointing toward laboratory experiments in which all the relevant parameters of the population can be known and controlled will have different needs than a group of students who will be working with "noisy" data from the field. As a result, analysis of variance might well receive far more emphasis in the one context than another. Given the urge most of us seem to have for imparting at least interval level characteristics to our data, regardless of the appropriateness of such an act, attention to measurement considerations is imperative from the very beginning of the class. At that point, one can progress to probability, which will in turn help students to understand significance testing. Descriptions of central tendency, norming and scaling, association, and correlation should certainly be covered in such a course. If we are truly concerned with the quality of our data, we will probably pay more attention to non-parametric statistics than is often the practice, even though they are not "in vogue" these days. Data handling procedures such as coding and file construction would be very useful for students and could certainly be encompassed in the course. Sampling and survey techniques are probably best left out of the basic course sequence if one is trying to keep it to six credits.

I find it hard to justify teaching students to calculate the various statistics by hand or desk calculator. I recognize that many teachers feel that the student who does so gets a better "feel" for the operations of the measure than one who merely utilizes a part of statistical package, yet I doubt that doing so is the best way to teach statistics. My feeling is that one ought to emphasize the requirements that underlie and the limitations that accompany each statistical measure rather than its computational formula. Teach from whatever formula is most illustrative of the relationships being tapped so that the student's understanding is most easily and economically achieved. Since the computational formulae are often not the ones that we would use to demonstrate why the measure works, or how it works, it seems to me that to teach students the computational approach is to waste time and effort and possibly to confuse the student unnecessarily. I would stress that to use statistics successfully as a part of the investigative process is really to make correctly a series of decisions pertaining to what kind of data one has or can generate, what kinds of relationships he or she wants to examine, and what kinds of statistical techniques are appropriately employed on the task; the actual computation is a mechanical operation that can be performed a variety of ways as the user prefers. This is the opposite of the "cookbook" approach to the application without understanding of statistical tests, yet it focuses more on understanding of concepts and context than it does on formal mathematical proofs.

If we recall that our goal is to help students "tool up" for subsequent educational undertakings, we would be well advised to make one further integration within this course sequence: the student would be asked to undertake, with his instructor's assistance, the preparation of a project (which utilizes his new investigative skills) for some *other* course he is currently taking. This way the student could work with substantive material from a class taught by a faculty member not particularly sophisticated in behavioral research tools and techniques and yet have close support from a trained researcher for this all-important initial venture into original investigation. I think it is hard to over-emphasize the importance of this step. It graphically demonstrates to the student that the tools he is learning can be of immediate benefit to him in a "substantive" course; with such feedback, it may be possible to begin to overcome the problem of atrophy that has plagued us in "tool" areas.

Another advantage may also obtain: should the students approach their task with enthusiasm, they may encourage other students to use the same approach. Should they be successful, faculty may begin to raise their expectations of what under-graduates can be expected to achieve. Possibly as a result, the overall level of intellectual rigor in our classrooms can be raised.

Conclusion

I have sought in this paper to consider the extent to which it is appropriate for us in the social and behavioral sciences to require significant computer science training for our undergraduate majors. Given the nature of the opportunities for original investigation accorded our average undergraduate, and the expectations held for his performance, I propose that he probably can make use of less computer science than he is often required to master. That which he does need to know might advantageously be presented in an integrated research skills package of no more than six semester credits covering methodology, computer science, and statistics.

I say this not to suggest that a six credit package is the *ideal*, but rather that it is *realistic*, given the environmental constraints many of us face today. That environment, as I see it, all too often is one in which undergraduates are not expected to do original investigation, in which faculty are not themselves prepared to guide rigorous behavioral research efforts, in which student-faculty ratios enervate attempts to work closely with small groups of undergraduates, and in which we tend to get students coming to our majors late in their academic careers and ill prepared to cope with behavioral research techniques.

Let there be no mistake: I do not suggest that we ought be pleased with the fact that we must work in such an environment. I both applaud and participate actively in efforts to change that environment. But I also believe that we have a responsibility to the majority of our students, those who will not be going on to graduate work in the field, to keep our requirements and expectations in line with the opportunities we can afford them at any point in time. Hopefully we will be able to improve our educational opportunities and can raise expectations and requirements for methodological rigor accordingly.

In suggesting that the undergraduate is unlikely to need more than this integrated package, I do not mean to denigrate the undergraduate's abilities. Indeed, one of the major virtues I see in such a package is that it might overcome some of the negative affect that social and behavioral science undergraduates often feel for mathematics in general, and I would strongly recommend that the statistics component of the package be built with an eye toward allowing the student to progress to advanced work in mathematics if he so desires. I am, however, reacting to what I see as the likelihood that this type of student will need (have a chance to utilize) such tools.

Two other needs must also be met for this approach to have maximum effect. The first is for development of various pieces of CAI for support of the course sequence instruction. One essential is an interactive tutorial program for BASIC that will prompt extensively but be more easily transportable than something like the PLATO system. Such a package for the various statistical techniques contained in the course could have several benefits. In addition to providing flexibly scheduled individual tutoring with immediate feedback, it could be employed to do much of the grading in the course. Instructors could be free to spend more time on consulting with individual students on research projects, and the need for paid course assistants might be reduced. Secondly, we need to develop readily available social science data bases for use in secondary analysis. The range of alternatives here goes from Dartmouth's Project IMPRESS through the services of the Inter-University Consortium for Political Research (ICPR) at Ann Arbor, to census tapes and survey data from purveyors such as the National Opinion Research Council (NORC), the American Institute of Public Opinion (AIPO), and others. If IMPRESS were readily transportable and if ICPR service were less expensive, the needs of the social and behavioral science community would be well served.

Changes such as the ones noted above are necessary for us to be able to implement undergraduate use of the computer in relatively common, prosaic ways: counting, sorting, and calculating. The future, though, undoubtedly holds new vistas for us. As we master new languages, such as SNOBOL, we may be able to work with words as readily as we now work with numbers, using the computer for textual analysis, pattern recognition, and other forms of content analysis, and as we become used to the notion of real-time computing we may open up new areas of application for ourselves and for our students. Through computer-based models and simulations, students with minimal computer sophistication will be able to manipulate variables and test our complex relationships in the classroom. As these developments take place, our curricula and pedagogy must also change if we are to meet our responsibility to our students.

In sum, then, this should not be seen as an attempt to impose arbitrary limits on undergraduates, who may well be able to do many more things than this paper discusses. It is, rather, a call to institutions of higher education and to us, as educators, to change expectations and provide opportunities commensurate with the undergraduate's ability to learn, question, and investigate, using all the tools modern technology can provide for the purpose.

3.
Improving Social and Behavioral Science Utilization of University Computer Centers

Richard A. Wiste   Norman E. Sondak
Northern Illinois University   *Worcester Polytechnic Institute*

The social and behavioral science (SBS) user, while an important and productive client of computer facilities, has often felt like a second class citizen at many university and college computer centers. From the standpoint of the SBS faculty member, this has often meant lower research productivity and limitation of educational processes. For the computer administration, this has often meant diminished curricular and budgetary support from an important institutional interest group. The existing situation has developed gradually over many years and tends to differ in detail from institution to institution. However, it seems possible to highlight eight somewhat interrelated facets of the relationship between the SBS user and his computer environment:

1. The tradition of university computer centers has been to support the physical sciences and engineering, which in turn have been primary sources of external funding.
2. There are often sharp intradisciplinary schisms over the proper role of computer related techniques in the social and behavioral sciences.
3. The selection of computer facilities without sufficient consultation with SBS users often results in real or imagined inadequacy of service.
4. SBS faculty are typically lacking in basic computer science skills.
5. Student orientations in the SBS are, for the most part, qualitatively and humanistically rather than quantitatively directed.

6. Operations and procedures at university computer centers are often established with limited regard to SBS needs or sensibilities.
7. The SBS is interested in the computer solely as a means to an end rather than as a study in itself.
8. The economics of computer support at the university are often structured in a manner unfavorable to the SBS.

Traditional Origins

The origin and early development of university computer facilities, often tied in with engineering, physical science, and mathematics departments, has resulted in recruitment and staffing policies that primarily reflect the needs, perspectives, and attitudes of these groups. While these groups typically represent as little as 20 percent of the university population, they often account for as much as 90 percent of the computer center professional staff. This has been an important factor contributing to the stronger traditional thrust for support for the physical science and engineering user rather than the SBS user.

In the past, when many educational computer facilities tended to be supported primarily by external research-related funding, such proportions could perhaps be justified on fiscal grounds. If the more recent tendency to regard computers as an institutional resource to be supported from internally distributed funds increases, this imbalance may lessen. Similarly, the increasing tendency of many state legislatures and budgetary commissions to scrutinize computer expenditures from the standpoint of their impact on undergraduate instruction may lessen the role of the physical sciences and engineering in providing financial support for the computer center.

One of the first things required of university computer center management is a self-conscious attempt to broaden the scope of computer processing at their institution and to have staff members and consultants available who are familiar with the needs and problems of the SBS user. These staff appointments should be at both the administrative decision-making level and the technical user support level. Unless this is done, the decision-making process may reach an irreversible stage before the SBS input or interest is recognized. For example, in large state universities, major resource decisions are usually made two years or more before installation. The SBS faculty member cannot effectively interact if these decisions are made on wholly technical and traditional usage grounds. There must be a clear realization that efficiency in the context of a university computing center has meaning only in relation to the pursuit of specific educational and scholarly objectives. The determination of policies on the grounds of "efficiency" by technical personnel isolated from a knowledge of classroom and research problems and priorities should be recognized as inappropriate. Computer center systems personnel uninformed about educational processes will have difficulty making sound acquisitions decisions.

Conversely, SBS users, instead of living off the largesse of intramurally obtained computer funds, can often be more aggressive in adding provisions for computer funds to grant requests and generally seeking to obtain outside support for computer activities. Moreover, particularly in graduate institutions, well-designed computer tool course sequences can serve as a source of SBS oriented computer center staff.

Intradisciplinary Schisms

Just as traditional patterns of usage in engineering and physical science have led to a natural acceptance of computers as an invaluable adjunct of analytical work of this type, traditional patterns of research in the SBS have also contributed toward a shaping of attitudes about computers among practitioners in these areas. Unfortunately, however, in many of the SBS disciplines this has resulted in attitudes ranging from passive acceptance to bitter hostility toward computer usage. Thus, in many SBS departments there are majorities or large minorities who not only do not use computers in their own research, but tend to regard computer usage in connection with the scholarly activities of others as evidence of the unsoundness of these activities. Those of a "traditional" or "anti-behavioral" persuasion may feel that a colleague using computers has abandoned the use of reasoned judgment and considered values in the study of human affairs for a mindless subservience to the machinations of a collection of electronic components. The fact that these attitudes tend to be far more prevalent among senior than among junior faculty gives hope for the future but accentuates the current problem. While these attitudes might tend to be more widespread in disciplines such as history and political science than in those such as economics and psychology, their existence must always be taken into account not only in considering incentives for individual SBS use, but also in guaging the willingness of departments to make budgetary sacrifices to support computer use.

While intradisciplinary methodological disputes are obviously not normally within the purview of computer center management, the director and his staff can shape policies with this situation in mind. In particular, communications efforts are better focused on interdisciplinary user groups than on departmental units. Similarly, management should be aware that for many SBS users, classroom computer utilization is a sufficiently marginal operation, from the standpoint of their own professional benefits, that the creation of substantial numbers of mutinous students disaffected by poor turnaround or cumbersome job submission procedures is ample cause to terminate such computer utilization.

Facilities

For the purpose of this paper "facilities" is used to refer to the total support system offered the user including traditional hardware, operating systems, compilers, and applications packages. The planning and development of computer facilities is generally a two-stage process in which an individual or special interest group first formulates a demand and provides sufficient justification to warrant further investigation. The second stage, administrative approval or rejection, involves a weighing of the relative costs and benefits of the desired facilities. The crucial consideration here is that the SBS is often at a disadvantage in participating in either of these two stages.

One reason is that SBS demand for any particular capability will not generally precede the existence of that capability at a particular institution. Only a small percentage of the SBS faculty have had any substantial computer involvement during their own formal professional training. Thus, their perceptions of what is possible, desirable, or necessary are largely shaped by those facilities and practices that have grown up at their own installations. The individual SBS faculty member may become aware of and desire certain facilities after reading papers or attending conferences, but this highly specific and atomized type of demand rarely receives effective expression. Even if the demand is articulated in some tentative manner, it is often easily rebuffed on technical grounds with which SBS faculty feel uncertain in dealing.

At the second stage of facilities acquisitions, a typical administrative response is to seek some indication of probable use through a questionnaire or survey of interested faculty. This approach is unrealistic when used to estimate future SBS usage patterns. For the same reason that the demand is not expressed before availability of a facility, the SBS faculty member receiving such a questionnaire is simply not properly equipped to respond. For example, the SBS department chairman confronted with a question on how many hours of CPU usage he expects in connection with a new simulation gaming system will normally find himself wholly lacking in any basis for intelligent response.

The typical SBS user is often most interested in such software support as statistical packages, simulations, and classroom oriented instructional routines. Active user groups in these areas can help to focus interests and serve as platforms for dissemeniation of information by the center staff. In presenting material to such groups, it is important to have output and examples of usage in connection with real SBS problems. Merely giving the name or a brief paragraph concerning some facility will not excite interest nor provide reliable estimates of probable use.

Conversely, no matter how open the computer center administration is to input from SBS users, no effective input will occur unless a few individuals take the initiative and responsibility for informing themselves and expressing their informed opinions in an appropriate forum. One of the greatest barriers to effective SBS input in acquisition decisions is often the reluctance of SBS faculty with large but relatively unsophisticated computing needs to suffer the embarrassment of appearing ignorant in technical discussions.

Minimal Computer Skills

The typical SBS faculty member is not trained in computer science, yet his applications often require sophisticated techniques for dealing with large scale data bases and complex statistical analyses. This often means that SBS users are compelled to rely on package programs transported to their installations. The SBS user interested in utilizing one of these packages, even if he himself was responsible for its acquisition, is likely to be wholly incapable of setting up even an optimally transportable system at his own installation. Moreover, even the SBS who possesses considerable statistical sophistication and intimate familiarity with his data is likely to encounter many vexing difficulties when attempting to use a package for the first time. Another problem associated with a lack of programming skills is the misuse of package programs in cases where simple routines would be much more economic and efficient.

The problem of lack of computer science skills on the part of SBS faculties can be self-correcting. As interest and usage increase, these skills will be acquired. The typical pattern in which faculty become involved with the computer are when the individual is involved in some research project that clearly requires computational support or when the faculty member, either as a result of colleagues' suggestions or through a conference or paper reference, decides to use some type of classroom computer aid. In both these cases, the user is completely problem oriented and has no particular desire to learn computer programming skills. It is crucial at this point that staff be available to help, or the novice user can be badly discouraged. Our experience has shown that the novice will often spend ten or more hours in attempting what low level staff can do in less than one hour. Often, the unassisted novice will waste physical resources in the same ratio as he wastes his own time. An all too frequent example is the use of expensive package routines for elementary data transformations that could be done far more efficiently and economically with simple FORTRAN or PL/I programs that a staff programmer could write in an extremely short time.

If assistance of this kind is funded and charged for in the same manner as other computer resources, both SBS users and the computer center will have increased incentive to eliminate many inefficient practices.

Student Orientation

While there are some students in SBS who are attracted to the computer, the typical SBS student associates computers with regimentation, impersonalization, and income taxes. When these unfavorable associations are combined with a fear of numbers and mathematics, the SBS instructor using the computer as part of his course is, when confronted with poor turnaround and restrictive systems, likely to find his educational innovation backfiring into a pedagogical and professional disaster. Moreover, when the social science student's initial experience with computers consists of long periods of waiting for output only to discover that some elementary keypunch or control card error has again deprived him of substantive results, he usually is sufficiently resourceful to structure the rest of his education in such a way as to avoid further computer involvement. To be sure, the SBS student could make more effective use of the computer if he were to take courses in computer science, but both faculty and student attitudes make such additional course loading extremely rare.

Since the SBS student is often hostile to the computer, interactive techniques with good HELP files and well conceived input error routines should be used whenever practical. The novice SBS faculty user may not be aware of all that can go wrong. A little staff assistance in the first efforts can greatly aid in creating reasonably good student reaction. If the SBS student is initially exposed to good computer techniques, he can be an excellent resource for further applications.

Operations

The operations philosophy of the typical computer center is designed around short jobs with high ratio of CPU time to I/O demand, and with input data files located in the job stream or on small permanently mounted data files. These jobs receive good turnaround and fast service. On the other hand, many SBS jobs, while needing minimal CPU time, have large I/O and main storage demands, and often require the mounting of tape or disc data sets. Moreover, the SBS user's initial interaction with the computer system is often at this complex level. Since the beginning SBS user (student or faculty) is often compelled to deal with packages requiring extensive use of a job control language at a time when he has no real understanding of that phase of computer operations, the combination of elementary setup and keypunch errors and a scheduling algorithm that places the job in a low priority queue leads to some initially disheartening experiences.

In addition, the main storage requirements for many SBS applications are extensive and not readily subject to compromise. For example, one commonly used package (SPSS) requires as much as 135K bytes for only the code of one of its subprograms. Hence, the user of such programs is often thrust into off-prime shift operations and limited turnaround. This difficulty is accentuated by the fact that such a large share of the SBS user's early submissions terminate with setup errors.

The resource scheduling algorithms have a profound effect on user service patterns. The SBS user can make good use of algorithms that allow a rapid initial error scan of the task and then permit rapid reentry of the job. The SBS user will be satisfied with standard turnaround for production runs if he is reasonably assured of receiving output rather than only an error listing. The need here is to supply the SBS user with turnaround during his initial error finding stage comparable to the fast turnaround received by programmers during initial debugging with batch compilers or compile-only runs. Some time slicing systems that give each job an initial allotment of time before rolling out longer jobs tend to produce this effect.

The SBS application may utilize large data bases requiring the mounting of selected tapes or disks. For classroom support, where hundreds of runs may be needed during a brief period of time, it is in the interest of both the user and the center that these be available on mounted volumes. Unless this is done, any kind of fastbatch or fast turnaround procedures for SBS will founder on the problem of time-consuming operator mounts. Simple administrative procedures should be instituted to insure sufficient computer center-faculty communication to allow intensively used large data sets to be available on mounted volumes for appropriate time intervals. Lessened systems and operations overhead associated with fastbatch runs of this type is likely to allow reduced charges that largely offset the cost of the disk storage space used. The SBS user who is willing to compromise on timing and is sufficiently knowledgeable to structure his data sets and input procedures appropriately is likely to find computer center staff more receptive to suggestions of this type.

Substantive Orientation

When the SBS faculty member uses the computer, the interest is naturally in teaching SBS or conducting SBS research and not in computer science. The effort involved in acquiring minimal computer science skills is considered an overhead burden. The efficiency of the computer as a pedagogical tool in SBS instruction is directly related to the ratio of this overhead burden to the substantive output obtained. The programming student learns a great deal about programming from examining his error listing on a debugging run. The student of legislative politics learns absolutely nothing about legislative politics from struggling with setup errors on his package program submissions. Computer center staff and procedures play an important role in determining just how much overhead is demanded of the SBS user.

The computer center staff must realize that the computer, like the library, is basically an auxiliary resource for the SBS scholar-teacher. The overhead for its use has to be kept within the bounds dictated by its advantages; otherwise, it will be ignored. Here again the most important factor is to provide adequate support so that the SBS user is not required to spend inordinate amounts of time in wrestling with technical problems. If ten dollars worth of consulting can save one hundred dollars worth of computing time or faculty time, it makes sense to devise accounting procedures that support such savings.

On the other hand, the SBS user should be alert to the long term benefits in terms of his own time and his institution's computer resources likely to accrue from his investing a few hours in increasing his understanding of the computer aspects of his work.

Computer Economics

Often the logic of costing for computer center operation is to determine what is perceived to be the normal flow of processing to make most effective use of resources and then to charge higher rates for special requirements. Again the SBS user, because of his often exceptional job configuration, can become a victim of such practices. In addition, lack of sophistication on the part of the SBS, coupled with inadequate computer center staff assistance, can result in unnecessarily high costs. For example, inappropriate data blocking procedures may escalate the number of I/O requests or main storage requirements beyond what is optimal or even reasonable for a given installation.

Interactive computing, which tends to be particularly appropriate for classroom SBS use, is more costly than batch processing in terms of machine resources. Traditionally, interactive computing has traded machine resources for more effective use of human resources. However, there are occasions when the additional costs are not justified in terms of additional results or educational benefits. In these and other cases a SBS user may require counseling regarding the most cost-effective use of his computer environment. For example, the BASIC language was designed for interactive program development but can be expensive for production runs. Interactive FORTRAN programs that achieve the same production results may be much more economical with only a small penalty in development effort. The SBS, who is typically familiar with no more than one language, is scarcely in a position to take advantage of existing opportunities to increase efficiency in this way, let alone take the lead in demanding facilities to allow such cost reductions.

Accounting algorithms are usually designed to include charges for CPU time consumed, main storage requested, job priority, I/O requests, mounts of tapes and disks, consumables such as paper, auxiliary storage, and other special resource demands. A minimum charge per submission is also common. Separate charges are usually made for terminal, communication lines, and connect time to the computer. The novice SBS computer user does not have a clear understanding of the degree to which these cost resource factors can be controlled by job specifications such as compiler size, data block size, buffers used, and batch versus interactive use. In some accounting algorithms, charges are non-linear with certain resource demands—three times the main storage usage may cost much more than three times the base charge. In many cases the SBS user is constrained to large storage requirements. This, coupled with high I/O charges, can result in excessive costs for runs that normally have small CPU time requirements. This costing procedure can discourage SBS jobs that might fit very well into a multiprogramming stream improving total center throughput without degrading service to the "number-crunching" user. A careful analysis of scheduling demands and accounting algorithms could result in better throughput and total revenue performance for the center if SBS jobs were judiciously integrated.

Summary

The best interests of the faculty, computer center, university administration, and the student can be served by creating an improved environment for the SBS user. The SBS special interest group will become a supporter of the computer center rather than an opponent or competitor for scarce budgetary resources. The throughput and total revenue performance of the computer center can be increased by the admixture of a variety of SBS applications complementing those already in the job stream with little or no disruption of current service. More students will be introduced to a powerful resource for learning and data analysis with consequent improvement in the quality of education at the host institution. A variety of research and supported activities can be opened to more SBS faculty. These and other points make the effort of understanding the problems of the SBS user a worthwhile investment for computer center management.

The SBS user, on the other hand, can do a great deal to improve his own computing center environment. By investing some of his time in the upgrading of his own skills he can realize a substantial return in the form of greater efficiency of his own efforts. He can increase meaningful throughput by using university facilities in a less wasteful fashion. Moreover, he can become a more effective representative of and advocate for the legitimate interests of social and behavioral science users in college and university computer centers.

4.
Computer Use in Undergraduate Psychology Curricula: Some Recommendations

B. James Starr
Howard University

Although the variety of actual and potential uses of computers in psychology has received a good deal of attention in the recent literature (e.g., Sidowski and Ross, 1969; Green, 1972; Sidowski, 1972, 1975; Starr, 1972), there is some reason to believe that computers may be underutilized in psychology (Cf. Sidowski, 1973; Castellan, Bailey, Lehman, Starr, and McClelland, 1976). Still, a number of innovative and significant uses have made an impact in the psychological literature. These applications seem to represent the efforts of a relatively small number of psychologists at a few institutions. The meaningful contributions by these few workers and the possible under-utilization by the larger community, taken together, suggest a number of considerations which, if acted on, might enhance the exploitation of this important tool within the discipline.

Inasmuch as my orientation is toward curricular matters, the objectives of this paper are readily defined. First, because we argue for curricular modification, the need for such change is examined and some substantive goals defined. Next, some of the possible impediments to meeting such goals are scrutinized. And, finally, a number of recommendations of potential benefit to effective use of computers in the curriculum are discussed.

Identification of Needs

A number of professionals with expertise in computer science applications in various disciplines have strongly stated the necessity of attempts to make the public "literate" with regard to computers (e.g., Zinn, 1972).

It is readily apparent that the computer has been meaningfully employed through a diversity of applications within psychology. Thus, the computer has been valuably implemented in clinical work (Johnson and Williams, 1975; Kleinmuntz, 1975); instruction (Lehman, Starr, and Young, 1975; Castellan *et al.*, 1976); process (e.g., experimental) control (Bailey and Polson, 1975; Castellan, 1975; Roemer, 1975); data analysis (Schucany, Minton, and Shannon, 1972; Leaf, 1974; Slysz, 1974; Gregg, 1975); modeling of behavior (Loehlin, 1968; Apter, 1970; Anderson and Bower, 1973); and the bookkeeping functions necessary in some of our work (Starr, 1970; Castellan, 1973). The foregoing list can provide little more than the flavor of the broad impact of computing in psychology. The works cited here, however, in many cases review developments in these areas. Moreover, a number of textbooks have been written by and for psychologists interested in computer usage (Green, 1963; Lehman and Bailey, 1968; Uttal, 1968). While a number of the contributions may be appreciated by individuals who are just "literate" in computer operation, few could be implemented in other environments with such limited knowledge. By virtue of this analysis, it is evident that it will be necessary for a number of individuals to achieve some higher level of facility regarding computer use.

Another factor documenting the need for developing a larger number of technically competent social science users is the ineluctable conclusion that an increasing number of applications are extremely difficult or impossible to handle by other means (see, e.g., Castellan, 1975; Kleinmuntz, 1975). It should be noted that the time may not be far off when the speed of data analysis outstrips the speed of data collection. Indeed, at a number of institutions where the computer is primarily a data analyzer, this has already occurred. It seems clear that continuing computer usage at current levels and ignoring the non-data-analytic capabilities of the machine may work to the detriment of psychology. In short, lack of sophistication regarding computer operation unnecessarily restricts the methodological armamentarium with which we can examine behavioral phenomena.

Impediments to Computer Training in Psychology

Most problems have features specific to their particular environment. When teaching about or using computers, these features often center on deficiencies in or uniqueness of the local software and hardware configurations. Problems that are created due to the local computing environment can not be dealt with here. Nonetheless, there are a number of common problems relating to software that can be discussed fruitfully. However, it is felt that the majority of problems that act in concert to block the development of more widespread computer use in our discipline are people problems, i.e., those emanating from both students and staff.

Student Impediments. A few years ago, I chaired a curriculum workshop group at a National Science Foundation supported Summer Institute on social science computing. As might befit academicians *sans* students, these faculty members discussed *student* problems impeding the curricular use of computers. What follows is in part a distillation of those discussions and in part an expression of my own biases.

One recurring difficulty facing those who would like to implement computer application courses or course enhancements in their curricula seems to be the relative discomfort of many undergraduate psychology majors with the formal, precise modes of thought necessary for programming and mathematics. While chemists, engineers, physicists, and others in traditionally "hard" sciences are exposed to heavy doses of formal problem-solving methods, psychology curricula generally minimize this type of exposure. Logic embodies the type of problem-solving orientation that is integral to the effective use of computers. There is, however, no logic requirement at many schools. Instead, in recent years there has been a decrease in requirements for students to take courses dealing with rigorous manipulation of symbols.

I have already noted the recurrent nature of this problem. Still, the last half-decade has been marked by fewer course requirements and a less demanding environment for our students (as documented, e.g., by the phenomenon of grade inflation). This legacy from an era of social consciousness and self-determination has not proven to be an invariably useful inheritance. One is hard put to argue against the laudability of the freedom fostered by the recent changes—whether one speaks of freedom to express a diversity of opinions in the classroom or freedom for students to chart their own course via fewer requirements and more electives. We would be remiss, however, if we did not recognize the mixed nature of this "blessing." If students are consistently rewarded for expressing a variety of opinions in many classes and equally consistently punished for failure to arrive at viable problem-solutions in others, how long can latter courses endure "free choice"? An obvious answer is "Not too long." In a pragmatic sense, a viable problem-solution accounts for the relevant facts, i.e., it works. Thus, opinion and problem-solution may not be equated. While it may be both easier and more comfortable to deal exclusively with substantive courses, it is not always the best alternative. Students must be made to realize that most problem solutions involve the use, in significant measure, of logical skills. These skills probably receive more attention in the "tool" courses (e.g., statistics, research methods, and computer programming courses) within our discipline than anywhere else. Insofar as students and faculty are partly motivated by a social consciousness concerned with "real-world" problem solution, the question becomes, "Can we hope to solve such problems while there is avoidance of the courses attempting to impart the requisite skills"? If the reader perceives a challenge in this question, the perception is not adventitious.

Another major impediment to the effective use of computers in the behavioral sciences lies in the lack of understanding of the principles of computer operation. To many undergraduates the computer is still a black box with decidedly magical qualities. The problem may go beyond a lack of computer literacy and reflect a fear of the unknown (or even the seemingly unknowable). At any rate, this obstacle can create difficulties in the area of computer-augmented instruction techniques. Such techniques are used to augment courses taught by traditional (i.e., non-computer) methods. The computer is used to support these more typical methods and not to do any actual teaching (Koh, 1974). Thus, if one would adopt these techniques for certain purposes, he is faced with the problem of rendering the computer "transparent" for his students. For example, the demonstration of a computer model of personality constructed according to some personality theory must be accompanied not only by a knowledge of that theory, but also by an at-least-rudimentary knowledge of how the model was implemented on the computer. Otherwise the demonstration would have little explanatory cogency. In the author's experience, this problem often manifests itself when he asks novice users to run a program. Even after receiving explicit oral and written instructions as well as demonstrations, a frequent response is, "But suppose something goes wrong when you're not here?" To solve this problem the novice must be convinced that the computer is not only a useful animal, but a friendly one as well. Its processes are understandable and, more importantly, controllable—by the novice himself.

Faculty Impediments. Inasmuch as many faculty members came through an education similar to that which exists today, some have developed attitudes like those which we examined for students in the immediately-preceding section. As Anderson points out in the first chapter in this volume, many social science departments are peopled by faculty members most of whom assayed graduate school prior to the widespread introduction of computers. These individuals often adopt a strategy of coping with the new technology by delegating computer work to their assistants. Because the faculty member's behavior in this situation clearly models the idea that computer work is truly unworthy of a professional's attention and personal involvement, the strategy is probably supportive of both student ambivalence and student negativism regarding computers. The problems outlined by Anderson might not be ameliorated in the near future by the infusion of new blood onto department faculties. It might seem that the problem will solve itself in this way, but this obvious and simple expedient does not seem to be in accord with the realities at our institutions of higher learning. The overproduction of doctoral level psychologists when coupled with the economic ill-health of many colleges and universities seems to have led to a significantly reduced turnover in staff.

Even faculty members with a positive attitude toward computer use and some computing experience often have difficulties in attempting to employ the computer for their work. These individuals seem to have a threefold problem. They must:

    (a) Familiarize themselves with the idiosyncracies of the local computer environment.

    (b) Become aware of both the hardware and the software that they might want to use in their work.

(c) If necessary, have the ability to import and implement new programs on their computer.

Although familiarization with the local computer setup is hard-bought at some institutions, most computer centers have both user's manuals and a variety of free seminars, often including rudimentary instruction in the languages available at that facility. The user's manual and general seminars have obvious utility. The value of a language seminar, especially for those already familiar with it, is less clear. However, it should be noted that such seminars often represent the *best* method for would-be faculty programmers to learn the unique aspects of the implementation of the language in that particular computer setting. Thus, such seminars may be a quick way to learn that certain features in a language can not be used at this facility. In the absence of widespread implementation of language systems incorporating solely those features advocated in the standard version, this is often the programmer's only recourse.

Apprising oneself of the available software and hardware applicable to psychological problems is often no mean task. Communications regarding psychological applications of computers are generally poor. Relevant articles appear in such diverse publications as *Artificial Intelligence, Behavior Research Methods and Instrumentation* (BRMI), *Behavioral Science, Communications of the ACM, Computer Decisions, Computer Surveys, Computing Reviews, Datamation, Educational Technology, Journal of Mathematical Psychology, Journal of the ACM, Modern Data,* and *Simulation and Games.* Little attempt has been made to centralize information for the psychologist interested in computers. A single journal, publishing only the variety of information on psychological computer applications, would be helpful in this regard. I envision such a publication as having regular departments or sections devoted to the major machine applications within the discipline (e.g., sections on developments in instructional uses, data analysis, experimentation, etc.). It should be noted that some centralization of computer-related articles has occurred in recent years. BRMI, under the editorship of Joseph B. Sidowski, has moved into the void and seems to be partly filling the call for articles on machine applications. BRMI has a section on computer technology, regularly publishes abstracts of computer programs, and annually publishes the Proceedings of the National Conference on the Use of On-Line Computers in Psychology. Unfortunately, this journal gives uneven coverage to the variety of computer uses, probably because the authors consider it inappropriate for certain applications. Although much useful information appears in BRMI, many psychologists regard BRMI as demanding a consistently high degree of technical competence of its readership.

A second and equally important mode of coping with the informational needs of the potential users involves the establishment of a well-publicized, general-purpose clearinghouse to foster better communications among workers developing innovative applications and the users in psychology. This type of clearinghouse could provide information on maximally compatible (across machines) and minimally expensive software (programming); the availability, expense, and advantages of various types of hardware; and specific computer-assisted instruction implementations. It could also act in the capacity of technical advisor for both applications designers and users. Some relatively poorly publicized, special-purpose clearinghouses (e.g., the National Program Library, CONDUIT, and Central Program Inventory for the Social Sciences at Wisconsin) do exist, but they do not seem to fill the diversity of needs among psychologist-users. The viability of a general-purpose clearinghouse is heavily dependent on the quality and quantity of the products it makes available.

For a psychologist to be able to import and implement new programs currently requires more than literacy. As a minimal requirement, he must be able to converse in a fairly sophisticated manner with staff about both his needs and the nature of the program and the hardware needed to support it. In the absence of the ready availability of trained personnel to help him, he must have a well-developed expertise in order to do the work himself. While either route can be formidable at times, both can be cleared by judicious planning to ease both the transportability and the implementation of programs. Such planning, of course, belongs more properly in the realm of what to do about the "software impediments" to broader usage of computers; therefore, it will be discussed in that section.

Software impediments. One manifestation of the underuse of computers is the wide variation in the local availability and use of the electronic data processing software. While "canned" data analytic programs account for a significant amount of computer usage, many researchers still perform non-computer analyses for a variety of reasons. Two of these reasons are of particular concern to us here. First, the researcher may lack even the minimal knowledge required for the use of prepackaged programs. For such individuals, the commentary in the last section is germane. Second, some computing milieus may have few or poor quality canned programs available. These problems may be related. A number of programs have clearly been written to satisfy the requirements of the programmer in his unique environment with little concern for the issues of the ease of either transportability or use. When such programs are exported, the ensuing difficulties are predictable. Although the discussion thus far has centered on data-analytic programs, it might just as well have dealt with instructional (or any other type of) software. The fact that the difficulties within different areas of application are similar suggests that there may be a common way of dealing with them. This analysis raises again the notion of a central clearinghouse, and recommends for consideration some functions it might serve.

A number of us involved in the publication of this volume have suggested elsewhere (Castellan *et al.,* 1976) the construction of specific guidelines to aid both developers and users of computer programs for instructional purposes. That paper also notes the value of using task forces to complete certain programming projects. Both the guidelines concept and the idea of task force units embody generally useful notions. The author believes that viable guidelines ought to be developed, under the auspices of the proposed general clearinghouse, in areas of endeavor (e.g., experimental control languages and programs) other than instructional computing. In addition, materials coming into the center for distribution should be subjected to rigorous checkout procedures. The materials disseminated by the clearinghouse should be accompanied by as much pertinent information as possible regarding the experience of previous users attempting to implement those materials in a computing environment similar to that of the person requesting the service. The user could be requested to report back to the center on the success of his attempt to adapt the program, language, etc., to his system or needs. He can also be required to report any problems encountered in the endeavor. Thus, a dialogue, albeit a formalized one involving some paper-work, would be established. As a consequence the use and ease of implementation of such material should increase considerably. Finally, it should be noted that the evolution of guidelines, checkout procedures, and performance evaluation forms, etc., is probably best done through the work of task forces.

This examination of problems impeding the expansion of computer usage within the discipline has suggested a number of possible solutions. From my vantage point, a variety of psychologists must become active in numerous ways for our field to benefit substantially from this important tool. Others are unlikely to do it. Psychologists must do it because at many institutions computer centers are still oriented toward their heaviest users in years past, i.e., the physical scientists. Computer center personnel, already overburdened in many instances, are not likely to assign high priority to the needs of psychologists as long as this group comprises a small and ill-informed minority of their users. Many natural scientists have routinely sought the opportunities to develop the necessary computer skills as something vital to their work. As long as the same does not hold true for social scientists, their requests for more or better software, service, or equipment are likely to emanate from a small group of competents. Such requests may be viewed with a jaundiced eye by decision-makers, who may regard them as representing pseudo-needs or esoteric interests. The possible constraining effect this might have on development of the discipline has been noted above. I have observed (Cf. Castellan *et al.,* 1976) that psychologists who have expertise regarding computers are often also resource people in the areas of research design and analysis (since these tap similar competencies). With a burgeoning awareness of the utility of computers within the field, such individuals are likely to bridle when asked to also translate for computer illiterates. This is probably most notably true for individuals who sought to develop their skills for a research career only to find themselves reduced to filling the role of service personnel. Any further demands on them would concomitantly reduce their freedom and increase their resentment. Moreover, service activity is not rewarded with advancement in a number of academic settiings.

Suggestions for Computer-Related Courses
for Psychology Undergraduates

The author feels that psychology students often neglect an important aspect of their development as problem-solvers by structuring their own training to avoid what we have been calling the "tool" courses. Anderson (this volume) also notes the dual problems of lack of motivation and anxiety regarding the technical demands that social science students often experience when confronted with such courses. Part of the source of anxiety these students feel has been traced above. Although I would like to see a course in logic installed as a university-wide requirement, I see it as a critical requisite for anyone seeking to function in a research environment. Thus, I suggest institution of a required course in logic for undergraduate psychology majors. Moreover, advisors ought to be encouraged to direct their students to take additional courses designed to develop logical and mathematical skills.

Anderson has mapped out in his first chapter in this volume a typology of curricular needs germane to social science computing. Anderson advocates a course that serves as an introduction to social science computing. Despite supplying us with a detailed outline of the proposed course, Anderson consciously chooses to avoid the knotty problem of which segment of the university community should teach it, noting that this type of decision awaits the assessment of actual needs and alternative solutions.

It is only on this last point that I disagree. While I agree that the assessment of needs and the preparation of solution strategies are crucial activities, it is difficult to find reason to believe that computer scientists (or anyone else) could better execute these functions for psychology than could psychologists themselves. Similar considerations with regard to statistical tools has led to a fairly widespread strategy of teaching statistics courses within psychology, perhaps based on the notion that no one understands the needs of the practitioner like another practitioner. This position strikes a sympathetic chord in me. In addition, Zinn (1972) has argued convincingly that computer scientists are unlikely to sustain the interest to engage in structuring curricula for users' disciplines. He also observes that psychologists probably do not have sufficient expertise to meet their own needs and suggests an interdisciplinary approach as a way of escaping the dilemma. This suggestion is laudable, but I am unaware of any major advances along these lines since Zinn's call for such a strategy. Moreover, I disagree with his contention that psychology lacks sufficient expertise within the discipline to deal with issues in compuer-related instruction. In the same paper Zinn noted that "Computers are more expensive, more complex, and *even more addictive than the teaching machines which diverted many a psychologist from his primary field of competence*" (1972, p. 650, italics added). It is precisely the addictive nature of the computer that has led to a wedding of the two interests by a number of psychologists. The lack of sufficient expertise within psychology is belied by the variety of sophisticated applications, albeit by a small core of workers and sometimes with the help of computer professionals, in the field. Finally, we restate the position articulated earlier: Psychologists may seek help, but they cannot wait for others to do for them; rather they must act as prime movers within their own discipline.

Beyond the introductory level, it is desirable that upper level undergraduate courses on important specialized applications (e.g., computer modeling, experimental control) be offered wherever this is feasible. However, in the absence of widespread use of such applications, there may be little apparent need to teach about them. Adopting some "usage" criterion for judging curricular inclusion of undergraduate courses over and above an introduction to social science computing clearly suggests that, at this time, only a course in data-analytic procedures could be so justified. This course may be viewed as minimal in terms of advanced offerings, at institutions lacking the resources to do more. Still, I adhere to the notion of the desirability of more advanced course offerings wherever this is possible. Such a strategy would allow a "boot-strapping" effect in terms of applications. Thus, through continual exposure to the few (and some of the limited) applications in some areas of endeavor, our students could begin to evolve better approaches to problem-solving in these areas.

Advanced Training in Computing for Psychology

Advanced training in the use of computers to deal with the specialized needs of psychology must to some extent be done on a "catch-as-catch-can" basis. This position recognizes the fact that few institutions have both the staff and the facilities to offer comprehensive training in this area. Notable exceptions, such as the quantitative psychology program at the University of Colorado, do exist (see Bailey and Polson, 1975). Again, wherever a reasonable degree of student interest, faculty ability, and useful hardware coincide, these training endeavors should be encouraged. This is especially critical at the graduate level, where the trainees would likely move to positions where they could gainfully employ their knowledge to the advantage of the discipline. Where possible such courses ought to be available to qualified undergraduates as well. The position also implies that psychologists avail themselves of courses and facilities in other disciplines. Thus, in certain areas (e.g., modeling in physiological psychology) collaborative efforts might emerge.

Elsewhere I have proposed (Starr 1972) the teaching of an algorithmic approach to problem-solving for graduate students. The approach would introduce the student to principles of computer operation, algorithmic logic (Starr, 1972), flowcharting (Chapin, 1970), and the use of prepackaged programs in either (or both) the batch-processing or interactive mode. Use of prepackaged programs in the batch-processing mode would likely require, in addition, an elementary knowledge of formatting. I developed this training method a number of years ago in an attempt to cope with the inadequacies in a number of graduate students who sought to use the computer but knew nothing of how to go about doing it. The scheme was designed as a stop-gap measure to help such students. The approach is deficient in light of the exigencies of the development of both our discipline and its practitioners. Current graduate students must know more than the minimum suggested. Still, the scheme embodies an introduction to computing. It may be profitably employed to help some of our colleagues with inadequate backgrounds in computing to obtain the skills necessary to use computers in their work. Moreover, it involves minimum cost, in terms of time, for these potential users.

In summary, the computer-oriented psychologist has often been indicted for enslaving himself to the machine. Although such dedication does occur and can be a danger, it is probably less of a danger than submitting to "tunnel vision" that prevents the broader employment of an important potential tool. By mobilizing our efforts on this front, we can benefit in many ways.

References

Anderson, J.R., and G.H. Bower. *Human Associative Memory.* Washington, D.C.: V.H. Winston, 1973.

Apter, M.J. *The Computer Simulation of Behavior.* New York: Harper and Row, 1970.

Bailey, D.E. and P.G. Polson. Real-Time Computing in Psychology at the University of Colorado. *American Psychologist,* 1975, *30,* 212-218.

Castellan, N.J., Jr. GRADER: An Automated Gradebook System, *Educational Technology,* 1973, *13,* 56-60.

Castellan, N.J., Jr. The Modern Minicomputer in Laboratory Automation. *American Psychologist,* 1975, *30,* 205-211.

Castellan, N.J. Jr., D.E. Bailey, R.S. Lehman, B.J. Starr, and G. McClelland. *The Current Use of Computers in Psychology,* CONDUIT, Iowa City, 1976.

Chapin, N. Flowcharting with the ANSI Standard: A Tutorial, *Computing Surveys,* 1970, *2,* 119-146.

Green, B.F., Jr. *Digital Computers in Research.* New York: McGraw-Hill, 1963.

Green, B.F., Jr. The Use of Time-Shared Terminals in Psychology. *Behavior Research Methods and Instrumentation,* 1972, *4,* 51-55.

Gregg, L.W. Computers: Large-Scale Usage in the Balance. *American Psychologist,* 1975, *30,* 199-204.

Johnson, J.H., and T.A. Williams. The Usage of On-Line Computer Technology in a Mental Health Admitting System. *American Psychologist,* 1975, *30,* 388-390.

Kleinmuntz, B. The Computer as Clinician. *American Psychologist,* 1975, *30,* 379-387.

Koh, Y.O. TUSTAT II: Tutorial System for Statistics with Time-Sharing Computers. *Proceedings of the Fifth Annual Conference on Computers in the Undergraduate Curricula,* Washington State University, Pullman, Washington, 1974.

Leaf, W.A. Statistical Analysis on a Large Time-Sharing System. *Behavior Research Methods and Instrumentation,* 1974, *6,* 205-208.

Lehman, R.S., and D.E. Bailey. *Digital Computing: FORTRAN IV and Its Applications in Behavioral Science.* New York: John Wiley, 1968.

Lehman, R.S., B.J. Starr, and K.C. Young. Computer Aids in Teaching Statistics and Methodology. *Behavior Research Methods and Instrumentation,* 1975, *7,* 93-102.

Loehlin, J.C. *Computer Models of Personality.* New York: Random House, 1968.

Roemer, R.A. Some Interactive Computer Applications in a Physiological Psychology Laboratory. *American Psychologist,* 1975, *30,* 295-298.

Schucany, W.R., P.D. Minton, and B.S. Shannon, Jr. A Survey of Statistical Packages. *Computing Surveys,* 1972, *4,* 65-79.

Sidowski, B. Various Uses of Minicomputers in Psychology. *Behavior Research Methods and Instrumentation,* 1972, *4,* 43-50.

Sidowski, J.B. Minicomputers in Psychology: Travelled Road and Destination. In B.J. Starr (Chair) Recent Developments in Non-Data-Analytic Applications of Computers, Symposium Presented at the Meeting of the Eastern Psychological Association, Washington, 1973.

Sidowski, J.B. Instrumentation and Computer Technology: Applications and Influences in Modern Psychology. *American Psychologist,* 1975, *30,* 191-196.

Sidowski, J.B., and S. Ross. Instrumentation in Psychology. *American Psychologist,* 1969, *24,* 187-198.

Slysz, W.D. An Evaluation of Statistical Software in the Social Sciences. *Communications of the Association for Computing Machinery,* 1974, *17,* 326-332.

Starr, B.J. Computerizing and Activities of Subjects for Psychological Research at a Large University. *Behavior Research Methods and Instrumentation,* 1970, *2,* 29-31.

Starr, B.J. Automated Problem-Solving for the Behavioral Sciences. *Behavior Research Methods and Instrumentation,* 1972, *4,* 161-164.

Uttal, W.R. *Real-Time Computers.* New York: Harper and Row, 1968.

Zinn, K. Computers in the Instructional Process: Directions for Research and Development. *Communications of the Association for Computing Machinery,* 1972, *15,* 648-651.

Note

[1] The author wishes to thank Sherman Ross and Leslie H. Hicks for their helpful comments on an earlier draft of this paper. Thanks are also due to Pat Jenkins and Stephanie Minor for their help in typing the final manuscript.

5.
Computer Use in the Undergraduate Curriculum in Political Science

Kendall L. Baker
University of Wyoming

James W. Hottois
University of San Diego

Stuart H. Rakoff
United Mine Workers of America

In this paper our goal is to assess the possibilities for computer use in the undergraduate curriculum in political science. We focus on three questions: the ways in which the computer can be used in political science courses; the benefits that can be derived from such usage; and the conditions that must exist in order to stimulate such usage.

The Place of the Computer in the Undergraduate Political Science Curriculum

One of the fundamental characteristics of political science majors is their limited background in mathematics, science, and statistics. Indeed, undergraduates often choose political science as a major in order to avoid exposure to such topics. Eulau and March (1969) have emphasized this point succinctly: "Students come to political science rather late (after many of the best have become committed to other fields); many of them migrate to political science because of inadequacies they have or feel in mathematics or science; many of them choose political science in order to prepare for a profession or simply as a liberal arts major without having any commitment to the field itself" (p. 109). As a consequence of this background, political science undergraduates are often, as Wildgen (1971) has noted, "scared stiff of computers" (p. 153).

In view of these conditions, it is difficult to imagine a course that dealt at length, and in depth, with computers in the undergraduate political science curriculum. Such a course would undoubtedly meet with substantial opposition; moreover, if implemented, it is likely that it would attract only a small minority of political science undergraduates. But there is another question: *should* such a course be part of the undergraduate political science curriculum? Our answer to this question is an unequivocal *no*. Political science, like history, English, philosophy, etc., provides basically a liberal arts rather than a pre-professional education. Few political science majors attend graduate school and many find jobs in professions quite unrelated to political science. The task of the undergraduate political science instructor, therefore, is to teach political science, not computer science. Computers are related to this goal only insofar as they provide tools for testing and understanding propositions about political phenomena. Consequently, our position is that, particularly at the undergraduate level, the computer must be viewed as a resource facility much like a library. We cannot expect most of our students to find this tool or facility inherently interesting or to have sufficient commitment to put forth the effort to become programmers in any sense of the term. Yet, if the computer is presented as a simple-to-use and non-threatening device (like the library), then our students probably will use it and find that their education is enhanced by it.

But how is this goal to be accomplished? In other words, how can the use of the computer in the classroom enrich and facilitate the learning experience of the undergraduate political science major? Our answer to this question is twofold: first, by using the computer as a data processor, the undergraduate can examine, on his own, generalizations discussed in class as well as questions that have been stimulated by reading and conversation. Second, by using the computer as a simulator, he can examine theories, policy proposals, etc., in terms of their consistency, consequences, and feasibility.

The undergraduate political science major usually does not have the time or training to perform truly original research. He has traditionally been the captive of the library, and his research papers have been regurgitations and distillations of what other people have said. If an undergraduate disagrees with a particular reported fact, he has usually been constrained by an inability to cite a counterfact. The student may have formulated a hypothesis about something but finds no way to test it. If the computer center were a resource place much like a library, then this need not be the case. It would be marvelous if the student could go to the computer to test previously untestable hypotheses. More importantly, it would be marvelous if we could say to an undergraduate major: "Here is a simple way for you to test your ideas. Go ahead and generate your own hypothesis." Or, "Don't take my word for it. Test it yourself." Here is a chance for the undergraduate political science major to share in the joy of discovery.

We do not propose that the computer be employed as a generator of student happiness, and we realize that computers can be frustrating to work with. However, in almost all areas of political science the computer and its attendant technology should be given serious consideration. Computers probably can contribute to motivating students to generate and to test their own hypotheses. Thus, the computer is obviously an important tool in any approach to undergraduate education that emphasizes inquiry and questioning rather than rote learning.

According to Guetzkow (1963), simulations of social phenomena are "operating representation(s) in reduced and/or simplified form of relations among social units by means of symbolic and/or replicate component parts" (p. 27). In a general sense, everything that political scientists do in the undergraduate classroom is simulation, attempts to present understandable representations of complex political phenomena. Yet, the systematic use of simulation as a means to achieving that understanding has been restricted, for the most part, to one subfield of political science, international politics. In simulations developed for courses in this area a student or group of students "play" a country and operate in a conflict paradigm established by the instructor. The aim of these man-man simulations is generally to teach by doing, and this technique has recently been effectively employed, with the aid of the computer, in other areas of political science as well.

At the introductory level, for example, computer simulations could be used to allow the student to explore some basic hypotheses or conceptualizations about politics. For instance, if students were able to make allocations for media advertisements, local party organization, and partisan distribution within an individual state or within the nation as a whole and then observe the results produced by these allocations, it is possible that they might have a greater appreciation of the impact of certain variables in election campaigns. Moreover, by working with simulations of various domestic and international policies and programs, students should be in a better position to examine and evaluate their consequences and implications; such an experience might also enable them to deal more effectively with new policies and programs. Finally, what better way to help a student learn the important factors that influence a state budgetary process than to compare the results of a simulation of that process with the results of a real-world system?

The existence of certain conditions might facilitate the more extensive and effective use of classroom simulations. One of these, of course, is the presence of adequate hardware. Most classroom simulations, for example, should probably be run on interactive systems. This allows the student to actually interact with the simulation program, to see " instant" reactions to his decisions, and to be able to immediately recycle the program to test a new strategy or hypothesis. Simulations can also be used at computer centers that are restricted to batch processing. The nature of one's facilities should not constitute a barrier to the use of this technique in the classroom. A second condition that might facilitate the more extensive use of simulation in the classroom would be the presence of students with programming skills. Such students would be able to test ideas, programs, policies, etc., by writing their own simulations. Yet, students with knowledge of programming are not essential to the use of simulation in the classroom, for a good deal of effective learning can take place using "canned" simulations.

In short, neither the absence of terminals nor the absence of students with backgrounds in computer programming should prevent instructors from attempting to use simulation at the undergraduate level. Many students, especially the better ones, learn by themselves, and computer simulation may provide a tool for this learning that is more efficient and rewarding than textbook or lecture description of alternative models.

**The Value of Using the Computer
at the Undergraduate Level**

In the last decade graduate departments of political science in the United States have increasingly required or encouraged aspiring Ph.D.'s to enroll in methods courses. Moreover, in the last several years, this curriculum development has been implemented at the undergraduate level at some colleges and universities. At some of these institutions, undergraduates are encouraged or required to take methods courses during their junior and senior years, while at others they are advised to take them at the outset of their college career. Although we believe the latter approach has more potential long range benefits, we should like to point out that either procedure has two major problems. First, a large number of undergraduate political scientists have little or no appreciation for the importance of methodological questions as tools for evaluating the substance of political science. Thus, many of them leave methodology at the door of the methods course. Second, many students in methods courses (here referring mainly to required methods courses) are poorly motivated before they enter the course. They have to take it, so they do.

As a consequence of these two conditions, the impact of undergraduate methods courses may be considerably less than desired. But, how can the situation be improved? Expose the student to methodological questions, no matter how simple, at a very early stage in his career. For example, in an introductory American government course a student says: "I don't believe that Americans vote for President mainly on the basis of their party preference." Now, if a data archive and a simple system for its use is handy, the instructor may say: "OK, here is the 1972 election study; go test your hypotheses." In preparing the report on this inquiry the student will have to confront some simple questions like "how do I calculate percentages?" and "is this table really different from that one?" We are immediately dealing with simple methodological and statistical questions. The persistent student whose hypothesis has not held up may start to raise questions about the wording of the items, and suddenly we are talking about reliability and validity. One of the main values, then, of using the computer as a tool in the undergraduate classroom is that it may stimulate in the student an appreciation of the importance of methodological questions.

A simplified introduction to the computer at the outset of the student's college career has yet another salutary effect. When he has been exposed to the computer in a way that is *both* interesting and non-threatening, an interest in learning more about controlling the computer may actually be generated. The student also finds that only a limited range of issues may be spoken to with a limited technical facility. Consequently, he may realize that he needs to develop more dexterity with the tool and thus he may enroll in a methods course.

In effect, then, what we are suggesting is really quite circular and reinforcing. The student is introduced to the computer in an introductory level course. This should generate interest in, or remove hesitations about, computer research methods and statistics courses. Following this, the student is exposed to a relatively systematic examination of the philosophy of political inquiry, quantitative and qualitative methods, and computer technology. From this course he moves into practical application in substantive courses of the skills he has learned; and, hopefully, this experience will move him back into advanced methodological and computer related courses. Political scientists often forget that when they are dealing with undergraduate majors, they are not dealing with people, for the most part, who are aspiring to the role of the professional political scientist. Our students want to learn about politics, and many of them want to engage in politics, but few of them wish to spend their lives as professional political scientists. Our role must, therefore, be one of facilitating undergraduate learning, and the computer should be viewed as an aid in this process.

Another value of the use of the computer in the undergraduate political science curriculum has been emphasized above, namely the joy of discovery. It has been our experience that students who are given the opportunity to work with the computer in substantive political science courses get a great deal of pleasure and benefit out of it. They seem to feel that in creating and testing their own hypotheses, they are engaging in quasi-original research. Rather than settling for what someone else thinks about a problem, they can, with proper facilities, examine their own ideas about the problem. Moreover, given the speed of the modern digital computer, they can evaluate a whole series of orthodox and unorthodox ideas and hypotheses in a relatively short period of time. They can also get an idea of the validity and reliability of someone else's conclusions about a problem or question, because in secondary analysis of data files, the student must confront the difficulty of doing a particular kind of research and evaluate such things as choice of variables, operationalizations, sample design, and statistical techniques.

We do not mean to imply, in any sense, that "the joy of discovery" can only occur when the computer is integrated into a course. This would be sheer nonsense. Clearly, library research can be equally exciting, and just as easily lead to a feeling that one is contributing something that is original. Moreover, good computer related research depends on a solid substantive background, and this can only be obtained by reading and evaluating the requisite literature available in the library. Our only point is that the computer is another resource facility that can contribute to understanding and stimulate thinking and that, as a result, it should be more heavily used at the undergraduate level.

Conditions Facilitating the Use of
the Computer at the Undergraduate Level

The principal theme of this paper has been that the use of the computer at the undergraduate level can supplement, expand, and enrich the political science curriculum. In order to achieve this goal, however, three conditions must exist: first, an adequate software system must be available; second, a relatively extensive data archive must exist; and third, there must be relatively amiable relations between the political science department and members of the university computer center.

Undergraduates should not have to learn computer programming in order to enjoy the fruits of being able to manipulate large or small data files. When the undergraduate is forced to write and debug his own program he certainly learns something about the algorithms that he is using, but he probably is not learning much that will contribute to his understanding of politics. The computer may, in this case, be standing in the way of his education. Many contemporary students, for example, are trying to escape from technology. Thus, they do not find computer programming inherently interesting and few of them can probably be convinced that it is essential to learn programming in order to learn about politics.

Consequently, if the computer is to be integrated into the undergraduate curriculum, it is essential that an efficient and relatively simple software system be available. There have been some important advances in this area in recent years. Probably the most notable work has taken place at Dartmouth College under the title of Project IMPRESS. Dartmouth is blessed with a well financed computer facility, a staff with impressive technical qualifications, and a genuine commitment to developing technology for undergraduate education. The IMPRESS project is impressive both in terms of the easy access which it provides to the student user and the cost of the hardware which is dedicated to it. IMPRESS works because Dartmouth has a large time-sharing system with many terminals easily available to students, and because the computer center was able to dedicate a large block of resources to the system. When operating under IMPRESS the student may access a data set through a typewriter terminal. If the student knows nothing at all about IMPRESS the system will instruct him in how to carry out the desired manipulations. Thus, IMPRESS is somewhat more than just a program-data-codebook interface. It is an interactive system that assumes that the user knows how to turn on the terminal and sign on the system. Once he has done this, the student, with instructional assistance from the system, is able to easily request information about a study and perform statistical manipulations on data from the study that is being used; and he is also able to transform the data in the study in various ways. All of this is accomplished with a few very simple commands that sound like the English language.

For most political scientists, IMPRESS is simply out of the question. Most of us are not blessed with Dartmouth's impressive physical and technological capabilities. However, it does represent an ideal that we should seek to emulate in our own ways and within the range of our own technical capabilities and campus facilities. Many of us have at least easy access to batch processing facilities, and, in recent years, there have been important software advances in this area, such as the Statistical Package for the Social Sciences (SPSS), and the University of Michigan package (OSIRIS) which can be usefully employed in the undergraduate program.

These systems are tied, for the most part, to large computers, and they provide students with a fairly simple and straightforward means of accessing large (or small) predefined data files. SPSS has all of the computing power of IMPRESS and it also matches IMPRESS in terms of the documentation. Like IMPRESS, it can also be employed by a fairly naive user, although it cannot instruct the user in the manner which IMPRESS (an interactive system) can.

The systems we have mentioned embody characteristics that we feel define the ideal situation for using the computer in training undergraduate political scientists. The software is sufficiently simple so that employment of the computer does not stand in the way of the student. Almost no investment in compter training is required for the student to use the computer. The student is able to access data quickly and easily and does not need to worry about dragging around boxes of cards, while the instructor does not need to worry about duplicating the cards. The data are documented with the output and the user does not need to supply his own data.

A second condition that would facilitate the more extensive use of computers at the undergraduate level is the existence of data archives. Undergraduates should not have to collect and keypunch their own data in order to learn about politics. We are convinced that, in most cases, the learning per hour is minimized while the drudgery per hour is maximized when the undergraduate is told to collect and keypunch data. We should also keep in mind that most good studies directed by experienced researchers usually take more than a semester to complete. Thus, it is our position that the development of data archives where computer compatible information is made easily available to undergraduate students is an absolute necessity.

The Inter-University Consortium for Political Research at the University of Michigan has provided us with a good centralized data archive whose materials are easily available to member institutions. Indeed, the efforts of the ICPR should probably be expanded. Yet, the ICPR is relatively expensive and, possibly as a result of this, few exclusively undergraduate institutions are members. Consequently, a more extensive system of regional data archive networks should be established. This would permit smaller institutions to make use of the data stored and collected by larger universities. Such regional archives are now in operation in a number of University settings, most notably in the State University of New York and the California State College system. In addition, more efforts should probably be devoted to the collection and storage of data on local political issues and problems. If computer related analysis is to contribute to the undergraduate curriculum, political science departments must be in a position to allow students to work with whatever data base they wish. They should not be forced to say to a student: "You may conduct a data project if it deals with national issues and questions of the following variety."

A final condition that we believe is central to the effective uses of the computer in the undergraduate classroom is the existence of friendly relations with the local computer center. Although this condition is discussed a number of times in the literature, there is, to our knowledge, no systematic study of the nature of the relationships between social scientists and computer scientists at colleges and universities in this country. Yet, on the basis of our own experiences and those of colleagues in varied institutional settings, it would seem that, in many instances, such relationships are less than ideal.

In view of this, what must computer scientists understand about political science use of computers and what services must they provide in order to facilitate the use of the computer by political science undergraduates? At the most fundamental level, it seems essential that they understand that a good deal of the use of the computer by political scientists involves data processing, and that, at present, only a limited number of political science undergraduates possess programming skills. Consequently, they should recognize that:

1. Substantial computer time should be available to political and other social scientists. What may be involved here is a close look at the computing center's accounting algorithms. Do they discriminate against the social scientist who runs a few jobs but whose jobs require large sectors of the computer?

2. The equipment necessary to use the computer (i.e., keypunches, card readers, line printers, teletypes) should be readily available to undergraduates. This means that the equipment should

be where the student is and plentiful enough so that the student can actually get to it.

3. In the case of political science undergraduates, it may be just as important to teach them how to make effective use of efficient "canned" programs as it is to teach them programming. It may be more important that they understand the rudiments of algorithmic thinking than that they understand the rudiments of programming.

4. At least one computer consultant with a solid background in social science should be available in the center or in the department. This consultant should be available either directly or indirectly to undergraduates.

5. If social scientists are to make use of interactive systems such as IMPRESS or interactive games and simulations, disk space must be provided for storing programs and data files. This is essential to providing easy access to archived information. In addition, terminal rooms, with consultants, should be established when time sharing capabilities are present.

Since computer scientists do not always seem to understand either the ways in which social scientists use the computer or their computer related needs, it might be useful to establish conferences and/or institutes at which social scientists are given an opportunity to discuss with computer scientists the relevance of the computer to their respective disciplines. Such institutes and conferences would be helpful in reducing some of the antagonism and hostility that apparently exists between these two groups. In instances where computer scientists do understand the needs of social scientists, but lack the necessary funds to meet these needs, appropriate funding agencies should be encouraged to provide developmental grants. Finally, in order to improve relationships between computer scientists and social scientists, it seems important that at least one social scientist always serve on the university computer committee; where such a committee does not exist, one member of the social science departments who has a strong background in computing should be appointed to serve as a liaison officer between the center and the social sciences.

References

Eulau, H., and J. March (Eds.) *Political Science.* Englewood Cliffs, N.J.: Prentice-Hall, 1969.

Guetzkow, H. *et al. Simulation in International Relations: Developments for Research and Teaching.* Englewood Cliffs, N.J.: Prentice-Hall, 1963.

Wildgen, J.K. Computers and Undergraduate Training in an Underdeveloped Area: The Case of Louisiana State University in New Orleans, in *Proceedings of the Conference on Computers in the Undergraduate Curriculum,* Dartmouth College, Hanover, N.H., 1971.

6.
Computer Applications in Teaching and Learning

Ronald L. Koteskey
Asbury College

Fred S. Halley
SUNY, Brockport

James M. Swanson
University of Texas, Austin

Robert J. Tracy
DePaul University

Some believe that computer technology, perhaps more than any other means at the present, holds promise that we can deal with the educational problems of today and tomorrow in a significant fashion (Holtzman, 1970). This view is not shared by others, who believe that the computer has a depersonalizing and alienating effect. The position of this paper is that the computer is a tool, neither good nor evil; and, like the slide rule or calculator, can be used as a time-saving device. Moreover, the computer can be used to perform tasks that would not even be attempted otherwise. On the other hand, it can be a waste of time and money, like using an expensive calculator to multiply a number by 1000 (Mesthene, 1968; Oettinger and Marks, 1969). This paper attempts to encourage the use of available computer technology by reporting successful, yet non-trivial, computer applications to teaching and learning.

Assumptions and Goals

At this point we make a series of assumptions about education. These are in the form of value judgments, unsupported in this paper, that could be easily challenged. They are used to review traditional educational practices and to illustrate instructional computer applications at the end of the paper.

The Individual Is of Greatest Importance. Keller (1968) has noted that traditional lecture, discussion, lockstep classes are potentially very depersonalizing. Each student is treated exactly the same; therefore, the slow are lost, the fast are bored, and the fortunate few "average" students learn the most. Everyone (the prepared and the unprepared) is studying the same material at the same time, going at the same rate of speed, etc. Of course, to receive credit in a course, the students should have studied the same content; but it may be inconvenient or impossible to study it at the time the teacher requires. The student may not have the necessary background, or he may already know the subject and have nothing to do until a new topic is introduced. If everyone were the same, the lockstep method would be fine, but it completely ignores the importance of the individual. A solution to this problem is to have a very low student-teacher ratio or to use student proctors as in the Keller Plan.

Cost Per Pupil Should Be Minimized. With rising teacher salaries and tightening educational budgets, most attempts to lower student-teacher ratios to increase individual attention are impractical. On-line computer-assisted instruction (CAI), one attempt to individualize instruction without lowering the student-teacher ratio, is not currently cost-competitive with conventional modes of instruction (see PLATO in Bitzer and Johnson, 1971). Kemeny (1972) has pointed out that CAI is often a misuse of expensive computer time. Efficient and effective instructional use of the computer in the educational process is a critical need as the cost per pupil increases.

Cheating Is Questionable. Aside from guilt feelings and lowering (or raising, depending on the value system) of self-esteem, the student who cheats is unlikely to learn essential material. The traditional method of teaching with everyone studying the same material, working the same problems, writing papers or reports on the same topic, and taking the same tests encourages cheating and makes it, from the student's viewpoint, a practical enterprise. Answers are compared, papers and reports are copied or purchased, and test questions move quickly along the student grapevine if they are not already in the files of fraternities and sororities. Students may pass courses, get good grades, but learn little.

The Student Should Know What Is Expected. Many teachers do not specify what they expect of the student other than that he "know everything" from the textbook and lectures. So, of course, the student does not know specifically his academic responsibility.

The teacher who has not specified behavioral objectives decides that the "ideal question" is one that discriminates the "good" from the "bad" students, i.e., half the students miss it. The basic strategy in making up a test question is not "What should the student know?" but "Will about half the students miss this?" Of course, this means that the teacher has failed with half his students. Therefore, teachers resort to footnotes, figure captions, and other insignificant details for testing. These teachers feel it is best to keep the student confused as to what he is to know. This situation may be avoided through proper use of criterion-referenced grading procedures.

The Normal Curve Is an Inappropriate Approach to Grading. Since the instructor typically has not specified behavioral objectives and students miss about half the questions on the typical well-constructed test, he resorts to the normal curve to determine grades. The normal curve is very useful in inferential statistics. But class grades obtained from a highly selected and usually small sample such as college students do not necessarily conform to a normal curve. Furthermore, if the student is in a slow class, he may get an "A" for the same work that would result in a "C" in a bright class. An alternative is to use a criterion-referenced or contractual procedure instead of normative grading.

Cooperation Should Be Encouraged. In the traditional classroom, competition often means that when one wins (gets an "A"), someone else must lose (get an "F"). Students who have been exposed to normative grading may become reluctant to help others because they realize their grade depends on their relative position in the class rather than on how much they know. As a result of normative grading, peer teaching and learning is minimized even though this is a valuable and effective pedagogical technique. The clear specification of behavioral objectives makes the teacher an ally rather than merely a judge in the attainment of these objectives.

Summary. The value judgments implicit in the above paragraphs are shared by many who use traditional educational methods. It is the experience of the authors that the goals implied above are not incompatible with computer technology and, in fact, computer applications may enhance the attainment of these goals.

Types of Usage for Computer Applications
in Teaching and Learning

While advances in computer and educational technology have created attractive new possibilities for the application of new knowledge in an effective manner, it has been stymied by strong resistance to change (Oettinger, 1966). The applications discussed below have been used successfully in actual classroom settings by one or more of the authors of this paper. There is no set pattern for implementing these techniques. The specific applications are dependent on the type of course, the instructor's goals, and student acceptance. The applications may play a major or minor part in a course. They may be used singularly or jointly to achieve instructional goals. Regardless of techniques opted, successful implementation is dependent upon both the instructor's and the student's understanding of how these techniques are to be used in the attainment of beneficial instructional goals. The applications listed below are intended as unobtrusive means to an instructional end rather than ends in themselves.

Examination Generation. The computer may be used to generate exams used to test student comprehension of subject matter in a variety of disciplines. This is most useful in courses where student understanding may be measured by means of multiple choice, true-false, or completion questions. Under control of the instructor, a question pool is organized into groups representing course content areas and stored in the computer. Programs are available that randomly sample within each content area to produce different, but "equivalent," examinations for each student and separate answer keys for the instructor (Wagener, 1973; Koteskey, 1972).

A variant of the above technique is to design the question pool so that it may be added to by several instructors rather than remaining the product of a single instructor. This is most useful when introductory sections of a course are being taught by different instructors and each may review and add to the question pool. To generate exams, the instructor specifies content areas to be sampled and can even specify specific questions from each content area. This cooperative technique involving several instructors eliminates the need for examination security since such a large pool of questions makes cheating without knowing the subject matter impossible. Some instructors even make the total question pool available to the students as a security aid.

Automatic Exam Grading. For multiple examinations produced by any method, the computer may be used to score and evaluate student performance. To do this, students take exams on optically scannable answer sheets, mark-sense, or portapunch cards to be processed by the computer. This procedure is applicable when a single exam is given to an entire class or when each student receives a different exam; in either case, answer keys produced during exam generation are used to score the student's tests (Towle *et al.,* 1973). Given the decline in support for graduate assistants, computerized grading is especially convenient for the instructor, and in large enrollment classes is often a necessity. Automatic grading programs can be used to provide summary statistics on student performance, such as histograms, standardized scores, and item analyses that may be desired by the instructor.

The above techniques utilize batch computing facilities for generation of student materials. An alternative technique is the use of time sharing computer terminals. Terminals further individualize the student's experience. A simple application may be made with the development of several forms of a test. When a student desires to take a form of the test, he obtains a copy from an instructor. The student then goes to a time sharing terminal and requests the computer program for his test. Responses to test questions are typed in to the computer by the student. As soon as the last question is finished, a previously established answer file is used to evaluate the student's performance. Almost instantaneously, the computer is able to report performance to the student along with diagnosis of errors.

A more sophisticated application of terminal testing is in the use of the computer for what Holtzman (1970) calls "Individually Tailored Testing" (pp. 137-200). In this application, previously prepared test forms are not used, but rather test questions, graded in difficulty, are stored in a computer. When a student goes to a terminal to take a test, questions are first printed out for the average student. As the student answers the questions, they are evaluated in terms of the difficulty he is having with the test. If it is too easy, harder questions are selected; if it is too difficult, easier questions are selected. In this manner, a student is tested within the range of his ability. He is scored on the basis of the correctness and difficulty of the questions he answered. This technique allows the computer to dynamically adjust the difficulty of a test to the ability of the student during the test itself.

Student Tracking. In large classes it often becomes difficult to maintain a record-keeping system that enables the instructor to keep track of the progress of his students. The computer may be used as a dynamic grade book and filing system that may be updated and corrected by the instructor. It is particularly useful in self-paced or self-instructional courses (Bruell, 1972). Such systems can produce graphs of class performance, compute scores, standardize test scores, and assign grades. The student data bank may be interrogated to find students who may be having difficulty with the course so that they may be offered extra help (Castellan, 1973).

The above applications of the computer can be used in practically any course. The following applications are better suited to statistical or methodology courses since they are based upon numerical methods.

Problem Generation. It is often desirable to supply individual students with separate sets of data for purposes of analysis and interpretation. Using the computer, it is possible to generate data sets by drawing random samples from populations, a procedure that produces a unique exercise for each student and thus discourages plagiarism, while at the same time offering considerable convenience for the instructor (Halley, 1972). Programs may be elaborate, so that entire word problems are printed on computer paper ready for student use, or more simple programs that create numeric outputs to be attached to preprinted problems may be used (Tracy and Salmon, 1974; Salmon and Tracy, 1975).

For each student exercise that is printed, a corresponding solution can be produced for the instructor's use in checking and grading. The solutions can contain not only the final answer to problems, but also intermediate summary statistics so that students' computation errors may be located and partial credit assigned. The printed output of the program can be designed so that the solutions can be conveniently separated from the exercises and the exercises easily separated from one another for distribution to students.

The programs are designed for the convenience of the instructor, and typically require no preparation of raw data. Instead, the instructor enters such information as the number of exercises to be produced, the difficulty level of exercises, and the parameters of the populations from which the data values are randomly generated. The parameter values can be chosen to produce marginal statistical significance, causing some of the generated exercises to yield statistically significant results and others to be nonsignificant (also see Lehman, 1972; Lehman *et al.*, 1974; Koteskey, 1974).

Computational Examination Generators. The above applications are primarily designed for homework, drill, and practice. However, the same general techniques may be utilized for exam generation and evaluation of student performance. This use of computers offers many of the same advantages as the problem generation procedure discussed above, specifically to produce individualized exams, discourage cheating, and to make exam production more convenient for the instructor. Kotesky (1972) has developed these procedures as a means of grading students solely in terms of the amount of material they master. Students are allowed to proceed to a new course topic only after they have mastered earlier material. Realizing this, the students study to learn the material well. The students take a test only when they are ready, so there is no such thing as a make-up test. The instructor meanwhile does not have to spend time making up tests and keys, since these are produced by the computer.

Program Packages. Program packages, often referred to as "canned programs," are generalized computer programs written and stored on a computer for use by persons not familiar with a programming language (Anderson and Coover, 1972; Service, 1972). For each program, there is documentation that instructs the person how to use the program. Program packages may be designed to run in batch or interactive modes, the latter mode being the most useful for student learning (Kemeny, 1972). Some are quite extensive and do almost any type of data analysis or statistical testing, while others are more specific and handle special applications.

Packaged programs are most useful in courses where it is not desirable to teach students computer programming, but it is desirable to have students use the computer (Halley, 1975). Once students are exposed to the utility of packaged programs to accomplish their objectives, they sometimes become interested in learning more about computers and computing languages.

Program packages may be applied in research methods courses where students analyze data they have collected. In courses where simulation packages (see discussion below) are used, students may use "canned" statistical programs to analyze the outcome of simulated experiments (see Swanson *et al.,* 1973). Also, in courses where it is desirable to analyze textual materials, programs for content analysis have been developed (Sedelow and Sedelow, 1972). When using someone else's "package," one must always check it carefully for accuracy and correctness. Many packages look nice on the outside but contain many errors.

Simulation. Computer programs may be used to simulate certain phenomena. In the area of statistics, for example, programs have been used to conduct sampling experiments based on random samples drawn from normal populations with specified parameters (e.g., Appelbaum and Guthrie, 1970; Garrett, 1970; Lehnes and Cooley, 1968; Wikoff, 1970). It is possible systematically to vary sample sizes and different parametric values to study their effects on a number of theoretical propositions. Such experiments, perhaps conducted in class, might be used to provide students with an intuitive understanding of theoretical concepts.

In addition, simulation techniques are being used to train students in experimental design in specific content areas (Main and Head, 1971; Cromer, 1973, 1974). This technique is used to introduce students to research design in a wide spectrum of the social sciences, encompassing areas in which research facilities may be limited (subject pools, apparatus, space, time, and cost constraints). The emphasis is on sequential experimental design in which students design subsequent studies based on prior experimental outcomes. For example, students are allowed to experiment with a model of the "cocktail party problem," concerning the ability of a person to attend to the conversation of one speaker in the midst of one or more other speakers. A computer model has been constructed to simulate current knowledge of this phenomenon and students are allowed to choose experimental designs and to input the design parameters into the model. For example, in one version of the model, students are allowed to manipulate such variables as: (1) the number of subjects to be run; (2) whether the accepted message (the message to be attended to) and the ignored message are presented to both ears or whether the two messages are directed to different ears; (3) the relative loudness of the messages; and (4) the content of the two messages. The model simulates the performance of the requested number of subjects under the specified conditions.

To complete the experiment, one or more additonal groups of subjects are simulated using different settings of the independent variables. The model outputs performance scores for each subject in each group, and the student may be required to interpret or to analyze the data in order to test his hypotheses. There are a number of other simulations that have been developed, dealing with imprinting, schizophrenia, and obesity.

Programming Skills for Problem-Solving. In this application, the student actually writes programs in a computer language. The availability of easy-to-learn programming languages frees the student from "busy work" at desk top calculators and enables the learning and understanding of statistical procedures to proceed at a more rapid rate. The implementation of these techniques is dependent upon the availability of easy-to-learn languages (BASIC) and access to time-sharing terminals (Kemeny, 1972). In addition, interpretation languages have been developed that may be used to write programs and include access to packages (Castellan, 1970; Swanson *et al.,* 1973).

Critique of Computer Applications

As can be seen from the variety of techniques above, computers allow wide variation in how courses are conducted. Even though courses are conducted differently, they all embody the basic philosophy stated in the first part of this paper.

Individualization. Contrary to what has been predicted, intelligent use of computers does not force people into the same mold. Individualization may, in fact, be enhanced by individualized testing that allows students to proceed at their own speed; repeatable testing that allows individual mastery of materials; unique problem generation that encourages each student to do the required work; and the provision of program packages that allow individual research and experimentation (statistical packages and simulation routines).

However desirable indivualization may be, there are possible disadvantages. Individualization places extreme responsibility on the student to pace himself. Without the traditional prodding of the instructor, students may procrastinate and get hopelessly behind, with the attendant consequences that they receive lower grades. Some would argue the desirability of student responsibility being reflected in course grades. Others would maintain that people need external pacing for attainment of difficult but important tasks. A method of accomplishing this latter is by providing a series of semi-threatening deadlines. With the exception of these deadlines and the end of the quarter, each student moves at his own speed.

Furthermore, a disadvantage exists for the instructor, as he may become less involved with his more interested and highly motivated students. The better students tend to complete individualized courses without contacting the instructor; the less able but motivated students tend to have extensive contact with the instructor, thereby distorting his view of overall student performance. A possible solution to this difficulty is to enlist the aid of the better students as tutors.

Cost Factors. A disadvantage of the techniques discussed above is that their initial implementation is costly in terms of time and expertise. The expertise factor may be less of a problem, since many packages currently under development possibly can be transported to the user's system. There still remains, however, the time expenditure for the individual instructor who must familiarize himself with available materials and decide, by consulting with his computer center staff, whether available packages can be implemented on his particular system. This is particularly problematic since these efforts are not usually recognized by colleagues as legitimate professional activities and thus are not rewarded.

Once the packages are working on the local computer system, the packages can have a dramatic effect on reducing instructional costs, especially if large class sections are being taught. Less instructor time is required in preparing exams. Less secretarial service is needed since exams are computer generated, and fewer assistants are needed because the computer scores the tests and keeps student records.

Cheating Minimized. Because exams and exercises are individualized, copying another student's answers is impractical. Furthermore, if the question pool is published in advance, there is no profit in students keeping examination files.

Computer Applications Encourage Specification of Course Goals. When the instructor goes through the process of designing a question pool to be placed in a computer file, he is forced to be specific concerning what the course covers. This clarification process enables him to more effectively communicate course expectations to students. With mystery removed, the student can now concentrate on learning the important material in the course. Similarly, mystery concerning the method of grading is removed as the criteria for grading are clearly specified. Moreover, use of the computer allows more rapid feedback on student performance.

Criterion Grading. Student grades now depend on absolute achievement, not on how well the rest of the class has done. The standards are set for each grade, and anything from all "A's" to all "F's" may be given. When the student receives a given grade, it means that he can do certain specified things, not that he fell at a given point in some unspecified class; thus, the grade has a different connotation than traditionally.

Cooperation Emphasized. Since there is no competition between students using these methods, cooperation is encouraged. Peer teaching and learning occurs openly and freely without the threat of one student's grade being enhanced at the expense of another's. Such cooperation is not encouraged under normative referenced procedures.

Without the threat of normative grading, the students feel that the professor is more fair and not to be flattered, out-guessed, or fooled; rather, the professor becomes an ally to be cooperated with in the attainment of clearly stated course goals. In this setting, without distraction of conflict, rivalry, and mysterious grading procedures, *esprit de corps* is likely to develop within the class.

Use of the computer produces a familiarity that promotes a positive attitude toward computers and their usage. The following note was received by an instructor during a course using these techniques:

"Dear Computer:
  Congratulations! You couldn't have picked a harder eight questions. May your transitors corrode, your wires melt, and your ability to pick easier questions improve.
                              Your truly human friend,
                                          Doug"

References

Anderson, R.E., and E.R. Coover. Wrapping Up the Package: Critical Thoughts on Applications Software for Social Science Data Analysis. *Computers and the Humanities,* 1972, *7, 2.*

Appelbaum, I., and D. Guthrie. Use of Computers in Undergraduate Statistics Instruction. *Proceedings of the Conference on Computers in the Undergraduate Curricula,* The University of Iowa, Iowa City, 1970.

Bitzer, D.L., and R.L. Johnson. Plato: A Computer-Based System Used in the Engineering of Education. *Proceedings of the IEEE,* 1971, *59,* 960-968.

Bruell, J. CUMREC: An Interpretive Program for Cumulative Records in the Classroom. Project C—BE, Technical Report #4, University of Texas, Austin, 1972.

Castellan, N.J., Jr. SMIS/SIS: The Symbolic Matrix Interpretive System and Statistical Interpretive System. *Common,* 1970, Seattle Proceedings, 64-73.

Castellan, N.J., Jr. GRADER: An Automated Gradebook System. *Educational Technology,* 1973, *13*(3), 56-60.

Cromer, A.O. Teaching Experimental Psychology with On-Line Computers. *Behavioral Research Methods & Instrumentation,* 1973, *5,* 195-197.

Cromer, A.O. Teaching Research Theory and Application Through On-Line Simulation, *Behavior Research Methods & Instrumentation,* 1974, *6,* 126-127.

Garrett, H.G. SAMDS: A Program to Generate Empirical Sampling Distributions of the Mean. *Proceedings of the Conference on Computers in the Undergraduate Curricula,* The University of Iowa, Iowa City, 1970.

Halley, F.S. Individualized Instruction in Basic Statistics: An Experiment in Computer Managed Instruction. *Proceedings of* the *1972 Conference on Computers in the Undergraduate Curricula,* Southern Regional Education Board, Atlanta, 1972.

Halley, F.S. Programs for Use in Teaching Research Methods for Small Computers. *Teaching Sociology,* 1975, *2,* 218-221.

Holtzman, W.H. (Ed.) *Computer Assisted Instruction, Testing, and Guidance.* New York: Harper and Row, 1970.

Keller, F.S. Good-bye Teacher. *Journal of Applied Behavioral Analysis,* 1968, *1,* 79-89.

Kemeny, J.G. *Man and the Computer.* New York: Charles Scribner's Sons, 1972.

Koteskey, R.L. *Computer-Generated Statistics Tests.* Baldwin, New York: Life Science Associates, 1972.

Koteskey, R.L. *Individualized Computer-Generated Workbooks for Statistics.* Baldwin, New York: Life Science Associates, 1975.

Lehman, R.S. The Use of the Unknown in Teaching Statistics, Eastern Psychological ssociation, Boston, 1972.

Lehman, R.S., B.J. Starr, and K.C. Young. Computer Aids in Teaching Statistics and Methodology, National Conference on the Use of On-Line Computers in Psychology, November, 1974.

Lohnes, P.R., and W.W. Cooley. *Introduction to Statistical Procedures with Computer Exercises.* New York: John Wiley, 1968.

Main, D.B., and S. Head. Computer Simulations in the Elementary Psychology Laboratory. *Proceedings of the Conference on Computers in the Undergraduate Curricula,* University Press of New England, Hanover, New Hampshire, 1971.

Mesthene, E.G. How Technology Will Shape the Future. *Science,* 1968, *161,* 135-143.

Oettinger, A.G. A Vision of Technology and Education. *Communications of the ACM,* 1966, *9,* 487-490.

Oettinger, G., and S. Marks. *Run, Computer, Run.* Cambridge: Harvard University Press, 1969.

Salmon, P.G. and R.J. Tracy. Computer-Generated Computation Exercises (BASIC). *Behavior Research Methods & Instrumentation,* 1975.

Sedelow, S.Y., and W.H. Sedelow. *Language Research and the Computer.* University of Kansas, Lawrence, 1972.

Service, J. *A User's Guide to the Statistical Analysis System* Raleigh, North Carolina: Sparks Press, 1972.

Swanson, J.M., S. Riederer, and H. Weekly. Using OMNITAB to Teach Applied Statistics. *Proceedings of the Fourth Conference on Computers in the Undergraduate Curricula,* The Claremont Colleges, Claremont, California, 1973.

Towle, N.J., P.S. Cohen, and L.R. Cohen. A Case Study in the Use of Computers to Personalize Instruction. *Proceedings of the Fourth Conference on Computers in the Undergraduate Curricula,* The Claremont Colleges, Claremont, California, 1973.

Tracy, R.J., and P.G. Salmon. *Computer-Generated Computation Exercises (FORTRAN).* Baldwin, New York: Life Science Associates, 1974.

Wagener, J.L. CAGEE: An Approach to Computer-Assisted Generation and Evaluation of Examination, Mimeograph, Department of Computer Science, SUNY College at Brockport, Brockport, New York, 1973.

Wikoff, L. Using the Computer in Basic Statistics Courses. *Proceedings of the Conference on Computers in the Undergraduate Curricula,* The University of Iowa, Iowa City, 1970.

PART II
Statistics and Methodology

7.
Social Science Data Processing: An Overview

James M. Sakoda
Brown University

Ronald E. Anderson
University of Minnesota

Francis Sim
Pennsylvania State University

Richard A. Wiste
Northern Illinois University

Basic Philosophy

The bulk of computer usage in the social sciences is in data analysis, rather than in areas such as model building. Part of this may be due to the state of social science theories, which are often verbal formulations not always conducive to representation as a viable model. An exception is population studies (Dyke and MacCluer, 1973). On the other hand, data to be analyzed do not come from experiments, which typically produce limited amounts of data, but from questionnaires and censuses that provide information on large numbers of variables for even larger numbers of cases. A typical national survey, such as those undertaken by the National Opinion Research Center, may contain a hundred questions, each of which can be treated as a variable, and 1500 respondents. Use of fewer cases leads to difficulties of analysis in the contingency table between two variables, with addition of controls for age, sex, etc. This requires setting up separate two way tables for each level of the control variable, and without sufficient numbers to begin with, refined analysis of the data is not possible. The number of variables could be reduced if important parameters were known and could be measured with confidence directly. In the absence of such parameters, indicators are sought. For example, to reflect socioeconomic status/income, information on income, education, and occupation are sought whenever possible. A procedure for reducing indicators to basic parameters, such as cluster analysis or factor analysis, can be used, but to take this step the initial indicator variables are needed.

Therefore, whether one is doing one's own research or teaching research methods to students, one must begin with the fact that the social scientist generally needs to deal with fairly sizeable files.

Serious social science students are generally encouraged to take a course in research methods and statistics. Statistical techniques are needed for analysis of data, but can only be used if the data are already tabulated. In the research methods course an attempt is usually made to teach the collection of data (e.g., by writing a questionnaire and administering it to fellow students). The actual processing of the data in the early days could be taught by coding sample data, punching cards, and running them through a sorter to obtain tabulations. The same task is now assumed by a computer, and if the skill and knowledge of data-processing is to be taught, use of the computer becomes necessary. To make the experience meaningful, it is desirable to allow students to deal with actual data rather than with simulated information, although simulated data for illustrative purposes have their place, also. One reason for this is that the task of analysis for the social scientist is not the relating of two variables that are well defined, but dealing with the problem of extracting meaningful relationships from a file containing many variables.

To meet this need of data collection and dissemination, program writing and implementation of computer usage is required. It is not sufficient, for example, to teach a student the rudiments of programming, since the programs that he is capable of writing would not begin to make a dent into the problems of file management and varieties of statistical analyses that he must perform.

The basic criterion for meeting this need must be feasibility. Given the resources of the instructor, students, and the available computer facility, ways must be found to make the use of computers possible. Primarily this means making the use of computers relatively easy for the instructor and students; only secondarily is it necessary to consider efficiency. Cost, which is tied to some extent to efficiency, is an important constraint, particularly for smaller colleges without adequate funds to acquire a large system.

Systems and Languages for Social Science Packages

To the casual observer of computer operations there appears to be two different modes—batch and interactive. The batch user typically submits cards at the computer center and returns some time later for his output from the center's high-speed printer. The interactive user sits at a typewriter terminal and continuously interacts with the computer in a language like BASIC or APL. APL is truly conversational in that it permits a programmer to get a line by line execution of the program, including input of data and output of results on the typewriter. BASIC provides line by line diagnostics. A programmer can also modify his program as he develops it. BASIC and APL are conversational languages in this sense. FORTRAN, a nonconversational language, requires that main programs and subroutines be compiled and filed before they can be executed. FORTRAN is sometimes available from a typewriter terminal in addition to or as a replacement for BASIC or APL. One might say that in using FORTRAN the mode is interactive, but not conversational.

In the interactive system, programs are written in either a conversational or nonconversational mode. A conversational program prints out messages to the user and requests appropriate responses from him. To the user, it makes little difference in which language the program is written. To the writer of the program, considerations such as availability of the language, its power, cost, personal preference, etc., will determine that language he will use.

In general, for mini-computers, BASIC is often the only language provided by manufacturers. In larger systems there is often a choice between BASIC, APL, and FORTRAN. APL has powerful mathematical features not possessed by FORTRAN or BASIC, but is the least likely to be available for use. APL also requires special symbols not found on many typewriter keyboards and typeballs and hence if it is to be used the appropriate equipment must be purchased. To the casual observer, then, the situation looks like this:

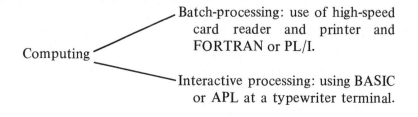

Computing
— Batch-processing: use of high-speed card reader and printer and FORTRAN or PL/I.
— Interactive processing: using BASIC or APL at a typewriter terminal.

In actuality the situation is a bit more complicated. In the interactive mode we have:

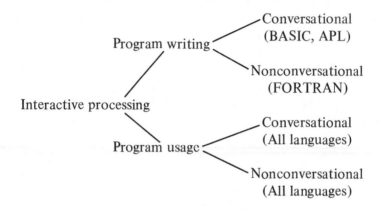

It would appear that a conversational program might better be written in FORTRAN rather than in BASIC, if there is a choice between two of them at the terminal, due to FORTRAN's greater power. Part of that power lies in its ability to provide subroutines that can be compiled and stored on a file, a capability that is missing in most BASIC systems.

Interactive processing of programs in any language carries a considerable amount of overhead, and most social science data processing production jobs, even for classes, can be performed more efficiently in the batch than the interactive mode. The problem for the social scientist is to attain some of the convenience of working from a terminal with the efficiency of batch processing using convenient-to-use large packages. There are a number of alternatives.

Fast Batch. Fast batch is designed to run many small student jobs and provide practically instantaneous turnaround time. Typically, students drop their program and data cards into a card reader, and wait for the high speed printer to print out results. To attain this high speed, an in-core compiler, such as WATFOR or PL/C, is used, and students are limited in the number of cards of input, number of lines of output, and the length of execution time. Fast batch is not interactive but provides instant turnaround desired by many users. It shares with interactive use many limitations on the type of program that can be run. It is generally not suitable for the use of large packages, such as SPSS, the Statistical Package for the Social Sciences.

Remote Job Entry of Remote Batch. A terminal consisting of a card reader and printer located some distance from the computing center provides input into and output from the regular batch system. To many social scientists this comes close to being the ideal setup, since they do not have to learn any new language in order to reap the advantage of not having to walk to the center and back again to check to see if their output is ready. The same service might be provided more slowly by a system of pickup and delivery.

Interactive Batch Processing. What is desired in a sophisticated system is interaction between the batch and interactive systems. In such a system a program written in FORTRAN or BASIC on a terminal could be sent to the batch stream to be processed efficiently there. The program could then be developed inter- actively, modified by the editing facility, and executed efficiently in batch mode. In some systems it is also possible to create a file of control cards for large packages, such as SPSS, at the terminal, and enter it into the batch stream for execution. It is also possible to have the output spooled on a disk file and made accessible from the terminal. Such a file can be scanned for errors using the editor. If an error is found, the control cards can be modified, again using the editor, and the user can then ask for a rerun of the job. If the run appears to be successful, the output could be sent to the high speed printer. Here we have what can be called interactive batch processing.

Possible drawbacks with this arrangement are the need to set up both an interactive and batch system, the need to have terminals on hand, and, in addition, the need to learn the terminal operations—logging on and off, typing conventions, file handling commands, editing commands, etc. In all, the student of social sciences must then learn the language of the batch operating system, the language of the package program, and the terminal interactive language. For unsophisticated users this may prove an excessive burden. But, for many, learning to manage the inter- active system greatly increases the user's ability to take full advantage of modern computing facilities.

Conversational Batch Processing. It should be possible to write a front-end processor that asks the user for control card information in conversational form and then creates a file of control cards for transfer to the batch stream for processing. This is the kind of conversational interaction that the user would appreciate. NORC, the National Opinion Research Center, is working on an interactive version of SPSS.

Interactive Integrated Packages

Most social science data processing is done in the batch mode. The large amount of data input and output, the extensive calculations, the large size of the program, the need for space for many tables, some of them fairly large, all militate against computing in the strictly interactive mode. Nonetheless, the trend is in the direction of taking advantage of remote terminals and interactive computing. This is more likely to take the form of preparation of input control cards from a terminal, using remote job entry to send the job to the batch stream for execution, and possibly again using the terminal to examine the output.

IMPRESS. An exception to reliance on batch processing is IMPRESS (Meyers, 1973), Dartmouth's interactive integrated social science system. Students at typewriter terminals can choose from dozens of data sets stored on disk files and perform statistical computations similar to those provided by SPSS. Its advantage is ease of use. As with other time-shared systems there are severe limitations on storage. For example, each user is entitled to only 16K words of core memory. The system is difficult to export because of its dependence upon Dartmouth's BASIC and Dartmouth's time-sharing system.

MISS. Another example of interactive statistical package is MISS (Anderson *et al.,* 1974), the Minnesota Interactive Statistical System. It is unique in that an integrated package is implemented on a mini-computer using the Libra time sharing system and the FOCAL interpreter, a FORTRAN-like language. While the system is suited to convenient student use, storage limitation does not permit large data sets or tables, which social science students are apt to need. The maximum raw data set is 700 words (e.g., 100 cases and seven variables), and the maximum size contingency table 10 by 10. This system is also difficult to export because it is not written in standard FORTRAN or BASIC.

Implementation

Almost all social science programs and packages for batch-processing are written in FORTRAN IV. There are good reasons for this. First, FORTRAN is an algebraic language, suitable for writing statistical routines. It has good input and output formatting capability, which permits proper handling of a variety of data sources, numeric or alphabetic. It provides for the use of subscripts in accessing data within a record or cell and within a two or three dimensional table. It allows for storing of precompiled subroutines. Second, FORTRAN is available on almost all medium and large size computers and even on some smaller ones. FORTRAN provides the greatest degree of portability of a program, not only because of its availability, but also because of existing standards for the language. PL/I has more features, such as dynamic allocation of storage, variable format items, list processing capabilities, non-integer fixed point arithmetic, and sophisticated character handling techniques. But PL/I is not as widely available as FORTRAN, particularly on small to medium size machines. For the foreseeable future both FORTRAN in scientific computing and COBOL in business data processing can be expected to be in active use as the dominant programming languages.

FORTRAN has some disadvantages as a programming language, but these generally can be overcome through programming techniques, use of assembly language subroutines, or the use of a more powerful operating system. FORTRAN's formatted input-output operation, for example, is costly in execution time. This shortcoming can be avoided by changing the data from formattted to unformatted form, although this makes the data less portable between computer systems. SPSS's system file, for example, is in unformatted or binary form, and does not require costly conversion. Another possibility is to write special input routines in assembler or symbolic machine language to achieve greater efficiency. Portability between systems can be maintained by having on hand the slower FORTRAN instructions or subroutines.

FORTRAN lacks dynamic storage allocation, i.e., the ability to create arrays of the desired size at run time. Standard FORTRAN IV provides adjustable dimensions for arrays within subroutines, but not in the main program, where space for arrays must be originally allocated. It is the lack of dynamic storage allocation that is at the base of artificial restrictions of table sizes, since FORTRAN arrays must be allocated at the time a program is written. Dynamic storage can be achieved first by treating all arrays as single dimensioned, and then cutting them out of a single large array as they are needed at run time. This technique requires both keeping track of where arrays begin as well as the calculation of addresses of multidimensional arrays. Relief from the addressing problem is possible by doing most of the calculations in subroutines, which are capable of using adjustable dimensions determined at run time. This technique is worked out in the DYSTAL system.

FORTRAN's input-output formatting procedures favor fixed column rather than free-format input or output. The trend in program packages is to allow users to write instructions in free-format form rather than to punch numbers into specific columns. This convenience can be achieved in FORTRAN by writing special parsing routines to locate the beginning and end of each word that is input. More recent versions of FORTRAN, however, have a free format input option (list-directed input-output). This shift to free formatting will help to bridge the gap between batch and interactive processing, since in the latter free-formatted input is the usual practice.

To fit a large program into a small machine, a heavy amount of overlaying of program segments is necessary. Overlay permits a large program to be brought into core memory one segment at a time. The prime requisite for overlaying is a program with a top-down or tree structure that can be cut up into convenient segments no larger than some desirable maximum. Some operating systems allow for more than one level of overlays so that subroutines within segments can also be overlaid among themselves. A top-down structure is one of the desirable features of good programming. Structured programming can be implemented in FORTRAN by judicious use of subroutines, by liberal use of indentations, and by adhering to a limited set of branching and looping conventions.

Another method of increasing the memory capacity of a computer is to provide virtual memory, i.e., to use auxiliary drum or disk memory as an extension of primary memory. Some operating systems provide virtual memory. It is also possible to program two-level store in FORTRAN, as it is done in the DYSTAL system.

From Programs to Packages

The use of computers by social scientists has generally followed the pattern of starting with simple programs, creating packages of programs, and then moving on to integrated social science packages. In many installations, programs for cross-tabulation, correlation matrix, multiple regression, analysis of variance, factor analysis, etc., have been written for local use. Packaged programs enable users to avoid the necessity of having to write programs of their own. For many of these enterprises it has been possible to make use of subroutine packages, such as IBM's scientific subroutine package, which contains subroutines for mathematical and statistical routines. It remains for the programmer to write the input and output portions of the program. The best known and most widely used package of statistical programs is the BMD package from the University of California (Dixon, 1973). A new and improved version of the package called BMDP has been announced (Engelman, 1974). Each program is a stand-alone entity, but all programs share a common input format and capabilities for transformation of variables that are frequently required by the social scientists. These programs do not face the problem of file maintenance, including the need to name variables and specify row and column headings for specific values and to make the labels as well as data available for use with a large number of different routines. But BMD will continue to be useful to many social scientists.

The late sixties saw the development of a number of integrated program packages designed to deal with the problem of file management and also to bring under the control of a single system the numerous statistical operations a social scientist is likely to want to use. The better known packages are SPSS, OSIRIS, DATATEXT, PSTAT, PICKLE, and TSAR (Anderson and Coover, 1972). The most widely distributed of these is SPSS (Nie, Bent, and Hull, 1970), which must be considered the most likely available social science package in universities and colleges with a large enough computer to support it. In a preliminary tabulation of a recent survey under the auspices of CONDUIT, Ronald E. Anderson reported that 74% of the sociology instructors contacted reported use of SPSS and 13% the use of BMD programs, and only small percentages reported using any of the other packages. The standard version of SPSS requires some 200K bytes of core memory, but a smaller version requiring only 100K bytes of core memory is also available. For social scientists the attraction of SPSS is that it is well-documented and relatively easy to use. It enables an instructor to set up a file on disk or tape, including labels for variables and specific values of variables, and allows students to select variables and make cross-tabulations, calculate means and standard deviations, calculate correlation coefficients, perform multiple regression analysis, and call for one of several varieties of factor analysis.

Advantages of SPSS. The popularity of SPSS is owed to a great extent to convenience of use. It is written in FORTRAN IV and easily transportable to IBM machines, on which it was first developed. Versions have also been written for a number of other machines, including CDC and Burroughs machines. It has a simple command structure, consisting of easily understandable single word commands followed by arguments in free format form. Only one routine is processed at a time, making it easy to overlay routines and also to add new routines as subroutines. It has a well-documented manual, providing material on use and interpretation of statistical methods, as well as on the mechanics of obtaining particular options. It started with many of the commonly-used statistical procedures and through updates now contains practically all of those likely to be employed by users. As a result of a series of updates, obvious errors have been eliminated. It has a good data transformation and recoding section, providing users with the capability of "Programming" calculations using variables and constants within the system. It provides for the maintenance of files and associated variables and value labels. Data and labels can be modified during the course of a run and also saved for future use on a disk file or on a magnetic tape. SPSS is now available on most large university campuses, and has become a common language for social science data processors.

SPSS enables the instructor to set up a data file, have students read the SPSS manual and start them off on the use of computers.

There is still need, however, for assistants to set up the file and help students correct errors and interpret results.

SPSS File Maintenance System. SPSS maintains three disk files. The system files contain a dictionary of variables and associated values, such as missing data, a list of labels for variables or for values of variables, and the data file in unformatted form. At run time, on the first pass (i.e., when the first routine is called), the label file and the data file are transferred to two separate temporary disk files. If any modifications of the data or labels are required, they are performed at this point.

There are some inefficiencies in the manner in which SPSS handles its disk files. First, a user with a program of his own is not able to use the system file because of the difficulty of locating the data file, which follows immediately after the dictionary and labels. In other words, the file is not compatible with most disk files maintained by others. Secondly, the need to keep two sets of label and data files carries inefficiencies of execution and space, since the scratch file is written and disk space is required to do this. Another source of inefficiency is the need to read in the same data each time a new procedure is called. In this sense SPSS is a multipass system, rather than a single-pass one.

Disadvantages of SPSS. SPSS has a number of shortcomings, which might be lumped together under lack of efficiency. In tests of execution time, SPSS generally falls about in the middle (Slysz, 1974). DATATEXT is generally more costly to run, while TSAR and the Census Bureau's CENT program are generally less costly. But these latter also provide fewer options. SPSS normally requires 200K bytes of core memory, and cannot be fit into small machines in the 32K to 64K byte range. SPSS is suitable for moderate size files running on a big machine. Very large files would be costly to run on SPSS so that there is room for an alternative efficient package. Even on a large machine with 256K to 512K bytes of memory and operating a multiprocessing system with the aid of virtual memory, a system as large as SPSS is apt to slow down computing operations to a noticeable degree.

Adaptations for SPSS

A number of efforts have been made to live with SPSS by making adaptations to overcome its shortcomings. For example,

DATATEXT has been used to maintain files in order to avoid the 500-variable restrictions imposed by SPSS. A number of efforts have been made to transform OSIRUS files to SPSS use. In the meantime, SPSS is providing a version capable of handling 1000-variable records. It has also made available the use of a large archival file of 5000 variables.

SOS and PUSH. SOS (DUALAB, 1974) is a front end program to SPSS that permits use of the hierarchically arranged public use samples of the U.S. Census of population and housing. In these files household records are followed by a varying number of person records. The neighborhood characteristics files have three levels of records—neighborhood, household, and person. SOS permits construction of a linear record out of selected variables from different types of records as they are read. One then processes these linear records with SPSS proper. PUSH (NIH, 1973) is a program to convert census public use samples to a desired linear form, picking off the variables as needed by the user. Both of these efforts point to the need for more general allowance by program packages for storage of data in hierarchical form, since in many instances information is gathered with main records containing within them a varying number of subrecords.

SCANSPSS. Another SPSS preprocessor is SCANSPSS (Liberal Arts Data Laboratory), developed at Pennsylvania State University. One of the problems of a batch processing system is the turnaround time of an hour or so to several hours. Many jobs consist of aborted runs due to errors in input control cards. SCANSPSS was written to fit into the fast batch partition, and to provide almost instant scanning of SPSS control cards for errors. The program is in its developmental phase.

An additional step has been taken in SCANSPSS to provide actual table making capabilities in the fast batch partition. SCANSPSS provides for processing of RECODE and CROSSTAB cards, and has the capability of inputting files on disk by means of a special INCLUDE card. Here SPSS control card language is being used to provide a miniature version of SPSS that will fit in the fast batch partition. This constitutes an attempt to write a new implementation of SPSS under restrictions necessary to fit the program into the fast batch mode.

Competing Systems

Systems in direct competition with SPSS on large computers appear doomed to lose out in the national and international competition as the predominant integrated social science package. BMD will probably continue to be used, particularly on small to medium size machines. Efforts continue, however, to tailor systems to achieve special advantages such as more efficient processing in a limited sphere. DUALABS, for example, has developed a frontend processor for the U.S. Census Bureau CENT program (NIH, 1974), which provides efficient tabulations, and has termed the combination CENT-AID. The question is whether other conveniences of SPSS can be added, while still retaining efficiency of processing.

It would appear that there will be efforts made to achieve a more efficient as well as convenient integrated package. One approach to this problem is to accept SPSS commands as the common language for the social sciences, and provide an implementation that combines both the efficiency and convenience features, a direction in which SCANSPSS is moving. For large systems such an effort may result in running SPSS in the fast batch mode, or it can be run at less cost using smaller amounts of core memory. Such a development is particularly important for colleges with small machines and in need of an integrated package.

MINITAB. Among attempts to cut down larger program packages to smaller ones is MINITAB, a shorter version of OMNITAB (Jowett, Chamberlain, and Mexas, 1972). It was developed by Ryan and Joiner (1973) at Pennsylvania State University. MINITAB provides for input of data into a two-dimensional work area, and an impressive number of simple commands to perform data transformations, random number generation, and statistical routines often used in teaching statistics. Its chief limitation is the size of the data storage, which typically provides 25 columns storing up to 200 numbers each. It is therefore more suitable for experimental data than for the processing of questionnaires and census material. The size of the program requires some 120K bytes of storage, and it is estimated that with overlay this can be cut down to about 80K bytes. Hence, in its present form it is not suitable for use with computers in the 32K to 64K range. Castellan (1970) has made a similar effort to write an interactive statistical system.

XTAB9. The chief virtue of XTAB9 is its small size and portability. It was developed by Sakoda on a 32K byte IBM 1130 system using Basic FORTRAN IV. It is a miniature system, compared with SPSS, but still providing for data conversions, labels for tables, six-way cross-tabulations, means, standard deviations, and correlation coefficients. It achieves efficiency through use of overlays, dynamic storage allocation, virtual memory, and two-byte integers. The most recent addition to it has been the ability to process a variety of hierarchically-structured files, including public use sample files and others structured in a similar fashion. It provides for creation of merged records as well as aggregation and tabulation of information from subrecords.

The Small College

Computing by social scientists at a small college faces great difficulties. The large size of most social science packages prevent their use of small machines and often on non-IBM machines. The computing staff is small and is not likely to include one well-versed in statistical computation. Small colleges are also usually not equipped to handle large files, which requires both magnetic tape and disk drives, and neither do they have the funds to acquire programs and data files. The development of miniature packages usable with machines with 32K to 64K bytes of core memory will help some small institutions that have their own computers. A small number of files, such as the National Opinion Research Center's annual general survey of public opinion, can be made available for class use.

But for many institutions the answer may lie in acquiring a few typewriter terminals and becoming connected to regional networks, similar to Project IMPRESS at Dartmouth. The problems of providing programming personnel, acquisition and preparation of data, and implementation of a complex system such as SPSS can be solved by making arrangements with a nearby larger institution or regional network service to pay for the amount of services used. As computer programs become more costly, the data files more numerous, and data transmission more efficient, this should become an increasingly attractive option for small colleges. One drawback for social scientists with such an arrangement is the need for a reasonably fast printer to provide adequate amounts of output.

Conclusion

The large integrated social science statistical package, particularly SPSS, has become the dominant means of introducing social science students to computer usage. Its primary advantage is ease of use compared with stand-alone programs. The predominant language for writing such packages is FORTRAN, and this is likely to continue in the foreseeable future. Computing in the social sciences is performed predominantly through batch processing, but the trend is increasingly in the direction of fast-batch processing and interactive usage. In most instances the basic processing will be done in the batch mode, with options of editing control cards at a terminal or inputting control cards through a conversational program. SPSS has disadvantages, and steps will continue to be made to offset them with makeshift arrangements until a system combining its convenience with greater efficiency is developed. In the meantime, small computer users are generally left without an integrated package which can be easily obtained and implemented on a variety of machines. It is hoped that some effort will be made to meet their needs.

References

Anderson, R.E. Bibliography on Social Science Computing. *Computing Reviews,* 1974, 247-261.

Anderson, R.E., and E.R. Coover. Wrapping Up the Package: Critical Thoughts on Applications Software for Social Data Analysis. *Computer and Humanities,* 1972, 7, 81-91.

Anderson, R.E. *et al.* The Minnesota Interactive Statistical System. *Behavior Research Methods & Instrumentation,* 1974, 6, 194-200.

Castellan, N.J., Jr. The Symbolic Matrix Interpretive System and the Statistical Interpretive System. *COMMON: Seattle Proceedings,* 1970, 64-73.

Dixon, W.J. *BMD, Biomedical Computer Programs,* University of California Press, Berkeley, California, 1973.

DUALAB (Data Use and Access Laboratories). *SOS: Statistical Package for the Social Sciences (SPSS)–Override System.* Suite 900, 1601 N. Kent Street, Arlington, Va. 22209, 1974.

Dyke, B., and J.W. MacCluer. *Computer Simulation in Human Population Studies.* New York: Academic Press, 1973.

Engleman, L. BMDP Programs. *SIGSOC Bulletin,* 1974, *5,* 10-13.

Francis, I. A Comparison of Several Analysis of Variance Programs. *Journal of the American Statistical Association,* 1973, *68,* 860-865.

Jowett, D., R.L. Chamberlain, and A.G. Mexas. OMNITAB: A Simple Language for Statistical Computations. *Journal of Statistical Computation and Simulation,* 1972, *1,* 129-147.

Liberal Arts Data Laboratory. *Use of SCANSPSS to Produce Cross-Tabulations,* The College of Arts and Science, Pennsylvania State University, (mimeographed), n.d.

Meyers, E.D., Jr. *Time Sharing Computation in the Social Sciences.* Englewood Cliffs, N.J.: Prentice Hall, 1973.

Nie, N., D.H. Bent, and C.H. Hull. *SPSS, Statistical Package for the Social Sciences.* New York: McGraw-Hill, 1970; revised, 1975.

NIH (National Institutes of Health). *Instruction Booklet for the Public Use Sample Helper (PUSH) Program,* U.S. Department of HEW, 1973.

NIH (National Institutes of Health). *Instruction Booklet for the Census Tabulation System—AID (CENT-AID) Program,* U.S. Department of HEW, 1974, 74-513.

Ryan, T.A., Jr., and B.L. Joiner. MINITAB: A Statistical Computing System for Students and Researchers. *The American Statistician,* 1973, *27,* 222-225.

Slysz, W.D. An Evaluation of Statistical Software in the social Sciences. *Communications of the ACM,* 1974, *17,* 326-332.

8.
Computer Aids in Teaching Statistics and Methodology

Richard S. Lehman
Franklin and Marshall College

B. James Starr   Kenneth C. Young[2]
Howard University   *Eastern Michigan University*

The purpose of this paper is to provide teachers of statistics a broad view of the alternative uses of the computer along with as much detailed, explicit information on "how-to" and "where-to-find" as we have been able to muster. We believe that we have comprehensively described the state-of-the-art in the field, although the scattered and fragmentary methods of publication preclude our reporting everything that is being done today. While our principal emphasis is on the introductory non-calculus course, most of the computer methods described are at least equally useful in higher level courses in statistics and research methodology. In fact, new approaches to teaching research skills to social science students tend to blur the distinctions between the introductory statistics course and methods or even content courses.

The use of computers in statistics instruction takes a number of different forms. Many courses are taught with a combination of approaches. For convenience, we have formed the initial presentation around the following categories: (a) the use of relatively large statistical packages; (b) the training of students to write their own programs, usually to compute some standard statistical measures; (c) the use of one of several "high level" statistical languages; (d) the use of the computer to simulate experimental data for student analysis on or off the computer; and (e) the use of computer-assisted or computer-managed procedures.

The first major section of this paper is devoted to a discussion of these five major educational strategies. A sixth approach, the use of computer demonstration exercises, is illustrated in some detail in the final section of this paper.

Statistical Packages

The use of large statistical packages such as SPSS (Statistical Package for the Social Sciences; Nie, Bent, and Hull, 1970)[3], BMD (Dixon, 1968)[4], SSP (IBM, 1966)[5], or OSIRIS II (Institute for Social Research, 1968)[6] is relatively rare in statistics courses *per se,* particularly at the introductory level. However, they deserve mention here because their impact on the teaching of statistics, both direct and indirect, has been enormous.

The computer's promise of freeing the social science researcher from tedious data manipulation and hand calculation of statistics has undoubtedly been fulfilled. Many social scientists and students have been able to employ SPSS and similar packages for these purposes. About 75% of sociology instructors who use computers have used SPSS. This widespread usage is remarkable in view of the fact that the package is only about five years old. The manual is already in its second edition (Nie, Hull, Jenkins, Steinbrenner, and Bent, 1975). Clearly, SPSS has filled a vital need in social science computing since its growth has followed fast on the heels of the growth in purchases of large scale computers by American colleges and universities in the late sixties and early seventies.

Since SPSS was designed as a research tool, its classroom usage has been limited primarily to upper level statistics and methodology courses. The greatest impact of SPSS on the teaching of statistics has been indirect. Its contribution to the ease of doing statistical computation, along with the development of computer techniques generally, has resulted in decreased emphasis on computational techniques in statistics courses. Consequently, more classroom time is available for greater emphasis on the realtionship between statistical understanding and the interpretation of results.

Furthermore, we can expect to see more of SPSS and similar packages in lower level courses, although these courses may not be labeled statistics. A "filtering-down" process seems to be taking place, causing advanced research methodology to be introduced at earlier and earlier stages in the curriculum.

A possible assumption underlying this movement is that if

students learn methodology at an early stage, they will have a better grasp of what social science is "really" about, develop a healthy skepticism about "received doctrine" in their field, and will be motivated by the "discovery method" inherent in this approach. Examples of this approach are IMPRESS (Meyers, 1969), a statistical package *cum* data base used for teaching sociology and political science at Dartmouth, and a new system at Notre Dame for the teaching of introductory economics (Jameson, Bonello, and Davisson, 1974). These courses blend the teaching of statistical principles, research methodology, and subject matter content in a way that defies classification in the traditional curriculum. At present they seem to be offered as an alternative to the traditional introductory course in sociology, political science, or economics, but we can expect to see descriptions of similar courses being offered as an alternative to the traditional introductory statistics course in the near future.

Since the SPSS is quite large (requiring about 200K bytes of memory in its full version), it cannot be implemented on small or medium sized computers. The second edition of the SPSS manual describes a mini-version (SPSSG) which requires 100K bytes of storage. Still, even at institutions with large computers it may be considered too expensive for student use because it takes so much core storage and is rather slow. Various smaller packages have appeared that perform many of the functions of SPSS and run on smaller machines. One such program is XTAB9[7], developed at Brown University by James Sakoda. XTAB9 computes cross-tabulation, chi square, percentages, means and standard deviations, one-way analysis of variance, and correlation coefficients. With extensive overlays, XTAB9 can fit into 12K words of storage, and can thus run on small computers or take a smaller partition on large ones.

Even if one of the large statistical packages like SPSS or BMD is not available, nearly every college or university computing center has a set of commonly used, and perhaps locally developed, statistical programs. Sometimes the documentation for such programs can be obtained in sufficient quantity to use as class handouts, and the instructor can build problem sets around the existing programs. But, unfortunately, the documentation is often either non-existent or inadequate. In such a case, the instructor who wishes to use local programs must either attempt (often with little success) to pressure his center into developing such documentation, or write his own, if he can figure out what the program is doing. (More often than not, if an instructor does develop the documentation for class use, he will soon discover that it makes its way to the computer center to be issued as *the* documentation for the program!)

The building of a course around major computational packages represents one or two general philosophical approaches to the use of computers. Typically, such a course uses the computer to remove completely arithmetic computations from the students, concentrating instruction instead upon research logic and the mechanics of computer use.

A second general philosophical approach to computer use is favored by many authors and instructors, including the authors of this paper. The argument for this position stresses that some computation must be included in a statistics course. To allow the computer to do all of the arithmetic has a number of undesirable consequences. First, by allowing the computer to do the work, we are implying to our students that arithmetic is *passé* and that they have no need for those skills. This in turn conjures up the disturbing vision of a generation of students who may be incapable of doing even elementary kinds of arithmetic without mechanical or electronic aid. This possibility is already being enhanced through the widespread availability of cheap hand-held calculators.

A second argument is represented by the Committee on the Undergraduate Program in Mathematics' (1972) careful study of the introductory noncalculus statistics course. They stress that extensive use of the computer as an arithmetic aid can obscure some important concepts in statistics. There is considerable benefit in actually experiencing the fact that the sums of squares and degrees of freedom add up properly in an analysis of variance, for example. Moreover, it seems reasonable to suppose that students who have worked out examples of statistical techniques would be likely to be better statistical programmers and better at catching errors generated by canned programs. We believe that experience in such hand calculations would lead to a higher level of understanding and sophistication.

Finally, computers are not always correct, despite the popular misconception. The ability to verify independently the correctness of a computer program, or to correct an erroneous one, depends upon human arithmetic. The students should be given those skills.

This second approach, represented by the remainder of the techniques discussed in this paper, typically has the students do some arithmetic themselves, and requires that they write and check their own programs.

There is no reason, of course, why the approaches cannot be combined in the same course. Initially, the students could be required to do hand computation, then write their own program, and finally use canned packages, perhaps on data provided by a data generation program as discussed below.

Student Programming Approaches

Another approach to the teaching of undergraduate statistics has been the development of courses that emphasize computer algorithms as a means of teaching statistical concepts. The method is to require students to write their own short programs to compute standard statistical measures. The assumption motivating this approach is that if students actually write programs to compute various statistics, they will develop a deeper understanding of the meaning of those measures and will be more sophisticated in their use of canned statistical packages later on.

The first introduction to the computer using this approach will most likely be the execution of a simple program that requires the student to do only the minimum work—merely logging onto the computer, perhaps supplying some simple information such as five numbers, or his name, and logging off.

If the students are to learn programming, or are relative novices, the next step will probably be either to modify an existing program or write a simple "original" program. A good problem is finding the mean of N numbers for this assignment—the students already know the procedure, and can follow the computer analog with little difficulty. The standard measures of central tendency (mean, median, mode) provide a graded series of exercises calling for progressively greater programming skills (see Starr, 1972).

Random Numbers. It is a good idea to introduce pseudo-random number generation early in the statistics course. The data used in the frequency distribution and later assignments are usually generated by the computer. If the students are writing programs or learning programming along with statistics, they must be given an introduction to random numbers early.

Many of the common programming languages provide easy access to a function that yields a pseudo-random number from a rectangular distribution. In an interactive environment, two of the most widely used languages, BASIC and APL, have rectangular random number functions as a part of their standard repertoire. In facilities where batch processing is the mode, often a function will have been developed that is callable from a standard language such as FORTRAN or PL/I. If a random number generator function is not available, several sources give appropriate algorithms (e.g., Bulgren, 1971; Lehman, 1968; Lehman, 1976; Lohnes and Cooley, 1968). Moreover, the output from rectangular pseudo-random generators may be modified algorithmically to simulate sampling from a variety of other distribution forms. Thus, Hemmerle (1967) provides the logic for generating numbers that behave as if they were drawn from normal, skewed, and Poisson-type distributors. Lehman (1968) presents methods for simulating normal, geometric, binomial, and bivariate normal distributions. Lehman (1976) presents all of these algorithms as well as a general multivariate normal procedure.

Random Variables and Distributions. For courses in which there is heavy emphasis upon probability theory and probability distributions, the computer offers an invaluable resource for the student. With a facility for random number generation available, students can write and/or run programs dealing with assignments such as relative frequency as an analog to probability, sampling from binomial, uniform, Poisson, and hypergeometric distributions, and empirically demonstrating the central limit theorem. Bulgren (1971), Carnahan, Luther, and Wilkes (1969), Lehman (1968), and Lehman (1976) offer a number of appropriate exercises and algorithms.

An interesting technique for students in a first semester course is to explore the central limit theorem. Students are asked to write a program that makes repeated samples of size N from a uniform distribution 1, 2, . . ., K, find the mean of each sample, and tally that mean into a frequency distribution (usually making use of a previously-written frequency distribution program). The program also computes the mean and standard deviation of the frequency distribution. The process is repeated for various numbers of means and values of N and K. The effects of sampling from distributions other than the rectangular can also be studied. The results often seem to be a better understanding of the central limit theorem and the relationships among sample size, the shape of the sampling distribution, and the size of the standard error.

Hypothesis Testing. Students may be required either to write and run, or merely run, a variety of programs dealing with various hypothesis testing procedures. An interesting kind of exercise involves sampling repeatedly from some statistical test. A frequency distribution of the obtained values of the statistic may be constructed, and a tally of the proportion of "rejections" of the null hypothesis will illustrate the concept of Type I error.

Both Bulgren (1971) and Lohnes and Cooley (1968) offer a selection of exercises for the student in Monte Carlo studies of hypothesis testing procedures as described above.

Many statistics teachers will object that student programming in the teaching of statistics is an unnecessary (even irrelevant) intrusion into an already crowded course. Still, the fact remains that in recent years an increasing number of instructors have decided that the benefits of programming outweigh the losses. Some institutions require a programming course early in the social science curriculum. In such cases it seems reasonable to combine the teaching of programming techniques with applications in the introductory statistics course.

Statistical Languages

An approach that stands midway between the use of large statistical packages and the student programming approach is the use of OMNITAB (Swanson, Ledlow, and Harris, 1973)[8], MINITAB (Ryan and Joiner, 1973)[9], OMNISIIRIMP (Harris, Swanson, and Duerr, 1974)[8], or SMIS/SIS (Castellan, 1970)[10]. These are statistically oriented computing systems somewhat similar to SPSS but permitting greater flexibility in their use and hence requiring somewhat greater statistical expertise and initiative on the part of the user. Because their control cards resemble high-level computer instructions (e.g., "ORDER THE DATA IN COLUMN 2"), their authors sometimes refer to them as languages.

These systems offer the promise of providing almost as much ease in computing as SPSS-like packages, while retaining an algorithmic control structure which should tend to maintain a greater awareness of the underlying computational procedures on the part of student users.

Like SPSS, OMNITAB requires a large computer and is considered rather slow, and hence expensive, for student use. However, MINITAB and OMNISHRIMP are smaller, faster systems that run on medium sized computers. We expect their use in statistics instruction to grow as they become more widely disseminated.

A similar "high level language" approach is that represented by SMIS/SIS (Castellan, 1970). This FORTRAN system operates upon a user-input data matrix, and provides 48 matrix manipulation operations and 25 statistical procedures. The system also provides access to user-written subroutines, making it locally modifiable. Castellan (1974) reports on the use of SMIS/SIS in both the type of undergraduate course being discussed here, and in a graduate multivariate analysis course.

Simulating Experimental Data

Another important computerized aid in teaching statistics need not involve the students with the computer in any direct way, but uses the computer as a fancy random number generator.

In this application, the computer not only eliminates the tedium of statistical computation but also eliminates the collection, input, storage, and manipulation of data from real experiments. It is particularly well suited to psychology, but applications exist in other fields as well.

A perennial problem to statistics instructors is the development of new sets of data to be used on problem sets and examinations, as class examples, and so forth. To make matters worse, whenever new data or problems are introduced, the instructor (or his assistant) must compute a new answer key. Another problem arises from the "sharing" of results of assignments across semesters, sections, and/or students. The use of computer-generated data with known solutions printed by the computer can greatly alleviate all of these problems.

Lehman (1973) has developed and used a set of data generator programs with a great deal of success in several courses. These programs include generators for single-variable independent-groups designs, generalized analysis of variance designs, and for both bivariate and multivariate experiments. The programs are written in FORTRAN, and are available to anyone who is interested.

One technique in using data generators is to provide unique sets of data for each student on a problem set or examination. Since the generators produce an "instructor's record" containing both the parameters of the population(s) sampled and the statistics for the particular sample obtained, grading the student's work is simplified. If the same population parameters are given for all sets of data for a given problem on a problem set, and if a little care is given to picking the parameter values, it is interesting to construct the classwide frequency distribution of obtained results that can illustrate Type I errors in a particularly meaningful way. In addition, since parameters are known, a wide variety of other important effects can be illustrated, including the effects of sample size, alpha level, or the magnitude of the "true" difference on power and Type II errors.

Another advantage to generating data from known populations is the development of an individualized approach to an advanced course. A course where students design hypothetical individual experiments, receive individual data, and conduct individual analyses has been described elsewhere (Lehman, 1972). The technique employs the data generators described earlier (and see Lehman, 1973). Since the course presents data to students who do not know its underlying properties, the approach is termed the use of an "unknown." The parallel to the standard technique in teaching chemistry is obvious, and makes for an interesting, exciting, and worthwhile statistics course.

On slightly grander scale, Suziedelis (1972; this volume) and Harper (1972) have developed complete data bases with known parameters for teaching quantitative procedures in social psychology and sociology, along with appropriate analytic systems to allow students to formulate and test meaningful hypotheses.

Another approach to data generation is represented by the highly developed EXPER SIM system from Michigan (Main, 1971; also see Rajecki, 1972). EXPER SIM, also known as the Michigan Experimental Simulation Supervisor (or MESS), is a set of sophisticated situations in specific substantive areas. The system presently includes simulations for imprinting, social facilitation, drug research, etiology of schizophrenia, and motivation. Each simulation includes a complete specification of the experimental setting, descriptions of built-in controls, and a number of variables (typically six to ten) that can be manipulated. EXPER SIM takes the variable settings that are given and generates sets of data, along with appropriate statistics if requested. The student may then analyze the data, just as if it were a real experiment. This is often followed by another "experiment," and so forth.

EXPER SIM has several features that are of interest to the instructor of statistics and experimental design. In the first place, the data are realistic, in the sense that the effects of the variables that can be manipulated are similar to the effects that those same variables have in the "real world." Secondly, the system is very easy to use, and is very tolerant of errors in input (even down to the level of misspellings and incorrect punctuation).

Third, the entire system is conceived as a subtle introduction to computer modeling; students are presented with a model of a behavioral domain and are to infer the underlying structure.

MESS is readily expandable so that new simulations can be added as only a single FORTRAN subroutine and perhaps a data file that gives certain constants and default values. Currently under development is a simulation writer program (SWIP) that will automatically produce the correct subroutine, thus making the introduction of new models a relatively simple matter for the instructor.

EXPER SIM has been exported to a number of other installations. It is now being given support through the Exxon Education Foundation, which is offering grants to institutions desiring to implement the system.[11]

Computer-assisted and -augmented Instruction

Although CAI (Computer-Assisted Instruction) has been highly touted by the mass media, its use in higher education has been limited. CAI refers to the use of the computer as an instructor, largely independent of student exposure to human teachers. The assumption underlying CAI development efforts is that students can master complex material better and faster if it is presented to them in easy stages with frequent quizzes and immediate feedback to student responses. The hallmark of CAI lies in such correction of student errors. The orientation of the present authors, on the other hand, is toward computer-augmented instruction (CAUI) as suggested by Koh (1974). As reflected in this paper, CAUI focusses on the use of the computer to augment teaching via the presentation of supplemental information. The technique is much less costly than CAI.

CAI has inherently high development and operating costs. The authors know of no general CAI systems for college level introductory statistics that are applicable on systems other than where they have been developed. There have undoubtedly been some courses developed, but the authors only know of one, at Illinois with the PLATO system. An interactive tutorial system, the Statistical Help and Instructional Program (SHIP), was in operation at the University of Colorado's Computer Laboratory for Instruction in Psychological Research (CLIPR), but it is no longer functional and it is doubtful that it can be exported to any other installation.

Since the publication of Keller's paper on self-paced instruction (Keller, 1968), the "Keller Method" has been introduced into a number of courses throughout the country. Somewhat surprisingly, very few reports have been made regarding the use of the Keller method in statistics and experimental design courses, or in using computers to help implement Keller Plan instruction. An exception, involving the Keller method in a quantitative methods course in economics and developed by one of the authors (Young, 1974), is described elsewhere in this volume.

One commerical publisher has developed an individualized set of materials for the first semester statistics course (Individual Learning Systems, 1971)[12]. The Individual Learning Systems (ILS) material consists of a set of eight paper bound texts, presenting 15 units of material. The topics cover the usual range found in the introductory statistics course. The format is that of short modules, followed by self-tests. At the end of each unit, the student is expected to pass an examination before he continues to the next unit. Considerable assistance for the instructor is provided with the materials, including an instructor's manual with many suggestions regarding the implementation of the course, and two forms of each unit examination. One of the authors (Starr) has used the ILS modules in a two-semester sequence in undergraduate statistics. The system works well for teaching the mechanics of computation; and, as such, helped to free both the instructor and the students for development of the rationale for various techniques during class time. Thus, the ILS materials formed an important component of a more comprehensive statistics course. The authors know of two related efforts, both of which use the computer.

Kotesky (1972) has developed and published a set of computer programs for generating multiple alternate forms for statistics tests, an essential element in a self-paced program. For the preparation of more traditional problem sets, but with unique data and solutions, Tracy and Salmon (1974) offer a set of FORTRAN programs for generating exercises. Both programs are available through Life Science Associates.[13]

Demonstration Programs and Laboratory Exercises

Although some of the earliest applications of the computer to the teaching of statistics consisted of demonstration programs and laboratory exercises, and although development of this type of material is in progress on many campuses, no one has yet succeeded in developing and disseminating a standard package of programs for that purpose. This lack is partly due to idiosyncratic differences in teaching that would require that such a package have a great many variations (or serve a very narrow market); it is partly due to technical problems of transportability; and it is partly due to the fact that developments in computer technology, particulary the rapid growth in time sharing, have tended to render obsolete the early programs. Until quite recently, most programs of this type were written in batch mode and student usage consisted of an examination of sample printouts.

Conversational time sharing programs have a distinct advantage in this type of use, since they permit student initiative in setting parameters and hence choosing variations in the demonstrations as they run. Other innovations have increased the availability of computers for in-class demonstrations and experiments. Mini-computers, phone lines into the classroom coupled with TV monitors, and kinescope projectors all provide an increasing number of instructors with the option of using the computer in class as a supplement to the lecture. For some demonstrations these devices may provide a medium that is superior to either batch-mode printouts or individual laboratory exercises.

In this section we discuss seven topics that are commonly suggested for the introductory statistics course (see Committee on the Undergraduate Program in Mathematics, 1972). For each topic, we either illustrate one possibility for computer enhancement in the form of demonstration or exercise, or suggest how the computer might be used.

Statistical Description. A useful technique in developing skill and understanding in descriptive statistics is to have students work in parallel with the computer. A program may be provided for the students that will construct a frequency distribution and compute the mean, variance, and standard deviation of a set of input data. If the computer and the student are given the same data, several interesting possibilities result. The program might, for example, compute the statistics using both raw-score and grouped-data techniques, thus allowing the student to see the possible biasing effects that grouping may have. If the program is provided with a variable interval size, the same data may be run with differing interval sizes, allowing experimentation with the effects of that variable on the shape of the obtained distributions and on the values of the statistics.

This step can be combined with the introduction to the computer, so that the first or second program that the student must use computes a frequency distribution. The accompanying assignment can require that one or two distributions be constructed by hand, and those plus several others be done by the computer.

Most computer center libraries contain descriptive statistics program that can be used.

An example of this sort of multi-purpose statistics program is the one David P. Doane of Oakland University called ANALYZ, prepared in BASIC on a Burroughs B5500. The program runs as a demonstration, with no programming required on the part of the student. When the user inputs N items of sample data, the program computes 17 measures of central tendency, dispersion, and skewness. Options in the program provide for ordering, standardizing and grouping the data, and constructing histograms. Listings and paper tape source code of the program may be obtained from Doane.[14]

Probability, Random Variables, and Distributions. A variety of programs might be employed to aid in the teaching of these topics. For example, one of the authors (Starr) has written a simple program (RPROB)[15] to check on the efficacy of a rectangular pseudo-random number generator and to introduce to students the frequency notion of probability. A series of numbers between 1 and 10 are generated. The program then calculates the frequency, simple probability, and cumulative probability of each number's occurrence. Theoretically, of course, each number should be equally probable but deviations from expectations are instructive. The program, consisting of 26 BASIC statements, has been run on a CDC 6400 but should be highly transportable. It requires two input parameters for execution. First, an arbitrary six digit number is used to seed the random number generator. The second parameter indicates the size of the sample of random numbers desired. A typical interaction is depicted in Figure 1. The program could be merged with (or code could be written for) a subroutine that would perform a chi-square test for goodness of fit to a rectangular distribution.

Figure 1

A Sample Run of Program RPROB

```
PROVIDE A 6-DIGIT NO. TO START THE RANDOM NO. GENERATOR
? 443865.  HOW MANY RANDOM NOS. WOULD YOU LIKE TO SAMPLE
? 1112
```

RAND. NOS. EQUAL TO...	FREQUENCY	PROBABILITY	CUM. PROBABILITY
1	118	.106115	.106115
2	100	8.99281E-2	.196403
3	107	.096223	.292266
4	108	9.71223E-2	.389388
5	131	.117806	.507194
6	117	.105216	.61241
7	109	9.80216E-2	.710432
8	94	8.4534E-2	.794964
9	122	.109712	.904676
10	106	9.53237E-2	1

```
STOP
```

A program may also be used to drive home the notion of statistical independence. To take a simple example, an instructor might specify a two-way table showing the relationship between, say, obesity and sex. The computer could be used to generate the probability of being male in the population, of being non-obese, and one single-cell probability such as obese and female. The student could then be required to supply all remaining probabilities. Each student could continue with such problems until he abstracts the principle that only when the products of the marginals exactly equal the cell probabilities for all cells is there true independence. The program, INDPRO,[15] can also be used as a demonstration to develop the rationale for the chi-square test of independence.

Special Probability Distributions. Programs to simulate coin-tossing or dice throwing are useful for introducing the binomial distribution. The program DICE[14], by Young, Doane, and Shapiro, illustrates basic notions of combinatorial probability by simulating a dice game. The purpose of the program is to provide a technique to assist students in gaining an intuitive understanding of combinatorial probabilities, sums of random variables, and the binomial distribution. The program summarizes the outcomes in printed histograms, summary statistics, and outcomes of each simulated game or experiment. It also produces a table of exact probabilities for any given number of trials and probability of success. Finally, it provides the option of making the simulated dice rolls into a game that focuses attention on the difference between the expected frequency of outcomes and actual outcomes. The program is written in time sharing BASIC on a Burroughs B5500. It consists of 273 statements. It is conversational in nature and all data input is by way of Teletype machine under program control. No programming is required by either student or faculty. Figure 2 is an illustration of the type of interaction between the user and the program. Additional interaction proceeds immediately after the material in the figure.

Other sophisticated programs and problems are available. Snell (1971) has described a series of more complex projects used in a probability theory course.

Sampling Distributions. An earlier section of this paper described how, in a course requiring student programming, students may be assigned a program to illustrate the central limit theorem.

Figure 2

An Example of the Operation
of the DICE Program

```
DO YOU WANT INSTRUCTIONS (Y OR N)   ?Y
WELCOME.  IN THIS RANDOM EXPERIMENT I WILL SIMULATE THE
ROLLING OF 1, 2, or 3 DICE.  YOU WILL TELL ME HOW MANY
TIMES TO ROLL.  THEN I WILL PRINT A HISTOGRAM OF THE
OUTCOMES.  I WILL ALSO SHOW VALUES FOR F(O) AND F(E),
WHERE
        F(O) IS THE ACTUAL FREQUENCY OF OUTCOMES OF EACH TYPE
        F(E) IS THE EXPECTED (BINOMIAL) FREQUENCY OF OUTCOMES

IF YOU WISH, THE DICE ROLLS CAN BE MADE INTO A GAME.  SHALL I
EXPLAIN THE GAME (Y OR N)     ?N
DO YOU WANT A GAME (1) OR A REGULAR SIMULATION (2)     ?2
ENTER A 2-DIGIT NUMBER TO START     ?23
HOW MANY DICE DO YOU WANT ME TO THROW (1, 2, or 3; 0-STOP) ?1
HOW MANY TIMES DO YOU WANT ME TO THROW     ?12
DO YOU WANT TO SEE EACH THROW     ?N

OUTCOMES FOR ONE DIE

           #     EXPTD      ACTUAL      HISTOGRAM
                 F(E)       F(O)

           1       2          1         *
           2       2          3         ***
           3       2          1         *
           4       2          4         ***
           5       2          1         *
           6       2          2         **
```

For courses that do not require student programming, the instructor can write such a demonstration or use a canned one. It is particularly helpful if the program contains graphical output to illustrate the process of convergence. This type of program is especially well-suited for an in-class demonstration if facilities permit. The CTL program developed by Young[16] is a program designed to illustrate the central limit theorem in class via television monitors. It permits the class to select arbitrary empirical distributions, and sample sizes; then it displays histograms of the sample distributions.

Such a program is exemplified by MONTE, a 258 statement

time sharing BASIC program written by Young and Doane. MONTE accepts a user-supplied empirical distribution, prints a histogram, and computes the mean and standard deviation for this "population." Next, the program draws (with replacement) a specified (i.e., user-controlled) number samples of specified size. Figure 3 provides a sample run of MONTE which has been implemented on a Burroughs B5500 and a DEC-10 computer.

Inferences Concerning Population Means. One of the more difficult concepts in the beginning statistics course is that of the power of a test. One good approach is to provide a program that will compute the power function for a single sample study, given a null hypothesis value, population variance, sample size, and significance level. The students are expected to run the program several times, using different values for some of the possible variables, and plot the resultant power curves. The educational result should be an understanding of the impact of significance level and sample size on power that rests more on the students' experience and less on "faith" (as is often the case in courses employing only lecture and text).

The POWER program by Lehman[17] fulfills the functions outlined above by accepting data representing values for a mean and standard deviation under the null hypothesis and a critical value for *Z*. With these data and a value for sample size, the program computes and prints Type II error probabilities and power probabilities for a range of alternative "true" population. POWER's output allows easy plotting of the power function.

The program is written in time sharing BASIC for a UNIVAC 70/46 computer. It includes an integration routine that avoids table look-up in computing normal curve areas. An illustrative run of the POWER program is shown in Figure 4.

Chi-Square and Contingency Tables. One of the interesting properties of the chi-square statistic is that its value is directly proportional to the size of the sample, assuming constant relative sizes of the cells in a contingency table. This can be readily demonstrated by adapting a chi-square computation program to allow the user to multiply the numbers in each cell of the contingency table by a user-supplied factor.

Correlation and Regression. A good bivariate scatterplot program is a valuable aid in presenting correlation and regression.

Figure 3

An Illustrative Run of the MONTE Program

THIS IS A MONTE CARLO SIMULATION WHICH DRAWS REPEATED RANDOM
SAMPLES, WITH REPLACEMENT, FROM A POPULATION. YOU MAY SPE-
CIFY THE GENERAL SHAPE OF THE POPULATION BY ENTERING FRE-
QUENCIES FOR EACH OF 10 CLASSES (GROUPED DATA). ASSUME THAT
THERE ARE A TOTAL OF 100 OBSERVATIONS TO BE ALLOCATED AMONG
THESE CLASSES.

PLEASE ENTER DESIRED FREQUENCIES FOR EACH CLASS:

FROM	TO	(NOT INC)	FROM	TO	(NOT INC)
0	10	?10	50	60	?10
10	20	?10	60	70	?10
20	30	?10	70	80	?10
30	40	?10	80	90	?10
40	50	?10	90	100	?10

THE HISTOGRAM FOR THIS POPULATION IS:

CLASS: FROM	TO	HISTOGRAM	CLASS: FROM	TO	HISTOGRAM
0	10	**********	50	60	**********
10	20	**********	60	70	**********
20	30	**********	70	80	**********
30	40	**********	80	90	**********
40	50	**********	90	100	**********

```
              POPULATION MEAN = 49.5785
              POPULATION S.D. = 29.34
```

ENTER THE SIZE OF EACH SAMPLE (N)?4
HOW MANY SAMPLES OF SIZE 4   SHOULD I DRAW?100
SHALL I PRINT OUT THE MEAN OF EACH SAMPLE (Y or N)?N

CLASS: FROM	TO	HISTOGRAM
----	---	
0	10	
10	20	
20	30	*******
30	40	**************
40	50	*******************************
50	60	***********************
60	70	*******************
70	80	****
80	90	*
90	100	

MEAN OF ALL SAMPLE MEANS DRAWN SO FAR - 49.5839
S.D. OF ALL SAMPLE MEANS DRAWN SO FAR - 13.2309
NUMBER OF SAMPLE DRAWS SO FAR - 100

Figure 4

An Example of an Execution
Using the POWER Program

```
ENTER YOUR NULL HYPOTHESIS VALUE?100
ENTER YOUR POPULATION STANDARD DEVIATION?15
ENTER THE CRITICAL Z FOR YOUR SIGNIFICANCE LEVEL? 1.96
ENTER YOUR SAMPLE SIZE?10

STANDARD ERROR = 4.74342
CRITICAL BOUNDS FOR TEST OF H(O):  U = 100   ARE
   90.7029 and 109.297
```

'TRUE' PARAMETER	BETA	POWER
55.00	0.000000	1.00000
59.50	0.000000	1.00000
64.00	0.000000	1.00000
68.50	0.000000	1.00000
73.00	0.000100	0.99990
77.50	0.002694	0.99731
82.00	0.033276	0.96672
86.50	0.187796	0.81220
91.00	0.524926	0.47507
95.50	0.842250	0.15775
100.00	0.950001	0.05000
104.50	0.842251	0.15775
109.00	0.524921	0.47508
113.50	0.187795	0.81221
118.00	0.033276	0.96672
122.50	0.002694	0.99731
127.00	0.000097	0.99990
131.50	0.000000	1.00000
136.00	0.000000	1.00000
140.50	0.000000	1.00000
145.00	0.000000	1.00000

```
RUN ANOTHER (YES,NO) ?NO
```

Most computer centers can supply one, although often it must be adapted. One possible exercise might be to have students prepare the plot of a set of data, and compute both the correlation coefficient and the values for regression. Then, the same data are submitted to the program as a check.

A more sophisticated approach would be to develop a program that embodies a bivariate normal data generator allowing the student to specify the population parameters and correlation. If the program then conducted a "standard" scatter plot and correlation analysis, several runs could allow a number of population correlation values to be compared. An even more advanced version of the same program could allow for truncation of the range of one or both variables by simply discarding any generated values that fall outside the allowable range.

Other Topics and Sources

In 1972, the Committee on the Undergraduate Program in Mathematics (CUPM) of the Mathematical Association of America published a document dealing with the teaching of non-calculus statistics courses (CUMP, 1972). It contains many ideas and suggestions, and should be considered a valuable reference source for all statistics instructors.

For the past several years, NSF has supported an annual Conference on Computers in the Undergraduate Curricula (CCUC). The conferences have been hosted by Iowa State University, Dartmouth College, Claremont Graduate School, Southern Regional Education Board, and Washington State University. Copies of the Proceedings of the conferences may be obtained from the respective host institutions. The Proceedings contain many reports of computing activities in undergraduate teaching, and are valuable sources of ideas and techniques—indeed, several of the efforts summarized here were first reported at CCUC.

The new publication, *Behavior Research Methods and Instrumentation,* often publishes papers describing computer techniques helpful in teaching statistics and methodology, as do *Educational and Psychological Measurement* and *Behavioral Science.*

Finally, the Special Interest Group on Social Science Computing (SIGSOC) of the Association for Computing Machinery has a special concern with the training of social and behavioral scientists.

Conclusion

At first, the computer was used by social scientists only as a data processing tool for research. While that role of the computer is valuable and has certainly led to an advancement in the sophistication of research technique, only in recent years has it had any significant impact on the process of teaching. We have here focused on the computer as an adjunct in the process of teaching statistics. The developments reported have not been in the use of CAI, but in allowing the power of the computer to expand the kinds of examples and exercises that are available for the instructor and student. We expect that these uses of the computer will continue to grow and develop as more instructors become aware of what the computer can do for them and their students.

Nearly all of the new procedures reported here have undergone some sort of evaluation procedure. While the evaluations have usually been informal, there have been almost unanimous reports of better student understanding, improved student morale, and an increase in the time available to the instructor to spend with the students. The only commonly reported difficulty has occurred in the first semester of use of a new procedure, when the computer programs are being developed or debugged.

In short, the review of these new teaching aids and their results indicates that there *are* better ways of teaching statistics and methodology. The course that is usually dreaded by all social science students can be made into an interesting educational experience that is even viewed as enjoyable by some.

We hope that this presentation of the current status of instructional computing in statistics will prove helpful. The authors will be pleased to hear from anyone who adapts some of these suggestions into his own teaching, or who has additional ideas to share.

Notes

[1] This work was in part supported by NSF Grant GZ-3431 for a College Faculty Workshop on Computer Science in Social and Behavioral Science Education at the University of Colorado, 1974.

[2] Authors are listed alphabetically.

[3] To obtain more information about SPSS, write:
National Opinion Research Center
6030 S. Ellis Avenue
Chicago, Illinois 60637

A magnetic tape of the program costs $500.00. Maintenance and updating service is $300.00 per year.

[4] More information on BMD is available from:
    Health Sciences Computing Facility
    University of California at Los Angeles
    Los Angeles, California 90024

[5] Further information on the Scientific Subroutine Package may be obtained from:
    IBM, Technical Publications Department
    112 East Post Road
    White Plains, N.Y. 10601

[6] Information on OSIRIS is available from:
    Institute for Social Research
    University of Michigan
    Ann Arbor, Michigan 48104

[7] To obtain further information about XTAB9, write:
    James Sakoda
    Department of Sociology
    Brown University
    Providence, Rhode Island 02912

[8] Information on both OMNITAB and OMNISHRIMP may be obtained from:
    George Culp
    CONDUIT Curriculum Coordinator
    Computation Center
    University of Texas at Austin
    Austin, Texas 78712

[9] To obtain further information about MINITAB, write:
    Thomas Ryan
    219 Pond Laboratory
    Pennsylvania State University
    University Park, Pennsylvania 16802

[10] Information on SMIS/SIS may be obtained from:
    N. John Castellan, Jr.
    Department of Psychology
    Indiana University
    Bloomington, Indiana 47401

[11] To obtain further information about EXPER SIM, write:
    Chairman
    Department of Psychology
    University of Michigan
    Ann Arbor, Michigan 48104

[12] Information on Individual Learning Systems Modules is available from:
    Individual Learning Systems
    P.O. Box 2399
    San Rafael, California 94902

[13] For information on the Kotesky (1972) and Tracy and Salmon (1974) programs, write:
    Life Science Associates
    Baldwin, New York 11510

[14] For further information concerning ANALYZ, DICE, and MONTE, availability of tapes, and an extensive student guide to them, write:
    David P. Doane
    School of Economics and Management
    Oakland University
    Rochester, Michigan 48063

[15] For listings and documentation for RPROB and INDPRO, write:
    B. James Starr
    Assoicate Professor
    Department of Psychology
    Howard University
    Washington, D.C. 20059

[16] For a listing of CTL, write:
 Kenneth C. Young
 Department of Operations Research
  and Information Systems
 Eastern Michigan University
 Ypsilanti, Michigan 48197

[17] For listing and an example assignment using the POWER program, write:
 Richard S. Lehman
 Department of Psychology
 Franklin and Marshall College
 Lancaster, Pennsylvania 17604

References

Bulgren, W., *A Computer-Assisted Approach to Elementary Statistics: Examples and Problems.* Belmont, California: Wadsworth, 1971.

Carnahan, B., H.A. Luther, and J.O. Wilkes. *Applied Numerical Methods.* New York: John Wiley, 1969.

Castellan, N.J., Jr. SMIS/SIS: The Symbolic Matrix Interpretive System and the Statistical Interpretive System, *COMMON, Seattle Proceedings,* 1970, 64-73.

Castellan, N.J., Jr. On the Instructional Use of SMIS/SIS (Symbolic Matrix Interpretive System and Statistical Interpretive System). In Gillings, J.L., and Barney, J.A. (Eds.), *Proceedings of the First Indiana University Computer Network Conference on Computer Related Curriculum Materials,* Bloomington, Indiana, 1974, 162-169.

Committee on the Undergraduate Program in Mathematics. *Introductory Statistics without Calculus.* Mathematical Association of America, Berkeley, California, 1972.

Dixon, W.J. (Ed.) *BMD: Biomedical Computer Programs.* Los Angeles: University of California Press, 1968.

Harper, D. The Computer Simulation of Sociological Surveys. *Behavioral Science,* 1972, *17,* 471-480.

Harris, G.S., J.M. Swanson, and J.L. Duerr. OMNI-SHRIMP: An Interpretive Language Which Mimics OMNITAB. *Behavior Research Methods & Instrumentation,* 1974, *6,* 200-204.

Hemmerle, W.J. *Statistical Computations on a Digital Computer.* Waltham, Mass.: Blaisdell, 1967.

IBM. *System/360 Scientific Subroutine Package Programmer's Manual.* White Plains, New York: IBM, 1960.

Individual Learning Systems. *Psychological Statistics.* San Rafael, California: Individual Learning Systems, 1971.

Institute for Social Research. *OSIRIS II User's Manual.* Institute for Social Research, University of Michigan, Ann Arbor, Michigan, 1968.

Jameson, K.P., F.J. Bonello, and W.I. Davisson. Teaching Introductory Economics with the Computer as a Laboratory. *Proceedings of the Conference on Computers in the Undergraduate Curricula,* Department on Computer Science, Washington State University, Pullman, Washington, 1974.

Keller, F.S. Goodbye, Teacher. *Journal of Applied Behavior Analysis,* 1968, *1,* pp. 79-89.

Koh, Y.O., TUSTAT II: Tutorial System for Statistics with Time-Sharing Computers. *Proceedings of the Fifth Annual Conference on Computers in the Undergraduate Curricula,* Washington State University, Pullman, Washington, 1974.

Kotesky, R.L. *Computer Generated Statistics Tests for Teaching to Mastery.* Baldwin, New York: Life Science Associates, 1972.

Lehman, R.S. The Use of the Unknown in Teaching Statistics, paper presented at the meeting of the Eastern Psychological Association, 1972.

Lehman, R.S. Computer Generates Data for Statistics. *Journal of College Science Teaching,* 1973.

Lehman, R.S. *Computer Modeling and Simulation: An Introduction.* Hillsdale, New Jersey: Erlbaum Associates, 1976.

Lohnes, P.R., and W.W. Cooley. *Introduction to Statistical Procedures: With Computer Exercises.* New York: John Wiley, 1968.

Main, D. A Computer Simulation Approach for Teaching Experimental Design. *Proceedings of the 79th Annual Convention of the American Psychological Association,* 1971.

Meyers, C.D. Project IMPRESS: Timesharing in the Social Sciences. *Proceedings of the Spring Joint Computer Conference,* 1969, pp. 673-680.

Nie, N.H., D.H. Bent, and C.H. Hull. *Statistical Package for the Social Sciences.* New York: McGraw-Hill, 1970.

Nie, N.H., L.H. Hull, J.G. Jenkins, K. Steinbrenner, and D.H. Bent. *Statistical Package for the Social Sciences* (2nd ed.). New York: McGraw-Hill, 1975.

Rajecki, D.W. EXPER SIM. Mimeographed paper, Department of Psychology, University of Michigan, Ann Arbor, Michigan, 1972.

Ryan, T.A., Jr., and B.L. Joiner. MINITAB: A Statistical Computing System for Students and Researchers. *The American Statistician,* 1973, *27,* 222-225.

Snell, J.L. Computing in Probability of Course. *Proceedings of the Second Annual Conference on Computers in the Undergraduate Curricula,* Project COMPUTE, Hanover, N.H., 1971.

Starr, B.J. Automated Problem Solving for the Behavioral Sciences. *Behavior Research Methods & Instrumentation,* 1972, *4,* 161-164.

Suziedelis, A. SIFT: Statistics by Interaction with Files from the Terminal, Mimeographed paper, Catholic University of America, Washington, D.C., 1972.

Swanson, J.M., A. Ledlow, and S. Harris. Using OMNITAB Interactively in a Statistics Laboratory. *Behavior Research Methods & Instrumentation,* 1973, *5,* 199-204.

Tracy, R.J., and P.G. Salmon. *Computer-Generated Computation Exercises for Elementary Statistics.* Baldwin, New York: Life Science Associates, 1974.

Young, K.C. Using a Computer to Help Implement the Keller Method of Instruction. *Educational Technology,* 1974, *14*(10), 53-55.

9.
Use of Computer-Generated Data for Instruction in Statistics

Antanas Suziedelis
The Catholic University of America

The purpose of this paper is to point out some important advantages of computer-generated data in the teaching of statistics, both at the introductory and advanced levels. This is not to suggest that artificial data should entirely supplant well-chosen examples drawn from actual data or exercises based on data collected by the students themselves. Lessons learned from the real-life "messy," "noisy" data are invaluable. Computer-generated data, however, has some very special pedagogical potential in leading students to understand the principles of statistics and also offer some practical benefits in the logistics of instruction.

Advantages of Artificial Data

Briefly, some of the pedagogical and practical benefits are the following:

a. Population parameters of data "sampled" by the computer are always *exactly* known, which is hardly ever the case with real data. This makes it much easier to convey some of the elementary concepts of statistics, e.g., type I vs. type II error, expected vs. obtained values, unbiased vs. biased estimates, relative power of individual statistics, etc. When the exact "truth" is known, it is possible very simply to demonstrate the fact that no statistic is ever entirely correct, as well as the fact that some statistics under some circumstances are more often more correct than others.

b. Since the basic concepts of inferential statistics (significance, confidence) are grounded in probability theory, the very fact that computer-generated data to a determinable degree are a product of chance is highly instructive. Here lies the ideal opportunity to demonstrate how statistics work in differentiating between signal and noise, and between real and error effects. Desired noise-to-signal proportions can be set and thus various conditions of real data can be simulated. It is instructive for students to see how sheer chance sometimes produces effects that appear to be real, and how some built-in, known real effects are sometimes entirely obscured or even cancelled by chance factors.

c. Students can work with samples of data that are both large and individual—obviously desirable conditions for instruction. Only with large samples is it possible to demonstrate satisfactory stability of statistical findings (best shown by replication—something hardly ever possible with real data within the confines of a course). And only individual data motivate students to carry out statistical procedures thoughtfully rather than just rehearsing along with the rest of the class. With data individually his own, each student is obliged to do all necessary statistical evaluation from beginning to end, including computation, interpretation, and conclusions, without being able to reach premature closure (e.g., "I obtained the same answer as the others, so it must be right.").

d. Use of computer-generated data introduces the student to computers in a somewhat more imaginative and provoking way than the usual data processing drills associated with such courses. Furthermore, since artificial data are always technically clean (no bad punches, irreconcilable responses, etc.), no time is lost as is usually the case with student-collected real data.

These and other advantages can perhaps be best shown by referring to actual experience in the use of computer-generated data in particular courses. Two examples are briefly presented.

Constant Parameter Data

For the introductory level, it seems sufficient to produce artificial data entirely automatically, without giving the student any options of control over the generating program. Such a specific program is much easier to write than a general-purpose data generator, and can be made as simple or elaborate as the instructor wishes.

One example of a constant parameter data file is the training file for the SIFT (*S*tatistics by *I*nteraction with *F*iles from the *T*erminal) package of interactive statistics programs designed at Catholic University for its DECsystem-10. The file contains 500 college freshman records, each record consisting of 20 pieces of information. Each time the generating program is executed[1], a new set of 500 freshman records is produced on the disk, immediately accessible for statistical analysis. The 20 variables are deliberately selected to exemplify various levels of measurement, have set population parameters, and are interrelated to a plausible degree with one another (e.g., IQ is positively correlated with CEEB, certain questionnaire responses are differentially associated with the sex of the respondent, etc.).

As the first task in the course, each student produces ("collects") his own data on the 500 freshmen and is required to work up a summary of his sample, for his own notes, in any way he thinks will help him to answer questions about his data if called upon to "testify" (e.g., Are northerners better students than westerners? How many freshmen favor co-ed dorms? Are there more men or women students on scholarships? etc.). He finds that he has to use a whole battery of descriptive statistical procedures: mean, mode, standard deviation, range, frequency count, cross-tabulation, even correlation. Some elect to make use of graphs. At this point, the emphasis is strictly on correct summarization of data, and a class period is devoted to pose to the students a whole series of simple questions (as above) about their samples. A few diligent students always have very complete descriptions available, and are amply rewarded by the fact that they are able to answer instantly any reasonable question about their "subjects."

A natural transition from description to inference follows. A class period is devoted to the comparison of the many different samples (as many as there are students in the class) drawn from the infinite pool of the freshman population. The point is made that each of the samples is completely independent of any other, and that in spite and because of that, the different samples in general are very similar (e.g., IQ means mostly within one point) and yet an occasional sample appears rather peculiar on some counts (e.g., southerners holding down half the scholarships available). Interestingly, somebody in the class gets stigmatized as the "guy with the wierd sample" whose data are not to be "trusted." A healthy discussion of some basic issues of statistical inference may follow, with the moral that large amounts of information make it possible to be very sure of what is really there, and that while being very sure, one can still be very wrong.

As the topic of inference is explicitly tackled, assignments are made on substantive questions: e.g., are eastern 18-year-old males more liberal on the issue of co-ed dorms than southern 18-year-old males? Purposefully, subsamples are defined so that they can be small, and questions are chosen that theoretically should produce perfectly null results. Invariably, students bring back answers which are *prima facie* contradictory ("yes, much more liberal," "no, in fact a little more conservative," etc.). The discussion then ensues on the concepts of amount of evidence (sample size), magnitude of evidence (what is "a little," "much"), and significance of evidence.

Beyond these exercises, meant to elucidate the general concepts and uses of statistics, the data file is further used to demonstrate particular procedures and theorems.

First, the ease of computing parallel, duplicate statistics on the same data makes it possible to show certain comparabilities and identities between particular statistics that are often underemphasized in textbooks, for example, that phi is a special case of the point-biserial, which is a special case of the Pearsonian, all computable by the same formula; that one-way analysis of variance and the eta tell the same story and are convertible to one another; that the t-test is a special case of the F-test; etc.

Second, the file is used to show the effects of various data conditions on particular statistics: restriction or truncation of range on correlation, recoding of missing data into modal values on the t-test, etc.

Last, some more abstract statistical theorems are demonstrated. We find that a constant parameter file can serve quite well as a laboratory for demonstrations and exercises throughout the course in introductory statistics.

Variable Parameter Data

A fixed parameter data file is only of limited use in advanced courses, where different kinds of data are needed to exemplify features of complex statistical procedures, e.g., various methods of

factor analysis and associated rotation methods, multiple discriminant function, canonical correlation, etc. For these purposes it is
desirable to be able to specify not only particular distribution
characteristics for each variable but, more importantly, the nature
and degrees of interrelationships among the variables generated.

A program of this type was developed specifically for use in a
course in multivariate methods at Catholic University, and its brief
description here might be helpful. The program takes its cues from
the general philosophy of multivariate analysis, i.e., to reduce
redundancy in the data by "boiling down" the many interrelated,
often overlapping variables to a fewer number of relatively
independent dimensions ("factors" in factor analysis, "functions"
in discriminant analysis, etc.). The mandate of the program
generating the data file is precisely the opposite: to take a limited
number of independent elements and to mix them in varying
specifiable proportions, together with desired amount of error,
into the generated variables, which thereby become complex,
interrelated, and overlapping.

The program produces any number of records (subjects), each
consisting of observations on a specified number of variables. Each
variable is built to contain specifiable proportions of any 10
available elements (dimensions, factors).

Suppose some 500 records are generated, each containing
observations on the six variables with variance composition
specified. We now can analyze these data by various correlational
techniques, with full knowledge at the start of what the results
should be. Thus, by examining the variance proportion table and
carrying out some simple calculations, we know the reliabilities,
commonalities, and validities for each variable, and also the
amount and the reasons for their intercorrelations. We find that
the variance proportion table is itself a useful tool for reviewing
these fundamental concepts.

Since build-in, *pure* relationships between variables are known,
it is easy to show subsequently how one or another statistical
technique works to extract this "truth" from the *noisy* data, and
to what extent it succeeds.

Following demonstrations of the uses and characteristics of
various techniques, students are given assignments to work
backwards and to reconstruct the variance proportion table from

data generated by the instructor with population specifications unknown to them. Similarly, students are given data and asked to answer questions such as these:

a. How many significant canonical functions link two given sets of variables, and which variables define them?

b. Which five of 10 predictors in the multiple regression problem may be safely eliminated from the predictor set without materially reducing the power of prediction? Which of these can be eliminated because they are virtual duplicates of other predictors and which are simply error variables artificially inflating the multiple correlation in that one sample?

Limitations and Conclusions

Like any other particular device of instruction, simulated data also has some pedagogical limitations. Practical experience has pointed up at least these caveats:

a. The flexibility and the potential of the tool may be seductive to the instructor, and he may overburden it with the onus of conveying to the students too many lessons at once. Our earlier version of the variable parameter data generator contained options for specifying complex distribution characteristics for the variables (skewness, truncation, biomodality, etc.). It quickly became apparent that such refinements introduced unnecessary complications into the exercises and tended to obscure the fundamentals of multivariate analysis. We have now opted for a generator that allows the specification of variance composition for each variable, but generates all variables as normally distributed with identical population means and standard deviations.

b. The generating program itself may take on the characteristics of a magical "black box" that "rigs" results. Earlier or later in the course it is desirable to explain how the generator works and to take the students through the algorithm of the simulation step by step. This is not time lost from the course: in fact, this offers a good opportunity to review the concepts of the central limits theorem, covariance, etc.

c. At least for some students, the method ushers in an additional unwelcome degree of abstraction, as one deals with artificial variables and artificial common elements having no reference to particular tests, items, and dimensions. The ultimate repair, of course, is to use examples from actual data at a later stage in the course. That brings about closure, and it is not uncommon for some students at that point to express surprise at how much they had learned from the simulation exercises. It is also useful to reduce the abstractness of the artificial files by attaching familiar labels to variables (Information, Comprehension, Digit Span, etc.) and to common elements (Verbal Ability, Memory, etc.) provided, of course, that such labels conform plausibly to the data structure generated.

Teachers of statistics in behavioral and social sciences will agree that in most courses we face two different constituencies of students, the nomothetics and the ideographs. The first have an affinity for quantitative methods; the second tend to regard statistics as an obstacle course. Our experience over the years with the use of simulated data in statistics reveals some interesting attitudinal effects. Some of the skeptics and cynics, who view statistics as a deft design to obscure the "truth," often are surprisingly intrigued and even "converted" as they see a particular method, such as factor analysis, extract from the sheer inscrutability of a large intercorrelation matrix the underlying structure built into the data generated. The believers often benefit from precisely the opposite "religion" as they see, especially on samples of limited size, how the carefully wrought sense of generated data gets unrecognizeably distorted by some complex statistical procedure. One never quite trusts the cookbook approach much after that.

Both are highly salutary effects.

References

Cohen, J. Some Statistical Issues in Psychological Research. In Wolman, B., *Handbook of Clinical Psychology.* New York: McGraw-Hill Book Company, 1965.

Suziedelis, A. *SIFT II: A Manual for Statistics by Interaction with Files from the Terminal.* Washington, D.C.: Catholic University of America, 1972.

Note

[1] FORTRAN source listings for the generator programs are

available from the author, Department of Psychology, Catholic University, Washington, D.C. 20064. Minor modification may be needed for compilation at other installations. The SIFT system, while also written in FORTRAN, capitalizes on unique features of the DECsystem-10 and would require extensive modification.

10.
Computer-Assisted Instruction in Experimental Design

Francis Campos
Lawrence University

With the advent of time-shared interactive computing came the promise of an educational revolution. By distributing the processing power of a single computer over many access terminals, the idea of a tutorial relationship between student and computer became a reality. This notion of computer-assisted instruction (CAI) held the possibility of lessons tailored to the particular needs of the individual student while freeing the instructor to pursue the broader goals of curriculum development.

A decade of experience with CAI has dulled some of that promise. In many areas of instruction, the limitations of the computer in interpreting natural language have prevented the development of realistic dialogue between student and computer. The field of artificial intelligence has not progressed to the point where a student's misunderstanding can be interpreted through algorithms or heuristics. The financial costs of development and continued implementation of CAI are decreasing, but limitations on educational resources have inhibited progress. These restrictions have limited not only the number but also the nature of CAI projects. As a result, applied mathematics, particularly elementary statistics, has received an inordinate amount of attention from CAI development.

A relatively neglected area of CAI development in statistics has been analysis of variance (Anova). Anova is a technique in inferential statistics that is essential to the design of experiments. The technique involves making decisions about the reliability of differences among means of sample data on the basis of variances.

131

In its simplest form it is a straightforward deduction from the central limit theorem; however, its complexity increases as the designs become more sophisticated.

This paper describes the implementation of computer-assisted instruction in analysis of variance, known as Casanova. The strategy and tactics of instruction are considered in the context of commercially available computing services and their limitations.

The minimal goal of a course in experimental design in psychology is to provide the student with the conceptual tools needed to critically evaluate the appropriateness of the design of an experiment and its data analysis in the experimental literature. A more demanding goal would be that the student could analyze data from a complex experiment of his own design. Accomplishing either of these goals requires relatively extensive treatment of Anova. While Anova is not the only technique for data analysis, it is the dominant technique in psychology. Furthermore, it provides a conceptual framework for the design of experiments using other techniques.

It can be argued that before a student can interpret data or criticize a design, he must understand the computations for an Anova. While a simple one-way Anova can be presented intuitively on the basis of the central limit theorem, the student can become confused when dealing with more complex designs for which the sources of variance are less obvious. The gap between verbal and mathematical understanding of Anova can be bridged by making the mathematical operations more concrete. By actually doing the calculations, the student can make the connection between the mathematical symbols used to represent a concept and the verbal statement of that concept. As he moves from simple to more complex Anovas, he can see the common elements among the various Anova techniques. In this fashion, his mastery of the computations provides a perspective from which to understand the logic of Anova.

A counter-argument is that doing these calculations by hand often buries the student in numbers. Since complex Anovas require extensive calculations, even the best student can lose his perspective on the problem when faced with numerous sheets of scratch paper and frustrated by minor arithmetic errors. In this situation, CAI has the potential to organize the scratch paper and reduce the errors.

Educational Considerations

By limiting the objectives of Casanova to teaching the calculations for Anova, it was possible to avoid many problems associated with natural language processing. The computer's responses to student input are well enough defined to avoid ambiguity of response, yet provide him with maximum control within the mathematical structure of the analysis. Since the organization of the solution to the problem can also be well defined, each problem is divided into a manageable number of subproblems. In this way the student is guided through a logical organization of the problem, but must himself decide on the correct computations for the subproblem.

A Casanova problem begins when the student selects one of the eight different Anova designs available. Casanova then generates simulated data that are based on parameters estimated from the results of an experiment. The purpose and design of each experiment is described in an accompanying workbook. These simulated data are presented to the student while the answers to the subproblems are stored for later verification against the student's answers. After he sees the data, the student receives instructions that define the first subproblem. He uses mathematical commands available to him to arrive at the answer using the computer to help him with the arithmetic. When he believes he has the correct answer for that subproblem, he signals the computer and the answer is verified. If he is correct, the instructions for the next subproblem are presented. If he is incorrect, he is again given control of the mathematical commands so that he can correct his error. At this point the student may ask for help and receive a message designed to diagnose the most common errors. When he feels he has recalculated the solution correctly, he may again verify his response against the stored answer.

A further step is taken to protect students who continue to obtain an incorrect answer. Even the student who knows how to solve a subproblem might be persevering in a clerical error. This and other possibilities are anticipated by allowing the student to see the correct answer to any subproblem once in each exercise. The limit on its use is effective in encouraging the student to use it cautiously. This option tends to humanize Casanova to a considerable extent. Furthermore, the workbook gives suggestions on how to work backward from the correct answer to try to identify one's mistake. The workbook also emphasizes the cumulative nature of the material as a reason for not passing by the error without attempting to understand its cause.

This organization of the exercises implements a number of tactical considerations appropriate to the war between students and statistics. First, the exercise is divided into subproblems that require one new concept. At first, the level of difficulty of subproblems is divided finely but becomes coarser as the complexity of the exercises increases. Early in the course, the large number of relatively simple subproblems ensures that the student takes on only one new concept at a time. Later, when the calculations are better learned, smaller steps are combined into a single subproblem so that the large perspective on a more complex analysis may be obtained. The goal is to avoid having the calculations obscure the problem, but to have them exemplify the mathematical abstractions. It is also intended that a reasonably high success rate be maintained throughout the course, even as new material is being introduced. The anxiety that often accompanies statistics is pleasantly reduced once the student feels that he has established some control over his solutions to the problems.

A second advantage to the subproblems is that they provide almost immediate feedback to the student's solution. Traditional homework exercises are graded hours or days after they were undertaken. This slow feedback allows misconceptions to persist longer, perhaps resulting in confusion later on. The immediate feedback given by Casanova identifies errors quickly. Casanova provides positive as well as negative feedback. A student may ask for help and receive a message intended to correct the more common errors for that subproblem. Here artificial intelligence would be particularly useful. If Casanova could use the incorrect answer to diagnose the error, for example dividing by N instead of N-1, then the feedback could be markedly more effective. However, an incorrect diagnosis could to a great deal of damage and such a technique has not been attempted.

It is important to note that the combination of subproblems accompanied by feedback ensures that the student who completes the exercise has done so correctly. Further precautions have been taken to avoid cumulative errors attributable to rounding error. If the student's error is small enough to be due to rounding, Casanova counts it as correct but supplies the exact answer for later use in the exercise. Because a completed exercise is a correct exercise, grading is simplified. To the student's benefit, there is no uncertainty about handing in an incorrect solution, a factor that would again tend to reduce the anxiety that may accompany statistics.

Another aspect of Casanova that helps contribute to understanding is the simplicity of the mathematical commands the student uses. The student asks for a command in abbreviated English, such as MULT for multiply and SUM for summation. All 13 commands are introduced in the first exercise and are used throughout the course; thus, there are no surprises accompanying more complex exercises. The commands are intended to be notation free so they can be used with any text, provided some modifications are made in the wording of the instructions. An advantage to this neutrality is that the student has a common basis for translating the summation notation of the text into arithmetic operations. The simplicity of the commands helps them become a bridge between the conceptual basis of the summation equations and the concrete basis of the calculations.

Another aspect of this CAI system is the integration of a workbook with Casanova. The workbook provides one or two examples of each design taken from the psychological literature. These examples serve to motivate the various exercises by providing easily understood instances of a design. They also serve as a basis for criticism of experimental design. The examples are presented in shortened versions, occasionally missing control groups and lacking in specifics of the methodology. This allows the student to go to the original research to see how well the author anticipated his criticisms. It is also instructive for the student to compare his simulated results with those of the empirical research. This will serve to reinforce the notion that Anova is a *statistical* inference technique and that errors are possible. Comparing the proportion of decisions to reject the null hypothesis in a large class is a vivid demonstration of power in statistical inference.

In addition to the variety of examples, a different set of simulated data is produced each time an exercise is started. This allows a student to repeat an exercise if he is not satisfied with his performance the first time. It again reinforces the notion that a replication of an experiment need not result in the same statistical decisions.

Using Casanova

Casanova has allowed a significant reduction in the time spent in lecture on the computational aspects of design. The manner in which computations are treated has changed as well. More emphasis can be placed on the conceptual rather than the arithmetic skills, allowing a better integration of a design with its analysis. More time can be spent making the connections between a concrete example and the requirements of a design. Such examples help students recognize when a particular design is appropriate to a situation.

The Casanova workbook, *Problems in Experimental Design Using CASANOVA,* provides examples of designs as well as supplementary material for student use of these programs. The introductory chapters explain how to use the commands and give suggestions for further criticism of the examples. The first exercise demonstrates the use of the commands for calculating variances.

The remaining eight chapters present examples of psychological research for various designs. Three of these chapters deal with completely randomized designs: one-way, two-way, and three-way Anovas. Also included are a one-way within subjects design, one within, one between subjects design, a hierarchical group, an analysis of covariance, and a latin square. The research examples cover a variety of topics including intermittent reward, imagery, concept formation, risky shift, and attribution theory. The workbook does not attempt to teach the calculations themselves. It must be accompanied by a text in experimental design.

Casanova is implemented on a Digital Equipment Corporation PDP-11/45 operating under RSTS. All the programs are written in BASIC-PLUS, an extended version of Dartmouth BASIC. Casanova uses as few of the extended features as possible and should be relatively transportable to other installations. All the programs use less than 8K of core; however the files for instructions and HELP messages require as much as 4K each. The use of record I/O could reduce storage requirements substantially.

Student ratings of Casanova have been positive. Undergraduate students report that the level of difficulty is appropriate and that it is well organized. Relative to the problems they worked by hand in a prerequisite introductory statistics course, they strongly preferred Casanova and recommended that it be used in the future. They also felt the workbook to be valuable. During the development of Casanova, only sketchy descriptions of the experiments were presented by the computer along with the data. The more extended examples in the workbook were seen as furthering their understanding of the application of the designs.

Unfortunately, the small size of our institution does not allow us to conduct a controlled experiment that would provide more precise evidence about the success of this endeavor. The opinion of this instructor, biased though it may be, is that the best students are learning as well as ever, but that the average and below average students are learning more than before. This would not be surprising, since the student who is having difficulty with the course can benefit most from the feedback process and organization of these exercises.

Casanova has allowed the instructor to redistribute the time he allots to this course. Although an occasional homework problem is assigned to be worked by hand, for example, individual comparisons, and the Casanova exercises are inspected by the instructor, an exercise that is completed is correct. Time formerly spent grading homework can be spent grading essay examinations and critical papers. The latter assignments help the student see that data analysis is more than just numbers and that experimental design is more than just data analysis. Students learn that statistics plays a crucial, but nevertheless small, role in the larger perspective of a scientific approach to psychology.

Reference

Meyers, J.L. *Fundamentals of Experimental Design,* 2nd ed. Boston, Mass.: Allyn and Bacon, 1972.

Note

[1] This project was supported in part by NSF Grant GY-10095 to Lawrence University and NSF Grant GZ-3431 to the University of Colorado. I would like to thank Jim Cox and Rick Cook for their able programming assistance, and Toni DiGeronimo and Paula Jackson for both critical and clerical contributions.

11.
The Use of Audio-Visual Techniques
in Computer Instruction
for Social Scientists

Michael A. Baer
University of Kentucky

Nona M. Newman
University of Newcastle

The Nature of the Problem

The development of computer usage in the social sciences has presented the discipline with several problems. Among these have been methods of instructing undergraduates in the applications of computers for social analysis. The social sciences have been slower than the natural sciences in developing instructional material in this area. Yet, as more faculty members develop familiarity with the use of computers and their applications, students in more social science courses are encouraged to use the facilities of the campus computing center to process data.

Most university computing centers have adapted themselves to this relatively new need by collecting or developing library programs that allow the computer novice to hurdle the obstacles that confront him. In addition to the individual programs that are collected and made available, there are several program packages for social scientists that have been distributed to a large number of universities. Students should have easy access to both the program libraries and these larger packages of program systems. For access to have any significance, there must also be a means of obtaining instruction in the use of the programs.

Here lies the problem of instructional methods. Many faculty members in the social sciences, though familiar with data processing techniques, are often not prepared to provide adequate instruction, and to supervise large classes in the use of canned programs. It is questionable whether even those instructors who are capable of clearly explaining the use of a package to students would be wisely using their time devoting numerous class hours to this purpose. This is particularly true since the material would need to be presented in several different classes, with some students repeating the material more than one or two times, as many upper level social science courses have few if any common prerequisites.

Traditional Solutions

One solution that has often been used in the institution by either a department or computing center is non-credit courses and seminars instructing students in the use of both the computer and the program packages. While this is more economical than providing individual instruction for each prospective user, an alternative often used by default, it is not always the most practical or most educationally desirable method.

First, the problem of scheduling such courses so that they are available to all students who need them is virtually impossible. There is always a conflict with the class and/or work schedule of a number of students. The cost of providing instructors for these basic seminars term after term may be prohibitive. Finally, seminars planned on a university-wide basis cannot be planned to fit into the schedule of any one particular course. It is desirable to present the material to students at the most logical point in their study. Frequently, students are able to grasp the details required to use the computer only after they have reached the point in a course where data processing is the next logical step. A student who is unfamiliar with data collection and the form that data may take is unlikely to retain information presented to him concerning the processing of data. In addition, while one or two instructional sessions in the use of a program package will certainly be helpful, students are likely to benefit by reviewing the same material in additional sessions after trying to use the computer.

The problem of instruction in the use of social science program packages extends beyond the undergraduate student. In a university environment, research workers in all fields are normally expected to carry out the whole of their research work themselves, including any computational work necessary. At any one time, even in a large university, the numbers wishing to learn to use a particular package may be quite small; but spread over a year, the numbers can be quite considerable. This becomes a problem when the research worker cannot, or will not, postpone his use of the computer for some months until sufficient like-minded colleagues have accumulated so that it is worthwhile for the computer center to put on a formal course. In addition, the documentation for these packages is usually reference-oriented and does not lend itself to use by the novice for self-teaching purposes, so that some sort of "course" is essential. Further, in the traditional kind of course, all learners are expected to learn the same things and reach the same standard. This is not necessarily appropriate if the package is one in which simple use is possible of a subset of the facilities, and where few users need to understand fully the complete capability of the package.

Searching for New Solutions

Because traditional solutions are not always satisfactory, at least two quite different methods, utilizing audio-visual techniques, have been produced and found relatively successful. The Computing Center and the Division of Media Services of the University of Kentucky have produced several instructional videotapes containing material related to computers and data processing.[2] Among these tapes were introductory sessions to two computing systems widely distributed and used by social scientists, OSIRIS and SPSS.[3] The Computing Laboratory of the University of Newcastle Upon Tyne has developed a series of slide-audiotape sessions for instruction on the use of SPSS.[4] At both universities the method of teaching SPSS, prior to the development of the audio-visual packages, had been through frequent series of formal non-credit courses, and individual aid to those persons attempting to wade through the manual between the courses.

While the goals of developing the courses at these two universities were quite similar, the criteria set forth for the two self-instructional packages differed somewhat. As SPSS, the *Statistical Package for the Social Sciences,* was involved in the developments at both institutions, we examine the use of videotape and of slide-tape presentations with SPSS in mind.

SPSS is a system of computer programs that offers capabilities of data mangement and analysis using techniques frequently employed by social scientists. It is distributed by the National

Opinion Research Center at the University of Chicago. Over 325 computing installations are using the SPSS package on IBM 360/370 computers and the package is issued in more than 15 different versions for operation on other computing systems.[5] In developing instructional material, both institutions had in mind the possibility of exporting their instructional package beyond their own universities. Thus, it was vital to make the material installation independent to their own institution. However, with no guarantee that other institutions would wish to use these materials, the method selected had to be more economical of staff time than the present system, so that as the user community grew more users could be helped without needing an expansion of the advisory service. It also had to be reasonably cheap, and here the value of the resources that would be saved was clearly relevant.

In addition to economy, it was important that the method enforced sequential learning, since SPSS has a natural structure. Finally, since a lot of information has to be conveyed, the method needed to contain sufficient variety to counteract the boredom that so easily sets in when studying stereotyped material.

The Two Solutions Compared and Contrasted

The development of videotape instructional sessions and the slide-tape presentation differed somewhat. This was largely because the slide-tape presentations aimed to give a more detailed coverage of the data description and simple analysis features of SPSS.

The production of the videotapes was approached with the idea of familiarizing students and faculty members alike with the SPSS package while requiring a minimum of staff time devoted to seminar and class presentations. Two one-half hour tapes were developed. The primary goal of the videotapes was to instruct the student in the basic operations of the SPSS package and to overcome the fear created by the several hundred page manual that accompanies the program system. The videotapes introduce the viewer to the basic cards that are necessary in carrying out a simple task in the SPSS system, and illustrate the system by working through several examples. These sample setups demonstrate the various types of parameter cards as well as the types of programs available in the system.

It was not expected that an individual totally unfamiliar with data processing would be able to process data with no problems after viewing the tapes. Nor was it expected that one could set up programs without referring to the manual after viewing the tapes. The tapes were, however, a means that could capture a clear presentation, encompassing well formulated examples. They also could be used at the convenience of the instructor and viewer for teaching the basics of a program system to the students.

The use of videotapes in an instructional situation provides an extremely flexible solution to many of the problems we have previously outlined. Because the tapes may be played over closed circuit equipment, large numbers of students in several classrooms can be accommodated at one time. The tapes can also be played over a portable machine and single monitors in any one classroom. Thus, they can be readily watched at any time convenient to a class. In addition, copies may be stored in a library where individual students may have access to the tapes and equipment for viewing at their own convenience. This is particularly helpful for a make-up session, or a review.

The slide-tape presentation was meant to be rather more than an introduction to SPSS, its purposes, and its manual. The student completing the series of slide-tape presentations would be expected to be able to carry out a task through the SPSS system with few problems. One additional factor used in developing the slide-tape presentation was that it should include facilities for practice sessions.

The use of SPSS at a relatively simple level was covered in eight sessions averaging 17 minutes each. Of these, one is introductory, aimed at giving a potential user some idea of whether the package provides the facilities he needs, one is concerned with data preparation prior to studying SPSS proper, and one deals with the use of SPSS at a specific installation. The remaining five cover data definition, transformation, and selection facilities of SPSS, and give a simple introduction to the use of SPSS procedures. Each session has an appropriate document to reinforce its ideas in summary. Following the third session, the user is asked to run a simple entirely predefined job on the computer, and after sessions four, six, seven, and eight there are simple examples for him to do. Users are expected to submit these, correctly done, to a computing laboratory adviser before proceeding.

The ability to allow students to have direct individual access to the instructional material is an extremely important aspect of the use of both types of presentation. The student may have first viewed the material in a group situation and, with a specific task in mind, selectively filtered information that was necessary for his particular goal or assignment. After achieving this specific goal, he may desire to use other features of a program system. Hopefully, the information he has retained will enable him to approach the manual and continue his progress. However, it might also be desirable for him to watch earlier sessions again, this time with an experienced eye picking out the more general aspects of the system. Thus, the replayable presentations may serve the purpose of providing a cumulative education over the course of several viewings.

Furthermore, in both cases, the flexibility of usage is not limited to the convenience of retrieval by students, but also extends to the production side. The materials that may be presented in a visually instructive and pleasant manner in either a slide-tape presentation or on videotape can far surpass the materials one might expect in live classes taught by a series of instructors each of whom was preparing his own examples and visual aids.

Conclusions

While there has yet to be any formal evaluation of the effectiveness of either method of presentation, the response from other installations who have previewed both sets of materials has been enthusiastic. Approximately 20 sets of the videotapes have been leased to other computing installations, and about 40 sets of the slide-tape presentation have been sold. In addition, many other user groups have requested further information or previewed the materials.

The use of these two techniques need not be mutually exclusive. The format of the current videotapes tends to give one an overall view of the program package under consideration. The slide-tape presentation gives one more in depth and specific information about the system. The two may in some circumstances be used in conjunction with each other.

These two techniques are attempts at the solution of a number of problems facing social scientists in their approach to the use of computers. The number of social scientists involved, their unpredictable schedules, and the similarity of their initial needs all tend to suggest that audio-visual instruction methods are appropriate. Furthermore, while the use of computer in social science education is increasing, we must remain aware that for many students and for many faculty members the computing center still carries an aura of the mystical. It is imperative that we adopt methods of convincing these individuals that it is not a complex task to use the computer in study or in research. One simple way may be through the use of readily available audio-visual instruction.

Notes

[1] We wish to thank the University of Surrey and the Leverhulme Trust for providing facilities and time during the preparation of this manuscript.

[2] The first production was an eight session short course in FORTRAN. A one-session program on teleprocessing was produced. In addition, the SPSS tapes described in this article and two sessions on OSIRIS have been produced. A modularized series of videotapes on OSIRIS III is currently under production.

[3] OSIRIS is a package of computer management and analysis programs distributed by the Inter-University Consortium for Political Research at the University of Michigan. SPSS is a package of programs distributed by the National Opinion Research Center, University of Chicago. The instructional manual is *SPSS: Statistical Package for the Social Sciences,* Norman Nie, *et al.* (New York: McGraw Hill Book Company, 1970). The videotaped instructional programs were produced at the University of Kentucky Division of Media Services under the direction of Michael Baer.

[4] The slide-audio tape sessions were produced at the University of Newcastle under the direction of Dr. Nona Newman. A slide-tape presentation involves using a slide-projector with an automatic slide-changing mechanism, which is linked with a cassette tape

recorder, capable of transmitting slide-changing pulses to the projector. The commentary is recorded on one track of the cassette, and pulses on the other, and these pulses cause the slides to be changed at appropriate points in the recording. Because the visual display is through the medium of 5 x 5 cm slides, the method is reasonably inexpensive.

[5] SPSS Newsletter, *National Opinion Research Center*, Chicago, Number 7, November, 1974, and accompanying list of User Installations.

PART III
Social Impact

12.
Computer Literacy

James R. Bohland
University of Oklahoma

Ronald E. Anderson
University of Minnesota

Introduction

Literacy long has refered to the ability to write and read. The significance of these abilities is that they are communication skills essential to a great many activities in modern societies. Reading and writing with various languages solved man's need to process large quantities of complex information in the attempt to communicate with others. In a parallel fashion, reading and writing languages that computer machinery can process solves man's need to communicate with computers. The ability to communicate effectively with computers appropriately is called *computer literacy.* Communication in this context encompasses both (1) the skill of writing commands and transmitting these to a computing device, and (2) the capacity to decipher computer output and understand at least the social significance of products of computerized information systems.

The computer literacy concept often is used to refer to general knowledge about computerization. For instance, a computer literacy panel of the Institute for the Future workshop defined computer literacy as "The understanding of basic computer functions in terms of what computers can and cannot do, with particular attention to their potential, as well as their limits, in meeting human needs." In this sense, it is a form of education in the interests both of the citizen-consumer and the designers of computer based information systems. Computerization increasingly raises questions of public policy, and informed citizens are essential for rational formulation of answers.

Computer education programs providing general computer knowledge are called here *general computer literacy.* In addition, educational programs are needed for providing specific task or employment skills for dealing effectively with computers. Such skills and knowledge are called here *functional computer literacy.* Of course, the skills and knowledge required varies from situation to situation or function to function.

The notion of functional literacy is borrowed from literacy programs in underdeveloped nations. Functional literacy programs are tailored to the particular needs of persons working in a specific environment. Communication skills are taught with the goal of facilitating the effectiveness of an individual in his work role. Functional computer literacy needs must necessarily be solved partially by the specific institutional work settings. However, as computer applications become more pervasive, broader educational programs become more useful. For instance, some nations, such as France and Israel, have instituted nationwide precollege computer literacy courses.

The two types of computer literacy identified above call for alternate curricula or instructional approaches. For the needs of general computer literacy, courses in the social impact of computers have been developed. These concerns are often called "computers and society," although some are appropriately called "computer appreciation" courses. For the needs of functional computer literacy, a tremendous variety of courses and training programs is offered. Our particular interest here is with functional computer literacy areas pertaining to the social sciences. Specifically, we are concerned with identifying content and materials for such educational programs. Despite the availability of computer science courses at most universities and colleges, not many courses in computer applications for the social and behavioral sciences are currently offered.

Literacy Objectives

Any plan for the functional literacy of students in the social and behavioral sciences must be flexible enough to accommodate the diversity between the different fields. To include both functional literacy and general literacy components is extremely difficult. Several factors work against any easy solution. First, as we have defined functional literacy, it involves a more specialized form of education. The range of interests within the social sciences makes it extremely difficult to define common needs and environments. Fragmentation rather than unity exists. Sociologists see their needs as unique, as do the political scientists, psychologists, etc.

Disciplinary ethnocentrism increases the demands for disciplinary relevance in technique and methods courses. This may eventually create proliferation and duplication of courses, as it did in statistics. If well-trained faculty are unavailable, the quality of instruction suffers and a generation of "cookbook" methodologists or technicians is created. In attempts to develop functional literacy, computer education could commit the same mistakes. If professionals in the social sciences can not agree on common needs or formulate methods of achieving them, duplication will occur, and the quality of education will suffer.

Staffing constitutes another problem area. Finding faculty who are capable of bridging the gap between the computer sciences and the social sciences is difficult. If proliferation occurs, the staffing problem would become acute. In the long run the problem must be solved by broadening graduate education in both the social and computer sciences. Until literacy programs are fully developed, the existing pool of instructors must be utilized. This means educational programs designed to broaden the scope of existing computer education.

The heterogeneity in the backgrounds, needs, and aptitudes of social science students further complicates the task of developing new programs. Also, although it is safe to assume that the influence of computers on the lives of the students will expand in the future, most people will not be required to know programming languages or be system analysts. Consequently, simply expanding the program language capabilities of students would not necessarily improve their functional literacy. An awareness and understanding of the potentials and limitations of computer technology in a variety of situations is needed. This can not be achieved by teaching three or more program languages rather than just one.

Disciplinary provincialism, staffing problems, and student diversity hamper the creation of integrated, innovative programs of computer literacy in the social sciences. Add to these a financial situation in higher education that is not conducive to new program development, and the task seems insurmountable. If, however, computer literacy is to be realized, present modes of computer education must be enriched, and this enrichment must come from within the social sciences. Responsibility for identifying specific needs and methods of accomplishing objectives lies with personnel in the social sciences, not the computer sciences.

Before progress can be made, it is essential that multi-disciplinary objectives be identified and clearly specified, and an implementation procedure created. Specifying objectives is the obvious first step. Several general objectives seem clear.

Programming Capabilities. Functional literacy does not necessarily mean a high level of proficiency in a number of program languages. However, if students are to be literate in computer techniques, one should have some experience with communicating in computer languages. Selection of the specific language should be left to the student or discipline because needs vary depending on the particular problems.

Analysis Language. Within the social sciences there is considerable variation in the languages employed in analysis. In some, numeric symbol systems are more common. Some, such as anthropology, rely less on numeric analysis but emphasize interpretation of oral or written verbal languages. In still others, such as geography, graphic communication is utilized. Functional literacy should include an introduction to computer analysis techniques that are applicable to all three language forms. It should also develop a higher skill level in the forms widely utilized in the student's discipline. For example, use of the computer for content analysis would have great value for anthropologists or historians. Conversely, the scope and capabilities of the computer for numeric analysis would be more meaningful to the demographer. To ensure effective communication across disciplines all students should be made aware of the potential uses of computer technology in each of the three areas: numeric, interpretive, and graphic.

Decision-making. Instruction in the decision-making capabilities of computers could range from simple gaming techniques to the more sophisticated forms of artificial intelligence. At a minimum, simulation and multivariate modeling procedures should be included. Simulation has no disciplinary boundaries, and the functionally literate computer person should have at least the basics of simulation modeling upon graduation.

Data Structure and Data Management. Some form of data management is a task that most college graduates will probably encounter some time within their vocational careers. The data base may be small or large depending on the situation, but procedures for organizing and handling data by automated procedures would be helpful.

Education. Within existing computer science programs the instructional capabilities of computers are seldom developed in any formalized manner. Yet, the instruction capabilities of the computer are enormous, and many social science students become involved in some form of instruction upon graduation. Computer-assisted instruction, record-keeping, examination pools, and other enhancement procedures would be valuable to students interested in pursuing a teaching position. Since many students would be required to use smaller computer systems, emphasizing the instructional capabilities of mini-computers would be particularly useful.

The five areas cited do not represent an exhaustive list. However, if all aspects of computer technology in each of the five are covered, a lengthy series of courses would be necessary. For this reason, we should begin to think in terms of alternatives to *courses* in computer literacy. Rather, basic topics and concepts must be identified and smaller units of study, modules, formulated.

A module would be a self-contained unit on a well defined computer concept or topic. Items such as computer graphics, simulation, computers in the post-industrial society, heuristic models, and others of a similar nature would serve as the subject matter. Each should be conceptually based, well documented with resource materials, and developed along sound pedagogical principles. One could design a course or a program of study tailored to specific needs by forming different modular combinations.

The development of a modular system would also help encourage the integration of computer related topics into substantive social science courses. As an example, some universities now have courses in futurology. A unit on computers in the post-industrial society should be an integral part of such a course. In most instances it is not included because the instructor is unfamiliar with the literature and concepts on this topic. Well designed modules would also help in the development of instructional personnel. More importantly, modules could change a trend in computer education that, if continued, can only increase public apprehension and frustration towards computer technology.

Summary

Computer literacy programs are at a critical threshold. Currently, the direction programs should follow is unclear. Lessons of the past should be sufficient warning. If we hope to make any substantial contribution toward educating the public about computer technology and its impact on the individual and society, old molds must be recast.

13.
The Computerized Society

Roberta Ash
DePaul University

Robert Ogden   Larry Gluck
DePaul University   *DePaul University*

The Purpose of the Course; Course Outline

"The Computerized Society" is an introduction to computer courses taught at DePaul since the winter of 1973. The purpose of the course is to provide the student with enough background in programming and related skills to establish a basis for making informed decisions in political matters related to information processing technology. In the words of the course syllabus: "It is our hope that, by the end of the course, the students will have confidence in their ability to make rational appraisals of the current uses and limitations of information-processing technology; that they will will be able to take part as citizens in articulating their feelings on how this technology should be used; and that their cognitive processes include systematic, step-by-step thinking as a means of problem-solving."

The purpose of the course is developed through a set of specific objectives:

(1) to understand the concept of algorithmic thinking;

(2) to see flow charting as an application of algorithmic processes;

(3) to write simple programs in BASIC, including decisions, loops, and "for-next" instructions;

(4) to have a reading knowledge of more complicated programs;

(5) to understand the concept of simulation and to be able to write simple simulations;

(6) to know the history of calculating devices and computers,

to see computer development in terms of social factors that shaped it, and to know the history of decisions about computers in our society;

(7) to understand the economic and political consequences of present systems of information retrieval;

(8) to know the present structure of the computer industry and the impact of that structure on computer development;

(9) to be able to identify present users of computer technology;

(10) to know the organization of computer work;

(11) to know some issues concerning artificial intelligence, robotics, and models of human problem-solving;

(12) to think about alternative uses of computers and an alternative organization of computer work; and

(13) to understand what types of problems computers can solve and how these problems must be formulated.

"The Computerized Society" is offered as part of the general education program at DePaul University, as one of a number of electives in the arts and sciences from which all students must select courses. The course includes the unique feature of being team taught by a sociologist and a mathematician. Students can take it for credit in either the natural or social sciences. Enrollment is usually about 35 to 40 students. The course devotes about five weeks each to information processing and the social impact of computers. Course topics are presented according to the following schedule:

Part I: Information-processing

(1) general concepts and history;

(2) a short introduction to binary arithmetic, logic circuits, hardware, and machine language;

(3) algorithms and flow charts;

(4) programming in BASIC with hands-on interactive experience with a Hewlett-Packard mini-computer (2000F);

(5) introduction to simulation; and

(6) artificial intelligence and robotics.

Part II: The Social Impact

(1) the present uses of computers;

(2) the structure of the computer industry and decision-making about computers;

(3) the issue of privacy;

(4) the impact on work and political structure;

(5) the organization of computer work; issues of hierarchy, creditation, and professionalism; and

(6) possible alternate uses.

Both instructors take part in all aspects of the course and are present in the classroom or computer lab at all times.

Information-Processing
Technology and the Structure of Society

An important feature of the course is our emphasis on how the computer (and related information-processing procedures) might change the *structure* of society. In other words, we emphasize how the nature of work, the distribution of political power, and even social class relations might change in conjunction with changes in information processing. We do not just point to possible effects on the individual or the "quality of life" experienced by the individual but also to possible effects on the relations between groups. In two versions of the course taught in 1974 and 1975 we used Kurt Vonnegut's *Player Piano* (Vonnegut, 1971) to make this point about social structure. Although dated in its treatment of computer technology, *Player Piano* stimulated discussion of how some features of contemporary American society indicate the potential for development in the direction of Vonnegut's anti-utopia: the enormous power vested in monopoly corporations; widespread un- and under-employment; meaningless quantification; educational tracking and channeling; the trivialization of women; cutthroat competition disguised as good-natured rivalry among junior executives and engineers, and so on.

In part, our model for the types of impact that computer technology might have is drawn from the historical cases of two other information processing technologies—writing and print. Writing was associated with rise of class societies (in the Near East, China, and Meso-America) and marks the loss of control by the illiterate mass of peasants and slaves over the recording of their own history and the recording of what they produced by their labor. For many centuries, writing was the prerogative of a small elite. Print, on the other hand, seems to have had a liberating effect and is associated with growing demands for popular participation, first in religion and subsequently in political life. Print was important in the organizing of the bourgeois revolutions (in 17th century England, in the American colonies, and in France) and in the creation of working class movements. At present, computer technology seems more like writing than like print in its effects—it seems associated with the concentration of political power in a state and corporate elite. But this situation need not always prevail; as computer literacy spreads, so that quantification can be used to rationalize production rather than mystify political issues, modern information-processing may be used as a tool for freeing people from coercion. Our model in this discussion suggests an *association* (and not a causal relationship) between information processing technology and social structure.

Another way in which we relate computers to social structure is by showing how the development of computers is not only conditioned by an internal logic but is much more strongly shaped by external social factors. For example, in our discussion of the development of the calculating devices that preceded computers, we show how they became especially important during the 16th and 17th century, with the rise of the bourgoisie (and its interest in ship building, navigation, commercial transactions, and so on) and the period of absolutist monarchies (with accompanying bureaucracies, systems of taxation, warfare using artillery, and so on). This line of analysis is continued using examples from the industrial revolution, industrial growth in the 19th century, and finally, the pressures of World War II that resulted in the birth of modern computers.

In a similar "externalist" vein we devote a lecture to the structure of the computer industry to show how the social organization of a field and the social context in which it develops shape it. The point is that computer technology does not develop in a value-free political vacuum but in a specific economic and political system in which powerful groups and organizations exercise various types of influence.

Exercises and Materials

To further the course goals and objectives we have included a number of exercises. Among the most effective exercises are the following:

1. Write a program for a task that is related to your major, your job, or any other interest of yours.

2. Privacy and Data Banks. Try to obtain an item of information about yourself (or your family) that is stored in the records of an organization. (The record system does not necessarily have to be computerized.) Credit bureaus, hospitals, schools, and law enforcement agencies are examples of the organizations that have records on individuals. Observe what procedures have to be followed to obtain your records; observe what kinds of officials act as "gatekeepers" and make decisions about whether you can obtain the information. If you do succeed in obtaining the information, decide whether it is complete and fair. What are your *legal* rights in obtaining records about yourself? Prepare a 1-2page description of your observations and be prepared to talk about it in class.

3. Discuss whether or not computer work—specifically programming and systems analysis—is a profession. Include in your answer (a) a definition of "profession"; (b) presentation of evidence to support your view; and (c) consideration of the consequences of your stand for programmers/analysts and for the society as a whole.

Teaching Experience

We would like to conclude with a brief discussion of our experiences in teaching this course. Every time that we have taught it (a total of five times) we have found the following:

1. Compared to other courses, this course stimulates greater interaction of students with each other, faculty with each other, and faculty with students.

2. Students learn new cognitive skills, namely logical step-by-step problem-solving procedures (a novelty for students with weak backgrounds in the mathematical sciences). They develop a much more active relationship to a discipline than is usual for many students who are otherwise often passive and who come to college with relatively little exposure to writing, notetaking, and other active ways of mastering knowledge. The rapid feedback provided by interactive BASIC and a time-sharing system (implemented on a Hewlett Packard with 24 teletype terminals) speeds up and reinforces these new cognitive habits.

3. Despite strenuous recruiting efforts, the course tends to attract students with a predisposition to "hard data" and quantified work (altogether too often males, whites, and/or science or business majors). Students enter the course with different levels of programming skills; about half are novices, a third have some experience (but usually less than they think they do), and a small number are actually very good programmers. The novices often end up performing just as well as their classmates, but the first few weeks are sometimes discouraging for them, since they have to put up with their classmates temporarily greater proficiency in programming and familiarity with the jargon.

References and
Suggested Readings

Garner, L. Computer Workers as Professionals. *Science for the People,* 1974, *6,* 28-32.

Gately, W.Y., and G.F. Bitters. *Basic for Beginners.* New York: McGraw-Hill, 1970.

Gotlieb, C.C., and A. Borodin. *Social Issues in Computing.* New York: Academic Press, 1973.

Norman, A., and J. Martin. *The Computerized Society.* Englewood Cliffs, New Jersey: Prentice-Hall, 1970.

Sharpe, W., and N. Jacob. *BASIC: An Introduction to Computer Programming Using the BASIC Language.* New York: Free Press, 1971.

Vonnegut, K. *Player Piano.* New York: Avon, 1971.

Note

[1] Preparation for the course, including research on the organization of computer work by Larry Garner (cited above), was supported by a grant from the Esso Foundation in 1972-1973.

14.
Sociology of Computing: Conceptual Framework and Curriculum Development

Francis Sim
Pennsylvania State University

Ronald E. Anderson
University of Minnesota

The connection between computing and social science in higher education is of long standing. Some of the earliest users of ILLIAC at the University of Illinois two and a half decades ago were social psychologists. Computer use—both in absolute and relative terms—has increased continually over the intervening decades in social science instruction and research. In some academic institutions, social science applications account for the majority of computer use. However, the vast bulk of the traffic between computation and social science has been service by the former to the latter; it has been the story of computing in social science. Relatively little effort has been given to flows in the other direction—to the study of computing as a phenomenon in human social life, to the social scientific study of computation. Computation has become a pre-eminent technology of social science, and one of the central facts of structure and change in modern society, without becoming one of the prominent objects of social science thought and research.

The little attention given to computation as a substantive object has occurred principally in terms of the "social impact" of computation on such factors as employment, workflow, and values. The emphasis has been on the effects of computing as technology. Further, this emphasis has reflected a rather thorough technological determinism. There has been much less organized and deliberate attention to the effects on computation of social organization and socio-personal dispositions. (Where these are noted, they are treated almost implicitly as non-rational responses that likely will be swept aside by the march of events, temporary holding actions against technological inevitability.) Moreover, beyond generalities concerning the potential powers of large-scale, high-speed computation, there has been little empirical attention to the revolutionary character of the technology, as being itself the stuff of social organization. While much has been said of information processing and communication capabilities, this has had little impact on our ability to see computation and computing systems as capable of entering into the structure of social life itself, as becoming part of social systems.

The computer is a communication system able to apply logical decision strategies to the processing of information within the system. If it were not for the computer's capacity for decision making, computing could be investigated simply as another communication technology. There are important parallels between the study of the social effects of mass communication and the study of the social effects of computation; and computers and mass communication are increasingly combined. Just the same, computers are unique technology: the first technology to combine capacities of large-scale information handling with control of task sequencing. New conceptualizations and new knowledge beyond our current understanding of technology are required to comprehend the social role of the computer.

These lacunae in our approach to computation seem related to the nature of that approach. We typically have treated computing as a practical problem, as a source of social, political, and economic potential for good and evil, rather than as a phenomenon that should be studied as a feature of the natural evolution of social life. This arises because it is difficult not to approach an emergent phenomenon of considerable obvious potential in a mood of prognostication about short-term practical outcomes.

In this paper, we attempt to sketch the possibilities for a "positive" empirical approach to computing in social phenomena. Our objective is to simultaneously foster basic research in this area and to encourage the development of curricula including the sociology of computing. In the past several years numerous courses have been taught under the labels "computers and society" and "social implications of computers" (e.g., Horowitz, Morgan, and Shaw, 1972). These courses and supporting curricular materials (e.g., Hamming, 1972; Martin and Norman, 1970; Nikolaieff, 1970; Pylyshyn, 1970) usually emanate from departments of computer science rather than social science, and the orientation is generally a combination of elementary knowledge about computing with discussions of the social problematic aspect of computerization. As social scientists we should have at least an equal concern with investigating computerization through empirical social research. Teaching about computers in society can't help but benefit from elaboration of analytical frameworks from a sociological point of view.

Before we can hope to develop high quality curricula in the sociology of computing, it is necessary to identify where social scientific knowledge and techniques can contribute to increased understanding in this new field. We have designed a possible course in the sociology of computing, an outline of which is contained in the appendix of this paper. Our major focus in this paper is on a conceptual base for such a course, especially the indication of theoretical frameworks.

We shall proceed in several main steps. First, we shall suggest how computation as a phenomenon is of interest to several areas and disciplines, including sociology, anthropology, political science, social psychology, and economics. Second, we shall turn to sociology in slightly more detail and catalog the possible specialties or areas where interest in computing should be high. Third, we shall attempt to say which major sociological perspectives should be most fruitful in, and invigorated by, the study of computation.

Economics

It seems almost unnecessary to assert that economics as a discipline in both its normative and empirical aspects has profound reasons for concern with computation. Electronic computers provide the means for technological realization of functionally rational action, even under uncertainty. The now mundane applications to routine operations in banking, and money-handling in general, have shown the penetration of clerical functions in this area. But more than that, it has been clear for some time that computers in interaction with men are an essential tool of modern economic decision (see, e.g., Silverman, 1966; Myers, 1967; Taviss,

1970). Their capacity for high speed decisions about large bodies of information according to complex rules provides tools that have become integral parts of contemporary economic decision systems. However, there are other problems concerning the integration of computation in economics that reveal non-rational aspects of the connection between computation and economic life. For example, some market functions, one might say some markets, have been thoroughly computerized, e.g., airline reservations; but others are much less so, e.g., stock ordering and transactions, where bookkeeping has been automated and the process of buying and selling has not. The problem of institutionalization of computation in various aspects of concrete economic systems in modern and pre-modern life should be a chief problem of the economics of development.

Political Science

It may be less obvious that there are comparable grounds for substantive interests in computing in political science. However, the character and nature of the political process and the structure of power may be profoundly affected by computerization, as is the relationship between the individual and the political system. Perhaps the first concern is nowhere better illustrated than it is in the setting that stimulated many of the most sophisticated information management innovations, *viz.*, command and control of military systems (see Merkle, 1971; and Debons, 1971). The developments of contemporary information processing techniques are affecting planning, administration, policing, judicial, and other functions (MacBride, 1967; Chartrand, 1971; Ernst, 1970; Greenberger, 1971). Access to computer data bases will become increasingly essential to participation in political work. As we noted above, military activities were among the earliest and most profoundly affected of all areas of social action. Relationships between agencies and levels of government are proliferated by needs for data exchange, and control is concentrated in the hands of those who can determine when and where information will be available. A particularly sensitive issue is the matter of invasion of privacy via sophisticated probes of massive, integrated files from multiple sources (Westin, 1967 and 1971; and Stone and Warner, 1969). These are only a sampling of the potential objects of interest by political scientists regarding computerization.

Social Psychology

The question of privacy is also of concern to social psychologists (Sawyer and Schechter, 1968), since it deals with the impact of the larger system and culture on the individual. Another principal area of interest in social psychology is the development of attitudes toward and values about computation, both concretely with regard to effects on occupations and relationships with public or private agencies (government data banks, commercial credit, etc.), and more generally as regards the "rationalization" of life. Similarly, there is concern about other effects on individual behavior and functioning, such as future shock, depersonalization, etc. (Anderson, 1972; Orcutt and Anderson, 1974). A subject that should be developed more extensively is the study of the communication relationship between the user as a person and the interaction partners represented by "the computer," and especially the meta-communicative aspects of such situations. It is worth noting that—up until now—there has been no obvious impact of computation on the substance of small-groups research within social psychology, in spite of the use of computing technique in the management and analysis of such research. This may well change in coming decades as computation diffuses from the organizational context in which it is now principally found (see below) into other areas of social life.

Anthropology

It might seem that at least anthropologists would still be free of the need to examine computing phenomena for their substantive work. However, there are at least two main ways in which computing becomes important to the substantive interests of anthropology. First, the roots of the historical and evolutionary processes that issue in modern electronic data processing lie in societies and cultures that usually have been ceded to the anthropologist. Certainly, we need much more comparative analysis of the emergence and development of clerical and computational techniques as a part of the process of rationalization of action and structure in social life. Second, comparative research also is required on the character and integration of computation in different contemporary societies. In addition, anthropology has long emphasized the salience of material culture in social evolution, and this in itself would justify extensive attention to computing and computerization.

Sociology

In sociology, as in these other disciplines, there are numerous substantive reasons for concern with computation. However, here we want to consider its relevance to more specific sub-areas of the discipline, in order to set the scene for discussion of the major areas of theoretical relevance of computing to sociology in the next section. It is not possible to cover all of the possible sub-areas, since they are numerous and there is not complete agreement on them, but we shall cover at least a representative group.

1. Clearly, computation is a phenomenon of the first order of importance in the study of organizations of many kinds—business, military, government, etc. (Greenberger, 1968; Whisler, 1970); it probably is of much less importance in connection with others, such as fraternal orders, civic groups, and other voluntary associations that do not have instrumental goals requiring heavy information processing. However, since instrumental objectives constitute a class of very great importance in this area, it is extremely important to consider computing activities as they affect organization and as they *are* organization. Thus, a much broader perspective is needed than is found in the many early studies on the impact of computer automation upon work and work-related activities (e.g., Evans, 1967; Faunce, 1960; Hill, 1969; Mueller, 1969; Shepard, 1970; Wiegman and Karsh, 1962).

2. There is considerable variation among social institutions with regard to the importance of computing as a phenomenon in understanding the nature and structure of the institution. At this point in time, computation has comparatively little bearing on study of the family or religion. In the latter case, it might be argued that administrative aspects of churches are affected by computing, but these belong under the study of complex organization above. A similar argument might be made with regard to politics, except as qualified by the remarks about political science above: there we emphasized the organizational aspects of politics, but there are also process features of persuasion, negotiation, and the like that do not much involve computation.

Computing in education is a matter of considerable controversy; plans for integration of computational techniques into the organization of teaching and learning have met with much less success than the use of large-scale computers in research or in organizational administration.

3. By comparison with areas mentioned above, the study of social deviance seems unlikely to be touched by computation as a phenomenon of substantive interest—again, except in connection with complex organizations that are commissioned to deal with deviant behavior, including delinquency and crime. However, the actual process of deviance of particular kinds is not intrinsically involved with computing. White collar crime that utilizes the possibility for sophisticated felony made available by computing technology in business may stand as another exception. But there seems little substantive relevance of computation for the study of juvenile delinquency, homosexuality, addiction, etc.

4. In a parallel way, computing is not very important in the study of social problems in the community or society. For example, the existence and social organization of poverty does not depend on electronic computing—most computers are not located in ghettoes. However, it is possible to bring the study of computation in social life into course work (and research) by treating "the computer" and its control as a social problem.

5. As yet, mass communication has been relatively little affected by computerization, although there is great potential for such developments (Parker, 1970; Sackman, 1971; Sackman and Nie, 1970). However, even when communication management has been greatly automated, there may be less effect of computation than might be expected off hand. Applications in this area will be aimed at transparency, and the decision mangement capacities of computing will be directed to the form rather than the substance of communication. Conversely, we shall suggest below that communication may be a good perspective from which to examine computing.

6. The last sub-area that we shall mention is occupations and professions. Here the main interest is with various computing specialties, and several studies have been done (Boguslaw, 1965; Mumford, 1972; Mumford and Banks, 1967). Clearly, such occupations could not exist as such without computers. However,

it is not as clear that this leads to specific and peculiar professional characteristics, beyond the demands of technological rationalization.

Other illustrations could be multiplied, but these suffice here for our needs. Our next purpose is to suggest the areas of sociological theory that seem to have the greatest potential for contributing to, and for being informed by, the study of computing as social phenomenon. The areas that seem to us to be most important as conceptual guidelines are bureaucracy, communication, and social values.

Bureaucracy. To begin with, it may seem wrong that we do not subsume the entire subject matter under the heading of the effects of technology on culture and social organization. However, it is our view that electronic computing is a technology of a fundamentally different kind from others, past and present.

Computing (as a set of technological facts) certainly affects organization, values, belief, social status, and roles.

Computation not only affects organization, in some ways it *is* organization. Especially in the case of the large, complex, formal organization, electronic computing is the realization of tendencies of development that span centuries and civilizations. Since the time of Max Weber, the study of formal organizations has taken bureaucracy as a touchstone or point of departure.

For Weber (1946), bureaucracy as a specifically rational instrument had certain fundamental features, including the following:

(1) administration (decision on dispositions of client cases) by explicit and recorded rules, rather than by preferences of individual administrators;

(2) separation of the person who administered from the office, access to the office governed by objective criteria instead of by relationship of some superior official, and absence of "ownership" of office;

(3) payment of officials in money, not in fees from services rendered, nor by compensation extracted from subject populations;

(4) hierarchical arrangement of offices such that lower ones are governed by higher ones; and

(5) vertical flow of communication through such offices.

It is readily apparent that such characteristics are never attained and perhaps not closely approached with great frequency by social systems manned by humans. It also seems apparent that some of the characteristics that cannot be achieved with any high degree of certainty of human individuals, short of exceptional preparation, are relatively easily implemented by means of computing technology. A computer program is a device to decide by explicit criteria, without attention to distracting features of the person, systems, or situation under consideration—it is a mechanism for applying rules, and potentially very complex sets of rules, to particular decisions, and of assuring that the same ones are used in the same ways until there are intentional and explicit decisions to change. Similarly, the flow of communications among components of the decision-making (administrative) structure may be completely specified in a program that is to be executed by a computer, as compared to one that is to be put into effect by human agents. Other problems concerning payment and appointment of office holders are similarly transformed for an automatic program execution facility. (Note that we have not suggested that electronic computation is rational as an administrative tool in any sense other than used by Weber—essentially that of calculation when values and ends are assumed or given.)

In many ways the computer program may be the ideal type of the bureaucrat that Weber formulated. On these grounds alone, the sociological study of computing in complex organizations would be completely justified. And the emphasis would be upon the extent and problems of the integration of the computational system into the social systems of the organization. It is well established that the introduction of large-scale electronic computing in a work organization leads to the modification of some jobs and the elimination of others. It is not so clearly understood that the work done by those jobs is still performed, but it is done by the computer program. If, when these tasks were performed by humans, they defined social positions and roles, then we must entertain the idea that they still define role relationships, but that these now involve automata.

Communication. The next theoretical approach to which computers should be linked is communication. Most computerized information systems function as centralized communication systems. The computer can be used as a communication channel and hence provides a unique resource for management of relationships with other people.

It is our suggestion that computer utilization can be largely modeled by the sociological concept of a mass communication system. (Some would classify computer communications as a 'specialized' rather than a 'mass' communication system because of its circumscribed audience.) This framework can be used to locate features of computing environments that lead to special problems.

A system of mass communications, including an information system where the communicator is a design/programmer and the communicatee is the computer user, has at least the following features:

a. one communicator and an audience (many communicatees);
b. most communicatees are not in contact with each other relative to the process, i.e., anonymity is the rule;
c. the communicatees mostly receive messages but do not send them, though they often do have to take some action to receive the message;
d. consequently, the communicatee cannot easily interrogate the communicator;
e. the communicator's message sending is managed, and has "latent" objectives,
f. while the communicatee's attention is less deliberate, though perhaps intense; and
g. communicatees come to attribute authority to the communicator, probably in part because of the features listed above, and other attendant features (i.e., ones suggested by, or essential to these, etc.).

More generally, these features do not act independently, they interact in their effects.

When the user "communicates" with the computer, the mass communication model is appropriate. In order to apply the model, however, it must be seen that the "communication" is best seen as between the user and a programmer, and that the machine is the medium (or channel). However, as in other mass communication situations, the communicatee tends to identify the medium and communicator. The situation we have described is one where there is "one" programmer (in the sense of a social role, just as in any mass communication system) and many users. The communications are not carried on at the same time, but that is not critical. The users are not in contact with each other during communication but seem to send messages to the computer. Most of the user messages, e.g., parameter setting, are really better seen as actions to elicit the programmer's message, and not as creative communications by the user, which is a consequence of the fact that the process of "communications" is totally managed and defined by the programmer.

Support for these points is provided by a laboratory study by Marshall and Maguire (1971), who modified the classic Crutchfield conformity experiment by substituting "computer aid" for peer pressure. The computer "aided" the subjects by suggesting incorrect answers for a series of perceptual judgment tasks. The information was simply presented in conjunction with the computerized administration of the experiment. Thus, the computer acted as an automated answer book; the subjects were not told how the computer acquired the answers or why they were being presented. Nonetheless, the subjects often adopted the computer judgment, following a response pattern very similar to experimental situations where there is information supplied by peers rather than computers. Apparently the subjects assumed that the computer was carrying out the orders of the experimenter and that this "authority" system possessed validity if not legitimation.

The meta messages of such systems tend to define the computer in an authority role and the user as a subordinate subject to sanctions for noncompliance. This suggests another kind of communication theory that could be applied to analyzing computerized systems, *viz.*, that developed by Bateson and others (e.g., Bateson, 1972). Meta messages are supplied by the context of any primary signal or message transmission. Sometimes the context or meta messages contradict the primary communication and hence place the audience or recipient in a "double bind." For instance, the rigidity and inflexibility of an interactive computer program may imply the message: "Understand or you're a dummy," when the program was supposedly designed to facilitate understanding in a step by step, individualized mode. Intolerant, unforgiving rigidity communicated through the essence of the contextual meta messages might explain the reticence of some possible users, e.g., extroverts and older age groups.

While further analysis along the lines suggested by meta-communication should be pursued, another line of research will be briefly mentioned. Recent work in engineering psychology (Chapanis, 1973; Waksman, 1974) concentrates upon conversational man-machine dialogues in order to clarify the nature of interpersonal communication. The research studies facets of factual information exchange when people solve a problem. It has been found (Waksman, 1974) that allowing the user to express intent in scientific computing contexts can improve the system effectiveness. Additional questions deserve exploration, including the following: How do communication patterns between man and machine vary with the person's ability? What sort of concessions will computers have to make for people at various levels of ability? How do communication patterns vary among different nationalities (Chapanis, 1973)?

Sociology of Technology and Social Values. The emergence of the rapidly growing technological sector of the computer world raises new social issues and potential ethical conflicts. When technology or any other social force becomes imbedded in an effectively normative environment, moral considerations arise. Technology is a significant ethical force because of the social meanings attached to it, and a powerful force when there is day to day social dependence upon it. Various moral dilemmas appear in the culture, as conflicts and disorders are perceived and attributed to technology. Although recent concerns have focused upon technology and its environmental impacts, attention will also be given to other issues, e.g., privacy invasion and impersonalization, which are raised anew by the computerization of social institutions.

This technology may not seem to conflict intrinsically with human values since it is purportedly a means toward whatever social end or value is desired. The impact of technology, however, has been considerably more pervasive due in part to unanticipated consequences and the simultaneous satisfaction of multiple or conflicting values. In addition and more importantly, advanced societies have had a tendency to treat complex technology and utilitarian norms as ends in themselves. Boulding (1969) and others argue that the resulting ethical void characterized by an absence of values, particularly those values that foster personal and social integration, may be the most serious problem.

Despite the apparent lack of an inherent conflict between technology and human values, numerous social critics and a large share of the public-at-large seem to perceive the existence of a fundamental disjuncture. For instance, technology is described as threatening to individual values such as creativity, individuality, emotional expressiveness, etc. Douglas (1971), Ellul (1964), Ferkis (1969), Rozak (1969), Mumford (1966) and numerous others elaborate upon a subtly overwhelming cultural dependency accompanying advancing technology. They also have emphasized the contrast between subjective and objective consciousness (see Rozak, 1969) and how science and technological premises have detracted from inner subjective experiences.

Such trends have been described by sociologists primarily in terms of the process of secularism. Sacred or spiritual values and norms serve as the moral foundation for structural integration in social systems. In contrast, utilitarian norms not only support sacred norms but increasingly in the form of institutionalized technology may become autonomous as well (Nisbet, 1970). Fromm (1968) identifies the problem as the trading of humanistic values for machine benefits. He argues that a one-sided emphasis on technique and material consumption results in self-estrangement and the loss of humanistic values bound up in spirituality or religious faith. Fromm claims that concentration on technical and material values results in the loss of emotional and expressive capacities, even though these qualities are still officially and ostensibly valued. He identifies these as "conscious and ineffective" values in contrast to "unconscious and effective" values such as comsumption, property, status, fun, and excitement. These later values are consistent with those generated, according to Fromm, by the technologically dominated cultural system.

Quite surprisingly, almost no concrete studies can be found that relate to the question of how interaction with machines affects personality, values, and social behavior. Yablonsky (1972) suggests that existence in a world of machine technology leads to dehumanization, which in essence is the lack of emotion, ambiguity, and ambivalence.

Although we lack precise knowledge about the causes of impersonal, dehumanized individual and interpersonal tendencies, people generally tend to see them as a consequence of growing technology and forbiddingly large organizations. This belief may not have foundation in actuality, but the fact of its acceptance in popular culture and among social critics is in itself very important. Not only will these perceptions of technology shape public policy regarding technology, but if people act as if it were true, similar consequences may occur. And even though we have little evidence to suggest the contention that machine technology leads to dehumanization, we have even less evidence to suggest that it is not true. Given these considerations, it is worthwhile to examine more thoroughly how in fact the public and its various sectors conceptualize and perceive the many facets of computer technology.

Conclusion

Social science has been inattentive to computation as a phenomenon of human social life to be studied in its own right. When it has been addressed by social scientists, computing is seen either as a methodological tool or as a technology having "social impact." It is our contention that computing itself should be examined as a form of social organization.

In earlier sections we sketched how the social sciences, and sociology in particular, would find substantive interest in computing. All of the social sciences have important reasons for analytical attention to the emergence of electronic computation as a major aspect of the natural evolution of socio-technology. Such areas as complex organizations, occupations and professions, mass communications, and social values at the present time are especially relevant to a social analysis of computing. Other areas and approaches to the sociology of computing may rapidly emerge, because fundamental shifts are still occurring in computer technology. The most obvious technological development now underway is that of microcomputing (Robinson, 1974; Vacroux, 1975), which promises to open up a vast new range of applications especially in research, communications, and commercial organizations. Etzioni (1975) and others have begun to speculate about the effects of a new wave of compact computers upon the organization of work, but microcomputing is also likely to lead to a variety of new devices in the less formal arenas of social life. Social science cannot afford to be inattentive to changes of such revolutionary character and proportions.

References

Anderson, R.E. Sociological Analysis of Public Attitudes Toward Computers and Information Files. *Joint Computer Conference Proceedings,* 1972, Spring, 649-657.

Bateson, G. *Steps to an Ecology of Mind.* New York: Ballantine Books, 1972.

Boguslaw, R. *The New Utopians: A Study of System Design and Social Change.* Englewood Cliffs, N.J.: Prentice-Hall, 1965.

Boulding, K.E. The Interplay of Technology and Values: The Emerging Superculture, in K. Bailer and N. Rescher (Eds.), *Values and the Future.* New York: Free Press, 1969.

Chapanis, A. The Communication of Factual Information Through Various Channels. *Information Storage and Retrieval,* 1973, *9,* 215-231.

Chartrand, R.L. *Systems Technology Applied to Social and Community Problems.* New York: Spartan Books, 1971.

Debons, A. Command and Control: Technology and Social Impact, in F. Lalt and M. Rubinoff (Eds.), *Advances in Computers.* New York: Academic Press, 1971.

Douglas, J. *The Technological Threat.* Englewood Cliffs, N.J.: Prentice-Hall, 1971.

Ellul, J. *The Technological Society.* New York: Alfred Knopf and Vintage Books, 1964.

Ernst, M.L. Computers, Business, and Society. *Management Review,* 1970, *59,* 4-12.

Etzioni, A. Effects of Small Computers on Scientists. *Science,* 1975, *189,* 4197.

Evans, T., and M. Stewart. *Pathway to Tomorrow: The Impact of Automation on People.* London: Pergamon Press, Ltd., 1967.

Faunce, W.A. Social Stratification and Attitudes Toward Change in Job Content. *Social Forces,* 1960, *39,* 140-148.

Ferkis, V. *Technological Man: The Myth and the Reality.* New York: Mentor, The New American Library, 1969.

Fromm, E. *The Revolution of Hope: Toward a Humanized Technology.* New York: Harper and Row, 1968.

Gotlieb, C.C., and A. Borodin. *Social Issues in Computing.* New York: Academic Press, 1975.

Greenberger, M. *Computers, Communication, and the Public Interest.* Baltimore: Johns Hopkins Press, 1971.

Greenberger, M. The Computer in Organizations, in C.A. Walker (Ed.) *Technology, Industry, and Man.* New York: McGraw-Hill, 1968.

Hamming, W. *Computers and Society.* New York: McGraw-Hill, 1972.

Hill, W.A. The Impact of EDP Systems on Office Employees: Some Empirical Conclusions. *Academy of Management,* 1969, March, 9-19.

Horowitz, E., H.L. Morgan, and A.C. Shaw. Computers and Society: A Proposed Course for Computer Scientists. *Communications of the ACM,* 1972, *15,* 257-61.

MacBride, R. *The Automated State: Computer Systems as a New Force in Society,* New York: The Chilton Book Company, 1967.

Marshall, C., and T.U. Maguire. The Computer as Social Pressure to Produce Conformity in a Simple Perceptual Task. *Audio-Visual Communication Review,* 1971, *19,* 19-29.

Martin, J., and A.R.D. Norman, *The Computerized Society.* Englewood Cliffs, N.J.: Prentice-Hall, 1970.

Merkle, J. *Command and Control: The Social Implication of Nuclear Defense.* New York: General Learning Press, 1971.

Mesthene, E.G. Technology and Humanistic Values. *Computers and the Humanities,* 1969, *4,* 1-10.

Mueller, E. *et al. Technological Advance in an Expanding Society.* University of Michigan, Institute for Social Research, 1969.

Mumford, E. *Job Satisfaction: A Study of Computer Specialists.* London: Longman, 1972.

Mumford, E., and O. Banks. *The Computer and the Clerk.* London: Routledge and Kegan Paul, 1967.

Mumford, L. *The Myth of the Machine.* New York: Harcourt, Brace, and World, 1966.

Myers, C.A. (Ed.) *The Impact of Computers on Management.* Cambridge: MIT Press, 1967.

Myers, C.A. *Computers in Knowledge-Based Fields.* Cambridge: MIT Press, 1970.

Nikolaieff, G. *Computers and Society.* New York: H.W. Wilson Company, 1970.

Nisbet, R. *The Social Bond.* New York: Knopf, 1970.

Orcutt, J.D., and R.E. Anderson. Human-Computer Relationships: Interactions and Attitudes. *Behavior Research Methods & Instrumentation,* 1974, *6,* 219-222.

Parker, E.B. Information Utilities and Mass Communication. In H. Sackman and N. Nie (Eds.), *The Information Utility and Social Choice.* Montvale, N.J.: AFIPS Press, 1970.

Pylyshyn, Z.W. *Perspective on the Computer Revolution.* Englewood Cliffs, N.J.: Prentice-Hall, 1970.

Robinson, A.L. Computers: First the Maxi, Then the Mini, Now It's the Micro. *Science,* 1974, *186,* 1102-4.

Rozak, T. *The Making of the Counterculture.* New York: Doubleday, 1969.

Sackman, H. *Mass Information Utilities and Social Excellence.* Princeton, N.J.: Auerbach, 1971.

Sackman, H., and N. Nie (Eds.) *The Information Utility and Social Choice.* Montvale, N.J.: AFIPS Press, 1970.

Sawyer, J., and H. Schechter. Computers, Privacy, and the National Data Center. *American Psychologist,* 1968, *23,* 810-818.

Shepard, J.M. *Automation and Alienation: A Study of Office and Factory Workers.* Cambridge: MIT Press, 1970.

Silverman, W. The Economic and Social Effects of Automation in an Organization. *The American Behavioral Scientist,* June 1966, 308.

Stone, M.G., and M. Warner. Politics, Privacy, and Computers. *Political Quarterly,* 1969, *40,* 256-67.

Taviss, I. (Ed.) *The Computer Impact.* Englewood Cliffs, N.J.: Prentice-Hall, 1970.

Vacroux, A.G. Microcomputers. *Scientific American,* May, 1975, 32-40.

Waksman, A. The Interface Problem in Interactive Systems. *Behavior Research Methods & Instrumentation,* 1974, *6,* 235-237.

Weber, M. *From Max Weber: Essays in Sociology* (Translated, edited, and with an introduction by H.H. Gerth and C.W. Mills.) New York: Galaxy Books, 1946.

Weizenbaum, J. Computers and Society. *Science,* 1972, *178,* 561-563.

Westin, A.F. *Privacy and Freedom.* New York: Atheneum, 1967.

Westin, A.F. (Ed.) *Information Technology in a Democracy.* Cambridge: Harvard University Press, 1971.

Whisler, T.L. *Information Technology and Organizational Change.* Belmont, California: Wadsworth, 1970.

Wiegman, J., and B. Karsh. Some Organizational Correlates of White Collar Automation. *Sociological Inquiry,* 1962, *32,* 108-116.

Yablonsky, L. *Robopaths.* New York: Penguin Books, 1972.

Appendix

A Course Outline for the Sociology of Computing

Objectives
The Course is designed to focus the tools and concepts of sociology upon the process of computing. Not only will the effects of computer technology be surveyed, but considerable attention will be devoted to the effects of social organization and social processes on computing. Students are expected to become acquainted with the diverse literature on the social impact of the computer and to gain experience in applying sociological analysis to computerized aspects of social institutions.

Outline
1. *The Concept of Computing*: History of rationalization of action covering the Weber (1946) notion of functional rationality and administration; decision making and required processing rules; clericism and the historical emergence of differentiated information reduction and processing; the correspondence between social information processing and computer information processing.
  (Note: Depending upon the background of the students, a brief history of computer technology should be provided. At this point an interesting discussion could pursue the interrelationship between computer languages, e.g., COBOL, FORTRAN, etc., and their corresponding activities within various institutional sectors.)
2. *Bureaucracy,* the role of computing in complex organizations: the nature of formal organizations, information flow, etc.; the structure of authority and evaluations.

3. *Communication Systems*: information processing theories; mass communication research and models; meta communication analysis.

4. *Sociology of Technology and Social Values*: Science and technology value systems, implications of computerization for interpersonal and personal value systems; relation to social attitudes toward computerization.

5. *Institutional Settings and Computerization:*

A. Industry: structural change, power, employment, occupations, manpower, job satisfactions, alienation.

B. Government: internal management and reorganization; external relationships with public or clients.

C. Education: problem-solving, testing, evaluation, control of students; bureaucratization of teaching.

D. Other institutions, including the military, health, law enforcement, religion, and family.

6. *Social Psychological Effects of Computing:*

A. Interaction patterns: impersonalization, intolerance of variation, dependency, restructuring of interpersonal interaction.

B. Learning: information, skills acquisition, reinforcement, attitude change.

C. Attitudes and values relevant to computing: beliefs about nature of and meaning of computing, resistance to computerization, shifts in value structures.

7. *Selected Topics:*

A. Data banks and information access: regulation and control, citizen understanding and behavior.

B. Inequity in access to computation: implications of power and control of computing resources.

C. Information complexity: vulnerability due to complexity and specialization (see Weizenbaum, 1972).

D. The computing industry: nature of industry, emerging professions, ethical issues.

Note

[1] This paper is based on a paper that appeared in the *SIGSOC BULLETIN*, Vol. 7, 1975-1976.

PART IV
Computer Based Enhancement
in Social and Behavioral
Science Education

15.
Experiment Simulation (EXPER SIM): The Development of a Future-Oriented Pedagogy

Dana B. Main[1]
West Virginia College of Graduate Studies

The Educational Challenge

The challenge for higher education is to prepare students for a fast-changing world. The teaching process must be viewed as much more than transmitting information to passively receiving students in the remote hope that if they are thus "educated" they will be able to deal with present and future problems. Nor is it wise to concentrate solely on the development of "saleable" skills that may assure a student a job at the time he is trained, but which may outdate him in the future under changed conditions. There is a need to make the "process" of education explicit to the student and to place it in a future-oriented context.

Students need effective experiences in making decisions with respect to future outcomes. This implies: (1) that students need to be active participants in the educational process, (2) that the pedagogical setting directs students to the future, (3) that problem-solving strategies be made explicit and open to search and exploration by students, and (4) that students gain ability in evaluating outcomes of decisions in terms of uncertainty reduction, utilities, and problem solution. Past knowledge and skill acquisition play a major role here, but the attempt is to develop independence, control, and adaptability in students.

How can we design a feasible education program that attempts to tackle these problems? I believe we need to think beyond the development of a course or even a set of courses, although that is often the most convenient place to begin. We need to think of the design of pedagogies that can be implemented in different kinds of

183

educational settings that may have different kinds of focuses. Educators who hold these ideas must examine their own sphere of influence and begin where they are.

Problems in Instructional Laboratory Courses

A few years ago, I was asked to coordinate a large multisection elementary laboratory course required of undergraduate psychology majors. The traditional format of elementary laboratory courses in the social and natural sciences has been one of introducing data collection techniques to students. Students are given access to a piece of equipment, a rat or two, and subjects from the unpaid subject pool and are instructed to conduct experiments following more or less previously constructed procedures. How well students follow the procedures and explain why the experiment did or did not "come out right" is the basis for evaluation of student progress.

It is difficult to assemble a set of experimental data collection techniques that are basic or pivotal to all later work in psychology. The field itself is too broad. If you concentrated on T-mazes, the clinicians complained. If you concentrated on psychophysics, the social psychologists complained. If you concentrated on survey techniques, the experimentalists complained, etc.

Further, we were not in an unlimited resource situation. There was not money to equip and maintain a technique oriented laboratory course for 250-300 students a term, even if it had philosophical virtue and that, of course, was what was most questionable.

However, there was some money for instructional computing.

There was a melting pot of graduate students from different areas in psychology eager to develop new concepts in teaching.

There were limited resources within the university available for development of new ideas, in particular, The Center for Research on Learning and Teaching.

There was freedom to proceed as one thought best, even though advice was often conflicting.

What there was not was a pedagogical philosophy.

Our challenge was to introduce students to research in psychology as a total decision process. Students needed to gain experience in formulating research goals, clarifying and stating problems, and developing hypotheses. They needed to construct the set of design procedures relevant to questions and hypotheses that they had posed, not just those that were posed for them. They needed to develop strategies in logical thinking.

They needed to anticipate the outcomes of experiments and how they would interpret each outcome. Would an outcome or set of outcomes support or refute a theory or theories? What uncertainty, if any, would be reduced by the experimental outcomes? How valuable is the potential experiment? Given each possible outcome, what should be the next experiment? Is there a way to organize one's questions and set priorities? What assumptions lurk behind those questions? Can these assumptions be organized into a theory or a model that would predict outcomes?

Can a pedagogy be designed where students gain experience with the full range of research decisions?

The Development of Computer Based Pedagogy

Suppose we re-organized the instructional sequence. Suppose instruction in data-collection techniques was largely delayed to more specialized advanced laboratory courses elected by students interested in that area of research. Suppose students at the elementary level were given an opportunity to think, question, and learn basic design principles. Would not the learning of data collection techniques be more meaningful if students could understand how data *they* collected would apply to questions that *they* had begun to pose?

For the past six years we have been developing and using a computer-based pedagogy that we call EXPER SIM (experiment simulation). There are two features associated with this pedagogy. One feature concerns the software. The other concerns classroom organization and instructional procedures that are not part of the software. The innovation is not one or the other feature, but both. Each feature will be discussed separately but the following description is a brief overview from the student's point of view.

The student receives a short description of a problem area together with further references in the literature. He also receives a summary of the following minimal information:

(1) a list of variables and their possible values that can be specified by the student;

(2) a list of possible dependent variables that he can choose to observe; and

(3) the range of the possible numbers of observations or subjects he is permitted to sample.

The student develops a research goal and a set of questions that he refines as hypotheses. For "between-groups designs," he specifies variables and values for each group, selects dependent or observable variables, and chooses his "N," number of subjects per group. If he has a "within group design," he also selects the number of repeated measures. Depending on the context, variables whose values are different from condition to condition are viewed as independent variables. Those that are held constant from condition to condition are viewed as control variables. They are both "manipulable variables" in that their values can be specified by the student. In models with more than one dependent variable available, he selects the variables whose values he will observe as "raw data." He submits his design to the computer and receives numbers that can be plausibly interpreted as data. He analyzes his data, makes inferences, and begins again. No knowledge of computer programming is required of him or his instructor. Data generation in response to a student's inquiries is a matter of minutes or even seconds. Cost on the University of Michigan system is around 75 cents per experiment using an on-line interactive mode, much less using a batch mode.

EXPER SIM: Software

As software development evolved at the University of Michigan we were in contact with similar work at other universities. In an attempt to avoid confusion we use the term EXPER SIM for the software *and* pedagogy. The particular set of programs developed at the University of Michigan by Robert Stout is called the Michigan Experiment Simulation Supervisor (MESS). The programs were developed and used on the University of Michigan's IBM 360/67 and are now running on the IBM 370. It is written in FORTRAN IV and requires 20,000 to 25,000 words of core. The set of programs developed at the University of Louisville by Art Cromer and John Thurmond is called the Louisville Experiment Simulation System (LESS). LESS was written for smaller computers requiring at least 8,000 words or core and bulk storage.

There is both a BASIC and FORTRAN version. Both programs have a supervisor or management program and a set of routing corresponding to different models in a library. Thus, new models can be added to either system by preparing a data check that links the models to the management program. This modularization means that the library can be extended, or models in the library can be removed or updated, without massive re-programming. It means that a library has a potential of containing models from other disciplines besides psychology. It means that the instructional model builder can devote attention to the substance of his model without having to worry about how it will be interfaced with the student. Models can be placed on both systems. The difference between MESS and LESS are the features of the supervisor programs. MESS is larger and more flexible. LESS, which was directed to smaller computers, enables students to have essentially the same educational experience, but requires a bit more of the student in its initial use. Between the two, EXPER SIM is available to virtually any computer capable of at least 8,000 words of core and bulk storage. Some universities have implemented both in order to evaluate the relative merits of each with respect to their needs.

When MESS was designed, several principal considerations were used in making decisions concerning program specifications. Robert Stout articulated them at the National Conference on On-Line Computers in Psychology in 1973 (Stout, 1974):

1. It should be possible for students with all degrees of sophistication to learn to use the system quickly; students should spend as much time as possible on the design and analysis of their experiments and as little time as possible puzzling over how to get the computer to do them. In particular, the program should require as few lines of input as possible, should allow students to describe conditions and groups using terms derived directly from the language of the problem area, should be highly tolerant of minor errors in spelling and syntax, should provide helpful error messages, and should provide output which is formatted and labeled in such a way as to be maximally intelligible.

2. The system should be capable of handling models from any area of psychology, and of any desired structure or degree of complexity. The program should allow a large number of independent and dependent variables, involving non-numeric dependent variables, and every kind of model structure from static analysis of variance and regression models to dynamic,

highly structured models such as finite automata or cognitive models like Newell and Simon's General Problem Solver.

3. The system should allow any general class of experimental design, including multivariate designs, repeated measure, confounded designs, and correlational experiments.

4. The system should provide a command language with as many options as possible to implement and modify models in the system.

Art Cromer, the designer for LESS, has adhered to these principles within the constraints of restrictions of smaller computers. In a personal communication, Cromer writes:

The Louisville Experiment Simulation System is a set of four basic programs plus the model programs. These programs can be thought of as the little brothers of the Michigan Experiment Simlulation Supervisor (MESS), in that they are both designed to implement the EXPER SIM concept but while MESS is written for large computers LESS is designed for small computers.

The LESS programs are written in BASIC and were developed on a Hewlett-Packard HP 2000C computer. The main program (called LESS) is the only program a student need know about, since this program is called up and run by the student at a terminal. LESS allows the selection of any model currently active, and controls the selection of variables and levels appropriate to that model. One central data file (called LESDAT) contains all of the information pertinent to each active model. This information is extracted by LESS and used in screening the user's choices before passing the data and control to the program containing the selected model. After the model program is completed, control returns to LESS for selection of additional levels in the same model, or selection of a new model. A program (called LESSIN) is used to: (1) initialize the data file before any programs are added to the system, or (2) to delete a specific model from the data file, or (3) to delete all models from the data file.

The third basic program in the LESS system (called LESPUT) allows an author to add the data for a new model to the data file. It prompts at each step of the way, making reminders and validity checks to help the authors enter the data correctly and verify it.

Cromer has also developed a FORTRAN version of LESS that is beginning to be transported. A FORTRAN program, DATA CALL, developed by Richard Johnson, was a forerunner of MESS and LESS. It did not have the management or supervisor program feature, but the basic logic behind the software and the pedagogy was a tremendous influence on EXPER SIM.

In the last three years EXPER SIM in the software form of MESS or LESS has been transported to a larger number of colleges and universities with different kinds of computer systems. The dissemination has been greatly facilitated by the Exxon Education Foundation's IMPACT program, which has solicited proposals from individuals at institutions interested in implementing EXPER SIM. Implementation at a college or university with a different system than that at University of Michigan or University of Louisville has taken about two weeks, depending on the level of sophistication of the staff receiving the programs. However, that time and effort is rapidly decreasing because we try to direct interested persons to individuals with similar systems who have worked out the compatibility problems. LESS has been transported to the following kinds of systems: CDC 6000 series, Hewlett Packard 2000, IBM 370, PDP 11, and PDP 10. MESS has been transported to IBM 370 and 360, PDP 10, CDC 6400 and 6600, Burroughs 6700 and 4700, UNIVAC, and Data General 1800. However, the number of different systems is growing as dissemination is currently underway. Cost of the programs, $100 or less, covers transportability expenses.

EXPER SIM: The Classroom Structure

As mentioned earlier, EXPER SIM is not a set of computer programs alone, but rather a pedagogy that uses the computer.

The design of the classroom structure is a very important ingredient. It is conceivable that MESS or LESS could be used in the following unimaginative way. Students could be given experiments designed by the instructor, told to "run" them on the computer and asked to write up results or fill in some laboratory report form. It could be used as a direct substitute for the assigned "lab" experiment in the traditional course. Or students could be asked to dream up any experiment within the constraints of allowable manipulable and observable variables, run them and turn in a report. In such approaches the computer software dictates the instruction, if indeed any occurs. Even worse, the goals for which the software was developed are not met.

I would like to describe a classroom structure that has been effective in elementary laboratory courses at the University of Michigan. I admit that I have a strong bias for this approach. Other structures may be just as effective in implementing pedagogical principles where they must apply to courses with different goals and where they take place in different institutional settings.

We turn sections of the course into simulated scientific communities where each student plays the role of an individual investigator. For a specified period of time, students can be given limited resources. This means that simulated costs for samples, for manipulation of certain variables, and for use of dependent variables can be constructed that reflect "real" monetary costs should data be actually collected in the research setting. The student must learn how to budget and allocate his resources with respect to this research goal. This procedure tends to minimize mindless experiments that explore combinations and permutations of manipulable variables with little or no forethought.

Given limited resources, a student needs to plan not just a single experiment, but an entire research program. He needs to set research goals and try to clarify the problem that he chooses to investigate.

We have the student write a research proposal using a format required by a federal agency. He needs to justify his proposed sequence of experiments. In order to do this well, he needs to anticipate the possible outcomes of his experiments, and develop contingency plans based on these outcomes. Looking ahead is then a valuable exercise. In doing this, he often revises his plans as he weighs the probabilities of outcomes and the utility of the potential information, given his research goal. We encourage him to examine the assumptions behind his hypotheses and his designs. This activity is individualized in the sense that students individually engage in problem clarification. However, we believe it is important to convey that scientists do not work in isolation, that they communicate and stimulate each other intellectually—that scientists work in a community.

Students learn quickly that if they combine their resources in collaborative experiments they can more effectively realize their goals under conditions of limited resources. This requires that they communicate their plans not just to the instructor but to their peers. The communication promotes better problem clarification as collaboration gets under way. The beauty is that collaboration follows naturally. Students are not asked by the instructor to work in assigned groups. They choose collaborators who have similar and/or complementary goals, ideas, and skills. In order to do this, a student needs to explain his ideas and justify them to another student who is likewise interacting with him. All of this can be done without touching the computer terminal. When they are ready, they submit the design of their first experiment to the computer and within minutes receive their first set of results. They now have the task of reducing the data, performing analyses, making inferences, and coming to conclusions. They have the task of communicating their findings not only to their collaborators but to the larger "scientific community" (their class). We have them ditto these reports and distribute them to the class. The first week's reports constitute Volume 1 of a scientific journal that they name. A student must not only understand his own experiment, but he must update himself with respect to the knowledge gained in the community and decide how or if he should modify his plans. The joy for the instructor is observing peer pressure for better clarification in the reports.

The next round of designs is submitted to the computer and the reports constitute Volume 2. If the student over-extends his budget, then he needs to write a budget-overrun proposal. In the end, we have them individually write reviews of the "literature" generated within their community, a task of which they are informed at the outset. Some students are motivated to include literature from real experiments. Depending on how many rounds have taken place, the volume of information may be quite large. Students need to develop organizing principles. An encyclopedic approach can be very wearisome.

We try to stimulate them into thinking about how the model generating the data is structured. Their inferences about the underlying model are communicated largely in descriptive terms, but many begin to be aware of the usefulness of modeling in structuring knowledge.

The EXPER SIM class as a simulated scientific community attempts to take advantage of several instructional components: (1) The student is responsible for a wide range of decisions in a rich but structured environment. To this extent, the pedagogy is individualized. (2) It is to the student's advantage, given his limited resources and the ever-looming review paper, that he work and communicate with his peers. In this way he develops not only communication skills but problem-solving strategies as he struggles to clarify problems, develop research hypotheses, refine his designs, interpret results, and make inferences. Individualized instruction need not mean learning in isolation. (3) The learning environment is structured to encourage the anticipation and plans for future events. Because the computer compresses the time of the data-collection step, the future quickly becomes the present and then the past. To this extent the pedagogy is future-oriented. (4) The role of the instructor is more of that of a consultant than a lecturer. Students consult about probelms that they have developed rather than passively receiving information pertaining to problems others have generated. Here is where the real teaching is done.

When I wander into an EXPER SIM class, the following scene is typical. A group of two or four students are around the terminal either entering a design or looking at the results coming out in the hard copy. They are talking to each other about the experiment—they are often arguing. Other students individually or in groups are pouring over output and there is often at least one other lively discussion taking place. The teaching fellow is rarely at the terminal but engaged in a discussion with one or more students, often on the other side of the room. My entrance even when I have guests rarely interrupts the activity. An extreme example occurred once. A photographer from our local newspaper was instructed to take pictures to accompany an article written by the science editor. Two students were in such an absorbed discussion that, although they were aware that the photographer was present, the poor man had to interrupt them in order to get their names. The interrruption was only momentary.

There are some further wrinkles in the simulated scientific community pedagogy that we have tried or are piloting. Success seems to be related to the organizational ability of the instructor. We have had student "editorial boards" that review the reports that go into the "journal volumes." Criteria for acceptance have to be developed by such students and communicated. We worried that some students would be treated punitively by the students on the "board," but our experience has been the opposite. Instead, board members often seek to be helpful in their suggestions. When we can manage it logistically, we extend the scientific community over several sections. In this case, members of a given class may be working on different models in the library. This gives students a choice of subject area, and the larger numbers of students increases the probability of a critical mass for that community. We have held "mini-conventions" within a section and between sections. This approach enables students to explore other ways of communicating ideas.

I have used the EXPER SIM pedagogy in a combined course in statistics and research design. Here students are introduced to statistical concepts and procedures as they begin to realize their need for them. Statistics is then viewed as a tool that helps communicate findings rather than as an arbitrary intellectual exercise.

In the introductory course described earlier, the statistics course follows the laboratory course, so students are naive about the subject. We can't teach this subject in the time allowed, but they gain some experience with sampling, variance, central tendency, the law of large numbers, the nature of distributions, and some simple inferential procedures. Many pursue a statistical concept on their own as they see its relevance to the inference task. Both MESS and LESS can interface with statistical software if that is desired.

At the University of Michigan-Flint, Harriet Braunstein has students place abstracts of their experiments in computer files that can be accessed by other students. I understand that students have great fun keeping score on how frequently their abstracts are accessed by their classmates.

These are some of the classroom procedures that have been developed, but new ones continue to arise as imaginative instructors attempt to make the most use of the software for particular purposes.

Future Expansion

If EXPER SIM is to have any real impact on college instruction, it must not be viewed as a closed software "package," but rather as a concept that stimulates and facilitates continual development. This means that new instructional models need to be devloped not only in psychology but in any discipline where it is desirable for students to make decisions in uncertain conditions. The approach is a "natural" for research design, methodology, and statistics courses. It has potential even in traditional content courses where students acquire knowledge of a subject by making research design inquiries of a model in a given subject area. Alfred Raphaelson at University of Michigan-Flint has used a motivation model (developed by Susan Mueller) in a traditional course on Motivation in the psychology curriculum. The DOPE model (by Howard Eichenbaum and Trudy Villars) is rich in the kinds of problems facing psychobiologists. It concerns the effects of drugs on learning where the subjects are experimental mice. It would be useful not only in a methodology course but in a psychobiology content course. The imprinting and social facilitation models (by D.W. Rajecki) are relevant in social psychology courses, and the schizophrenia model (by David Malin) may be quite useful in clinical and social psychology courses.

Richard Nussloch (1974) conducted a study where one class was exposed to an imprinting model through computer simulation and another class to the literature on which the imprinting model was based. He was primarily concerned with studying the differences in problem-solving strategies and indeed found that students in computer-simulation courses were better at designing experiments related to the hypothesis, better at formulating an overall design, and better at identifying relevant independent variables than students who only studied the literature. Moreover, students in the computer simulation class also performed better than students in the literature class on a straight content test.

EXPER SIM needs to be evaluated not by its present models, but by its potential to encourage and facilitate instructional modeling in other areas of psychology and other disciplines, and by the quality of this endeavor.

We reasoned that the creative college instructor who is well informed in his subject and who is concerned about instructional improvement is an ideal candidate for contributing to the expansion of the EXPER SIM library. Such a person, however, may or may not be familar or comfortable with computers. His knowledge of modeling may be restricted. But he does have several things going for him: He is a doer. He is concerned with self-improvement. He knows his subject. He knows his students.

He has an intangible love for teaching. We have had enough faith in him to give him a textbook, a classroom, and a teaching assignment. I believe we can extend that faith to his ability to create good instructional models. He may stumble at first and have a few false starts—but, in the end, this is the individual that will get the job done and make the greatest contribution to higher education.

How then can the process be facilitated? We have concerned ourselves at this point with the problem of the college instructor's unfamiliarity with the computer. We have approached the problem in two ways. The modularization of the MESS and LESS software in such that the instructional model builder does not have to concern himself with the problem of interfacing the student with his model. He concentrates on his model, writes a FORTRAN subroutine or works with a programmer who writes the subroutine, and then attaches the subroutine to MESS or LESS.

If his model is a simple additive model, he can place it directly in the LESS library without going through a programmer. There are other programs, such as MODLER developed by Gerald Shure, in which an instructor and his students can develop models interactively, depending on the complexity of the model.

The Simulation Writer Interactive Program (SWIP), first begun at the University of Michigan by Robert Stout and being completed at Butler Hospital in Providence, Rhode Island, is an interactive FORTRAN IV program that also enables the model builder to bypass the programmer. The program has many options and is capable of handling a wide range of models, such as Markov, analysis of variance, regression, and time series models. In time it is anticipated that there will be a need for post-professional short courses for instructors who wish to expand their knowledge of modeling. Such a development will have a very positive impact on higher education—because the most stimulating teaching occurs when the instructor is also learning.

Decisions in Instructional Model Building

Regardless of the specific kind of model that an instructor and his students are engaged in developing, we have identified certain kinds of decisions that an instructional model builder must make. Each decision must be made with educational goals in mind.

Nature of the Output. One of the first decisions that an instructional model builder must make is whether the outputs are to represent observable data or theoretical abstractions. The model outputs in the current MESS and LESS libraries are numbers that can be plausibly interpreted as "data." If the student were to conduct experiments in the real world, the outputs of these experiments would be the same in kind as those he obtained from a simulated experiment. Our principal experience with EXPER SIM has been in methodology courses, where it was important for students to make inferences about theory from data. It is conceivable, however, that an educational goal would have students deal with abstractions rather than observables. In any event, it is a decision the model builder must make.

If the decision is to have the output relate to observable data, then the model builder must decide what level of transformation the data takes. For example, is the output a subject's "score," or a number related to events on which the student must compute a score? Is the transformation at a higher level, such as a mean, or a correlation coefficient? What level of transformation the output takes depends on the kinds of problems the instructor wants his students to approach. The decisions must be made with respect to the educational goals or objectives.

Probabilistic-Deterministic Models. Another decision facing the instructional model builder is whether the model outputs are probabilistic or deterministic in nature. If the student submits the same design to the computer a second time, will he get the exact same output, or a different output.

Again, because we were using EXPER SIM in methodology courses and we wanted students to have to confront problems with sampling error, all of our models have probabilistic outcomes in that it is extremely unlikely that a repeated experiment will yield the same output. How variable the output is on repeated experiments depends upon the algorithm. Models can be deterministic until the last stage that specifies the sampling error or they can be probabilistic to that stage. The choice depends upon the model builder's scientific philosophy and modeling style.

I have often been asked: Why build models that generate simulated data? Why not have students explore a data bank where the numbers are "real" data?

I quickly respond that this is possible as far as our software supervisor is concerned. Students can have a very similar experience with data banks as they do with data generated from a model.

However, there are problems in depending solely on data banks. One is that much knowledge in psychology as well as other fields is simply not contained in data banks. The next is that data banks often require a tremendous storage where algorithms do not. This requirement is very restrictive on smaller computers and may be quite expensive on larger computers.

But my principal concern is more fundamental. The data in a cell of a data bank are fixed. Repeated observation of the data in that cell yields a constant output. I worry that students may infer a constant or deterministic process underlying the data which, especially in the social sciences, is simply not the case. The experience may imply that sample data no matter how extensive, are, in themselves, an "answer" or the "truth."

Relevance to the "Real World." All of the models in EXPER SIM libraries are based on a literature. By this I mean that data generated from the models are comparable to what has been published. The degree of validity of the model is another consideration for the instructional model builder. If the field is controversial, the literature often contains conflicting reports. The very selection of literature upon which to base a model reflects the model builder's theoretical biases. Further, the literature on a subject is often incomplete, even if it has been studied extensively. In this case, logical extrapolations must be made. Documentation of models should, at the minimum, include the literature on which the model was based. It should go further, however, and differentiate between what was based directly on empirical studies and logical extrapolations.

In short, the model should reflect the model builder's state of knowledge. It also means that it reflects his certainty about his state of knowledge. What then affects the model builder's certainty?

The credibility of the investigators who have contributed their findings to the literature is one factor. The degree to which a number of studies in the literature have yielded data that are predicted by a theory is another factor. These are hard judgmental questions demanded of a scholar who is asked, "What do you know and how certain are you?" This is a question students have a right to ask their instructors. A model explicitly reflects the instructor's knowledge and uncertainty.

Probability of Missing Data. The instructional model builder may want his students to cope with the problem of missing data. Missing data are the bane of a scientist's existence—and certainly not a joyful experience for students.

We have used the probability of missing data in the DOPE and social facilitation models. We have linked it to certain combinations of variables such that when the student thinks about the problem carefully he can design experiments that minimize missing data. For example, drug dosage, strain of mice, and drug type are associated with the probability of missing data in the DOPE model. The student can overdose his sample and kill all or part of his sample. He learns to carefully design a set of procedures that minimizes this catastrophe.

Conditions of No Data. The instructional model builder will want to pay close attention to those conditions in which no data results from the design. On the simplest level, he will want to note those combinations of variables that are impossible in the real world. For example, when a student thoughtlessly designs experiments calling for identical twins of opposite sex in the Schizophrenia model, he is told that he has specified an illegal combination of variables or a set of variables where data are impossible. He must examine his design for flaws. I might point out that some students perniciously pursue such impossible combinations as a personal test of the integrity of the model. Rest assured that if you have not identified all illegal combinations, your students will certainly find them and challenge you.

If there are certain experimental procedures that you want to make sure that the students consider, an illegal default value can be assigned the variable. Every variable has a default that the program uses unless the student specifies another value. The default may be a constant or may vary in some way across the allowable range. If a default is assigned that is not in the allowable range, then the only way data can be obtained is to consciously specify a value for the variable. This will consistently draw attention to the variable. For example, many students in a real or simulated animal learning experiment have wondered why the animals are just sitting there, until they discover that they have forgotten to turn the shock on or put food pellets in the receptacle. Such an experience tends to develop careful consideration of all of the experimental procedures.

Unfolding Strategy. In the first three models, schizophrenia, imprinting, and motivation, the entire set of manipulable and observable variables are given the student at the outset. We became convinced that students were not given an opportunity to operationalize other variables in their probe of the model. Students were constantly asking about other variables that were not programmed in the model. How could we give students the opportunity to infer and operationalize new variables in a manageable way?

The approach Rajecki took in the social facilitation model was as follows. He designed three stages. In the first stage, the student is given a list of manipulable variables and a description of the dependent variable. He begins to learn something about the phenomena of social facilitation. In the second stage, the list of dependent variables is expanded and he can observe the phenomena in different ways. He may be developing some theories about the social facilitation as a process, but he needs to manipulate and observe variables that are not on his list.

In the third stage, he is given no variable names. When he has an idea, he discusses it with his instructor who has a list of the remaining manipulable and observable variables. After this consultation, the instructor gives him a code for a new variable. If, in the discussion, the instructor believes he has inferred one of the unknown variables, he gives him the code name for the variable. If the student has inadequately operationalized a variable, or is simply out of the ball park, he is given a code for a "no effect" variable. If the student's design yields a positive effect, he may wish to pursue it further. If it yields a negative effect, he must worry whether he had operationalized a relevant variable or had simply designed an inadequate experiment with respect to that variable. The consultation period is important. If the student has a good idea, but his variable is not in the program, the instructor may choose to tell him so and direct him to something close to his idea that is in the program. If the student persists in a poor or unclear operationalization of a variable, he experiences the consequences from an inconclusive experiment.

With the unfolding strategy only some of the variables in the model are revealed and others are revealed at a later time after students have gained initial experience. This "revelation" can be explicit as in stage two or it can occur after students have had an opportunity to infer them.

Simulated Costs. The instructional model builder may want to include a simulated cost algorithm in his model. Here he can assign costs to the use of subjects, and differential costs related to the values of variables and to dependent or observable variables, that reflect "real" monetary costs. The calculated costs for each experiment can be printed as part of the output.

Summary

EXPER SIM represents an attempt to develop a pedagogy that orients students toward the future. The computer is used not to ask or answer questions, but to hold knowledge represented by models. Students probe this knowledge with experimental designs and make inferences about the knowledge from data generated from the models. It is important that they consider possible outcomes of their designs, how probable these outcomes are and how valuable or costly is the information. The computer makes it possible to bring anticipated future outcomes into the present and then the past and the process is repeated.

Students are active participants in the inquiry process, rather than passive receivers of the results of someone else's inquiry. Not only do they gain knowledge of a subject but they gain experience in developing strategies for the acquisition of knowledge. Computer simulation and carefully designed classroom procedures can bring experiences previously reserved only for graduate students or outstanding undergraduates to a larger number of undergraduates at the beginning of their college years. EXPER SIM needs to be expanded and will most certainly be improved as it dynamically grows. Hopefully, it will stimulate ideas and development of other future-oriented pedagogies as well.

References

Main, D.B. (Ed.) *EXPER SIM on Michigan Experiment Simulation Supervisor.* Xerox College Publishing, 1974.

Nussloch, R., R. Kaplan, and D.D. Main. Casual Critiques or Active Arguments? A Comparison of the Use of Computer Data Generator and Journal Article Criticism in the Science Classroom. *Proceedings of the Conference on Computers in the Undergraduate Curricula,* Washington State University, Pullman, June 1974.

Shure, G., and K. Brainerd. MODELR: Model Building and Model Modification for Instruction. *Behavior Research Methods & Instrumentation,* 1975, 7, 221-225.

Stout, R. SWIP: Modeling on the Simulation Writer Interactive Program. *Behavior Research Methods & Instrumentation,* 1975, 7, 226-228.

Stout, R. Modeling and the Michigan Experimental Simulation Supervisor: An Overview and Some Prospects. *Behavioral Research Methods & Instrumentation,* 1974, 6, 121-123.

Thurmond, J.B., and A.O. Cromer. Models and Modeling with the Louisville Experiment Simulation System (LESS). *Behavior Research Methods & Instrumentation,* 1975, 7, 229-232.

Note

[1] This paper was written while Professor Main was at the University of Michigan.

16.
Computer Graphics and Instructional Enhancement: Theory and Methodology

James R. Bohland[1]
University of Oklahoma

My comments in this paper are restricted to a discussion of two parallel developments in computing and the educational advantages obtained by adjoining them. The two are: the use of computers to enhance instruction, and their use in giving graphic representation to information. Both have fairly recent histories. However, both have begun to achieve some prominence in today's computer priorities. Unfortunately, recent development in the two fields have been achieved independently. Only occasionally are graphics integrated with computer based instructional models.

Instructional computing is beginning to achieve a solid foundation of concepts and principles. Simulation models, numeric analysis packages, and experimental design systems have been developed to take advantage of the computer to supplement the present educational environment. When properly integrated with other instructional procedures, they provide the student with a meaningful heuristic.

This paper suggests the educational value of the packages might be increased by supplementing their linguistic and numeric output with graphic output. Graphic languages, when properly integrated with other instructional models and languages, can greatly enhance the comprehension of abstractions. Most educators would concur with this, but the instructional strategies needed to attain this integration have not been formulated. Procedures integrating conceptual pedagogies with graphics constitutes an important development. Certainly models are one means of facilitating conceptual learning. If well designed, they help the student understand the associations, concepts, and theory underlying a given process.

Recognition of the capabilities of models in instructional environments is the basis for the assumption regarding the utility of graphics in teaching. Graphics, be they pictures, maps, graphs, etc., are models; symbolic generalization about reality. They convey important information about form and process. The map is a good example of the graphic as a model (Georgie, 1967; Beard, 1967). It reduces the complexities in spatial associations to a general schematic by the use of symbolic notation. As a model it has many of the attributes of more formal mathematical models. It also has certain perceptual advantages over other model languages. The perceptual aspect is important. By translating numeric or verbal languages to graphic output via the computer, a wider range of the student's senses are utilized.

Assuming for a moment that the assumption about graphics and learning has been scientifically validated—why computer graphics? Why not permit the student to translate between languages and produce his own graphic output? In a number of instances and for some ages this is desirable. The computer does, however, have certain advantages. These are important not only from a graphic standpoint but also from an educational one.

1. Speed and efficiency—the computer produces high resolution, low-error graphics rapidly. High speed output means the student can have visual images shortly after or during a particular activity. Moreover, the student is not bored by being forced to do menial drafting tasks, i.e., the proverbial complaint about "busy work."

2. Standardization of quality—graphics drawn by the computer vary little in their quality. Consequently, the output can be evaluated on the basis of content rather than drafting ability. This subjective element of the evaluation process is eliminated or reduced from present proportions. The student who may not have drafting skills is not penalized.

3. Versatility—with existing computer software a wide range of output is available. Consequently, high quality graphics can be obtained by students who would be unable to do so by hand. For example, few have the skills necessary to draft three-dimensional surfaces; however, these can be easily accomplished on the computer.

4. Interactive capabilities—a well designed graphics system will enable the user to interact with the model to edit in real-time environments. With these capabilities the user can easily modify output prior to final printing.

These attributes make the computer an effective tool for producing high quality graphic presentations. When integrated with a well designed, imaginative instructional strategy, computer graphics can be an excellent addition to our present educational environment.

This paper is divided into three sections. First, some basic principles of graphic languages are discussed. The discussion centers on the concepts important in designing good graphics for improving communication.

Some basic data surface concepts are discussed in the second section. The user must be familiar with the characteristics of the surfaces being drawn by the computer to avoid misrepresentations. In the third section, examples of different types of graphic output are presented and their use for enhancing instruction discussed.

One point should be stressed at the outset. The emphasis, particularly of sections II and III, is on computer mapping. Although this may seem rather limiting, it need not be. Many social and behavioral scientists deal with aggregate areal data. The convention in most disciplines, with the notable exception of geography, is to use tabular formats to present data to students or colleagues. This procedure takes from the data a basic element of information, its spatial pattern. In many instances this is an informative and important bit of information. Moreover, from a pedagogical perspective, the impact of a visual representation of areal data (Figure 1) is much more effective than having a student read a lengthy table (Table 1).

Besides this rather obvious reason for using maps, computer mapping routines are more versatile than the restricted definition of a map would imply. A map is more than a simple diagrammatical representation of some piece of territory. We speak, for example, of "mapping" causal linkages in models, "mapping" flow patterns in computer charts, or "mapping" cognitive processes. In this context a map is an abstraction of a particular chunk of information expressed in a symbolic form. The abstraction may or may not be areal data. In either case a map of the phenomenon

Figure 1

Data on federal tax taken from Table 1 as shown on Line Printer Map of United States. Software: *SYMAP*.

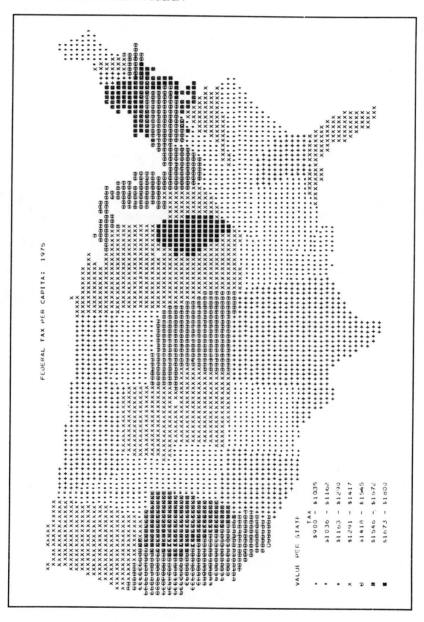

Table 1

State	Tax Per Capita ($)	State	Tax Per Capita ($)	State	Tax Per Capita ($)
Alabama	1026	Maine	1075	Ohio	1441
Arizona	1256	Maryland	1615	Oklahoma	1181
Arkansas	970	Massachusetts	1535	Oregon	1371
California	1526	Michigan	1539	Pennsylvania	1426
Colorado	1368	Minnesota	1382	Rhode Island	1457
Connecticut	1800	Mississippi	908	South Carolina	1041
Delaware	1743	Missouri	1362	South Dakota	1081
Florida	1378	Montana	1183	Tennessee	1147
Georgia	1217	Nebraska	1420	Texas	1264
Idaho	1087	Nevada	1612	Utah	1072
Illinois	1704	New Hampshire	1399	Vermont	1167
Indiana	1441	New Jersey	1760	Virginia	1355
Iowa	1405	New Mexico	1024	Washington	1402
Kansas	1432	New York	1636	West Virginia	1091
Kentucky	1094	North Carolina	1145	Wisconsin	1331
Louisanna	1064	North Dakota	1288	Wyoming	1295

Source: *National Journal 1976*

imparts information about concepts like pattern, auto-correlation, contiguity, distance, and direction.

Since these concepts are significant to many disciplines, a map and its use need not be restricted to the narrower definition of the model. As Georgie (1967, p. 49) notes. "The usefulness of maps (graphics) as models is of considerable pedagogical value, but it is also of conceptual value, and may even be of literal value. Language and maps come together in some measure in the use of graphs and algebraic geometry generally. Perhaps the most important aspect of the use of maps lies in its more direct appeal to the eye. *The use of words is secondary rather than primary, and the two can clearly be used together* [emphasis added] and where this is done, we can place the interpretation of 'scientific theory' on the result."

I. Information, Perception, and Computer Graphics:
Concepts and Theory

"A picture is worth a thousand words." This old adage appears to have stood the test of time. Most of us who have attempted to convey information to a group have encountered the situation where words are ineffective. One turns to a diagram, map, photo, graph, or whatever to help convey the basic concepts. At that moment our intuitive feeling about pictures is reinforced. By "picture" I mean more than photos or grey tone representations. It is used to represent all forms of graphic images.

Does there exist support for this adage? Kennedy (1974) emphasizes that the role of pictures in learning is an area of much speculation and little scientific proof. The evidence, however, appears to suggest that pictures can enhance the flow and retention of information.

Haber supports this view. He concludes (1970): (1) recognition memory for pictures is virtually perfect; (2) it probably lasts indefinitely; and (3) it does not seem to be mediated by verbal coding or labeling of the content of the pictures. This gives strong justification for the use of pictures in the educational process; however, there is not total agreement on all points. It is true that memory for pictures is high. However, it is not indefinite. For short-term time, at any rate, retention of image is higher (approximately 90 percent after a week) than for the written word.

Some research also indicates that pictorial recognition requires no learning and is not culture specific (Hochberg and Brooks, 1962). This is particularly significant from an educational perspective. It reduces the effects of prior learning differentials among students. This conclusion has been challenged, however, and evidence to the contrary exists. This does not, however, negate the conclusions of most research in this area, which is: Pictures are an effective means of providing useful information.

Information and Graphics. Before proceeding it should be recognized that there are two aspects of picture perception. Pictures contain information and thus constitute a language just like numeric or linguistic languages. This is important to the educational perspective. Pictures or graphics, however, also have an aesthetic dimension. The two are not totally independent but the distinction is relevant to the design of graphic displays. Aesthetic pictures may not be effective for transmitting information. The reverse is also not always true.

What then constitutes an effective graphic? Where and what type of information is present in graphic displays?

The contemporary definition of information is a derivation of Shannon's (1948) original statement. Information is related to the uncertainty present in a particular channel. Information is transmitted when an unknown event occurs, an unpredictable event. The result conforming to some predefined expectation does not convey any information. Only when unexpected signals occur is information present.

On first inspection this definition seems alien to our scientific paradigm. To predict accurately from a model has always been thought to be an important part of science. And, prediction constitutes the embodiment of developing new information. In fact, this association is reversed, or in a more colloquial sense— "the melody is right but the words are all wrong." Science is interested in redundancy, the absence of information. Prediction is possible only when a high rate of redundancy occurs in data. When information is maximized, a complete state of entropy exists, the antithesis of our classical definition of science and the "scientific method."

It is somewhat overstating the case by saying science is interested only in redundancy. Science is interested in information but as it occurs in a redundant framework. Only when information, that piece of the unexpected, is framed by a predictable set of circumstances is it possible to understand the meaning of that new piece. Residuals from a regression model, for example, only have meaning if the model provides a predictable framework for the association between certain variables. If the model does not have sufficient predictability (redundancy), the information imparted by residuals has little meaning.

Information theory in the context of scientific methodology is a useful analog for education. The model of inquiry implicit in logical positivism is one some feel is an appropriate educational paradigm. Consequently, the concepts of information theory important to scientific investigation have some relevance to the design of instructional strategies. The role of redundancy in providing an interpretable framework from which a student evaluates new information is a concept central to good instruction.

How these information concepts relate to graphics within an educational framework is another question, one central to this presentation.

If numeric data are presented in an illustration, this quite obviously constitutes a source of information. The designer of the illustration, to maximize its educational value, must be aware of both the signals and noise present in the data before translating it to graphic language (see section II for a discussion of methods for signal enhancement in data). There is, however, information contained in the geometry or form of the image and this is also quite relevant to information transmission.

Information contained in graphic form is a function of the organization of the entire graphic. In a pictorial account, uncertainty or information is concentrated at contours (in pictures, contours are areas of tone change while in line drawings a line outlining a form is a contour) and where the contour changes direction.

This makes intuitive sense if one considers maps. For example, in the four maps in Figure 2, Map A is highly redundant. It has no information. According to information concepts, Map C contains more information than B, and the information in D is so great it is difficult to interpret. These four maps illustrate a simple concept but one that is central to good graphic output. The information in

Figure 2

Four maps showing different levels of surface complexity. Map A is highly redundant while map D has information overload.

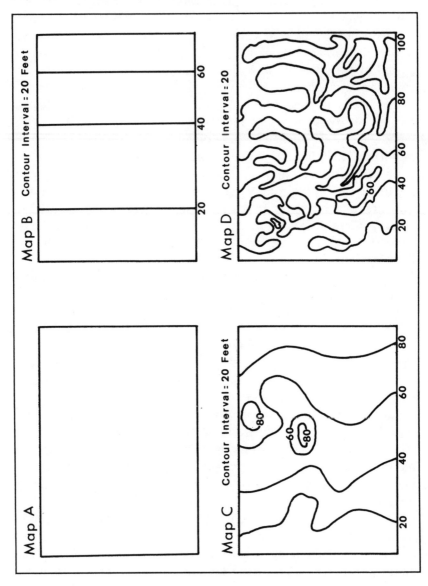

the geometry of the graphic should not constitute a major source of noise in the illustration.

Understanding information concepts as they relate to the geometry of the graphic constitutes an important aspect of graphics, if they are to be used in an educational environment. On this point psychologists stress that information in pictures cannot be discussed in isolation. Perceptual "goodness," the ease of recognition of form, is as important as information in using pictures as an instructional language. For example, research indicates that forms are easily distinguished and retained if they are "good" from a perceptual perspective. *Such representations contain little information.* As Hochberg and McAlister (1953) conclude: perception or organization of a stimulus is inversely related to the information contained in that figure.

Given the significance of "perceptual goodness" in image recognition, how can it be measured? No simple measurement techniques exist; however, there are certain principles of form recognition based upon gestalt psychology. Proximity, similarity, continuity, common fate, and closure are five principles that can be used to organize visual form concepts.

Other factors, such as experience of the observer, are also important to form recognition and must be considered. However, these principles serve as a basic framework for understanding the perceptual organization of graphic materials. They highlight an important point about graphic languages—the geometry of the illustration is as important as the surface being illustrated. Or, to paraphrase a famous line—"the graphic is the message."

The important aspect of information theory and visual perception concepts is that they converge to the same basic conclusion. Where learning is concerned, information and redundancy must be viewed as interdependent concepts. To be an effective language for enhancing the educational process, a good figure must have minimal uncertainty. Complex representations violate both the principles implicit in information theory and visual perception. Consequently, graphics can become ineffective instructional languages. A simple principle to remember is that the objective of a model is to generalize the significant aspects of a complex system. The principle applies to graphic as well as mathematical models.

II. Surface Characteristics, Preprocessing,
and Graphic Design

Peucker (1972) has three simple principles to be used as guidelines in preparing graphics.

1. Know what information is important and know it in a fashion that can be implemented.
2. Use procedures adequate to the expected results.
3. Produce the results in a form that one is able to interpret.

The first principle deals with knowledge of data surfaces, their characteristics, trends, and composition. The second principle concerns data processing prior to translating to graphic language. This so-called preprocessing stage is used to enrich the information in a surface by eliminating or reducing noise and/or amplifying important signals. The last principle relates to the actual drafting of the representation, or in the case of computer graphics, designing the program so as to secure the best possible graphic output. Each of these principles has concepts that are uniquely significant to it. Some, like scale, are important in all three.

Surface Characteristics. The most important aspect of any empirical analysis is knowledge of data. Validity and reliability are familiar concepts to all social and behavioral scientists. These, of course, are closely tied to sample design and procedures. In graphics, sampling not only determines the value of a particular parcel of data, it also characterizes the surface. This latter point is the prime determinant for selecting the proper projection for illustrating data.

Figure 3 illustrates a basic sampling/surface identification problem arising from improper sample procedures. If the three-dimensional block represents the real data surface and the three graphs represent surfaces inferred from three different samples, it is obvious that incorrect inferences have been made. It is also clear the errors may have been avoided by prior knowledge of the surface.

Prior judgments concerning the continuity of the surface are particularly important. Is the surface continuous or discontinuous, i.e., discrete? This differential is, of course, central to many statistical procedures. It influences the selection of the proper statistical model. Likewise, in graphics it is the prime determinant of the appropriate graphic model.

Figure 3

Illustration of the effect of location of sample points when sampling a surface with cyclical patterns. Three different representatives are derived from the same surface by using different Software: *SYMVU.*

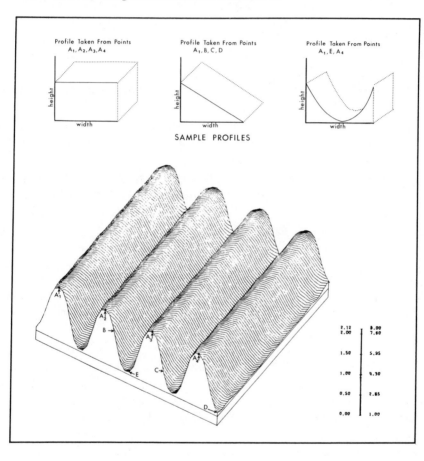

Discontinuous surfaces are correctly illustrated by conformant maps. Data are assigned to specific data zones or units of area. The statistical equivalent would be cells in a contingency table or cross-tabulation tables. Continuous surfaces, on the other hand, are correctly illustrated by isarithmic (contour) maps. Interpretation of isarithmic representations assumes that a regular interpolation function exists between points of known information (contour lines). Figures 4 and 5 illustrate proper graphic representation of discontinuous and continuous surface.

There are numerous examples, both spatial and non-spatial, of continuous and discontinuous surfaces. Intelligence indices, for example, are assumed to be along a continuum, as are age and various sociometric scales. Sex, on the other hand, is discrete, as is occupation and family size. Area examples of continuous surfaces are temperature, elevation, and to some extent socio-economic variables like transportation costs from a point. Discontinuous surfaces are exemplified by items like urban population, state revenues, or other data assigned to a bounded area.

The nature of the data surface is not always clear-cut as these. One may have little prior knowledge of the surface, and justification of a particular configuration may be impossible. Where sufficient empirical data exist, procedures such as auto-correlation can help in these situations. In other cases the user must make a subjective judgment.

A critical factor to consider in any surface assumption is the scale of data collection and presentation. Assumptions about continuity vary with scale. For example, consider housing values in a metropolitan area. One may assume a continuous surface for these values if the entire urban area is being considered. If, however, the scale is larger and only one block is being sampled, housing values are more correctly assumed as discrete, i.e., defined for a particular data zone—the residential lot.

Scale is also important for non-spatial data, although it is usually not stated in terms like scale. For example, if one is analyzing an individual's voting patterns in an election, the data are discrete; he can only vote in given categories. If, however, one's analysis covers several elections, the data become continuous, i.e., he votes Republican 61 percent of the time, she votes Democratic 38 percent, etc. Only the scale of analysis changes.

Figure 4

Choropleth map of federal aid to disabled. County is the discrete unit of analysis. Software: *SYMAP.*

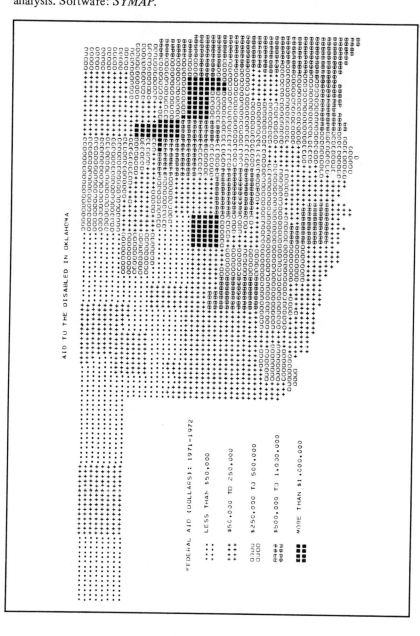

Figure 5

Contour map of tornadoes touching ground in Oklahoma. Data is represented as a continuous surface. Software: *SYMAP*.

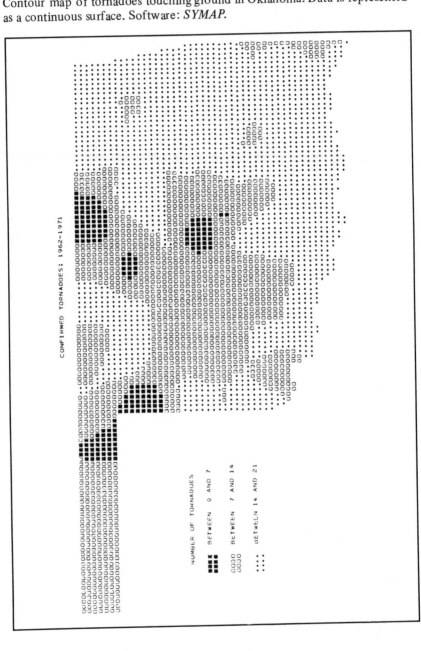

The change, however, does modify the assumption about the data surface.

Assumptions about the nature of the data surface must be stated and understood clearly, or errors in the graphic language can occur. Using continuous surface projections to display discrete surfaces is as erroneous as using double negatives in literature.

Preprocessing. The second stage in Peucker's design is for transforming raw data into interpretable patterns. A variety of techniques exist to maximize the interpretability of data. Simple descriptive statistics to complex multi-variate procedures are used. From a graphics standpoint these can be divided into two groups. In one case the intent is to enhance the relevant signals in the data. Others are used to reduce noise, that is, to filter from the data the information, random or systematic, irrelevant to the objectives of the presentation. Although these constitute different approaches, one may wish to use both for a particular problem, and some techniques accomplish both tasks.

A bevy of statistical and mathematical procedures can be used for enhancing information. Most standard statistical procedures process data so that we can make judgments about what information is significant. If wrapped in good theory (a redundancy framework), the significant information is more interpretable.

If one is concerned with two-dimensional surfaces, additional procedures are important. Interpolation to new data points constitutes a common procedure for signal enhancement. By interpolation the amount of data is increased and one may be better equipped to separate noise from signals. Also, many computer graphic algorithms require sample points to be in some type of regular lattice, e.g., contour algorithms.

In addition to interpolation, a variety of filtering processes can be used. Most are designed to eliminate noise, but for some distributions the distinction between noise and signals is nebulous (Tobler 1967, 1969). Trend surface analysis, binomial smoothing, and spectral analysis are procedures used to amplify signals. Spectral analysis has considerable potential and is currently used for one-dimensional spectra. Attempts have been made to use it for two-dimensional surfaces (Rayner, 1971) but several problems still exist. The potential is great and it may become a powerful technique for synthesizing the information content of a complex surface.

Graphic Design. The principles of visual perception and how these apply to graphic design were discussed in section I. The important design principle is not to let the translation to a graphic language weaken the interpretability of the information. Good sample procedures, surface assumptions, and data processing can be seriously depreciated if the final graphic output is poor.

There are many aspects of design that are universal and not a function of the device used in production. Computer graphics do, however, have some special problems of design that must be considered.

1. Line printer versus plotter output. This problem may be eliminated if both options are not available at the computing center. Each output device does, however, have certain advantages. The line printer is cheaper, faster, and is available at most centers. Plotters, on the other hand, are more versatile and the resolution of the output is much higher than printer output.

2. Line versus grey tone. Should the form of an object be filled with grey tones or should simple outlines be used? Grey tones can help distinguish broader patterns but details may be covered by the tones.

3. Planametric versus other perspectives. Many programs permit perspectives other than two-dimensional planametric views. These may be more appealing visually but they may not be suitable for certain audiences. Many people have difficulties visualizing information in this type of presentation.

4. Scale. Scale is a problem that is not unique to graphics; however, plotter and printer size form constraints that are not found in other devices. One may be forced to fit the output into too small a design because of this. If so, other alternatives should be employed.

5. Symbolization. The basic problem with symbolization in computer graphics is with line printers. The symbol options are limited to the character strip on the printer. Even when overprinting is considered, this limits the number of usable symbols. This particular symbolization problem can greatly affect the recognition of forms in the illustration.

6. Encoding of boundaries and lines. Encoding is not strictly a

design problem, but it becomes relevant to the final output because it influences the amount of detail in the output. If students are involved in coding of the geometry of the graphic, a system that is easy, understandable, and doesn't require large amounts of time should be used.

Good design is a function of a number of factors. If the intent is to improve the learning environment for students, the concepts discussed in section I should be utilized. Familiar forms and geometric shapes should be employed. New projections, different orientations to familiar shapes, and uncommon symbolization are to be avoided. The intent is to communicate ideas and concepts. Good graphics can help the process. Poor ones can hinder it.

III. Computer Graphics: Examples of Instructional Use

The supply of quality graphic software is increasing rapidly. Consequently, persons desiring to supplement existing instructional strategies with graphics have to choose from a number of alternatives. The choice should be based on the efficacy of the software in achieving pedagogical objectives; however, to make such judgments requires some prior knowledge of existing software and their appropriateness for achieving specific goals. This section of the report examines some of the existing software and its applicability to different goals.

It must be recognized that software selection is constrained by hardware considerations. The absence of a digital plotter or CRT scope, for example, reduces the available options. However, the absence of sophisticated hardware should not dissuade one from utilizing graphics; besides, printers have two advantages. They are inexpensive and fast. In large classes speed and cost are important graphic parameters.

Speed of response time is extremely critical when graphics are integrated into an inquiry approach to instruction. Delays in the inquiry-feedback process reduce the pedagogical advantages of graphics. Graphics provide visual reinforcement to verbal or written descriptions; accordingly, if the time lag between the different communication modes is great, the effectiveness of each is reduced.

Response time can be maximized in an interactive or time sharing system. In these systems response to student queries is rapid, and the pictorial image becomes a functioning part of the communication system. An interactive mode also permits experimentation by students without major time or cost penalties. The ability to interact and change parameters is particularly ideal for graphics because previewing can eliminate useless plotting, thereby lowering cost.

Movement along a vector can be shown when CRTs are utilized; consequently, process as well as pattern can be visualized. In fact, in a properly designed system viewers become involved in the process unfolding before them. Students become participants rather than stoical observers of static patterns. The advantages of participating in experiences are well known in education, and although interactive graphics cannot replace real-world participation, problem-solving experiences can be replicated in real-time decision environments. Moreover, by using graphics as an instructional language, the response to a particular choice is displayed in a form that helps one obtain a quick grasp of the outcome of a given choice.

Interactive systems provide interesting and meaningful educational experiences; however, graphics need not be restricted to the interactive mode. Creative use of graphics is not a function of the hardware capabilities. Innovative ways of incorporating computer graphics into instruction can occur without relying on the most advanced forms of computer technology.

How can graphics be employed in instruction? A variety of possibilities exist. Three broad areas are discussed in this section: (1) graphic representation of spatial data, (2) graphic representations of simulations, and (3) graphic representations of mathematical or statistical functions. These three are not exhaustive or mutually exclusive catagories of usage. Rather, they are offered as illustrations of ways that graphics can be incorporated into instruction.

Spatial Data. Spatial data are common to non-geographic as well as geographic problems. Data collected by area units, such as counties or states, are by definition spatial; however, non-areal data can be transformed into spatial frameworks, for example, taxonomical space. As an example, Figure 6 illustrates the location of individuals. Graphics such as Figure 6 can be achieved with minimal effort with existing plotting software.

Figure 6

Three dimensional plot showing life satisfaction (Z) as a function of income
(Y) and age (X). Software: *GRAFPAC.*

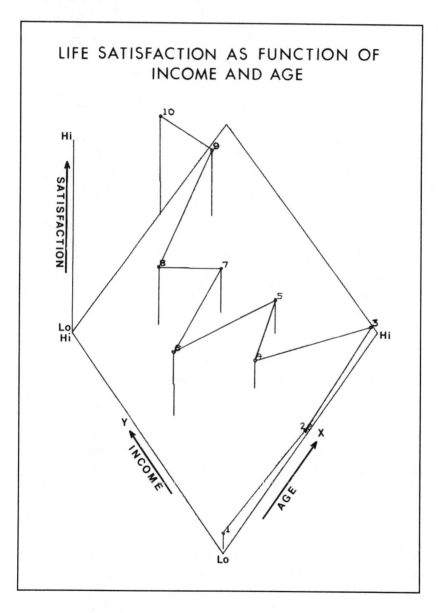

Computer cartography is the branch of computer graphics concerned primarily with displaying data that has a definite geographic basis. The software development in this branch of the science is extensive and has applicability beyond simply the plotting of geographic data. A complete review of cartographic software is beyond the scope of this paper, but some examples are presented to illustrate some of the available alternatives.

If data are assigned to a specific data zone or unit area, maps can be produced from printers as well as plotters. Figure 7, illustrating federal revenue flows in 1945, was produced by SYMAP, one of the more versatile printer software packages. [A bibliographic description of all software mentioned is included at the end of the paper.] Figure 8 shows the same data produced on a digital plotter. The software in this case is CALFORM, a graphics package, like SYMAP, developed at the Harvard Graphics Center.

This type of graphic format is a good supplement to tabular data distributed to students. Students obtain a quick visual impression of patterns, which helps them postulate explanations for data variations. Even a cursory examination of the revenue flow patterns in Figures 7 and 8 generates hypotheses about factors contributing to the variation in federal spending.

Contour representations of surface also can be obtained from both printers and plotters. Although the data in Figures 7 and 8 could be displayed as a contour map, contour images should be reserved for representation of continuous surfaces. There are many examples of continuous data surfaces; Figure 9, for example, shows the distribution of Native Americans in Oklahoma by a three-dimensional representation.

Most surfaces can be displayed three-dimensionally. The addition of depth perspection dramatizes the gradients of change occurring along a surface, so that students can easily visualize the slope characteristics of a surface. The peaks and the troughs in the Native American population surface of Oklahoma are easily recognized in the three-dimensional map shown in Figure 9. The rates of change between nodes of concentration and areas with small numbers of Indians is clearly shown by the slope variations in the surface.

The visual impression of the three-dimensional representation of

Figure 7

Federal revenue flows as shown on a line printer map. Software: *SYMAP*.

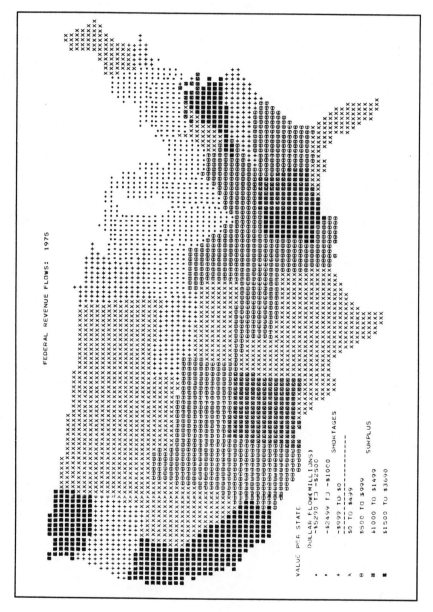

Figure 8

Federal revenue flows as shown on a map produced by a Digital plotter. Same data as in Figure 7 but new class internals highlight different aspects of the pattern. Software: *CALFORM.*

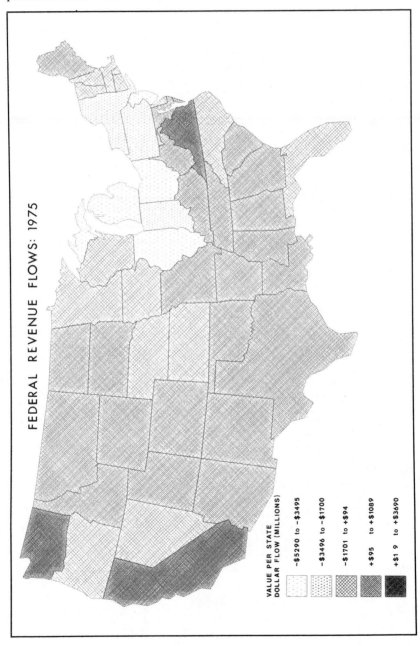

Figure 9

Three dimensional map of a continuous surface. Software: *SYMVU*.

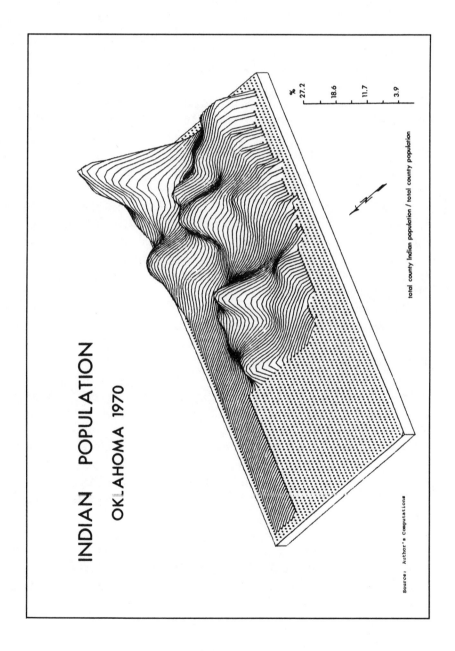

Native Americans makes it more appealing than the two-dimensional contour map in Figure 5. However, three-dimensional representations have some shortcomings that reduce their instructional effectiveness. Information can be hidden between intervening peaks in the surface. Also, if perspective drawings are used, the surface is distorted in order to achieve the perception of depth. Furthermore, many students find it difficult to orient three-dimensional images. The angle of view and the surface representation may be so different from the normal graphic perspective that some students are unable to grasp quickly the meaning of the image. Because of these problems, three-dimensional representations must be used with caution. The perceptual qualities of the imagery must be fully researched before they are utilized on a massive scale.

Statistical and Mathematical Functions. Anyone using bivariate or multivariate statistics has been introduced to graphic representation of statistical functions. The scatter diagram is familiar to most of us, and the command—"plot your data to *see* what the relationship looks like"—is an unconscious recognition of the utility of graphic languages.

Computer graphics is encountered most widely in bivariate statistics. Scattergrams, residual plots, histograms, or frequency curves are common options in statistical packages. However, even at the bivariate level the use of graphics has been unimaginative. There is considerable room for innovative graphic designs in statistical analysis. The use of FACES, introduced by Chernoff (1963) and included in the TROLL system, represents an imaginative way to show variable relationships. Features of the face, such as width, height, or position of mouth, are set to vary with the value of a series of variables (Figure 10). The resultant facial expressions give a visual representation of the associations.

Displaying multivariate functions in their true perspective is, of course, limited to three-dimensional situations. Three variable plots, such as Figure 6, are easily produced with computer graphic software. Such plots enable the user to maintain a proper perspective on variable representations. Unfortunately, most statistical packages do not have three-dimensional plot options; however, if digital plotters are available, three-dimensional plotting can be easily interfaced with multivariate statistical procedures.

Figure 10

Four examples of Chernoff faces showing differences in the mean (length of mouth); variance (length of nose); and range (face width) in four different data sets.

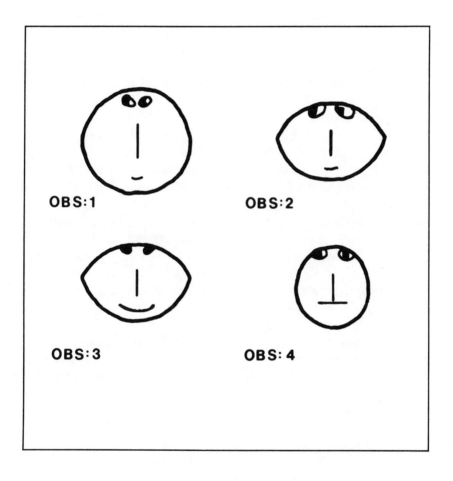

Mathematical as well as statistical functions are easily shown graphically. The visual representation of simple or complex mathematical functions gives the student new insight into abstract operations. An interesting application of graphic plots of mathematical functions is computer art. Creative visual images can be created by integrating a series of mathematical functions. For example, the software package called DABBLE enables the average user to create a wide variety of interesting creations using mathematical functions (Figure 11).

Graphics and Simulation. Perhaps the greatest educational use of computer graphics is displaying simulation results. Most simulations involve the interaction of several variables within a time and/or spatial framework, and either framework is easily adapted to graphical display. By allowing students to visualize processes, or at least stages within a process, an added dimension to the learning experience is achieved. Moreover, the student can participate in an ongoing event, and can be evaluated on the basis of his/her ability to obtain a specific outcome. The popularity of the new wave of computerized games, tennis, hockey, etc., is indicative of the enthusiasm generated by combining graphics with simulation.

Although interactive systems are ideally suited to combining graphics with simulation, the patterns displayed by a printer can be useful in illustrating simulated processes. The checkerboard model discussed elsewhere in this book is an example of how graphics can be used to display the output from simulations. Examples of this use of graphics are common. LANDUSE displays the land use patterns around market centers (Figure 12). The area devoted to a particular crop is determined on the basis of an estimating equation; the results are output in the form of a map of the different land uses.

An extensive discussion of simulations that employ graphics as the primary or secondary language form is not possible in this brief review. The two cases mentioned here are simply illustrative of how graphics can be used to show certain patterns. Experience suggests that graphics are the best language for conveying information about certain types of simulations.

Figure 11

Example of computer art produced by using a series of mathematical functions. Software: *DABBLE*.

ART FORM
produced by
DABBLE

Figure 12

Line printer map showing distribution of 3 different land uses around a market center. Map is example of output from the teaching package, *LANDUSE*.

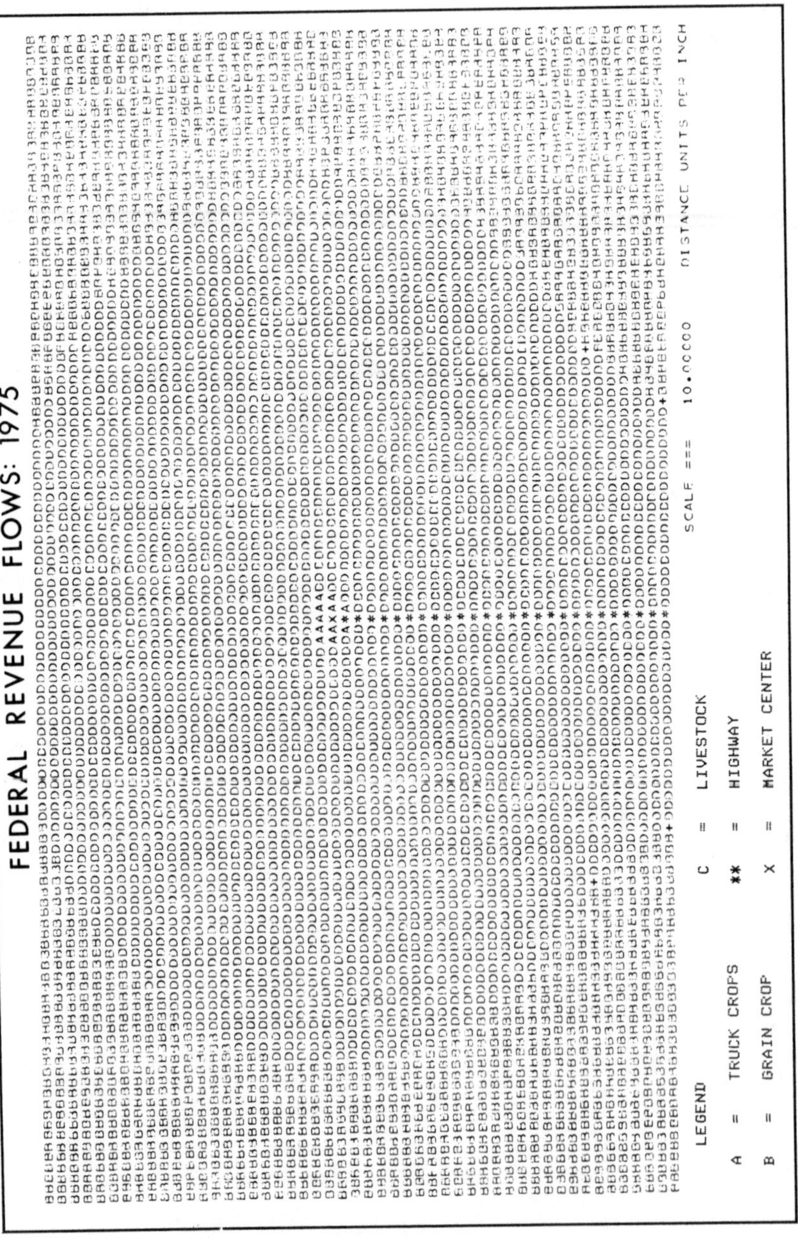

Summary

In the beginning of this chapter the claim was made that computer graphics had certain characteristics that made them suitable as an instructional language. Hopefully, some support for this assertation has been presented in this chapter. I feel strongly that computer graphics offers the instructor a means of expanding the educational experience of the student. However, computer graphics is not a crutch that can be used to support instruction that is conceptually sterile. In the headlong rush to use computer-assisted instructional systems, many fail to differentiate between efficiency and efficacy. Enhancing instruction by using computer graphics must be based on pedagogical as well as economic principles.

References

Beard, C. Maps as Models. In *Models in Geography,* Parts I, II, and V. *Physical and Information Models,* R. Charley and P. Haggett (Eds.). London: Methuen, 1967, 672-719.

Chernoff, H. The Use of Faces to Represent Points in K-Dimensional Space Graphically. *Journal of the American Statistical Association,* June 1963, Vol. 68, 360-361.

Georgie, F.H. The Use of Models in Science. In *Models in Geography,* Parts I, II, and V. *Physical and Information Models,* R. Charley and P. Haggett (Eds.). London: Methuen, 1967, 43-56.

Haber, R.A. How We Remember What We See. *Scientific American,* May 1970, Vol. 222, 104-115.

Hochberg, J., and U. Brooks. Pictorial Recognition as an Unlearned Ability: A Study of One Child's Performance. *American Journal of Psychology,* 1962, Vol. 75, 624-628.

Hochberg, J., and E. McAlister. A Quantitative Approach to Figural Goodness. *Journal of Experimental Psychology,* 1953, Vol. 46, 361-364.

Kennedy, J.M. *A Psychology of Picture Perception.* San Francisco: Jossey-Bass, 1974.

Peucker, T. Computer Cartography, Commission on College Geography, Resource Paper No. 17, Association of American Geographers, Washington, D.C., 1972.

Rayner, J.N. *An Introduction to Spectral Analysis*. London: Monographs in Spatial and Environmental Systems Analysis, 1971.

Shannon, C.E. A Mathematical Theory of Communication. *Bell System Technical Journal*, 1948, Vol. 27, 379-423 and 623-656.

Tobler, W. Of Maps and Matrices. *Journal of Regional Science*, 1967, Vol. 7, 275-280.

Tobler, W. Geographical Filters and Their Inverses. *Geographical Analysis,* 1969, Vol. I, 234-253.

Software Cited

Title	Source of Software
CITY	North Carolina Educational Computing Service
CALFORM	Harvard Laboratory for Computer Graphics
DABBLE	Thomas Pricket, University of Oklahoma Computing Center
FACES	Computer Research Center for Economics and Management Research, National Bureau of Economic Research
LANDUSE	see *LANDUSE: A Computer Program for Laboratory Use in Economic Geography Courses*, Duane Marble and Bruce Anderson, Technical Paper No. 8, Association of American Geographers, Washington, D.C., 1972.
SYMAP	Harvard Laboratory for Computer Graphics
SYMVU	Harvard Laboratory for Computer Graphics
TROLL	Computer Research Center for Economics and Management Research, National Bureau of Economic Research.

Note

[1] The author gratefully acknowledges the assistance of Thomas Pricket, University of Oklahoma, in preparing portions of the graphics for this paper.

17.
ALL: Automated Learning Laboratory

B. James Starr
Howard University

Sally A. Flanik
Howard University

Many of the smaller institutions offering instruction in psychology have neither the budget nor the facilities to support laboratory courses. Nonetheless, many such institutions have access to one or more time-sharing terminals. As Green (1972) has pointed out, this milieu is suitable for the use of the computer as an instructional aid. Recent years have witnessed the creation of a variety of computer programs directed toward instruction in various areas of psychology. Thus, Lehman, Starr, and Young (1975) have presented a review of such programs in the teaching of statistics and research methods (see the paper by Lehman, Starr, and Young in this volume). Relatively few programs have been developed and disseminated for other areas of psychology. This paper briefly describes a few of these endeavors and then discusses a program developed by the authors that treats response learning in a computer *qua* laboratory setting.

Some programs have been developed for use in various experimental psychology courses. An ambitious and apparently successful package of programs for use in a course in cognitive psychology was written by Bewley (1973, 1974). Six experiments provide the instructional vehicle for this package. Computer programs, written in time-sharing BASIC for use from a teletype terminal, present the tasks to the students. The students then evaluate their performances *vis-a-vis* that of the model. The procedures lead the students to experimentation both with features of the model and with other human subjects. The package contains experiments on pattern recognition, short- and long-term memory, concept learning, decision-making, and problem-solving (see the paper by Bewley in this volume).

Another important package has been developed by Main (1971; see also the Main paper in this volume). The EXPER SIM program was developed at the University of Michigan to teach students experimental design. The system allows students to engage in repeated experimentation in specific rescarch areas via computer modeling. This permits students to conduct many more "experiments" than would be normal in a typical course. Moreover, the student may actually pursue a "program" of research with regard to a specific area and may learn from the work of others. Thus, the student in many ways really enters a microcosm of the world of research. Perhaps the most interesting feature from the viewpoint of the present authors is that the outcomes are modified (i.e., made substantively accurate) with changes in the "real world" state of knowledge in the area. The system currently has imprinting, social facilitation, drug research, etiology of schizophrenia, and motivation as research areas. Others are to be added to this list.

Green (1972) has described and presented a variety of programs that provide useful experiences for students in problem-solving, concept formation, and decision-making. The programs operate on the responses of the students who serve as research subjects. As with the other programs described here, the student not only gains first-hand experience as a research subject (and/or research in Bewley's package and EXPER SIM), but he also produces computer output that is useful for didactic purposes.

The authors' own effort, the ALL program, was designed to give beginning students a variety of controlled experience with principles of response learning in an actual learning situation. ALL is used to run students through one of several simple learning tasks and record the performance of each individual in two formats. The student receives a record of his performance and the instructor obtains a summary record of the performance of all participants in the experiment.

Stimuli and Tasks

ALL's stimuli are numerical. The program prints out two numbers and the student is asked to respond with a third number.

Currently, the program comprises four tasks. These elementary tasks are analogs of simple response learning tasks that have long been used in research on rats and/or college sophomores. The student may receive stimuli where he is required to respond with the number that appears first (or second, i.e., a position learning task). A second task involves the student's responding with an absolute item (say, the number "4" each time). The remaining two tasks pose serial learning problems. The student must respond with the next item in the series. The simpler version of this problem employs an additive or multiplicative (positive or negative) constant to generate the series. The complex version creates the appropriate numerical stimuli by using first an additive constant and then a (different) multiplicative one.

The program can be used to vary both the type of reinforcement and the schedule of reinforcement. These variables permit manipulation and thus provide a basis for research with regard to their effect on acquisition and extinction of the desired behaviors. Thus, the student may receive positive (RIGHT) or negative (WRONG) reinforcement, or both. In addition, the reinforcement may be continuous or partial (with both fixed- and variable-ratio types available under partial reinforcement). The fixed-ratio schedule may involve the reinforcement of every other (appropriate) trial or every third, fourth, or fifth (appropriate) trial. Reinforcement may also occur on a variable-ratio schedule with a mean fixed by the experimenter.

Suggestions for Use

Although there were originally two versions of ALL, only one will be detailed here. (Other versions are briefly described below.) The two versions differ only in the way in which the program parameters are selected. In the random version, the task and the type and schedule of reinforcement are all randomly selected. The instructor does not control the selection process. While this version may be advantageous in environments where the program may be run by individuals who lack computer skills, much of the power and instructional value (in terms of controlled experimentation) of this approach would be lost. Therefore, the random version is not further described here.

The fixed version can easily be used to run experiments. Given the present program structure, a variety of one-factor and higher-order investigations are conceivable. The data so generated might provide the springboard for various important experiences. Thus, a number of data analytic skills could be developed or sharpened. Specialized techniques involving curves and curve-fitting are applicable. Moreover, the student gains two invaluable experiences. One tangible benefit is that the student has examined an integrated research venture from start to finish, with relatively little energy expenditure in terms of data collection. In most of his classes the student is exposed only to selected aspects of a research endeavor. Furthermore, the student may also have the advantage of viewing the process from the vantage point of both the experimenter and the research subject.

ALL shares this capacity to offer the student a dualistic experiential research role with Bewley's (1973, 1974) package. It also provides the opportunity for the student to be paced through an orderly progression, going from these roles to a point where he can engage in some programmatic research (as with EXPER SIM) in the area of response learning. ALL is one of few programs focusing on concepts propaedeutic to the study of learning. By integrating aspects of computer-assisted instruction and process (e.g., experimental) control (Scholz, 1972), it attempts to give the student a flavor of the research process.

Description of Function

The fixed version of ALL permits the instructor or experimenter to specify the experimental conditions prior to program run. The instructor responds to a number of interrogations by the computer with values for parameters that together determine the nature of the particular investigation. Thus, parameters are entered indicating the type and schedule of reinforcement, the type of task, the number of acquisition trials, the number of extinction trials, the maximum number of subjects to be run under these conditions, and constants to be used in the serial tasks. An additional parameter is used to help generate the starting point for the task, i.e., the first stimulus number for the task. In all, there are 12 major variables.

After entry of the parameters, the program spaces the paper, allowing removal of the information prior to running the first research subject. When the research subject enters, the program requests his name and student number. Following this an introductory message is printed and the task is initiated. The student responds and the appropriate type of reinforcement is meted out according to the selected schedule. The process continues until the student has obtained the required number of acquisition trials. Next the procedure is continued without reinforcement until the specified number of extinction trials is reached.

After the student has completed the requisite number of trials, the bookkeeping routine prints out the student's name and number and a summary of the number and percentage of correct responses during both acquisition and extinction. This module also updates the file to be printed for the instructor and spaces the paper to allow the student to remove and carry off his record.

When there are no further subjects to be run, the instructor enters "LAST SUBJECT" (unnecessary when specified number of subjects have been run). This leads to printing of the summary information on all the research subjects employed in the study.

Programming Details and Availability

The version of ALL described here is written in time-sharing BASIC and has been run on an IBM 370/145 computer. Its immediate ancestors have been used on both IBM 360/50 and CDC 6400 machines. The program is written as a number of modular routines that, despite the absence of a standard for the BASIC language, appear to be reasonably transportable. The program involves about 350 lines and occupies about 16.4K bytes of file storage.

A third version of ALL, consisting of the modules employed in the version described here plus several other modules, is also available. It is expected that this version would be more appealing to users with some programming skill and limitations on storage allocations at their facilities. The modular structure will allow for on-site merging of only those routines actually required during a particular computer run. The additional modules consist of a number of other tasks and a statistical routine. The statistical routine provides for the computation of various univariate (e.g., median, skewness index) and bivariate (e.g., correlation between acquisition and extinction performances) statistics. The additional task routines include choosing the largest (or smallest) number from the stimuli presented and a maze learning task. Another modification currently being added to this version will lead to research designs involving "random effects" independent variables. Thus, for example, the researcher will have the option of specifying the levels of fixed-ratio partial reinforcement to be used in his design or of having the computer randomly select these levels.

A variety of other changes, potentially useful in certain settings, have been contemplated. Although the authors may eventually incorporate some of these alterations, they are briefly described here with the hope that they may be of more immediate benefit to interested users.

Clearly, a language more flexible than BASIC would have a number of advantages. First, certain aspects of the coding could be simplified through the use of statements allowing multiple branches. Second, using a language with more output flexibility in terms of computer graphics and a cathode-ray tube (CRT) would allow the inclusion of some discrimination learning tasks. Another possible set of tasks might involve the choice of vowels (or consonants) from letter sets. In addition, options for various criteria for acquisition and extinction might be built in to any of these versions.

ALL is available on both paper tape and microfiche. The documentation and program can be obtained, at a cost of $5, from:

Sally A. Flanik
Department of Psychology
Howard University
Washington, D.C. 20059

Please specify whether paper tape, microfiche, or hardcopy only is desired. Unless another version of ALL is specified, the fixed version described here will be sent. That's ALL.

References

Bewley, W.L. The Use of Time-Shared Terminals in a Human Learning Course. *Proceedings of the Fourth Conference on*

Computers in the Undergraduate Curricula, The Claremont Colleges, Claremont, California, 1973.

Bewley, W.L. *Cognitive Psychology: A Computer-Oriented Laboratory Manual*, Project COMPUTe, Hanover, N.H., 1974.

Green, B.F., Jr. The Use of Time-Shared Terminals in Psychology. *Behavior Research Methods & Instrumentation*, 1972, *4*, 51-55.

Lehman, R.S., B.J. Starr, and K.E. Young. Computer Aids in Teaching Statistics and Methodology. *Behavior Research Methods & Instrumentation*, 1975, *7*, 93-102.

Main, D. A Computer Simulation Approach for Teaching Experimental Design. *Proceedings of the 79th Annual Convention of the American Psychological Association*, American Psychological Association, Washington, D.C., 1971.

Scholz, K.W. Computerized Process Control in Behavioral Science Research. *Behavior Research Methods & Instrumentation*, 1972, *4*, 203-208.

18.
A Case for Computer Modeling in the Political Science Classroom

James W. Hottois
University of San Diego

Stuart H. Rakoff
United Mine Workers of America

This paper deals with the shortcomings of readily usable materials for computer-related undergraduate instruction in political science, and proposes a solution in one instructional area. A study by EDUCOM (1972) has identified the vicious circle that must be broken if progress along these lines is to be made. Starting from the premise that the effectiveness of the computer in education must be demonstrated, and then asking how effectiveness can be shown, we are led to recognize that effectiveness requires good material, which in turn requires good people devoting large blocks of time and effort, which in turn requires professional support and recognition for these activities, as well as funds. But, to complete the circle, these rewards and supports will not be available until effectiveness can be demonstrated convincingly.

Despite the odds against such progress, recent developments have begun to break the circle and lend some hope to the future for computer-related instructional materials in political science. A survey of the available materials indicates that they tend to fall into two categories. First, we find several inductive, data-analysis based packages, and second, a number of simulations and games in various subject areas, particularly international politics.

By far, most of the materials developed have been of the data-analysis type. The packages produced at Minnesota, the Iowa package, Dartmouth's IMPRESS, the VOTER project at Michigan, the ICPR data analysis learning packages, the SUNY II learning packages, and other individual packages that follow these lines all share a number of similarities. They are essentially empirical, theory-free sets of data along with an accompanying set of programs or routines to do simple statistical analysis, usually cross-tabulation with some contingency statistics. The approach is to let the student search through the data, generate hypotheses, and then test them with the data set and programs in the package.

While this inductive approach is no doubt better than failing to introduce students to data at all, and while it certainly does emulate the empirical analysis typical of the profession, it may in the long run do a disservice to both the student and the discipline of political science. The exercises in these packages rarely require the student to get involved in the serious questions of political research and theory-building, and therefore present a view of political science that can be accepted as either revealing the essential irrelevance of quantitative analysis or as reinforcing a negative view of political science as number-crunching. Neither of these is the attitude we should strive to leave with our undergraduate students.

Simulations and games, on the other hand, solve some of these problems but also raise others. Based on an explicit statement of the relationships involved in a process, simulations at least begin to consider the problems of theory in a somewhat systematic fashion. William Coplin and Michael O'Leary (1972a) have specified five goals that use of a simulation, in this case PRINCE, can help to achieve: "(1) Introducing the student to basic facts about contemporary international relations; (2) Providing the student with a *framework* for understanding these facts; (3) Introducing *social science methods* and informing the student of *current theory and research* in international relations; (4) Improving the student's *decision-making and planning skills*; and (5) Helping the student to deal with the problems of effectively *organizing a group* to undertake complex decision-making" (Coplin and O'Leary, 1972a, p. 459). Yet, a close analysis of PRINCE suggests that it neither introduces students to social science methods nor to theory (goal 3). Rather, PRINCE focuses primarily on goals (4) and (5) only secondarily on goals (1) and (2). The "framework" provided by PRINCE is not explicitly related to current theory and, in fact, it may not be possible to so relate it. Many others have acknowledged the power of a well-designed simulation in an undergraduate course, especially one for which the underlying model is simple and elegant. These models and simulations are most common, for social sciences, in the field of economics, where a number of such models have been translated into games and simulations of various market and macro processes. But political science lacks many of these elegant models. Thus, simulations of political phenomenon tend to be somewhat less well grounded in theory. Instead, they tend to emphasize a set of almost *ad hoc* parameters that act upon student decisions as the students play the simulation, either against the program or through the algorithm of the program against other students. Constructing such a complex system is a time-consuming and expensive undertaking, which probably explains why comparatively fewer simulations for classroom use have been developed than the relatively easily produced data-analysis packages.

Most of the simulations produced by political scientists have been for research rather than teaching purposes. The classroom simulations might more appropriately be called simulation games, for their central feature seems to be using a computerized model to process student decisions and provide stimulae for a new round of inputs, rather than allowing the student or researcher to explore what happens to the modeled process under different sets of conditions. The best developed simulation games have been in the field of international politics, including PRINCE, the Inter-Nation Simulation of Harold Guetzkow, and Robert Noel's game.

In all simulation games, the underlying model or theory is almost transparent to the student, and none of the simulation games is designed to allow the student to evaluate and change the behavior of the model as opposed to changing his own behavior. The simulation becomes a black box that may in the end not teach the student very much at all about the underlying theory.

As indicated above, the full potential of the computer in the undergraduate political science curriculum has not begun to be tapped. In particular, the use of the computer to allow the student and instructor to formulate and test alternative models of the political system has hardly been appreciated. The solution is to develop interactive models.

The primary benefits of well-designed interactive models seem to be: (1) an increase in student interest in the subject matter; (2)

development of student appreciation of the complexity of policy-makers' problems; (3) utilization of a greater number of and more sophisticated economic models; (4) improvement in ability to illustrate the practical value of theory and statistics in dealing with complex problems; (5) a stimulus to the faculty to be more precise in specifying economic relationships (programming requires the development of precise, functional forms and parameter specifications, which causes somewhat more deliberation on the part of the instructor); and (6) greater repetition and variety in expressing the same basic educational messages (Naylor and Baird, 1971).

While these goals were outlined for a set of interactive models in economics, if they are seen broadly, they might be applied to political science. They have the advantage of involving both the instructor and students in more precise reading, definition, and evaluation of the theoretical and empirical literature in a field. Interactive models permit comparison of the assertions of different writers against actual data sets. Well developed programs would also allow the student to propose and test his own models. In all of this, the gap between empirical research and theory building is bridged because the student is forced to deal with data within a rather precisely formulated theoretical framework. Thus, the shortcomings of data analysis packages and black box simulations are avoided, while the advantages of both are attained.

Interactive modeling might be employed in any number of standard political science courses. The only requirements are that a body of theory be available for the students to interact with and that data be available to the students. We have chosen to demonstrate the relevance of interactive modeling in the voting behavior area. This could include courses in voting behavior, Presidential elections, the Presidency, or political behavior. We chose voting behavior as an illustrative course for a number of reasons. There is a rich theoretical literature in the field with sharp and easily identified disagreements between major points of view. Those disagreements, in turn, reflect upon serious issues regarding representative democracy. Yet, the number of commonly accepted explanatory models is relatively small; and, for the most part, they have been developed and tested using similar data sets. Moreover, the study of voting behavior has been heavily dependent upon quantitative techniques and data, and the necessary data are readily available through the Inter-University Consortium for Political Research.

Our plan in the following sections of this paper is to outline briefly the theoretical frameworks employed in voting behavior in order to define the parameters of the field. The discussion of theoretical frameworks is related to a discussion of the different simulations that have been developed as a part of the literature. The intent of this section is to show the relevance of interactive modeling in instruction in voting behavior and to suggest the shortcomings of existing simulations as teaching tools. Thus, this section is both developmental and critical in its approach. Then, we outline a system for interactive modeling referred to as TAMIVOC (Testing Alternative Models of Individual Vote Choice). TAMIVOC provides a bridge between the data analysis packages currently found in the field and the theory that defines the study of voting behavior.

Models of Voting Behavior

This section seeks to outline the major theoretical positions in the voting behavior literature and to describe and criticize computer models or simulations related to that literature. The discussion is divided into three parts. First we consider the analytic frameworks from which the models are drawn. Much of this discussion is based on the groundwork supplied by Shaffer (1972). Next, we analyze the models in terms of their applications. Is a particular model intended to explore a theory of elections? Is it "explanatory?" Or, does a model seek to simulate candidate strategies given hypotheses about the behavior of voters? Is it a "strategy" game? Finally, we discuss the difference between simulation and modeling in order to show that some of the work reported as simulation is actually not simulation in a strict definitional sense.

The literature on voting behavior has three different analytic perspectives, each of which represents a main current in the micro-level study of voting behavior. These approaches view the voter as either a psychological, a sociological, or a rational being.

The approach with the widest currency in political science is the psychological approach proposed by researchers at the Survey

Research Center (SRC), University of Michigan. The model has its fullest explication in *The American Voter* (Campbell *et al.*, 1964). This psychological approach proposes that the voting act is caused by numerous factors that combine until very few are left just prior to the voting act. The final causes, or "components," of voting choice are: (1) attitude toward Democratic candidate; (2) attitude toward Republican candidate; (3) group-related attitudes; (4) attitudes toward the parties as managers of government; (5) attitudes on domestic issues; (6) attitudes on foreign policy issues (Campbell *et al.*, p. 271). The SRC approach hypothesies that each voter balances his partisan predispositions on each component against his partisan predispositions on each other component in arriving at a voting choice. That is, the voter seeks balance within the cognitive field surrounding the voting choice.

The SRC model has certain obvious faults. Shaffer has pointed out that the six components are highly inter-correlated, suggesting that each component "reflects a more general dimension of attitude than its name would imply" (1972, p. 135). However, Campbell *et al.*, (1964) demonstrated that the components were not highly dependent upon party identification, and Shaffer (1972) fails to suggest a viable alternative explanation for their findings. More seriously, one might question the SRC model because it gives relatively equal weight to each of the components. Some work has suggested, for example, that domestic issues are almost always more important than foreign policy issues in affecting voters' decisions. Finally, the SRC model is not dynamic. It does not account for trends in the electorate and it is not sensitive to the issue of component differentiation.

Several models have drawn from the SRC approach. Shaffer (1972) operationalized the SRC model using 1964 election data collected by SRC. The SRC model predicted the votes of the survey respondents correctly in 19.5% of the cases. The greatest error appeared in the prediction of abstention, where non-voting was notably underpredicted.

Coombs, Fried, and Robinovitz (1968) draw upon the SRC model for the basic "voter decision module" in their election simulation. Rather than relying on a summation of the six components, the authors utilized the theory of cognitive balance that underlies the model. They look at the emphasis a candidate gives to an issue compared to the emphasis the voter gives to the issue. The result of the first comparison is then compared to the voters' party preference and strength of party preference to obtain probabilities about whether the respondent will vote. The result is then fed into a longer electoral process model. Unhappily, there is no mention as to whether the authors ever actually wrote the programs for the model or how well the model actually worked. The same algorithm was applied earlier by John Kessel.

Kessel (1966) suggested a novel application of the SRC approach. Kessel's model employs game theory and collapses the SRC six components into three for each candidate. The components for each party's candidate in a two-party system are: (1) candidate's personal qualities; (2) orientation toward the party itself; and (3) orientation toward issues. The model assumes that candidates act rationally in attempting to maximize their strengths and minimize their weaknesses. The outcome is a prediction of partisan advantage that may be transformed into a percentage of vote and compared to the actual two-party vote. This model rests upon micropolitical theory. But, unlike the others just described, the model does not predict individual vote preferences. Thus, it is essentially macro-level.

The Kessel model is tautological as defined and as operationalized by Klassen and McGrath in *Elect* (1973). It is not possible to determine whether the utilities in the voter preference matrix existed at the beginning of the campaign or whether they were created by the candidate's strategy choices during the campaign. The SRC model posits that the components exist just prior to the voting act and thus are outcomes of campaign forces rather elements of them. Kessel may have been cognizant of this difficulty, since he suggested some modifications of the algorithm that would make it into a "campaign game." Klassen and McGrath have incorporated some of those modifications into "Elect 3" (discussed below). The modifications do not, however, speak to the basic problem of locating voter attitudes PRIOR to the beginning of the campaign.

Paul F. Lazersfeld and his colleagues have suggested a sociological approach to voting analysis, first in *The People's Choice* (Lazersfeld, Berelson, Gaudet, 1944) and then in *Voting* (Berelson, Lazersfeld, and McPhee, 1954). The sociological perspective focuses upon the voter as a member of various strata or groups. Sociologists of voting have noted that the members of a group tend to vote the same way over long periods of time. In some situations a voter comes under "cross pressures." Cross pressure can occur if the voter occupies statuses that pull him in different directions or if he has issue positions that are not congruent with a single party's position. The sociology of voting relies on the interaction between group members or reference group theory to explain the consistency of group voting.

The best known model of voting behavior is the so-called simulmatics model developed by Pool, Abelson, and Popkin (1965). The simulmatics model rests squarely on the two basic precepts of the sociological approach: groups are consistent and stable in their partisan predispositions, and cross-pressured voters will tend not to vote as a way of avoiding the psychological (or sociological?) conflict which cross-pressures imply.

The first step in the simulmatics approach involves development of a classification system. In the model a voter is classified as one of 480 possible voter types. Survey data are then used to determine the position of any particular voter-type concerning any one of 52 issue clusters. The result is a 480 x 52 matrix of voter-types and issue-clusters.

Using the theory of cross-pressures, the simulmatics group created a series of predictive equations comparing the issue stands of various groups to their propensity to vote Democratic. Since cross-pressures predicted abstention, they included estimates of the cross-pressures' effect in causing potential voters to abstain. A new set of equations is prepared for each issue and each voter type that is hypothesized to be affected by the issue. The outcome can be stated in terms of electoral votes by creating pseudo-states.

The simulmatics model is impressive in its sophistication and in its adaptability as a predictive device. Yet, the model has some serious shortcomings. The theoretical basis of the model rests upon the notion of a static electorate and fails to account for shifts in the electorate (Key, 1955). More seriously, the sociological model fails to take account of short-term forces operating on the electorate. Finally, the simulmatics model in operation is both issue and election specific, since a different set of equations and assumptions is necessary for each new run of the model.

William McPhee suggested a sociological model that has not had wide currency in political science. McPhee's model, which includes several feedback loops, seeks to simulate the forces acting on the electorate over several voting periods. The model includes three processes that act on a voter; (1) "simulation process" where the appeals of candidates or issues of the campaign are brought to bear upon the voter; (2) "discussion process" where the voter (denoted as ego) tests his preferences in discussion with some significant other (alter); and (3) "learning process" where the voter internalizes his decision for the current election as a predisposition for the next election.

The model was operationalized and tested against real election data and hypothetical data (McPhee and Ferguson, 1962). The power of the McPhee model is in its representation of a social system and in the way it incorporates election dynamics—both within a single election period and over several elections. The model does not provide useful predictions of a particular election nor is it amenable to use with survey data without extensive modification.

Finally, we come to models of electoral behavior that posit voters who behave according to rational principles. The most thorough theorizing in this area remains Anthony Downs' *An Economic Theory of Democracy* (1957). Downs' basic premise may be stated simply: in deciding whether and how to vote, a voter compares his expected utility payoff if party A is in office to his expected utility if party B holds office. He then votes for whichever party will provide him with the greatest benefit. If there is no differential, the voter abstains. This simple model is then modified in order to account for the uncertainty of future events, the costs of gathering information, and the normative value of voting. It is these latter modifications that make the model complex and difficult to operationalize.

Shaffer has constructed a model of Downs' voting system based upon 1964 Survey Research Center election study data. Shaffer (1972) estimated six parameters of voting behavior: (1) differential intensity index; (2) information cost index; (3) perceived closeness index; (4) long-run participation value index; (5) ideological congruence index; and (6) performance rating.

Shaffer used his model to test the relative importance of each of the parameters in the voting choice. He found that with all parameters weighted equally 42.3 percent of the votes were predicted accurately. The only change that made a noticeable difference was the removal of the information cost parameter that raised "the predictive accuracy of the simulation to 58.6 percent." Shaffer concluded that the Downs model, without the information cost parameter, was a better predictor of voter choice than any of the other then available models.

Each of the models discussed here was developed to achieve different purposes. The majority of election simulations have been oriented toward explanation. Some voting models are primarily strategy oriented. Some models are predictive.

All of the studies reported above have been referred to by their authors as "simulations." But many of them are not simulations in a strict definitional sense of that term. Simulations generally are understood to include process as one aspect of the system that they model (Evan, Wallace, and Sutherland, 1967). As such, simulations generally pass through successive states in a chronological sequence of state histories. A simulation may be differentiated from a model that is a symbolic representation of some systems without the additional requirement of a state history.

Shaffer's (1972) six-component model represents a complex model rather than a simulation in the sense just described. The six-component model does not pass through successive states and no state history is produced. The model itself is static. Using the same restrictive definition, both the simulations approach and Kessel's (1966) approach modeled in "ELECT 1-2" (Klassen and McGrath, 1973) may be classified as static models. Neither model involves process and neither produces successive system states.

Four of the models reviewed above are easily recognized as computer simulations using the strict criteria employed here. Shaffer's Downsian model is a simulation to the extent that the model has clearly specified processes between decision points. The fact that Shaffer does not monitor the state of his system at any particular point is of little importance since it is possible to do so.

Coombs' (1968) model is also a clear application of computer simulation. The model includes several clear decision points and creates a state history through successive stages of the campaign which is being modeled.

"ELECT 3" (Kessel, 1966; Klassen and McGrath, 1973) may also be considered in the category of simulations. The game allows a player-candidate to make various decisions during the course of a campaign and then periodically feeds back information concerning the state of the system resulting from his campaign decisions.

Finally, McPhee's (1962) model must clearly be placed within the simulation category. The model is intended to represent the long-term forces acting upon the electorate across several electoral periods. The state of the system may be monitored at the end of any particular election.

The teaching algorithms most clearly fitting our restrictive definition of simulation possess a common characteristic. They are all strategy, rational-actor oriented. Elect 1-2-3 (Klassen and McGrath, 1973) is the only election model widely available for classroom use. Like PRINCE (Coplin and O'Leary, 1972) it presents the student with a black box that somehow turns strategy decisions into outcomes. Unlike PRINCE, Elect 1-2-3 is based on a well developed theoretical framework. Yet, Elect tells the student no more about that theoretical framework than PRINCE does about its theory. Indeed, the suggested readings accompanying Elect emphasize campaign strategy rather than electoral behavior. Thus, the only commonly available classroom oriented model (or simulation) of voting shares the weakness of inter-nation simulations. Elect is atheoretical like PRINCE.

The Models and Classroom Applications

The models reviewed above are primarily of two types. With the exception of Kessel's model, each is either a switching or additive (or linear) model. Kessel's model is multiplicative and is based upon the following equation:

OUTCOME = (vector of candidate A's strategies) x (matrix of voter preferences) x (vector of candidate B's strategies)

The switching-type models are by far the most interesting and complex. In a switching model different conditions lead to different paths in the model. Thus, in the Downs model a voter with zero or near zero party differential is switched to a routine to determine whether there is any long-term participation value for that voter. The result of that inquiry may in turn lead to a decision to vote or not depending upon the long-term value of participation for the voter. The McPhee model is also a switching-type model.

Switching models are more amenable to simulation than other sorts of models. They represent process as a flow of various decisions and results interacting with each other within some system of interactions. By their very nature they go beyond a static, moment-of-time description of a system. And, as such, they generally represent the forces of a campaign or series of campaigns better than other sorts of models. However, the complexities of switching models make them difficult to operationalize. There are virtually no data available that allow the analyst to estimate the parameters of the system being modeled.

It is interesting to note that neither McPhee's model nor Coombs' model (which also involves switching) has had wide currency in the discipline. Switching models are also difficult for students to operationalize. The complexity of the models makes estimation of the various parameters nearly impossible for any but the most experienced analyst.

Additive or linear models permit simpler classroom presentation and do not restrict hypothesis testing. The psychological models drawing from the SRC six-components approach are all additive. The basic equations in the sociology of voting may also be expressed in additive form. Additive models permit instructors to introduce modeling to students who are relatively unsophisticated in mathematics or statistical analysis. This is important, since a primary goal in classroom applications is to provide students with a device that allows them to develop a sense of the politics of elections as a system rather than as a series of discrete variables. An equally important goal is to introduce students to the idea of modeling within a simple but meaningful framework. Students do not need to be distracted, at the outset at least, with questions of technique.

TAMIVOC

With this background we turn to a description of a system for testing alternative models of individual vote choice—TAMIVOC. TAMIVOC may be operationalized on either interactive or batch processing systems, with either large or small core; it requires access to election data of the sort supplied by the ICPR and requires peripheral storage on small core machines.

TAMIVOC presents the student with a straightforward problem: What characteristics of a voter best predict his vote and what is the relative importance of the different characteristics determining a voter's choice. TAMIVOC gauges student success by comparing predicted to reported votes.

TAMIVOC operates with a simple algorithm:

$$VOTE = WD_1 + WD_2 + \ldots + WD_N$$

Where VOTE = Predicted vote for Democratic or Republican candidate or no vote.

Di = the ith characteristic (or variable) that the student feels should impact upon the voting choice. This must be expressed as either a pro-Democratic (+1) or pro-Republician (-1) or "no difference" (0) score.

W = the weight (0 to 1) that the student wishes attached to the Di element.

The student must specify the values of VOTE, e.g., which values of Di are to be understood as a pro-Democratic, a pro-Republican, and (optionally) an abstention. The student may choose to seek to predict any one of the following:

(1) Democratic-Republican split.
(2) Democratic-Republican-abstention split.
(3) vote-abstain.

Routines are included for recoding the desired variables along with instructions for the recoding. The weight parameter (w) is optional and assumes a value of 1 if none is entered.

The availability of the weighting parameter is important for at least two reasons. First, the weighting allows students to test their hunches about the relative importance of various characteristics in the voter's decision-making. Second, it allows students to run sensitivity tests on the models that they construct in order to determine empirically the relative importance of various characteristics.

The student may also choose to use normalized scores. If this option is chosen, the program first recodes the data, computing means and standard deviations. It then transforms the Di's into Z-scores before doing the calculations. The new equation is:

$$VOTE = WZ_1 + WZ_2 + \ldots + WZ_N.$$

The use of Z-scores itself affects the impact of a variable upon the outcome of the equation according to the distribution of the characteristic, as recoded, in the population.

Classroom application of TAMIVOC is relatively straight-forward. The student and instructor must carefully consider the voting behavior literature, focusing particularly on the predictive utility of the different theories. The instructor must provide the student with a short explanation of linear models, relating them to the TAMIVOC algorithm. And, of course, some instruction in the mechanics of computers must take place, as well as a discussion of the information requested by TAMIVOC. The interactive version of TAMIVOC can provide the student with prompts.

It is best to start with a simple problem. For instance, a student might be asked to test a model that predicted vote choice simply as a function of party identification and the vote in the previous Presidential election. First, the student would choose the election for which he wished to test this model, assuming that data for multiple elections are available. Then, having entered with a well-defined verbal theory, the student would operationalize the two concepts in the theory, party identification and previous vote. In this case, the translation from concept to indicator is straightforward.

The next step is for the student to recode the values of these indicators to conform to a consistent Republican-Democratic scale, which runs, say, from -1 to +1. In interactive models the program would ask for and the student would input the values for the recodes. Then the student would be asked for and input the regression coefficients to be associated with each of these variables. How much will he weight party identification as opposed to previous vote? A good first experience might be for the instructor to suggest initial values for these parameters that yielded only fair results, and then allow the student to change them on subsequent trials. Finally, the student must specify the range of values for the calculated dependent variable, vote choice, which are to be associated with Republican or Democratic votes, and those associated with non-voting. As an aid to this, the program will calculate and print at this point the range that predicted vote could take, based upon the selected recodes and parameters.

Figure 1

Table of TAMIVOC Results

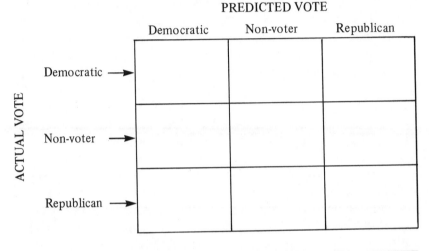

PREDICTED VOTE

The program will now access and process the proper data set and variables, and will recode the variables according to the input specifications. Having read and recoded the data, the program will then calculate a predicted vote for each subject, compare that predicted vote to the reported vote of that respondent, and on the basis of the comparison, increment one cell of Figure 1.

The student then receives his output, in the form of a filled-in table, a percentage breakdown of that table, some contingency statistics for the table, and a listing of the mean and standard deviation of each of his variables.

With this information, the student is able to evaluate the predictive ability of the model he has tested, and in interactive applications he will then be asked if he wants to re-enter the program to modify either his selection of variables, his recoding scheme, or his parameters. If he does, he will be returned to the beginning of the program and asked for the changes he wishes to make. If not, he will be asked if he wants to test the model against a different data set, and if so, will enter the name of that data set and begin again. If he has completed his testing, he will sign-off and return to write up the results and his conclusions.

After this initial rather structured exposure to the operation of the TAMIVOC system, the student is prepared to move to more complex verbal theories, either drawn from the literature or based upon his own reading and thought, and test them using the system. In any case, it is important for the instructor to monitor the process, especially in terms of the statement of the verbal models and the operationalization of the concepts. The TAMIVOC system should be seen as an adjunct to the instructor, not as a substitute.

Advantages of TAMIVOC

The bulk of this paper has focused on two basic points. First, we have raised several objections to computer-related instructional materials described as either data anlysis packages or simulations. Second, we have explored the rich body of literature on voting behavior and its application in computer simulations. The thrust of our critique of existing CRI materials is that they are atheoretical, treating theory as something that is never made explicit in the first instance or something in a black box in the second. We believe that TAMIVOC takes theory out of the black box and forces students to treat it as something explicit in understanding political behavior.

TAMIVOC draws on the voting behavior literature, yet it is not based on a single theory or, necessarily, a single data set. It forces the student to become aware of the important literature on voting behavior and also provides impetus for instructors to make explicit the nuances of that literature. Unlike either simulations or data analysis packages, TAMIVOC forces students to model complex relationships between variables while focusing on the prediction of voter behavior that is the primary concern of the voting behavior literature. TAMIVOC does this within the confines of a simple linear model, yet, as the review of the literature indicates,the most common explanations of voting behavior rely upon linear models.

TAMIVOC differs from other classroom simulations in an important respect. TAMIVOC is not a strategy game. This is an important consideration because strategy simulations such as PRINCE (Coplin and O'Leary, 1972) and Elect (Klassen and McGrath 1973) force the user into the role of political actor. TAMIVOC forces the user into the role of political scientist. Data analysis packages accomplish part of this goal. But they focus on the empiricist tendencies within political science and fail to alert students to the role of theory in the search for explanation. TAMIVOC directs the user's attention toward the role of theory in prediction and explanation.

References

Berelson, B.R., P.F. Lazersfeld, and W. McPhee. *Voting*. Chicago: University of Chicago Press, 1954.

Campbell, A.P., E. Converse, W.E. Miller, and D.E. Stokes. *The American Voter*. New York: John Wiley & Sons, 1964.

Coombs, S.L., M. Fried, and S.H. Robinovitz. An Approach to Election Simulation Through a Modular System. William D. Coplin (Ed.), *Simulation in the Study of Politics*. Chicago: Markham Publishing Co., 1968.

Coplin, W.D., and M.K. O'Leary. Educational Use of PRINCE. *CCUC*, 1972a, 459-562.

Coplin, W.D., and M.K. O'Leary. *Everyman's* PRINCE. Belmont, California: Duxbury Press, 1972b.

Downs, A. *An Economic Theory of Democracy*. New York: Harper & Row, 1957.

EDUCOM. Factors Inhibiting the Use of Computers in Instruction: EDUCOM, Princeton, N.J., 1972.

Evans, II, G.W., F. Wallace, and G.L. Sutherland. *Simulation Using Digital Computers*. Englewood Cliffs, N.J.: Prentice-Hall, 1967.

Kessel, J.H., A Game Theory Analysis of Campaign Strategy. In M. Kent Jennings and L. Harmon Zeigler (Eds.), *The Electoral Process*. Englewood Cliffs, N.J.: Prentice-Hall, 1966.

Key, Jr., V.O., A Theory of Critical Elections. *Journal of Politics*, 1955, *17*, 3-18.

Klassen, D., and J. McGrath. ELECT 1-2-3 (State University of New York, 1973). Distributed as part of the HUNTINGTON II project.

Lazersfeld, P., B. Berelson, and H. Gaudet. *The People's Choice*. New York: Columbia University Press, 1944.

McPhee, W., and J. Ferguson. Political Immunization. In W. McPhee and W.A. Glaser (Eds.), *Public Opinion and Congressional Elections*. New York: The Free Press, 1962.

Naylor, J.A., and W.M. Baird. Interactive Simulation-Games in Economics, *CCUC,* 1971.

Pool, I. deS., R.P. Abelson, and S. Popkin. *Candidates, Issues, and Strategies: A Computer Simulation of the 1960 and 1964 Presidential Election.* Cambridge: MIT Press, 1965.

Shaffer, W.R. *Computer Simulations of Voting Behavior.* New York: Oxford University Press, 1972.

19.
An Interactive Computer Program for Theory Building in Sociology

Fred S. Halley
SUNY Brockport

This paper presents a generalized interactive modeling program for student theory building. First, its logic and instructional applications are differentiated from other uses of computers in sociology. Next, the program and its usage are described. Last, the statistical assumptions, other applications, and limitations of the program are discussed.

A frequent criticism of the use of computers for instruction in sociology is that computers are not helpful in teaching theory. While most will agree that computers have been successfully employed for statistical analysis of empirical data in the process of theory verification, their implementation has been primarily for research rather than instructional applications. The use of computers in the theory verification process has been important and it has played a vital role in theory development. In general, the data analytic applications in social research have paralleled data analytic instructional applications of the computer.

Typical among these are systems that provide easy-to-use student access to large data bases, such as Project IMPRESS (Cline and Meyers, 1976; Davis, 1971) and Gilchrist's NORC/Roper inquiry system (Gilchrist, 1974). Other applications have attempted to teach students the use of program packages, such as SPSS or DATA-TEXT for the analysis of collected data (Anderson and McTavish, 1970; Halley, 1975). Computers have been employed to aid in the clarification of statistical concepts (i.e., Erickson and Jacobsen, 1973); but, as an overall objective, the statistical application is a sub-area of data analysis.

By using simulation techniques, more direct theory teaching applications have been developed. Theoretical models have been translated into programming languages. Often these applications take on the characteristics of games that follow rules specified by the modeled theories. Others are more technical and allow student parameters to be entered into the model and results computed (see Dollar, Hanes and Accola, 1974; and Hansen and Davidson, 1974). Geographers, economists, biologists, physicists, and engineers have made greater use of simulation for teaching theory than have sociologists. However, most of the simulation approaches have been substantive specific. The program presented here is substantive general, but it does impose a particular type of theoretic model.

The logic of computer programs used for instruction has largely followed the logic of programs used for research. Usually these researches have consisted of large data bases which were used for either theory verification (as the last step in a deductive scheme) or for theory development (the generation of theory from data, or induction). As a result, computer-augmented *a priori* theory development has received little attention for instruction. Wallace (1971) has graphically portrayed the relationships between induction and deduction in the process of generating sociology. In his terms (Wallace, 1971, Chapters 2 and 3) computer applications have primarily been used to induce theory; the other half of the process, deduction (Wallace, Chapter 4), has not been well addressed by instructional computer programs.

Dubin has provided a systematic approach to theory building (1969, pp. 147-206) which may be employed as a guide to the construction of a computer program to aid in the *a priori* development of theory. Although the computer program provided by the author only partially addresses Dubin's outline, it does provide a simple, perhaps oversimplified, interactive computer program for students to use in learning how to build theories.

Dubin prefers to call concepts "units" because of ambiguities among the common usages of concepts, conceptual frames of reference, and conceptual frameworks (Dubin, p. 27). For the purpose of this paper the word concept will be used in place of Dubin's more neutral word, unit. For Dubin, theories are made up of systematically-related concepts. This is not to say that the phenomena about which we theorize are systematic in nature, but only that we set up our theories in a systematic way. The concepts in a theory are related to each other in a logical system where each relationship is specified. Using a deductive system, we endeavor to manipulate the concepts on an *a priori* level and arrive at a testable theory. Ultimately, we hope to find the same systematic relationships between conceptual indicators, or operational definitions, at an empirical level as we expected at an *a priori* level. While this brief statement of deductive scientific method does not adequately relate Dubin's detailed guide for theory building, it does provide a brief introduction to traditional theory development.

Systematic verbal statements of theories are problematic because they lack a dynamic component. While systematic theories acknowledge that concepts (or units) affect each other, the nature of the interaction and its results often resist verbal statement. To aid in the statement and understanding of interaction within theoretical systems, a theory modeling program (THEory MODeling) has been written that dynamically relates hypothesized conceptual indicators of a given theoretical model and reports hypothetical outcomes.

THEMOD provides the student with a tool to investigate the implications of his *a priori* theory building. It is written in an interactive language (BASIC), which makes it possible to use the computer from a typewriter-like terminal. In this manner, THEMOD and the student can interact with each other. The student may select up to five conceptual indicators. After this is done, THEMOD asks for hypothetical means and standard deviations for conceptual indicators. These are supplied by the student. The student is then interrogated by THEMOD for the degree of relationship (in the form of r coefficients) between each of the conceptual indicators. When this is completed, the student has been required to supply the parameters of his theoretical system in terms of relationship, magnitude, and variance. From a pedagogical point of view, this is beneficial, because it forces the student to be specific about what are sometimes fuzzy theoretic notions of relationships between concepts and possible empirical indicators of the concepts. Moreover, once THEMOD has been given specific information about a theoretic system, it can dynamically relate the conceptual indicators so that each indicator (or unit) affects all the other indicators as specified by the student's model. This is accomplished by using a multiple regression technique and modifying means provided by the student and returning an altered system via the terminal.

As with most initial attempts at theory building, students will probably be disappointed with their first efforts. THEMOD will probably provide long-range implications that are quite different from the student's original expectations. Too strong a relationship may have been specified between a set of conceptual indicators; a mean of the wrong magnitude may have been selected; or an improper standard deviation may have been stated. After running a model, THEMOD allows the student to change the initial assumptions made in his model. Means, r coefficients, and standard deviations may be altered. The new model may then be run and compared to previous results. In this manner, a student may create a model, examine its implications, and re-run it with altered parameters. This provides students with the opportunity to "play" with a theory and learn by experimentation. It is my contention that this is not only helpful in learning theory, but is also a valuable first step in the clarification of theory for empirical research.

An Example

To illustrate THEMOD, a brief portion of a simple example of a previously-formulated theory is used. Georg Simmel has suggested that three person groups (triads) are naturally unstable and break down into more stable two person relationships (dyads). If the instructor of a theory course were teaching this sociological version of "three is a crowd" he might use THEMOD as an instructional tool to allow his students to discover some of the more subtle aspects of Simmel's work. Following Dubin, there are three concepts, each representing a group member. The problem is to explore their relations at an *a priori* level. To do this, each concept needs a conceptual indicator. In this example it is easiest to think of the conceptual indicators, or operationalizations, as persons. Most appropriate for the three person group would be the three hypothetical persons, Tom, Dick, and Harry. For the purpose of this illustration, suppose that interaction is measured on an interval scale and that all three persons have initial scores (means) of 50 with standard deviations of 3. Moreover, for the initial illustration, it is assumed that all three persons are interacting with each other in an equally positive manner with r coefficients of .1. Triads are supposed to disintegrate. But this triad has been purposely set up with a theoretical assumption of equilibrium.

Below is a terminal printout from a run of THEMOD for the triad described above. Student inputs are in bold face type. As may be seen, the program reports that it has been retrieved from the computer system and asks the student if he is familiar with it. If the student answers no, he is told he is welcome to use it, but readings are suggested for him to get the fullest benefit from the program. The student is requested to specify the number of conceptual indicators he will be using in his model (in this case, three). He is then queried for a name for each of the conceptual indicators; TOM, DICK, and HARRY are entered.

> WELCOME TO THE DYNAMIC THEORY MODELING PRO-
> GRAM.
> ARE YOU FAMILIAR WITH THIS PROGRAM (YES OR NO)?
> **YES**
> GOOD. NOW WE CAN GET STARTED
> AFTER THIS MESSAGE, TYPE IN AN INDICATOR FOR
> EACH OF THE CONCEPTS YOU WILL BE USING IN YOUR
> MODEL. UP TO 5 MAY BE ENTERED. INDICATORS MUST
> BE 10 LETTERS OR LESS
>
> ENTER NUMBER OF INDICATORS? **3**
>
> ENTER NAMES AFTER ? MARKS
>
> ? **TOM**
> ? **DICK**
> ? **HARRY**

After the conceptual indicators are named, the program can refer to them by name rather than a number. To build a set of regression equations, it is necessary to have the hypothetical means, standard deviations, and correlation coefficients for the model. As may be seen below, the means and standard deviations are solicited from the student by the names of the conceptual indicators. Once they are entered, the program goes on to request correlation coefficients for all possible relationships between the conceptual indicators.

BELOW, A LIST OF EACH OF YOUR INDICATORS WILL BE PRINTED. FOR EACH ONE, ENTER A REASONABLE MEAN AND STANDARD DEVIATION SEPARATED BY COMMAS. EXAMPLE: INCOME? 11500,1250

TOM? **50,3**
DICK? **50,3**
HARRY? **50,3**

NOW IT IS TIME TO SPECIFY THE RELATIONSHIP BE-TWEEN EACH OF YOUR CONCEPTUAL INDICATORS. YOU WILL BE ASKED TO SUPPLY A CORRELATION COEFFI-CIENT FOR EACH PAIR OF VARIABLES. IF YOU DO NOT KNOW THE RELATIONSHIP, ENTER A 0

TOM AND DICK? **.1**
TOM AND HARRY? **.1**
DICK AND HARRY? **.1**

At this point the program is ready to be used, but the student may not know the commands for using the program. If the student responds NO when questioned about his knowledge of the program commands, he is given the list of commands shown below. If he responds YES, he is simply asked for the first command.

DO YOU KNOW THE COMMANDS FOR THE SIMULATOR (YES OR NO)? **NO**

THE COMMANDS ARE:
RUN—RUNS THE MODEL

PRINT—PRINTS THE CURRENT VALUES FOR EACH INDICATOR
DONE—STOPS EXECUTION OF THE SIMULATION PRO-GRAM
CSD—ALLOWS THE CHANGE OF AN INITIAL STANDARD DEVIATION
CM—ALLOWS CHANGE OF AN INITIAL MEAN
CCC—ALLOWS CHANGE OF AN INITIAL CORRELATION

CLEAR–CLEARS ALL VALUES AND RESTARTS PRO-
GRAM
BETA–PRINTS BETA MATRIX

When the RUN command is entered, the initial means are
printed for each of the conceptual indicators. The student is then
given the option of altering the mean for the duration of this run.
In our example, not shown here, no alterations were made and
Simmel's model was run with all parameters equal. The correlation
coefficients were slightly positive (.1) for each of the relationships.
The result was not the reduction of a triad to a dyad, but a
strengthening of the triad. The hypothetical interaction scores
increased from 50 to a little more than 59. This demonstrates, on
an *a priori* level, that triads do not always degenerate into dyads,
but that under special conditions, they become stronger. The
changing of different parameters brings about different results,
and numerous examples of student-computer interaction could be
presented in this paper.

Implications of THEMOD

Since the THEMOD user supplies his own conceptual indicators,
the program is substantively free. Theories from various substantive areas may be explored with THEMOD. For instance, if one
were interested in deviance, he might want to take a Durkheimian
approach and enter conceptual indicators such as rate of social
mobility, anomie, economic stability, and crime with their
hypothetical means and standard deviations. The relationship
between each of the conceptual indicators would be expressed by
r coefficients requested by the program. The student could then
use the THEMOD commands to explore the theory.

THEMOD does not require applications that are based in
classical theory. Quite often, students approach instructors with
"theories" about phenomena that are of current interest to them.
Usually these are in the form of some vague ideas inspired by
course work, reading, and the student's current situation. Suggesting that the student formalize and explore his theory using
THEMOD provides a useful way of encouraging a student to
seriously consider the implicatons of his construction of social
reality. It allows the student to create a theoretical realm of his

own that may be explored and modified. Hopefully such activity will help students realize the difference between theorizing and philosophizing.

While the computer program and its associated statistics are moderately sophisticated, the sophistication should not hinder student usage. The student only needs to have elementary knowledge of the statistics mean, standard deviation, and correlation coefficient. While multiple regression is used in running student models, all computations are done by the computer and the student only needs to know how to interpret results for his problem. To be sure, statistical expertise would make a THEMOD exercise a more meaningful experience. However, the use of THEMOD by a statistically naive, but theoretically interested, student can demonstrate the importance of formal techniques for theory building to the statistically shy student.

A discussion of the statistical techniques used to compute new scores for each run of the program is important in relation to some of the limitations and advantages of the program. The program collects means, standard deviations, and a correlation matrix from the user. Standardized beta weights are first computed from the standardized betas, means, and standard deviations using the method described by Meyers (1973, pp. 354-355). This technique is repeated for each variable so that a vector of betas and their associated intercepts is calculated for each conceptual indicator supplied by the user.

Once betas and intercepts are computed, a regression equation is computed for each conceptual indicator. A new score for each conceptual indicator is computed by adding the conceptual indicator to the sum of the betas times their appropriate indicator scores. Once a new mean has been calculated for all the conceptual indicators, the results are printed and the student is asked for a new command. In this manner, conceptual indicators are allowed to interact with each other as specified in the original correlation matrix. The degree of effect among indicators is determined by the strength of relationship (r) and the amount of variability (standard deviation) specified by the user.

Conclusion

Since THEMOD utilizes a parametric statistical technique, the kinds of conceptual indicators selected must be operationalized at an interval or ratio level of measure. Concepts such as marital status, age, and sex would not be appropriate for exploration using THEMOD. Although dummy variables are often used in parametric techniques, it is doubtful if it would be helpful to a student to say that male and female should be given a mean of 1.5 and a standard deviation of .5. Nevertheless, THEMOD might be used in cases of ordinal operationalization if the student and instructor are aware of the broken assumption. For instance, in theories dealing with occupational prestige, alienation, or morale, where measures are usually ordinal, for purposes of theory exploration, parametric assumptions could be ignored.

References

Anderson, R.E., and D.G. McTavish. Sociology, Computers, and Mass Undergraduate Education. *Proceedings of a Conference on Computers in the Undergraduate Curricula,* The University of Iowa, Iowa City, Iowa, 1970.

Cline, H.F., and E.D. Meyers, Jr. Probelm-Solving Computer Systems for Instruction in Sociology. *The American Sociologist,* 1976, *5,* 365-370.

Davis, J.A. Using the IMPRESS System to Teach Sociology. *Proceedings of the Second Annual Conference on Computers in the Undergraduate Curricula,* Dartmouth College, Hanover, New Hampshire, 1971, 382-387.

Dollar, C., L. Hanes, and W.V. Accola. Making It in the Ghetto: A Computer Simulation. *Proceedings of the Conference of Computers in the Undergraduate Curricula,* Washington State University, Pullman, Washington, 1974, 185-194.

Dubin, R. *Theory Building: A Practical Guide to the Construction and Testing of Theoretical Models.* New York: Free Press, 1969.

Erickson, M.L., and R.B. Jacobsen. On Computer Applications and Statistics in Sociology. *Teaching Sociology,* 1973, *1,* 84-102.

Gilchrist, C.J. "Introductory Sociology" and "Implementing Elaboration," presentations at the 1974 A.S.A. Annual Meeting for *A Workshop on Computer Applications in Teaching and Learning.* Communications relating to these applications may be sent to C. Jack Gilchrist, Sociology Department, Montana State University, Bozeman, Montana 59715.

Halley, F.S. Programs for Use in Teaching Research Methods for Small Computers. *Teaching Sociology,* 1975, *2,* 218-221.

Hansen, R.G., and S. Davidson. Simulating the Propagation and Diffusion of an Idea by the Monte Carlo Method. *Proceedings of the Conference of Computers in the Undergraduate Curricula,* Washington State University, Pullman, Washington, 1974, 109-121.

Meyers, E.C. *Time-Sharing Computation in the Social Sciences.* Englewood Cliffs, N.J.: Prentice-Hall, 1973.

Wallace, W.L., *The Logic of Science in Sociology.* Chicago: Aldine-Atherton, 1971.

20.
Some Interactive Computer Programs for an Introductory Econometrics Course

James Ciecka
DePaul University

Introduction

The purpose of this paper is to show how certain abstract assumptions arising in mathematical statistics can be concretely interpreted by using interactive computer programs. In particular, the paper focuses on the usual assumptions for a single equation least squares regression model. The nature of the usual assumptions is a source of problems for students in introductory courses because of the difficulty of bridging the gap between abstract mathematical assumptions on the one hand, and an intuitively clear notion of the conclusions that result from those assumptions, on the other hand. The interactive computer programs described below are a vehicle through which we can move from abstract to more concrete knowledge. These programs allow students to specify assumptions and immediately see the consequences of their specifications in terms of the quality of the resulting least squares estimates. The programs also allow students to experiment with various sets of assumptions without getting involved with complex mathematical deductions.

Least Squares Assumptions

The usual assumptions (Wonnacott and Wonnacott, 1970) for a simple regression model can be stated as follows:

(1) $Y_i = \alpha + \beta X_i + e_i$ $\qquad$ $i = 1, \ldots, n$

where α and β are unknown constants, Y is the dependent variable, X is the independent variable that is non-stochastic in nature, and e is a random variable.

(2) $E(e_i) = 0$ $i = 1, \ldots, n$
(3) $E(e_i^2) = \sigma^2$ $i = 1, \ldots, n$
(4) $E(e_i e_j) = 0$ $i \neq j \; i, j = 1, \ldots, n$

The least squares estimators are linear, unbiased, and possess smaller variance than any other linear and unbiased estimators if assumptions (1)-(4) are met (Johnston, 1972). Violation of assumption (2) can bias the estimators, (say) $\hat{\alpha}$ and $\hat{\beta}$, of the "true" paramater values α and β. If we have that

$$E(e_i) = k \qquad k \neq 0 \qquad i = 1, \ldots, n$$

then the least squares estimator of α is biased but the estimator of β remains unbiased. However, the estimators of both α and β become biased (Murphy, 1973) when:

$$E(e_i) = k_i \qquad k_i \neq 0 \qquad i = 1, \ldots, n$$

Violations of assumptions (3) and (4) do not bias the least squares estimators of either α or β, but rather increase their variance (Murphy, 1973). In such cases, a regression done with only one set of data often yields results that are quite different than the actual values of α and β.

A final assumption regarding the distribution of the random variable e is made in order to test hypotheses about α and β. We assume that e_i is normally distributed. From the previous assumptions we can conclude that:

(5) $e_i \sim n(0, \sigma^2)$ $i = 1, \ldots, n$

Finally, it can be shown that the random variable

$$\frac{\hat{\beta} - \beta}{\dfrac{s}{\sqrt{\sum_i (X_i - \overline{X})^2}}} \qquad \text{where} \quad s = \sqrt{\sum_i [Y_i - (\hat{\alpha} + \hat{\beta} X_i)]^2}$$

has a t distribution with (n-2) degrees of freedom (Johnston, 1972). This allows us to test hypotheses about β, but the test is only valid when assumptions (1)-(5) are all fulfilled.

Now that the least squares assumptions have been stated, let us consider the concept of unbiasedness as an example of the difficulty caused by the abstract nature of assumptions (1)-(5) and the equally abstract conclusions derived from them.

A simple formal argument proves that $\hat{\beta}$ is indeed an unbiased estimator of β. However, it leaves many students rather uninspired and confused. In order to clarify this proof, the probability density function for $\hat{\beta}$ is often sketched as depicted in Figure 1.

Figure 1

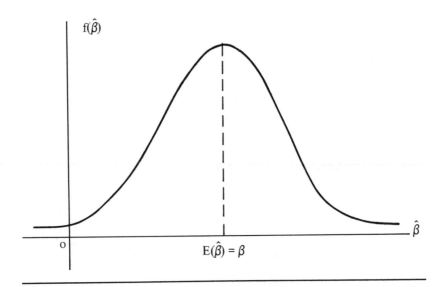

In this illustration, $\hat{\beta}$ is viewed as a random variable (i.e., it can take on many possible values) with its mean value depicted as β. Thus, $\hat{\beta}$ is an unbiased estimator of β. Although Figure 1 is helpful, the concept of unbiasedness could possibly be more clearly illustrated by an interactive computer program. Such a program would:

(a) allow users to choose a linear function by specifying the actual or "true" values of α and β;

(b) choose values of X_i randomly and the corresponding values of e_i that satisfy assumptions (1)-(5);

(c) calculate the least squares estimates $\hat{\alpha}$ and $\hat{\beta}$; and

(d) repeat steps (a)-(c) several times at the user's direction.

Each time a least squares estimator $\hat{\beta}$ is calculated, its value would be printed, and finally the average value would be calculated and printed. The user could easily compare the latter value with the value of β. When assumptions (1)-(5) are fulfilled, the average value of $\hat{\beta}$ should be "close" to β since $\hat{\beta}$ is an unbiased estimator of β. The program also would allow students to experiment by changing any of the assumptions (1)-(5) and then observe the effect on the estimated $\hat{\beta}$ values. In this way, users have a concrete illustration of which assumptions must be fulfilled in order for $\hat{\beta}$ to be an unbiased estimator of β, which assumptions can be violated and still maintain the property of unbiasedness, and finally, how violation of certain assumptions will lead to a specific amount of bias in $\hat{\beta}$.

In the following section, several interactive computer programs are described. Each program asks the user to specify a linear function by giving the values of α and β and also the value of $E(e_i)$. In addition, each program, except the one illustrating the problem of unequal variances, calls for the user to specify the value of σ. The common characteristic of each program is that comparisons can be made between the "true" values of α and β (which are specified by the user) and the calculated values $\hat{\alpha}$ and $\hat{\beta}$ that result from various regression assumptions made by the user. These comparisons do not involve mathematical expressions, but rather numerical quantities that result from assumptions that are stated in the form of mathematical expressions. By observing such numerical quantities many students get a clearer notion of the meaning of underlying abstract mathematical assumptions.

Programs

The program REG 1 illustrates the ideal regression situation. All regression assumptions are built into the program. The X_i's are non-stochastic and take on randomly selected values, and a set of random variables e_i is generated for each X_i as illustrated in Figure 2.

After asking the user to furnish values for α, β, $E(e_i)$, and σ, the values of Y_i are calculated such that $Y_i = \alpha + \beta X_i + e_i$. The least squares estimates $\hat{\alpha}$ and $\hat{\beta}$ are calculated and printed. The values of $\hat{\alpha}$ and $\hat{\beta}$ should be quite "close" to α and β, respectively, since all regression assumptions are fulfilled. After running the program a few times with the same values of α, β, $E(c_1)$, and σ, the user is invited to experiment. For example, the user may vary σ while retaining the same values for α, β, and $E(e_i)$. After running the program a few times it becomes apparent that the variances of $\hat{\alpha}$ and $\hat{\beta}$ change directly with the size of σ. Another user option would be to specify that $E(e_i) \neq 0$ and observe the resulting bias in the least squares estimates.

The consequences of $var(e_i) \neq \sigma^2$ $i = 1, \ldots, n$ are illustrated in

Figure 2

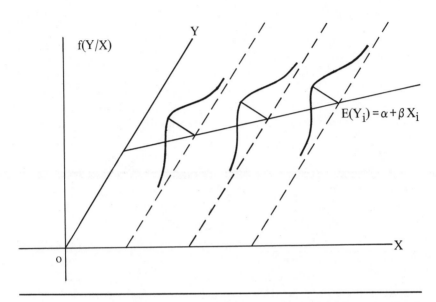

the program REG 2. In particular, the assumption $\text{var}(e_i) = k^2 X_i^2$ is built into the program. The user supplies the variance of the first random variable as well as the actual values of α and β and $E(e_i)$. The program's output contains three sets of estimates:

(1) least squares assuming $\text{var}(e_i) = \sigma^2$ $i = 1, \dots, n$
(2) least squares assuming $\text{var}(e_i) = k^2 X_i^2$ $i = 1, \dots, n$
(3) weighted least squares assuming $\text{var}(e_i) =$
    $k^2 X_i^2$ $i = 1, \dots, n$

The first estimates are ideal in the sense that all assumptions are fulfilled. The second set of estimates is influenced by unequal variances of the random variable e_i. The final set of estimates is arrived at by applying a technique (weighted least square) designed to remedy the unequal variance problem. This program allows the user to make several important comparisons. The algebraic difference between the estimators calculated in (1) and the actual values of α and β is a measure of how far least squares estimates miss their mark even under ideal regression conditions. The difference between the estimators calculated in (2) and the actual values of α and β gives the user an idea of the quality of least squares estimates when the unequal variances problem exists. The difference between the estimators in (1) and (2) gives the user a measure of the error solely attributable to unequal variances of the random variable e_i. A comparison between the estimates calculated in (3) and those in (2) indicates how successful the weighted least square technique was in eliminating estimation errors. Finally, the remaining error after application of weighted least squares is determined by comparing the estimates in (1) with (3).

Table 1 summarizes the foregoing comparisons. In that table, $\hat{\alpha}$ and $\hat{\beta}$ denote the estimates obtained from (1), the estimates from (2) are denoted by $\hat{\alpha}_{uv}$ and $\hat{\beta}_{uv}$ and the estimates from (3) are denoted by $\hat{\alpha}_w$ and $\hat{\beta}_w$.

Table 1

(1)	(2)	(3)=(1)-(2)	(4)	(5)=(4)-(2)	(6)=(3)-(5)
$\hat{\alpha}_{uv} - \alpha$	$\hat{\alpha} - \alpha$	$\hat{\alpha}_{uv} - \hat{\alpha}$	$\hat{\alpha}_w - \alpha$	$\hat{\alpha}_w - \hat{\alpha}$	$\hat{\alpha}_{uv} - \hat{\alpha}_w$
$\hat{\beta}_{uv} - \beta$	$\hat{\beta} - \beta$	$\hat{\beta}_{uv} - \hat{\beta}$	$\hat{\beta}_w - \hat{\beta}$	$\hat{\beta}_w - \hat{\beta}$	$\hat{\beta}_{uv} - \hat{\beta}_w$

Column (1). Difference between least squares estimates when there are unequal variances and true parameter values.

Column (2). Difference between least squares estimates when the variance is constant and the "true" parameter values specified by the user.

Column (3). The error in estimation due to unequal variances.

Column (4). Difference between weighted least squares estimates when there are unequal variances and "true" parameter values.

Column (5). The error in estimation due to unequal variances after the application of weighted least squares.

Column (6). Improvement of weighted least squares estimates *vis-a-vis* ordinary least squares when there are unequal variances.

The unequal variance problem is depicted in Figure 3. Notice that the absolute value of the random variables e_i increases as X_i increases. This is precisely the meaning of the $\text{var}(e_i) = k^2 X_i^2$ assumption.

Figure 3

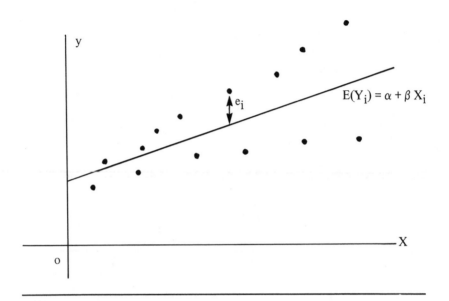

The serial correlation problem $E(e_i e_j) \neq 0$ $i \neq j$ $i, j = 1, \ldots, n$ is illustrated in a program called REG 3 that assumes the auto-regressive scheme

$$e_i = k e_{i-1} + v_i$$

where $E(v_i) = 0$ and $E(v_i v_j) = 0$ $i \neq j$ $i, j = 1, \ldots, n$. The student types in α, β, $E(e_i)$, and σ, and the program's printout contains the least squares estimates with and without serial correlation and with the application of the generalized first differences technique. Thus, three different sets of estimates are printed as was the case for REG 2. In addition, the Durbin-Watson statistic is calculated for each set of estimates. This allows students to make the usual test for serial correlation. Figure 4 illustrates the serial correlation problem.

The figure exhibits negative values for e_i for small X_i values and positive values of e_i for large X_i values. The least squares line $Y_i = \hat{\alpha} + \hat{\beta} X_i$ fits the data quite well but is nevertheless very far from the actual linear relationship $E(Y_i) = \alpha + \beta X_i$. Table 2 summarizes the types of comparisons one can make from the information generated in the program.

Figure 4

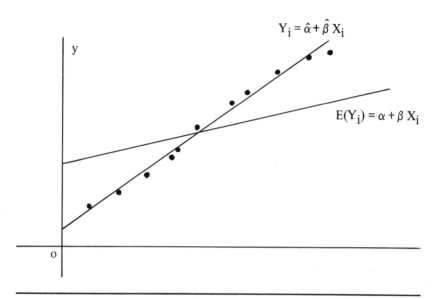

Table 2

(1)	(2)	(3)=(1)-(2)	(4)	(5)=(4)-(2)	(6)=(3)-(5)
$\hat{\alpha}_{SC} - \alpha$	$\hat{\alpha} - \alpha$	$\hat{\alpha}_{SC} - \hat{\alpha}$	$\hat{\alpha}_{FD} - \alpha$	$\hat{\alpha}_{FD} - \hat{\alpha}$	$\hat{\alpha}_{SC} - \hat{\alpha}_{FD}$
$\hat{\beta}_{SC} - \beta$	$\hat{\beta} - \beta$	$\hat{\beta}_{SC} - \hat{\beta}$	$\hat{\beta}_{FD} - \beta$	$\hat{\beta}_{FD} - \hat{\beta}$	$\hat{\beta}_{SC} - \hat{\beta}_{FD}$

Column (1). Difference between least squares estimates when the error term is serially correlated and the "true" parameter values.

Column (2). Difference between least squares estimates when there is no serial correlation and the "true" parameter values.

Column (3). Error in estimation due to serial correlation.

Column (4). Difference between generalized first difference estimates when the data is serially correlated and the "true" parameter values.

Column (5). Error in estimation due to serial correlation after application of generalized first differences.

Column (6). Improvement of generalized first difference estimates *vis-a-vis* ordinary least squares estimates when there is serial correlation.

Students' t values are calculated in REG 4 under the assumption that the random variable is normal, uniform, and negative exponential. The student enters the values of α, β, and the null hypothesis value of β (say) β_0. The standard error of $\hat{\beta}$, the number of degrees of freedom, and the value of $(\hat{\beta} - \beta_0)$ are printed in addition to the t values. REG 4 also provides the user with three sets of estimates of α and β—one set for each assumed distribution of the random variable e_i. A t value is also printed for each estimate of β. This allows students to test their null hypothesis for three different cases, but the results of the tests will, in general, depend on the assumed distribution of e_i. For example, a null hypothesis may be rejected when e_i is normally distributed, but it may be accepted when the distribution is uniform. Of course, when e_i is uniformly or negative exponentially distributed, a t test is not valid and an incorrect statistical decision can be made.

Conclusion

Each program described provides students with an illustration of an assumption or theorem from linear regression theory. By allowing the user to specify the "true" parameters, comparisons can be made between those values and the least squares regression values when: (a) all assumptions are fulfilled, (b) certain assumptions are violated, and (c) standard correction techniques are applied. This allows students to get a "feel" for the severity of certain regression problems as well as for correction techniques.

References

Johnston, J. *Econometric Methods*, 2nd edition. New York: McGraw-Hill Book Company, 1972.

Murphy, J.L. *Introductory Econometrics*. Homewood, Illinois: Richard D. Irwin, Inc., 1973.

Wonnacott, R.J., and T.H. Wonnacott. *Econometrics*. New York: John Wiley and Sons, 1970.

21.
A Computer Oriented Introduction
to Cognitive Psychology

William L. Bewley

Minnesota Educational Computing Consortium

This paper describes a new kind of laboratory manual for psychology. The volume is called *Cognitive Psychology: A Computer-Oriented Laboratory Manual.* It was written with support from COMPUTe, a curriculum development project based at Dartmouth and funded by NSF. The computer programs on which the manual is based were initially developed at the 1972 NSF Summer Institute on Computers in the Social and Behavioral Sciences at the University of Colorado.

The manual provides a laboratory introduction to cognitive psychology. The material is presented by means of six experiments, each of which is run on a time-shared computer system using the BASIC language and a teletype terminal as the input/output device. In each experiment, a computer program presents a task to the student and a simulation of a model of human information processing relevant to the task. Most of the programs are designed so that features of the tasks and the models can be changed by the student, allowing the running of experiments on the model or on other humans.

This paper is divided into four sections. The first is concerned with technical details of the computer programs and with the question of transportability to different systems. The second section describes the organization of the manual. Section three briefly describes the six experiments that can be run. The fourth section presents a rationale for the instructional use of the computer, discussing what students should learn from the manual and why the computer is needed to help them learn.

Technical Details and Transportation

As mentioned in the introduction, the computer programs on which the manual is based were written for a time-shared computer, and they use a teletype terminal for input and output. CRT output would be desirable because of its speed and silence, but all of the experiments require that the student obtain a "hard copy" of the output.

The programs were originally written in BASIC for the PDP-11 RSTS System. They were later translated into Dartmouth BASIC for use on the Dartmouth Time-Sharing System and to KRONOS BASIC for use at the University of Colorado. They are presently installed on the UNIVAC 1110 time-sharing system in Minnesota. No insurmountable problems have been encountered in these translations, most of the difficulty being related to idiosyncratic system functions for measuring clock time. CONDUIT has recently standardized the programs, making them even more transportable.

Each of the programs requires at least 8K of storage and from 30 to 60 minutes of terminal time to run.

Organization of the Manual

The manual is really two manuals, one for students and the other for instructors. Each is approximately 100 pages long. The main body of the student manual consists of material relating to the six experiments. The material for each experiment includes a brief abstract, a description of the experimental procedure, a description of the model, a set of study questions designed to encourage critical evaluation of the model and independent experimentation, and a general discussion that briefly describes alternative models and suggests further reading. In addition to material on the six experiments, the student manual contains an introduction describing the relation of each experiment to a general information processing model, and two appendices, one dealing with a suggested format for lab reports and the other with the minimum chi-square procedure for goodness of fit.

The instructor manual contains program listings and documentation, remedies for a few potential transportability problems, and answers to the study questions contained in the student manual.

The Experiments

The six experiments were chosen to cover the range of cognitive activity represented in current general conceptions of the human information processing system, e.g., Atkinson and Shiffrin (1968), Norman and Rumelhart (1970), and Atkinson, Herrmann, and Wescourt (1974).

Each experiment is conducted using a computer program that presents an experimental task to both a student and a simulation of an information-processing model. The task and model associated with each experiment are summarized below.

Experiment 1. Pattern Recognition. The task is a partial replication of the visual search experiment of Neisser (1963). Students search through 50 six-letter lines for the presence or absence of 1 or 2 target letters in a context which is visually similar to or different from the target. If, for example, "Z" was the target, a line with visually similar context might be "EXIMZW"; a line with visually different context might be "CDGOZU."

The student is allowed to specify the target, the number of targets, and the context from a standard set of alternatives (those in Neisser's experiment). The student can also specify nonstandard target and context letters and choose to run a subject and the simulation or the simulation alone.

The program records search latencies for both the student and the simulation.

The model is a nonlearning version of the Selfridge (1959) Pandemonium. It has a memory that associates visual features, e.g., straight lines, curves, and angles, with letter names. It assumes feature extraction with hierarchical and parallel processing of features. These assumptions lead to certain predictions about search latencies. The student is asked to evaluate the model by comparing search latencies with those of the model. The student also evaluates the model by comparing its capabilities with those of template matching and scene analysis models (e.g., Guzman, 1969, Winston, 1970, 1973).

A more detailed description of this experiment can be found in Bewley (1974).

Experiment 2. Short-term Memory. The task is based on the continuous memory experiment of Atkinson and Shiffrin (1968).

Students are presented with a series of paired-associate trials, in which they are first asked to recall the response most recently paired with a stimulus and then to study the pairing of a new response with that stimulus. The independent variable is the "lag" or time between study and recall. The dependent variable is the probability of correct recall at each of the six lags. These data are recorded for both the student and the model.

The student can choose to run the standard experiment, in which the stimuli are six two-digit numbers and the possible responses are all letters of the alphabet, or he can choose to specify any even number of stimuli from two to twelve. The sequence of stimulus presentation can also be specified. The student can choose to run a subject and the simulation or the simulation alone.

The model is the buffer model of Atkinson and Shiffrin (1968). This model assumes that incoming information passes through three different memory stores: a sensory register, the short-term store, and the long-term store. The short-term store is assumed to contain a limited capacity rehearsal buffer.

There are four model parameters that can be manipulated by the student: (1) r, the capacity of the rehearsal buffer; (2) a, the probability that information in the sensory register enters the rehearsal buffer; (3) $\emptyset$, the rate at which information is transferred from short-term store to long-term store; and (4) T, the rate at which information is lost from long-term store. The student runs experiments with the simulation, manipulating parameters in an attempt to make the model's behavior match the student's and to determine the effect of each parameter on the model's behavior.

The manual's discussion of this experiment suggests that rehearsal is an information-processing strategy evoked by the nature of the continuous memory task. The Reitman (1970) queueing model, which has no rehearsal mechanism, is presented as an example of a short-term memory model appropriate for tasks in which rehearsal is less appropriate, e.g., the memory span task.

Experiment 3. Long-term Memory. The task is the Palermo and Eberhart (1968) paired-associate task. Subjects learn a list of number-bigram pairs, e.g., "61-VM," by the study-test method. Most of the pairings follow a rule that relates a particular number to a letter, e.g., if "6" is the first number in the stimulus, "V" is the first letter in the response. A few of the pairings, the "irregular pairs," violate the rule. Of the pairs that follow the rule, some are not presented during the study phase. These are called "omitted regular pairs." In order to respond correctly to these pairs, the student must learn the rule. The regular pairs that are presented during the study phase are called "presented regular pairs." Each of the presented regular pairs is presented once during the study phase; each irregular pair is presented twice.

The dependent variable is the proportion of correct responses for irregular pairs, omitted regular pairs, and presented regular pairs.

The purpose of the experiment is to provide an experimental analogy to children's learning of morphological rules. Ervin (1964) found that children tend to learn the past tense inflections of the more frequent irregular verbs (verbs for which there is no rule for forming past tense, e.g., came, went, did) before those for regular verbs (verbs for which there is a rule for forming past tense inflections, e.g., kissed, hugged, loved). When children learn how to inflect the regular verbs, however, they begin to make mistakes on irregular verbs, e.g., comed, goed, doed. The nature of the mistakes suggests that they are "overregularizing"–applying the rule too broadly. If the same thing happens in the paired associate experiment, students should learn the irregular pairs first and then, when they learn the rule for the regular pairs (as indicated by correct responses on the omitted regular pairs), they should make overregularizing errors on the irregular pairs.

The model is the Hintzman (1968) discrimination net model. This model, which is a modification of the Feigenbaum (1963) EPAM model, assumes that stimulus discrimination is the primary process in learning. Long-term memory is represented as a discrimination net consisting of a hierarchy of test nodes that look for the presence of particular positions of the stimulus. The net for the pair "61-VM" is shown on page 282. The test node in line 1 is looking for the presence of "6" in the first position of the stimulus. If a "6" is found (the outcome of the test is positive), control is transferred to line 2, where the response is stored. If the outcome of the test is negative, control is transferred to line 3, which indicates that the correct response is not known.

The model learns by adding new test nodes or by changing

Line	S/R	Position	Positive	Negative
1	6	1	2	3
2	VM			
3	?			

stored responses. There are three parameters: (1) A, the probability that a new test node is added following an incorrect response; (2) B, the probability that if a new test node is not added following an incorrect response that the stored response is changed; and (3) C, the probability that a new test node is added following a correct response.

There are two computer programs associated with this experiment. The first, which is called PAL, presents the paired associate task to the student and the model but provides for no changes of the task or model parameters. The second program, SAL, allows the student to manipulate parameter values, to run either a subject and the simulation or the simulation alone, to specify the number of simulations to be run, to define list length and stimulus-response pairs, and to specify the maximum number of trials allowed. The student uses PAL to compare human behavior with model behavior on the Palermo and Eberhart (1968) paired associate task. SAL is used to run experiments with the model and with other paired associate tasks.

The manual's discussion of this experiment points out the weaknesses of the discrimination net as a model of long-term memory (e.g., it has no rule learning strategies) and points to Anderson and Bower (1973), Kintsch (1972), Quillian (1969), and Rumelhart, Lindsay, and Norman (1972), as alternative models.

Experiment 4: Concept Learning. The task is the blank trials concept identification task of Levine (1966). Students are given a series of concept learning trials, each consisting of a pair of four-dimensional stimuli, e.g., a large black T on the left and a small white X on the right. They are told that one of the two stimuli is an example of the concept they are to learn. Some of the trials are "blank" trials in that the students receive no feedback on their response. The purpose of the blank trials is to provide information on the student's current hypothesis about the identity of the concept.

The dependent variables are those employed by Levine (1966); the percentage of blank trials showing one of the possible hypotheses, the probability that the current hypothesis is retained following positive and negative feedback trials, and the number of hypotheses in the subject's pool of possible hypotheses.

There are really four models associated with this experiment: (1) the sampling with replacement model of Restle (1962), (2) the local consistency model of Gregg and Simon (1967), (3) the consistency check model of Trabasso and Bower (1966), and (4) the focusing model of Levine (1966). All are "hypothesis models" in that they assume that the subject selects hypotheses about the correct concept from a pool of hypotheses. They differ primarily in the strategies used to select hypotheses.

The student can choose to run either a subject or one of the four models. If one of the models is chosen, the student can specify the number of replications to be run and the level of detail in the output. Level of detail ranges from the printing of summary statistics at the end of the simulation to the printing of the stimuli, the model's current pool of hypotheses, hypothesis selected by the model, and the model's response. If the computer system has more than 8K storage, it is also possible to install an attention mechanism that allows a choice of the number and identity of stimulus dimensions to be attended to. This mechanism requires only 14 additional lines.

The manual presents S-R theory, e.g., Hull (1920), and mediated S-R theories, e.g., Kendler and Kendler (1962) and Zeaman and House (1963), as alternatives to hypothesis theories. It suggests that S-R theories and hypothesis theories might represent alternative concept learning strategies, with strategy selection being controlled by factors such as the nature of the task and instructions.

Experiment 5. Decision Making. The task for this experiment is a game similar to the famous Prisoner's Dilemma Game. There are two players, the student and the computer. To play the game, each player makes one of two possible choices. The outcome of the game is determined by the payoff matrix shown on page 284.

If both players make the same choice, both receive an equal number of points—4 for choice 1 and 0 for choice 2. If the players make different choices, the player making choice 2 receives 3 points and the opponent receives 1 point.

Computer

		1	2
Student	1	4,4	1,3
	2	3,1	0,0

The experiment involves playing 75 of these games. There are two independent variables. The first is the type of feedback the student receives after each game. With OWN feedback, the student is told the number of points he received in the last game and his total points. RELATIVE feedback tells the student the number of points received in the last game and the *difference* between his total points and the computer's total points.

The second independent variable is the pattern of the computer's responses. There are two patterns, U and inverted -U. The pattern refers to changes in the frequency of "1" choices by the computer over the 75 games. In the U pattern, the frequency is high in the early and late games and low in the middle games. This is reversed for the inverted U pattern: the frequency is low in the early and late games and high in the middle.

The student can set values for these variables and has the option of running a subject and a simulation of the associated model or a simulation alone.

The model is a combination of the social motives model of Messick and McCLintock (1968) and a stochastic learning model of choice behavior described by Rapoport (1967). The social motives portion of the model assumes that there are two possible motives in the game: (1) a motive for own gain, in which the player attempts to maximize his own points; and (2) a motive for relative gain in which the player attempts to maximize the difference between his points and those of the opponent. The motive for own gain leads the player to make choice 1; the motive for relative gain leads to choice 2.

The probability of a player holding one of the two motives is determined by the opponent's response, using a linear operator equation taken from stochastic learning theory:

$$P(g + 1) = AP(g) + (1-a) L.$$

P(g) is the probability of a motive at the beginning of game g. P(g + 1) is the probability at the beginning of game G + 1. A and L are parameters that determine the rate and direction of probability change, respectively.

The model plays against the computer with its preprogrammed responses (determined by the response pattern variable) just as the student plays against the computer. The student can specify values for A and L parameters in attempting to obtain the best fit of model behavior to student behavior and to determine the influence of the parameters on the model's behavior.

Prescriptive decision models for game situations, and descriptive models are presented as alternative decision-making models.

Material on non-game decision-making is also mentioned, e.g., Coombs, Dawes, and Tversky (1970), Edwards and Tversky (1967), and Raiffa (1968).

Experiment 6. Problem-Solving. The task is the missionaries and cannibals problem. In a typical problem, there might be three missionaries, three cannibals, and a boat that holds a maximum of two people at the bank of a river. All six people and the boat are to be transferred to the opposite bank without ever having the cannibals outnumber the missionaries on either bank.

The program allows the student to specify any number of missionaries and cannibals and any boat capacity. It also allows the student to choose between running a subject or a simulation. If a subject is run, the program records errors and response time at each step of the solution. Errors at each step are recorded for a simulation.

The model is the General Problem Solver (GPS) of Ernst and Newell (1969). The model uses means-end analysis as a heuristic to choose from among several operators appropriate to the missionaries and cannibals problem, e.g., "move 1 missionary and 1 cannibal to the right bank." Operators are chosen and applied by using three recursively-connected procedures: TRANSFORM, REDUCE, and APPLY. TRANSFORM attempts to transform the current problem situation into the desired problem situation. In order to do this, it calls on the REDUCE procedure to reduce the difference between the two situations. REDUCE calls on APPLY to apply an operator judged appropriate for reducing the difference.

As the simulation of the GPS model attempts to solve the problem, it prints a trace of its activity, indicating the current procedure and operator. If the model solves the problem, the program prints the number of errors at each step of the solution. The student uses the trace and the error data to compare the model's behavior with student problem-solving behavior.

The manual suggests that means-end analysis and the operators are information-processing strategies and discusses the influence of a person's perception of the task and his past experience on strategy selection in problem-solving. Functional fixedness and habitual set are used as examples.

The S-R theory of Maltzmann (1955) and Gestalt theory (Kohler, 1925) are presented as alternative models.

Rationale

A legitimate and important question to ask about any computer-oriented curriculum is whether the computer is really needed. Can students learn anything from the computer-oriented curriculum that could not be learned from a traditional curriculum? Does the new learning, if any, balance the added cost?

A cognitive psychology course must include some discussion of the models relevant to the field. In most courses, presentation and analysis of models and associated data is the primary activity. This manual hopefully includes at least some of the models most frequently discussed.

As usually presented by lecture and written description, these models can be extremely difficult for the student to comprehend. They are abstract and complicated. They are also dynamic, representing processes rather than static structures. It is difficult to capture this feature in a verbal description.

The manual's use of the computer helps students comprehend the models and their behavior by representing them in a concrete and dynamic form. The students learn by experimenting with the models. They can manipulate parameters and tasks and then observe the effects of their manipulations. The effects that can be observed include the operation of the model because the models are presented as "glass boxes" rather than "black boxes." Students can see Pandemonium analyze the visual features of input letters and watch items enter and leave the rehearsal buffer; they can observe trial-by-trial changes in the contents of the hypothesis pool and in the probability of holding the "own gain" motive; they can follow the sequence of GPS procedure and operator activation. The result of all this is that the student will learn more about the models and about cognitive psychology.

The computer may also help students learn how to learn and think. The computer allows the student to evaluate the adequacy of models and to tinker with the models in an attempt to test hypotheses about the causes of their behavior. While testing hypotheses and trying to solve problems with the models, the students should be learning something about how to test hypotheses and solve problems.

In addition to providing an opportunity for students to test hypotheses and solve problems, the computer may be providing models for learning and thinking. College students have no doubt mastered rehearsal as a memory mnemonic, but have they all discovered the power of focusing or means-end analysis as problem-solving strategies? Are they even aware of the fact that they can use strategies and that some are more appropriate for certain tasks than others? Have they ever thought about the use of critical tests in drawing conclusions from partial evidence, as suggested by Pandemonium and the discrimination net? This idea, that the computer may provide models for learning and thinking, has been developed further by Bewley, Holznagel, and Klassen (1975).

Whether the value added by the use of the computer outweighs the cost of requiring the computer is a judgment that will have to be made by potential users of the manual. As the reader might expect, I believe that it does.

I also believe that at some institutions the cost of requiring the computer may be insignificant. When I developed the manual, I was teaching at Lawrence University, a small (1500 students) liberal arts college in Wisconsin. I had little laboratory space and no equipment suitable for a cognitive psychology course serving 60 students. There were eight terminals and a PDP-11 sitting around, though, and I found that I could run the laboratory on the terminals free of charge. If there had been a charge, the cost would have been at least partly offset by savings on lab space and equipment. A description of my experience with this course, using an early version of the manual, can be found in Bewley (1973).

References

Anderson, J.R., and G.H. Bower. *Human Associative Memory*. Washington, D.C.: V.H. Winston, 1973.

Atkinson, R.C., and R. Shiffrin. Human Memory: A Proposed System and Its Control Processes. In K.W. Spence and J.T. Spence (Eds.), *The Psychology of Learning and Motivation: Advances in Research and Theory*, Vol. 2. New York: Academic Press, 1968.

Atkinson, R.C., D.J. Herrmann, and K.T. Wescourt. Search Processes in Recognition Memory. In R.L. Solso (Ed.), *Theories in Cognitive Psychology: The Loyola Symposium*. Potomac, Maryland: Lawrence Erlbaum Associates, 1974.

Bewley, W.L. The Use of Time-Shared Terminals in a Human-Learning Course. *Proceedings of the Fourth Conference on Computers in the Undergraduate Curricula*, Claremont Colleges, 1973.

Bewley, W.L. Computer-Based Experiments in Cognitive Psychology. *Creative Computing*, Nov.-Dec., 1974, 36-42.

Bewley, W.L., D. Holznagel, and D.L. Klassen. Toward a Cognitive-Developmental Rationale for the Instructional Use of Computer Simulations. *Proceedings of the 2nd World Conference on Computers in Education*, Marseilles, France, September 1975.

Coombs, C.H., R.M. Dawes, and A. Tversky. *Mathematical Psychology: An Introduction*. Englewood Cliffs, N.J.: Prentice Hall, 1970.

Edwards, W., and A. Tversky (Eds.) *Decision Making*. Harmondsworth, Middlesex, England: Penguin Books, 1967.

Ernst, G.W., and A. Newell. *GPS: A Case Study in Generality and Problem Solving*. New York: Academic Press, 1969.

Ervin, S.M. Imitation and Structural Change in Children's Language. In E.G. Lenneberg (Ed.). *New Directions in the Study of Language*. Cambridge: M.I.T. Press, 1964.

Feigenbaum, E.A. The Simulation of Verbal Learning Behavior. In E.A. Feigenbaum and J. Feldman (Eds.), *Computers and Thought*. New York: McGraw-Hill Book Co., 1963.

Gregg, L.W., and H.A. Simon. Process Models and Stochastic Theories of Simple Concept Formation. *Journal of Mathematical Psychology*, 1967, *4*, 246-276.

Guzman, A. Decomposition of a Visual Scene into Three-Dimensional Bodies." In A. Grasselli (Ed.), *Automatic Interpretation and Classification of Images.* New York: Academic Press, 1969.

Hintzman, D.L. Explorations with a Discrimination Net Model for Paired-Associate Learning. *Journal of Mathematical Psychology,* 1968, *5,* 123-162.

Hull, C.L. Quantitative Aspects of the Evolution of Concepts. *Psychological Monographs, 28,* Whole No. 123, 1920.

Kendler, H.H., and T.S. Kendler. Vertical and Horizontal Processes in Problem-Solving. *Psychological Review,* 1962, *69,* 1-16.

Kintsch W. Notes on the Structure of Semantic Memory. In E. Tulving and W. Donaldson (Eds.), *Organization of Memory.* New York: Academic Press, 1972.

Kohler, W. *The Mentality of Apes.* London: Routledge and Kegan Paul, 1925, 2nd ed., available in paperback from Vintage Books, New York, 1959.

Levine, M. Hypothesis Behavior by Humans During Discrimination Learning. *Journal of Experimental Psychology,* 1966, *71,* 331-338.

Maltzmann, I. Thinking: From a Behavioristic Point of View. *Psychological Review,* 1955, *66,* 367-386.

Messick, D.M., and C.G. McClintock. Motivational Bases of Choice in Experimental Games. *Journal of Experimental Social Psychology,* 1968, *4,* 1-25.

Neisser, U. Decision-Time Without Reaction-Time: Experiments in Visual Scanning. *American Journal of Psychology,* 1963, *76,* 376-385.

Norman, D.A., and D.E. Rumelhart. A System for Perception and Memory. In D.A. Norman (Ed.), *Models of Human Memory.* New York: Academic Press, 1970.

Palermo, D.S., and V.L. Eberhart. On the Learning of Morphological Rules: An Experimental Analogy. *Journal of Verbal Learning and Verbal Behavior,* 1968, *7,* 337-344.

Quillian, M.R. The Teachable Language Comprehender: A Simulation Program and Theory of Language. *Communications of the ACM,* 1969, *12,* 459-476.

Raiffa, E. *Decision Analysis: Introductory Lectures on Choices Under Uncertainty.* Reading, Mass.: Addison-Wesley, 1968.

Rapoport Amnon. Optimal Policies for the Prisoner's Dilemma. *Psychological Review,* 1967, *74,* 136-148.

Reitman, J.S. Computer Simulation of an Information Processing Model of Short-Term Memory. In D.A. Norman (Ed.), *Models of Human Memory*. New York: Academic Press, 1970.

Restle, F.A. The Selection of Strategies in Cue Learning. *Psychological Review*, 1962, *69*, 320-343.

Rumelhart, D.E., P.H. Lindsay, and D.A. Norman. A Process Model for Long-Term Memory. In E. Tulving and W. Donaldson (Eds.), *Organization of Memory*. New York: Academic Press, 1972.

Selfridge, O. Pandemonium: A Paradigm for Learning. In *Symposium on the Mechanization of Thought Processes*. London: HM Stationery Office, 1959.

Trabasso, T., and G.H. Bower. Presolution Dimensional Shifts in Concept Identification: A Test of the Sampling with Replacement Axiom in All-or-None Models. *Journal of Mathematical Psychology*, 1966, *2*, 163-173.

Winston, P.H. Learning Structural Descriptions from Examples. M.I.T. Artificial Intelligence Laboratory Project, AI-TR-231, 1970.

Winston, P.H. Learning to Identify Toy Block Structures. In R.L. Solso (Ed.), *Contemporary Issues in Cognitive Psychology: The Loyola Symposium*. Washington, D.C.: V.H. Winston, 1973.

Zeaman, D. and B.T. House. The Role of Attention in Retardate Discrimination Learning. In N.R. Ellis (Ed.), *Handbook of Mental Deficiency*. New York: McGraw-Hill, 1963, 159-223.

22.
Computer Construction of Test Forms: Sampling from Item Pools[1]

Phillip L. Emerson
Cleveland State University

Introduction

For several years, a computerized testing and scoring system has been used in sections of an introductory psychology course with 150 to 200 students. The system seems to have solved several of the familiar problems involved in ordinary testing and grading procedures with large classes. The test-generation part of the system is similar to that described by Prosser and Jensen (1971). The test-scoring part of the system maintains cumulative records of test scores for each student throughout the school term. This feature was included because it aids the student in keeping track of his progress as he checks the updated printout posted after each test. Many of the implementation details were determined by the questions of whether such a system could be implemented on a scale small enough to be adoptable by the decision of an individual instructor for a single course. Experience with an earlier form of the system has been reported (Emerson, 1974). The main modifications since then have been (a) conversion for lower-case printing of test forms, (b) the use of tape files rather than punch cards for record keeping and item files, and (c) an increase in the size of the item pool.

Facilities

The crucial facilities needed for the system, or a similar one, are a central computer installation with batch processing and a fair amount of primary memory, a high-speed printer, and some means of machine reading of test responses. Most universities have such facilities.

The specific facilities used in the project reported here are an IBM 370/145 system with the usual card reader, two tape drives, a high-speed line printer with the lower-case "T" train option, and direct access disk storage. The most demanding of the several programs uses 320K bytes of primary (virtual) memory, plus 21000 64-byte records of temporary direct-access disk storage. This program is used only once, to generate the final examination. The programs used repeatedly are less demanding, one using 128K bytes of primary memory and 2000 80-byte records of indexed direct-access temporary disk storage, the other using 384K bytes of primary memory only. The entry of test response data for scoring and updating of records is via IBM cards punched from answer sheets by an IBM-1230 optical scanner mated to a 534 keypunch machine.

The programs are written in FORTRAN, but use some non-standard programming features. In particular, they use "DEFINE FILE" statements as well as alphanumeric-binary conversion depending on the 32-bit FORTRAN integer representation on IBM computers. Conversion to run at a non-IBM installation, assuming comparable facilities, would probably require changes in a dozen or so statements in each of several programs.

Test Generation and Scoring

The main idea of the project is to store an item pool of test questions in the computer, and then to have the computer generate and print individual test-question forms by selecting randomly for each form a different subset of the available items. At test time, each student in the class gets a different form of the test covering the current material, significantly reducing the student's temptation to copy answers. The system also permits retesting on the same material at the option of the student, since the retest forms are new random subsets from the item pool.

After the test, the students are allowed to keep the question forms, but turn in the IBM answer sheets on which they have recorded their answers, student identification, and test form numbers. The answer-sheet information is transferred by optical scanner to punched cards for input to the computer for scoring. Even before computer scoring, the students obtain feedback information, since a list of the correct answers for each used form number is posted immediately after the examination period. There is no need to be secretive, since make-up tests can be given with forms whose correct answers are not yet posted.

The scoring program reads the punch-card test responses, and also a gradebook record file from tape containing the scores, to date, on each test for each student. It scores the tests, updates the records, and writes out a new record file to be used as input the next time. It also prints out information to be posted as the official results of the test. This is a list with each line containing a student identification number, name, form number, correct answers for that form, any wrong answers given by the student, the score for the current test, and the cumulative record of scores on all tests to date. The scoring program, when updating a record, checks first to see whether there is already a score for the test. If so, the old score is replaced by the new only if the new is higher than the old. Thus, it gives credit to the student for his highest score when he is tested more than once over the same material. We give students the option of two tests on each of the ten divisions of the assigned reading. In addition to these two 20-item tests each week, there is a 50-item final examination, where a given form consists of five randomly chosen items from each of the ten item pools, one for each division. There is no retest option with the final examination.

Test-Retest Rationale

The main reason for the adoption of the test-retest procedure was the supposition that material to be read, learned, and understood is less likely to evaporate into a cognitive vacuum if parts of it answer questions not far out of the circle of focal attention. The procedure seems to help create the opportune state of having relevant questions in mind at the time of exposure to the source information; and there may be other, somewhat different, cognitive effects of posing questions. In addition, there is a motivational one. Repeatedly exposing the student to samples from a pool of test items exploits his natural curiosity concerning the kinds of questions that will appear on tests. If the items are of good quality and the pool is rather large, there is at the same time very little encouragement for the use of mnemonic tricks that circumvent the semantic content. In the procedure used, the students may expect to see some of the items on the retest that have appeared on the test. However, the extent of such expectations can be controlled by variation of the sizes of the test, retest, and item pool.

The remainder of this section is a discussion of probabilities associated with items reappearing on retests. A test of *m* items is randomly selected from the same pool of *n* items, and a retest of *k* items is randomly selected from the same pool of *n* items (*m*, *k* < *n*). The retest selection is independent of the first test selection, and the number of items that appear both on the test and the retest is a random variable, denoted there by *x*.

Figure 1

The subset structure in selecting a test of size m and a retest of size k from an item pool of size n.

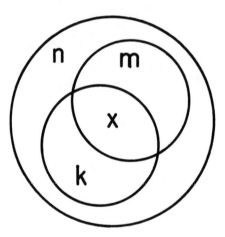

The formal sampling process arises in several applications (Feller, 1957, p. 41, p. 118). The distribution of *x* is of the hypergeometric form, and the probability of any particular value of *x* is given by

$$p(x) = \binom{m}{x} \binom{n-m}{k-x} / \binom{n}{k} \tag{1}$$

The reasoning behind equation (1) goes somewhat as follows (see Figure 1). There are $\binom{n}{k}$ ways of selecting the second sample, of size k. There are $\binom{m}{n}$ ways of selecting x items from the subset of size m. For each of these $\binom{m}{x}$ ways of getting x items from the subset of size m, there are $\binom{n-m}{k-m}$ ways of getting the other k-x items from the difference subset of size n-m. Hence, there are $\binom{m}{x}$ $\binom{n-m}{k-x}$ ways, altogether, of selecting a retest of size k whose intersection with the size-m test is exactly of size x.

From equation (1), we find that the jth factorial moment, $E(x^{[j]})$, where

$$x^{[j]} = x(x\text{-}1)\,(x\text{-}2) \ldots (x\text{-}j\text{+}1),$$

is expressible as

$$E(x^{[j]}) = m^{[j]}\,k^{[j]}\,/n^{[j]} \tag{2}$$

Expressions for the mean, μ, and variance σ^2, are readily obtained from equation (2), i.e.,

$$\mu = km/n \tag{3}$$
$$\sigma^2 = m(n\text{-}m)k(n\text{-}k)/n^2\,(n\text{-}1) \tag{4}$$

Now, apply these preliminaries to some of the questions that arise in the test-retest procedure. The item pool for each chapter is approximately of size $n = 80$. The test and retest for each chapter are of equal size, $m = k = 20$. Thus, the expected number of items reappearing on the retest is 5, and the standard deviation is 1.69. For the test and retest both of size 20, equation (3) may be used to estimate the size of the item pool necessary to reduce the mean number of items reappearing on the retest to some desired number, say two. Thus, $n = (20)^2/2$, or 200 is the required size.

On independent repetitions of the test-retest procedure for each of a series of units or textbook chapters, the total number of repeated items on all retests is a variable of interest. Because of the independence, the means and variances are additive. In our implementation, there are ten such repetitions, one for each of the ten chapters of the text. Hence, for all ten of the 20-item retests together (i.e., 200 total items) the mean and standard deviation of the number of "familiar items" are 50 and 5.34, respectively. The relative sizes of the confidence intervals decrease in proportion to the square root of the number of chapters, thus tending to average out the inequities of extreme deviations from the mean on individual chapters. However, students tend to get together and compare their original test forms, which we allow them to keep, thereby increasing the sizes of their samples from the item pool before the retest. Equations (3) and (4) can be used to obtain an idea of how much a student can expect to profit from the opportunity of seeing one form of the original test, in addition to his own. Since the two test forms are generated independently by random selection from an item pool of size n, and are of the same size, say m, the expected size of the intersection of items on the two forms is m^2/n, and the expected size of the union is therefore $2m-m^2/n$. In our case, $m = 20$, and $n = 80$, so that two test forms expose a student to 35 items from the 80-item pool on the average, as opposed to only 20 from a single test form. We may infer the expected number of "familiar items" on the retest in this case by taking $m = 35$, $k = 20$, and $n = 80$ in equation (3). It turns out to be about nine as opposed to five for the case of pre-exposure only to one form of the original test. This kind of reasoning is elaborated for a different purpose in the following paragraph.

In addition to the 20-item test and retest for each of the ten chapters, we include a 50-item final examination constructed by randomly selecting five items from each of the item pools for individual chapters. Let y be the number of items, in these five, that appeared previously on the corresponding test, retest, or both. The conditional expectation of y is

$$E(y|x) = \frac{5[2(20)-x]}{80}$$

where x is the size of the intersection of items appearing on the test and retest. Then

$$E(y) = \frac{200}{80} - \frac{5}{80} E(x),$$

or $E(y) = 2.2$. Summing over the ten chapters, we arrive at a figure of 22 as the mean number of items on the final that have been seen previously. This assumes that a student is exposed only to items on his own tests and retests, so it is reasonable to increase the estimate a little. Hence, we guess that the average number of familiar items on the 50-item final examination is about 25.

For the weekly tests and retests, we went against the advice of Prosser and Jensen (1971), who recommended that the item pool be at least six times as large as the test forms to be generated from it. In our case, the initial item pool was only about 5/2 the size of the test forms, although this factor has increased to about 4 with later additions to the item pools. The consequent relatively high rate of reappearance of items on the retests is not entirely a defect. It encourages students to regard the test questions as a learning resource rather than merely as tools whereby the instructor may estimate achievement.

Costs

The approximations made here are quite rough, but sufficiently realistic to decide whether or not the system is merely an expensive boondoggle. Included are the time and expenses that an instructor might expect to incur if he planned to adopt such a system already in existence. Excluded are the additional time and expenses that went into the original implementation, and any effort that might be required to modify the present system extensively.

The item pool. The first requirement is for a sizeable pool of good-quality test items. Our initial pool contained about 500 items for the whole course, and it does not seem advisable to try to get by with fewer. If the instructor were to sit down and create 500 test items from scratch, the item pool could be very expensive. But there are alternate ways of acquiring the necessary item pool. Many instructors have built up such pools over several years of teaching, and numerous instructor manuals provided by the textbook publishers include such pools, though usually not of the required size. In our initial implementation, the publisher of the textbook furnished us with 50 items per chapter, printed on 3 x 5 cards. It was necessary, however, to weed out or modify some items with a view toward presenting arbitrary subsets of them as test forms printed in upper case alphanumeric characters. Moreover, we had to get them into machine readable form on punch cards. A generous estimate of the amount of time involved in these processes would be 15 minutes per item. Thus, the cost of our initial item pool was on the order of $1000. If another instructor were to teach the same course, using the same textbook, he would naturally want to use the same item pool, since he could figure its cost as negligible. It would be a matter of duplicating the tape files, a computer run costing perhaps twenty dollars.

Computer time. Over the whole school term for good production runs, we use about two hours of CPU time, print about 8000 pages on the line printer, and punch about 1200 cards. To these figures might be added about 10 minutes of CPU time, 500 printed pages, and 4000 punched cards, used in setting the system up initially with the item pool stored on tape and printed for easy reference. The total cost of these computer services would probably run about $500.

Clerical work. There are a number of tasks that an assistant can perform. These involve filing and posting of computer output, preparation and submission of decks for computer runs, correction of answer-sheet errors in the identification fields, and the like. There seem to be five to ten hours per week of this kind of work.

Consultation time. If the system is operational at a given installation, an instructor who has never used it before probably would need about eight hours of consultation with someone who has had the experience; roughly four hours initially to get things set up and for clarification of the process; and about four hours in small pieces scattered over the school term as new questions arise. If the system were not already operational at the installation, additional consultation would be required to implement it. This would involve programmer and systems personnel associated with the installation, and the amount of time would depend on the facilities and operating policies at the installation.

Costs per test form. Assume that the system is operational at an installation and that the item pool is available in usable form. Then, with a class of about 200 students, the cost of using the system for a school term would consist of about $20 to get the item pools duplicated, about $500 for computer runs over the school term, and roughly $400 for clerical work, errand running, etc. These figures can be rounded to a total of $1000, which can be regarded as a base figure to be corrected under different circumstances. Our cost per student per test administration then comes to about 25 cents. This figure should be fairly stable under changes in class size and number of tests given over the school term, since the total computer time and clerical work should both be approximately proportional to class size and number of tests. The total expense contains some small overhead components, and there should be some improvement of the rate with larger classes. For classes of size 50 to 300, it seems unlikely that the more customary systems are much cheaper than this, considering (a) the time it takes the instructor to put together a test in handwriting or by selection of cards from a file, (b) the typing and reproduction expenses, (c) the recording and totalling of scores in the gradebook, and (d) the construction and administration of special make-up exams, etc.

Assume that an adequate item pool is available, perhaps from the textbook publisher, but not in machine-readable form. The editing and keypunching necessary to make it usable was estimated above to be about $1000. For use in only one school term by one section of 200 students, this would raise the cost per test form to about 50 cents. However, if the same course were to be taught using the same textbook and item pool for five school terms (i.e., to 1000 students), the expense of the item pool could be distributed, and the cost per test form would descend to about 30 cents. The effective lifetime of an item pool might be limited by the normal process of textbooks going out of print, and the issuance of revised editions. Some kind of amortization might be the best way to estimate the costs, if more exact estimates are needed, taking into account the salvageability of some of the items.

A possible way to extend the lifetime of the item pool indefinitely would be to make a larger initial investment for the construction of a large set of items written in such a way as to be independent of the particular textbook used. This idea has some broad beneficial implications, but there are difficulties with it. Particularly at the introductory level, courses are expected to be relatively self-contained, in that all necessary resources are to be clearly indicated and made easily available to the student. It seems likely that no particular introductory text that might be adopted would adequately prepare a student for tests made up from items of this more general kind of item pool. The scheme might be more appropriate for courses at the upper-division or graduate level.

Consultation and programming costs involved in implementing the system for the first time at an installation could be treated in a similar way, to obtain an approximate increment in the cost per test form. This expense should be distributable over a longer time period and a greater number of users than is that of the item pool. It does not seem likely that it would normally amount to more than one or two cents per test form.

The above estimate of 25 to 30 cents per test form is quite different from the five cents estimated by Prosser and Jensen (1971). The main discrepancy is due to our attempt to include all the expenses of the testing and grading system. They included only materials and computer services in order to make a fair comparison with the materials and services involved in just the typing and duplication of tests by conventional methods. A second discrepancy is in the number of test forms generated per computer run; they assumed 1000, while we assumed 200. A third discrepancy is that they exploited special features of the version of FORTRAN available at their installation, to reduce the execution time of input and output processing in their programs. Only the third discrepancy is one of system efficiency, but it, together with other possible small differences in efficiency of the object programs, may well account for as much as ten cents of the difference in costs per test form. They estimated the cost of tests per student per school term to be about one dollar. We estimate it to be about five dollars, taking into account the discrepancies indicated above. Considering the fact that we have attempted to include all costs of the testing and grading activity in the course, five dollars is not very expensive.

Psychometric Consequences

There are two main functions of tests in a course, and they seem to conflict sometimes in practice. The first, we call certification. It is primarily predictive in nature, the test results being used in later decisions involving the destiny of the individual. For example, course grades are used as admission criteria by graduate schools; they can encourage or discourage a student to take more courses or major in a discipline; and they partially determine whether or not an individual's college career continues to completion. Given that test results are used in such important decisions, it is important that tests be designed and conducted insofar as possible in accordance with the psychometric ideals of reliability and validity. The degree of unfairness of using tests for such purposes is mainly a direct function of the inaccuracy of the tests.

The second main function of tests in a course is for suggesting relevant questions and providing feedback to consolidate or perturb the student's scholarly habits or cognitive tactics. This function might be called rectification. Accuracy is an ideal here, too, but timeliness now becomes equally important. Thus, a possible tradeoff arises in the use of tests in their rectifying function.

Modern innovations in educational testing practices tend to emphasize rectification, while relaxing the requirements for the certification function. In the long run, there probably will be an appropriate reduction of confidence in the certifying value of test scores and grades. But in the short run, some of those personally affected might well complain of fraudulent exploitation. The design goals of the system reported here were aimed primarily in the direction of improvements with respect to rectification. But it can be argued that there is no necessary compromise in the other direction.

The main feature that might be regarded as a psychometric weakness is the intentional injection of an additional random component, as individual test forms are obtained by selection of random subsets from the item pool. But one effect of this feature is to reduce cheating, a prevalent phenomenon that psychometric theory ignores for the most part. Thus, the system better approximates the conditions under which the application of the theory is justified. Moreover, the increased frequency of tests increases the size of the sample of behavior from which the final evaluation is made. This increased sample size would roughly compensate for the injected random component, even if cheating were no problem.

Evaluative Observations

In operation, the system seems to meet all the design goals. The net effect from the instructor's point of view seems to be relief, during the actual conduct of the course, from much of the planning, execution, and supervision involved in the more customary testing and grading procedures. Additionally, there is continual confidence in the clarity of operational communication of the tasks, criteria, and feedback to the students. The regular weekly test-retest routine seems to obviate repeated reminders of impending tests and exhortations against total reliance on a few concentrated cramming sessions.

The students' attitudes toward the testing and grading procedure are also favorable. This is evident from sporadic comments during the school term as well as from a course-evaluation questionnaire administered during the last week. Of the 15 items on the questionnaire having anything to do with testing and grading, 13 are of a direct evaluative nature, e.g., "The testing and grading system was fair," and "The test-retest procedure encouraged unproductive study habits." In each case, the preponderance of responses has been favorable. The other two items are: "I studied more for the retests than for the tests," and "The most helpful study aid was old tests." In both cases, very many responses have been in affirmation of the statement (74% and 83%, respectively). These responses indicate that our test-retest procedure, as it actually works, might be called more aptly a "pretest-test" procedure.

The main evaluative observations of the system to date are thus positive, and the instructor intends to continue using it.

Some Possible Variations

In the foregoing discussion, rather particular experiences have been related concerning a system used several times by the author. Some of its features were determined by design goals, but others by convenience and perhaps personal bias. Other educators[2] have discussed and implemented computer-based test-construction systems which differ in various ways from the one reported here. Some of the more obvious possible variations are as follows.

Programming languages. Some say that COBOL is more convenient than FORTRAN for the storage and retrieval of bodies of alphanumeric information. SNOBOL is even more convenient from the programmer's point of view, if there is much manipulation and transformation to be done. However, object-code efficiency is a matter of concern in the applications in question, since the programs are executed repeatedly for a large number of production runs. Hence, compiler languages such as COBOL, FORTRAN, and PL/1 are more logical choices than are, for example, SNOBOL, or BASIC.

Shuffling. It is possible to give every student exactly the same set of questions, but each in a different random order. This scheme has a number of advantages, such as (a) statistical item-analysis is facilitated, (b) one can get by with smaller item pools, and (c) post-test key changes seem more fair. These advantages are offset, however, by the need for additional sets of items if there are to be retests and make-up tests.

It would also be possible simply to randomly permute the presented alternatives of each question, but this would rule out alternatives of the form "all of the above," etc.

Item classification. In the system reported here, items are classified with respect to one attribute only, the subject matter of the successive chapters in the textbook. Each final-examination test form is then constructed by selecting randomly an equal number of items from each of these classes. Would there be advantages in the use of other attributes as well? Selection of equal numbers of items from groupings with respect to level of difficulty could help to make the different test forms more equivalent. The items might also be classified with respect to different objectives of a course. For example, it might be reasonable in some courses to define classes of items which test (a) concept mastery or vocabulary, (b) inferential skills or reasoning ability, and (c) problem solving. Each test form would then consist of three subtests, and the separate subtest scores might be of diagnostic value to the students and the instructor.

In view of the cost analysis of the system reported here, however, it would appear that the expenses of additional attributes of classification might place the item pool beyond the budget allowable for a course taught by a single instructor. This variation might be more feasible in larger permanent organizational units.

Items with variable arguments. Another extension of the system would generate alternate forms of a particular item, by random selection from a set of substrings, for insertion at one or more "variable-string" locations in the item. For courses in subjects requiring arithmetical or symbolical manipulations according to some procedures to be learned, this extension could be of value. We foresee no significant application of it, however, with the kinds of items that are used in introductory psychology courses.

Conclusion

The results of the trial of the computerized system indicates that it does solve some of the usual problems of testing and grading with a large class. It permits increases in the frequency of tests, immediacy of feedback, and accessibility and currency of cumulative records, with concomitant decreases in opportunities for cheating, clerical and administrative work, lag time between the initial planning and the administration of the tests, extra work associated with make-up exams, and the need for secretarial and typing services. Instructor and student attitudes toward the system are generally favorable, and it appears to be feasible economically under prevailing conditions. Given the appropriate computer facilities at a university, an individual instructor could consider the adoption of such a system for a large class that he teaches regularly.

References

Emerson, P.L. Experience with Computer Generation and Scoring of Tests for a Large Class. *Educational and Psychological Measurement*, 1974, *34*, 703-709.

Feller, W. *An Introduction to Probability Theory and Its Applications*. New York: John Wiley, 1957.

Prosser, F., and D.D. Jensen. Computer Generated Repeatable Tests. *AFIPS Conference Proceedings*, 1971, *38*, 295-301.

Notes

[1] The development of the system described here was aided by a grant from the Center for Effective Learning, Cleveland State University, for the purchase of computer tapes.

[2] John Luoma, Al Berger, Thomas Heines, Richard Wiersba, and Richard Black, to mention some at Cleveland State University.

23.
Write Your Own Book and Revise It Every Semester — Or Instruction Personalized by and for the Teacher as well as for the Student

Ronald L. Koteskey
Asbury College

Personalized instruction has become very popular during the last few years, but the question remains as to how personalized it really is. It usually refers to a more or less self-paced, unit by unit, presentation of the material, the same material to everyone in the class and often the same material to all classes. The problems of difficulty level, topical coverage, and modification of materials still remain, even in personalized instruction. A partial solution to these problems in teaching a course in elementary statistics is presented in this paper. It involves allowing the instructors to choose topics, set parameters, reword questions, give answers or not, set sample sizes, and specify the number of decimal places given. Following this, the computer generates a unique workbook or test for each student and a corresponding detailed answer key for the instructor.

Problems Still Remaining

Although personalized instruction has many advantages, a number of problems still remain and are regularly encountered by those attempting to use it. The units prepared for a certain type of student may be inappropriate for others. As long as one has a group of students with interests and abilities similar to the standardization groups, all is well. But if one has a group of students with low ability, or an honors group, all may be lost. The instructor has no way of controlling the difficulty level of the material unless he switches to another series of modules, which may not be as well written, not cover the desired topics, or any of a number of similar problems.

More control is given to the instructor over the topics covered. However, still more control would be desirable. The instructor uses only the modules or units he wishes to cover, chooses from a self-selection textbook, or has his own individualized book of selected reprints printed (if his class is large enough). If a topic is not covered as thoroughly as the instructor wishes, he switches to a different series, prepares additional material himself, or remains frustrated.

When the instructor wishes to present material in a different order within a unit or module, he again has a difficult time. Sometimes he would even like to reword the way something is presented or reword a question to make it clearer to his classes, but copyright laws prevent such changes. The best he can do is assign supplementary reading or duplicate some of his own remarks for the student to read along with the available material. Using selections from different series, supplementary material, duplicated remarks, etc., all lead the student to see the course in a piecemeal fashion, making it difficult for him to get a unified view of the subject. These facts make it evident that personalized instruction leaves many problems unsolved. Although it is called personalized, most instructors use the same modules, the students in a given class all read the same material, and each class covers about the same thing except that they do it at their own individual rates of speed.

A Partial Solution for One Course

The above problems related to the uniformity of personalized instruction are accentuated in statistics. Often an instructor wishes to teach one set of techniques but is forced to include others that the textbook or module authors have included as "necessary" background for their explanations. Also, when all students are doing the same set of problems, copying of solutions usually results, to the detriment of the student, since actual experience working problems is often essential to understanding given procedures. This is especially true if the problems are too difficult for the students. In this case, it becomes much easier to copy than to try to understand. If a student copies to get the problem correct, but never understands it, he is unprepared to advance to the next step in the course.

An attempt has been made to further individualize the psychological statistics course by allowing each instructor to write his own workbook for his own type of teaching, and a different one for each individual class if he wishes. He can easily revise it each semester or add to it during the semester if necessary. This has been done by writing a series of subroutines that use the computer to generate individualized workbooks and tests according to the specifications of each instructor. Each instructor writes his own workbook for his own course—or, rather, the computer does it for him. Furthermore, each workbook or test is unique and even has the student's own name on it.

Materials. A library of subroutines has been developed with one subroutine for each of the techniques commonly taught in a statistics course. Each subroutine generates the problem for the student on the right half of the page and the solution worked out in detail for the instructor on the left half, so that they can be easily separated with a paper cutter. Each problem is unique in that the numbers in it have been chosen randomly from the same population, one specified by the instructor when he called the subroutine. Instructions as to what the student is to do in the problem are automatically printed in the subroutine, or the instructor can write his own instructions, put them in the program just before he calls the subroutine, and have the ones in the subroutine suppressed.

The following subroutines have been developed and used.

1. Constructing frequency distributions.
2. Percentiles and percentile ranks from frequency distributions.
3. Measures of central tendency (mean, mode, and median; either from raw scores or from frequency distributions).
4. Measures of variability (range and standard deviation; either from raw scores or from frequency distributions).
5. Normal curve, sampling error, and confidence intervals.
6. Random *t*.
7. Correlation, regression, and prediction (Pearson *r* and rank order).
8. Correlated *t*.
9. Chi-square.
10. Mann-Whitney U test.

11. Wilcoxon signed-ranks test.
12. Analysis of variance (single and double classification and the Scheffé test).

Others can be developed as the need arises. Workbooks for a whole introductory course can be generated for a cost of just about what students would ordinarily pay for the usual workbook.

Procedure. These materials have been prepared to allow maximum individualization by the instructor with a minimum of effort. On the basis of his own perspective of statistics and available text materials, he decides what topics will be covered in his particular course for that semester. If that topic is not covered in the available subroutines, a new subroutine must be written; but if it is in the subroutine library, he simply decides how many exercises on that topic he wants. He then decides whether or not he likes the wording of the instructions to the student in the subroutine. If so, he uses one parameter in the subroutine call. If not, he uses a different parameter and writes new instructions to be printed. He then decides on the parameters for each problem, specifying means, standard deviations, correlation coefficients, etc., for the populations. He specifies sample sizes, giving all students the same size samples, or letting the computer pick sample sizes randomly between two values he has chosen. He chooses whether or not the student is to be given the final answer to the problem on his side of the page. Finally, he chooses how many decimal places there will be in the scores given to the student.

In specifying the above, the instructor takes into account his goals for that particular class and unit. If he is stressing calculation skills, he may want to give more decimal places in the problems, using very small and very large numbers, or he may wish to give a mixture of positive and negative numbers. If he is stressing understanding of statistical concepts, difficult calculations may interfere with that type of learning so he may use only positive integers in the problems. These goals may change in the various units of the course. For instance, calculation skills may be emphasized early in the course and understanding of concepts during the latter parts.

The instructions referred to above are coded into a subroutine call for each problem desired and the computer does the rest. If the instructor wishes, he can code each subroutine call in the same particular way and the computer sets all parameters, etc., automatically. When the instructor receives the workbooks from the computer center, he cuts each one in half with a paper cutter, keeping the answers and giving the problems to the student. When the student has worked his problems, he can be given partial credit for them if desired since the computer has printed step-by-step solutions to the problem on the answer key. If the teacher prefers mastery teaching, he can check the answer and if it is incorrect he can send the student back to work on it some more or quickly locate and point out the student's error before he sends him back for further work. Student proctors can easily be taught to do this.

Finally, the subroutines can be used to generate individualized tests in the course. The instructor then makes up his tests and keys using the same procedures as to write his workbooks. He also can generate quickly supplementary exercises if he sees that his students are not understanding a given concept even as he is teaching the course. Of course, he will incorporate these supplementary exercises into his workbook as he revises it for the next semester.

Advantages of this system. Of course, the major advantage of these materials is individualization, for the teacher as well as for the student. The instructor can adjust his instructional materials to his teaching, rather than modifying his teaching to fit available materials. Furthermore, he can continually change his teaching; each semester is a new experience with new topics added, old ones dropped; new parameters, systematically varied to see what happens; giving the students no answers, some answers, or all the answers; traditional teaching one time, mastery teaching the next; etc. Innovation becomes easy, since the instructor can easily answer the question, "I wonder what would happen if . . . ," when applied to his teaching.

The student gets actual individualized materials with this system. He receives his workbook with "Prepared for 'John Student,' Fall, 1977," printed right on it. He gets a unique workbook or test with the same type of problems that the other students have, but with the specifics of each problem different so that the answers are all different. Although students' workbooks are different, they are generated from the same populations, so that they are similar enough for students to help each other, thus encouraging cooperation without copying. Cheating (copying) is minimized because it takes a great deal of effort on the part of the one giving the answers; he has to work each problem over again. Students are able to help each other because they know how to work that type of problem, but they cannot copy, since all answers are different.

There are other advantages as well. Much time is saved for the instructor, since he no longer has to make up tests or exercises along with their solutions. He simply specifies parameters and how many of each he wants—and the computer does the rest. When the class pools their exercises or problems from their workbooks, sampling experiments can be done, because each exercise or problem was drawn from populations with identical parameters. If the instructor has systematically varied the parameters, this helps get the basics of sampling theory across to the students. Since the workbooks are generated using batch processing on the computer, a large computer with time sharing and many terminals is not necessary.

In conclusion, these subroutines allow great individualization with little effort. They allow the instructor to more fully express himself in his teaching while giving the student more personalized materials. Of course, this is only the first step since it involves only workbooks. The next step is a similar type of generation of text material as well with the instructor picking topics, types of explanation for each (mathematical derivations, intuitive, etc.), setting parameters for examples, etc.

Note

[1] Requests for further information should be sent to Ronald L. Koteskey, Department of Psychology, Asbury College, Wilmore, Kentucky 40390.

24.
Political Science and Computers:
An Application

Steven Parker
Western Illinois University

Introduction

An on-going problem faced by planners of social science curricula concerns the relationship between a discipline's "subject matter" and "methodology" courses. One field in which this has been especially obvious is that of Political Science. In subject matter courses the student is instructed in such matters as the character and functioning of the U.S. Congress or the Presidency, while in the other type he examines the means by which knowledge is gained: how to gather data, the means of analysis, etc.

In each of these "tracks" the courses progress from the introductory through the advanced levels, but a problem often remains regarding their fit. When should shifts be made from subject matter to methods courses and back again? How do methods courses complement and enhance research projects executed in the subject matter courses? The answers to such questions vary from institution to institution, but the overall trend seems to be toward the increasing integration of methods materials into the subject matter courses themselves, i.e., toward actually breaking down the artificial barriers created by the two-track system. A good example is project SETUPS (APSA, 1974). One reason for this is that students simply must have quantitative and analytical training if they are to function competently and compete effectively upon graduation. Another reason for the growing integration may well be that the material in the courses is, in reality, not as discrete as it is often thought to be.

For several years, Western Illinois University (enrollment 14,000), has been operating on the assumption that more interchange between the two tracks is a worthwhile goal. For its Political Science Department, this has meant diversifying its introductory American Government course to include methods material. The project has focused on structuring empirical analysis into the course itself. This paper examines the program's major dimensions and on-going findings.

The program can be briefly summarized. Students in this course participate in an exercise involving computer analysis of survey data, such as the biennial election studies of the Center for Political Studies (1970, 1972). The project is suited for that section of the course dealing with elections and public opinion, and in it students develop their own hypotheses, that they then test using the school's IBM 360/50 computer.

The program is administered centrally by one staff member, who goes into each of the course sections and gives several lectures on the theory and method of computer utilization in Political Science. He, along with graduate assistants, also monitors student progress. These tasks are performed in place of one course preparation. Guided by the work of Kenneth Janda (1969), the exercise relies upon simple cross-tabulation, and it is administered to approximately 1500 students per academic year.

Objectives

Two goals have guided the program, and they both concern breaking down the artificial barriers between substance and method. The first deals with making the student more active in the education process. Instead of simply taking in the pre-packaged ideas of others, he now has to take a positive role in his own education process by formulating and testing his own hypotheses.

The second goal also has a psychological basis, but pivots on the fear of failure. Many students stay away from methods courses because of a fear of them and of the use of computers. The student tells himself that he cannot master this field, and thus does not. We have sought to interrupt this self-fulfilling prophecy by exposing the student to a relatively simple, computer-based project in the very first introductory course. By experiencing success, which most do, the student learns that he need not necessarily fear this mode of analysis. By making the tool work for him once, we structure the situation so that he may want to employ it again. Thus, further interchange between the two tracks is facilitated.

These objectives, then, revolve around overcoming the real, but too often over-exaggerated, distinction between substance and method. Where this distinction is concerned, however, one might hear the objection raised that by taking the time to teach certain methods in such a course, one is merely decreasing the amount of time available for instruction in the subject matter itself. At Western this problem has been overcome by developing the exercise along highly programmed lines, the most important part of which relies on "learning kits" distributed to every student. The use of such kits is one of several functional requisites identified by our experience.

Functional Requisites

Although the objectives and basic operations of such a program are relatively straightforward, the reader can imagine the many possibilities for confusion and breakdown, especially given the large number of students being served. Given the many potential obstacles, it is relevant that our years of experience have enabled us to isolate a number of functional requisites: procedures and conditions the absence of which would likely be harmful to the program. First of all, there must be a ready availability of real data sets, and thus the election studies conducted by the Center for Political Studies (1970, 1972) provide a primary data base.

Given the introductory nature of the course and the project, a second requirement has been the use of canned programs, specifically Dixon's *Biomedical* package (1970) and Nie's *Statistical Package for the Social Sciences* (1970). Canned programs have their limitations, but for the novice working under carefully controlled conditions there is hardly any substitute. A third requisite involves faculty commitment. Without this, none of the other requisites can be satisfied, since the faculty as a whole controls the allocation of resources.

The final requisite concerns packaging of the program and the means of its presentation. Several alternative approaches are available here, but Western's experience has isolated the effectiveness of programmed learning packages or kits that can be incorporated into the exercises themselves. As with most programmed material, the kit breaks the exercise down into a number of discrete steps so that the student can follow the logic and flow in a serial manner.

The materials in the kit are as follows:

a. *Instructional manual.* The first, and probably most important, component is a short instruction manual and workbook. This contains all the technical information necessary for use of a canned program. In addition, it introduces a sample hypothesis and guides the student through an elementary analysis of it.

b. *Codebook.* The second component is a mini-codebook for the study being used. During the period reported on here, analysis decks for the Center for Political Studies' 1970 and 1972 election studies were employed.

c. *Input list.* The third component is an input list. It is presented on a sample coding form, and it sets forth all of the job and control cards necessary to examine the sample hypothesis. The cumulative nature and interdependence of these pieces should by now have become apparent. Here the student learns what instructions to give the computer in order to test the sample hypothesis presented in the workbook and operationalized via the codebook.

d. *Printout.* Each student is provided with a sample printout for the sample hypothesis.

e. *Worksheet.* Finally, there is a worksheet asking various questions about the student's own hypothesis and data. When completed, this is submitted to the professor.

The most important aspect is the interdependence and coordination between all of the pieces in the package. Around a common set of procedures and a sample hypothesis revolve the workbook and manual, the codebook from which the variables for the hypothesis were chosen, an input list for the given sample hypothesis, and finally a sample output. A copy of the entire instructional package is available from the author.

After two hours of in-class lecture, a thorough reading of materials in the package and the viewing of a short (12 minutes) videotape made by the author on how to use the keypunch machine, each student uses his codebook to generate a hypothesis of his own, which he then tests by following the procedures learned.

Findings

Our findings indicate that the program is well received by both students and professors, with colleagues being convinced that the execution of a project of this nature during the section of the course dealing with electoral behavior definitely heightens the student's appreciation for the dynamics involved.

Evaluation of student reaction has been based upon a short questionnaire administered to participants at the time of completion of the project. While space does not permit a full-scale tabulation and analysis of results here, the most significant findings gleaned over the three-year period may be briefly summarized. The device uses a five-point scale and finds more than 90 percent of the students rating the project as either "interesting" or "very interesting." Figures were almost as positive for an item scaling their views on how "worthwhile" the experience had been. It is also of significance that when students are asked to rate the degree to which the course itself is "worthwhile" (using identical categories), they consistently have a much less positive reaction. That is, there are approximately 20 percent fewer choices of the top two ratings, which are the only "favorable" ones. Thus, it appears that students ordinarily seem to have a better experience with the data experience than with the course of which it is a part. Significantly, this holds true regardless of what grade the student expects or what his major happens to be. Tentatively, one might conclude that because the new addition has consistently received a more positive reception than its parent, the latter benefits from its presence.

Conclusions

The first, and most basic, conclusion that may be drawn from the foregoing is that computer-assisted data analysis may, under the right conditions, be successfully included as an integral part of introductory courses. Secondly, the Western experience indicates that the conditions for effective implementation of such a program include the following:

—the availability of real data sets;

—the availability of canned programs such as those in the BMD and SPSS series;

—faculty commitment;

—administrative procedures focusing responsibility on one person; and

—the extensive use of detailed, programmed learning packages.

A third conclusion is that when these varying pre-conditions are met, student response is likely to be very positive. This would appear to be due largely to the fact that the student is being given a chance to be active in his own education, rather than simply a passive recipient.

A final conclusion stems from the others. It would appear that we can use such programs not only to help teach the "substance" of various introductory courses, but also to lessen the fear many students have for methodology. The computer exercise, presented simply and at the introductory level, can have the impact of "de-mystifying" much quantification and the computer.

References

American Political Science Association. *SETUPS: Supplementary Empirical Teaching Units in Political Science*. Washington, D.C.: American Political Science Association, 1974.

Center for Political Studies. *American National Election Study*, Center for Political Studies, Ann Arbor, Michigan, 1970.

Center for Political Studies. *1972 American National Election Study*, Center for Political Studies, Ann Arbor, Michigan, 1972.

Dixon, D. *Biomedical Computer Programs*. Los Angeles: University of California Press, 1970.

Janda, K. *Data Processing: Applications to Political Research*. Evanston, Illinois: Northwestern University Press, 1969.

Nie, N., D. Bent, and C. Hull. *Statistical Package for the Social Sciences*. New York: McGraw-Hill Book Company, 1970.

PART V
Simulation and Modeling

25.
Simulation and Modeling in the Classroom

Richard S. Lehman
Franklin & Marshall College

While many psychologists still regard the computer as only a tool for large-scale data analysis, there is an increasing awareness that it may serve in other areas as well. The growing use of computers as on-line control and recording devices is one example, as is the rapidly expanding literature on simulation and modeling using the computer. This paper focuses on two aspects of the latter development—the appearance of courses where models and simulations are taught explicitly, and the use of models and simulations in the teaching of other, more "traditional," content areas.

In two respects, this paper may be regarded as a case study on the educational application of simulation. In the first place, only psychology is discussed. The same kind of impact is being felt in the other social sciences as well, so that the discussion could be paralleled in other fields with minor changes in emphasis and examples. Second, no attempt of or claim to exhaustiveness is made here. The examples used are just that—other illustrations could be selected from among the growing literature in all fields.

Models As an Aid in Content Areas

The development of a conceptual model or algorithm, a quite direct result of the development of computer models in research, has resulted in new formulations of theoretical positions. For example, Hunt, Marin, and Stone's (1966) book had a strong impact both on later formulations of theoretical positions and on the terminology used in the field of induction and artificial intelligence. Likewise, Neisser's (1967) presentation is algorithmic in nature and readily leads to class discussion formulated around the idea of the perceptual system as an active processor of information. In both of these cases, while no actual simulations are postulated, modeling in its broader sense has had a significant impact.

This section of the paper surveys four topics traditionally covered in an undergraduate psychology program. In each area, the applicability of several recent computer simulations are illustrated.

Statistics and Research Design. Computer simulations are employed in several ways in the teaching of statistics and research design. Simulations of experimental situations are used to generate data for student analysis. The various statistical distributions can be simulated to provide data for problem sets. A full discussion of the use of the computer in teaching statistics can be found in the paper by Lehman, Starr, and Young, in this volume.

Learning. Models of various learning phenomena have appeared recently that may be incorporated in a course on learning.

One of these, the Stimulus and Association Learner (SAL) by Hintzman (1968) deals with paried associated (P-A) learning. The model itself embodies a discrimination net theory of P-A learning, closely related to Feigenbaum and Simon's EPAM (Elementary Perceiver and Memorizer; see, for example, Feigenbaum, 1963). In this model, a network of branches is constructed in learning; to retrieve the response for a given stimulus, a series of tests is made to uniquely identify a stimulus. (For example, "Is the first letter an X? If so, do I have a response for X? What is the second letter? Do I have a response for this pair of letters? etc.") If there is no stored response, the model specifies guessing, and constructing of a new testing node upon being informed of the correct response.

Hintzman's paper describes three versions of SAL, based upon increasing sophistication of both theory and program. The general structure and discussion of the theory given by Hintzman would form a good foundation for a class discussion or student report on this particular approach to theorizing in P-A learning. In addition, the models themselves, or at least SAL-I, are not complex and can be understood by students with a modest background in computer programming.

Lehman (1976) presents a FORTRAN version of SAL-I and SAL-II that is readily transportable. With the program available, students can actually run the model without having to know anything about programming. They can be encouraged to repeat some of the simple experiments described by Hintzman for themselves to gain an understanding of some of the elementary phenomena of P-A learning.

A related learning model is that by Anderson (1972) called FRAN (for Free Recall in an Associative Net). FRAN is another model in the general EPAM-SAL style, based on a network of associations in memory. The presentation of the model itself might, like SAL, serve as the basis for a class discussion or reports on associative models of free recall. The program for FRAN, as well as the conceptual model, is somewhat more complex than any of the versions of SAL. It is less likely that a version of the FRAN program could be readily understood by undergraduates, or even by graduate students, unless they were thoroughly familiar with the LISP programming language. FRAN is written in LISP/360, which limits its transportability to other computers.

Anderson and Bower (1973), in a masterful volume destined to have a profound influence on learning theory, summarize the work with SAL- and FRAN-type simulations. An entire high-level learning course could be built around their work.

Bewley (1974) has developed an excellent collection of simulations for classroom use. Devoted to the general topic of cognitive psychology, this combination workbook and handbook should see wide use in learning courses.

Another valuable contribution is the text by Uhr (1973). This book, applicable not only to learning but to courses in perception and cognitive theory as well, presents a wealth of example programs. The programs are written in a special language called EASEY. EASEY programs are readable, and may be operable on a system with a SNOBOL compiler, the language in which the EASEY compiler is itself written.

Social. Green (1972) presents a discussion of the three-person common-target game, in a version for a single S interacting with two simulated stooges. In the common-target game, E presents a number "target" and each S responds with a number (e.g., between 1 and 10), so that the Ss' numbers total the target. The Ss are not allowed to interact, but must develop a strategy for playing the game. Joyner (1970) presents a model of the process embodying an algorithm allowing the simulated player to test and evaluate strategies during the operation of the program. The Green (1972) version, on the other hand, is a greatly simplified model using one of three predefined strategies instead of having the program formulate and test them. In terms of teaching utility, the full model (Joyner) deals with the broader issue of concept learning in the common-target game and could serve as a useful springboard for discussion. Green's model, on the other hand, is immediately useful on an interactive terminal, and would allow a student to play the role of a subject in the game, with the computer serving as the other two *S*s.

In a related fashion, Fox (1972) presents some research in two-person zero-sum game playing, using a computer program as the opponent. The program plays either a rational or non-rational strategy, depending upon the situation. While Fox used the model in research to investigate *S*s' learning of strategies for play, the model is admirably suited to classroom use as well. Students often have difficulty in understanding the nature of the simple two-person game when it is discussed abstractly in readings or lecture. A few minutes with the computer as an opponent would be very helpful in their understanding of the game.

Perception. The field of perception is being influenced a great deal by computer modeling. The impact of Neisser's book has already been mentioned. The consideration of perception as active information processing has led to a large number of models. Some of the models have never been actually implemented as operating computer programs, but are conceptual descriptions of information processing processes applied to perception.

An operating perception simulation, PATREC, a pattern-recognizer developed by Wallingford (1972), will serve as an example. PATREC is a feature-detecting model based on the neurological evidence for receptive fields in the visual system that selectively responds to certain features of a visual display. It is written in FORTRAN, and should be operable on a great number of computer systems.

Even in the absence of an operating version of PATREC, Wallingford's paper, assigned as class reading, could stimulate discussion of the nature of simulation (the paper makes it clear that no direct physical parallelism is assumed), and also of what a system capable of recognition must accomplish.

If PATREC were available and could be modified, it would also be interesting to change its set of receptive fields and allow students to explore the kinds of features essential for the recognition of certain classes of visual stimuli. PATREC might also be compared with a template-matching program, if one were available; or it might be feasible to compare PATREC with a parallel processing model, such as Selfridge's PANDEMONIUM (1959).

A perception course could be developed by using Uhr (1973) as a text. It would have to be supplemented by other materials, but the presentation of several models of pattern recognition can serve as a major focus of organization for the entire course.

A Course in Simulation and Modeling

The use of simulation techniques and results in teaching content courses is only a part of the contemporary story; the other part is the development of courses and seminars whose subject matter is simulation *per se.* This section of the paper discusses these courses by presenting a generalized outline of a course, discussing several different kinds of courses, and briefly summarizing the characteristics of several books that might be considered as texts.

A Course Outline. In the recent history of psychology, if the computer was introduced to students at all, it was typically in its role as a research tool. Theoretical developments, such as those cited above, and many others, have led to a wider appreciation that the computer can also serve in the theory development and simulation role. This realization has led to pressure for courses addressing the topic of simulation directly.

An outline for a course in simulation is presented below, followed by a discussion of the way the outline might be tailored to suite several different kinds of courses. One assumption should be noted—students entering the course must have some background in psychology, in elementary statistics, and in basic computer programming.

A. *Introduction and overview*
    1. Nature of simulation and modeling

       2. Goals, aims, and uses of simulation and modeling

B. *The process of developing a computer simulation*
    1. Problem definition
       a.   The use(s) to be made of the simulation
       b.   Process study
    2. Data requirements and representation
    3. System design
    4. Coding and debugging
    5. Some selected programming techniques (e.g., lists, trees, random number generation, string processing, etc.) if desired and appropriate.

C. *Selected applications areas*
    1. Problem solving
    2. Learning and memory
    3. Group processes
    4. Voting behavior
    5. Social engineering
    6. Organizational processes
    7. Economic systems
    8. Ecology
    9. Demography
   10. Pattern recognition
   11. Artificial intelligence
   12. Linguistics
   13. Game playing
   14. Operations research
   15. Belief systems
   16. Choice and preference

D. *Evaluation and use*
    1. Evaluation procedures (indistinguishability tests, subjective criteria, etc.)
    2. Consideration of various example models in light of evaluation criteria
    3. Using simulations
       a.   Theory building
       b.   Theory testing
       c.   Prediction
       d.   Etc.

E. *Impact of computer modeling and simulation*

    1. Business and industry
    2. Social and behavioral sciences
    3. Society at large
F. *The future of computer simulation*

Several different course organizations, reflecting different emphases, can be derived from the outline.

1. *Survey course.* This course would emphasize an assortment of topics in Section C (Applications). The selection would be made on the basis of the interests of the students and/or instructor. Some coverage of Sections A, D, E, and F would also be included, but the bulk of the course, perhaps one-half or more of the total time, would be in applications survey. The presentation could be lecture with assigned outside readings, or perhaps by student reports in seminar fashion.

2. *Theoretical course.* Here the emphasis is on the computer simulation as a theoretical statement or as a test of a theoretical position. The materials in Sections A and D are the most relevant here, with examples drawn from the Section C topics as appropriate.

3. *"How-To" course.* The emphasis in this kind of course is on Section B. Typically, the students might be required to develop and program a simulation on some topic of interest to them.

4. *"How-To" and survey course.* The author has taught a combination "how-to" and survey course by requiring that students pick an area of interest, write a "library-type" survey paper to present in seminar, and develop and orally present a related simulation program.

5. *Other organizations.* The four preceding courses were developed around the topic outline. Other organizations are possible. For example, a course might be organized around various kinds of models (e.g., strictly mathematical models, process models, mechanical models, man-machine interactive models, man-man simulation games, etc.).

Sources and Resources. A large number of published materials can serve as resource material for a course in simulation and modeling. The selection of a text is a difficult matter for any course; it is particularly so for a course in a rapidly developing field like simulation. Any text should be supplemented by readings in the current literature.

A survey course might choose as a major text a book like Feigenbaum and Feldman (1963) which, while somewhat dated, introduces a broad range of topics. Other choices might include Guetzkow, Kotler, and Schultz (1972) if the course is interdisciplinary, or perhaps Shank and Colby (1973), Uhr (1973), or Apter (1970) for more specialized courses.

A "how to" course requiring a major programming project might choose Emshoff and Sisson (1970) or Lehman (1976). These books devote considerable space to the detailed procedures involved in actually programming a simulation and comparatively less space to surveys of existing simulations.

The theoretically focussed course offers the most difficulty in text selection. Most of the references just cited offer one or more chapters devoted to the theoretical and metatheoretical aspects of simulation. Additional key readings would include Abelson (1968) and Fridja (1967).

Developing a course in simulation and modeling requires a great deal of effort by the instructor. Unless the course is to be devoted to a detailed investigation of a narrow area (learning and cognition, for example), the necessary materials will be found scattered through a bewildering array of books, journals, and technical memoranda. Inspecting the references provided in the survey books and papers mentioned above will indicate the most likely sources for current developments.

Conclusion

This paper is but a small beginning. Simulations are finding their way into the everyday world of the psychologist at an increasing rate. Theoretical development in every subfield of the discipline is being influenced, often profoundly, by the computer. This summary of and introduction to the field will hopefully offer an instructor a view of how he might incorporate simulation into his teaching, by either the inclusion in existing content courses, or perhaps by developing a new course in simulation itself.

References

Abelson, R.P. Simulation of Social Behavior. In G. Lindzey, and E. Aronson (Eds.) *The Handbook of Social Psychology,*

Second Edition (Vol. 2). Reading, Mass.: Addison-Wesley, 1968.

Anderson, J.R. FRAN: A Simulation Model of Free Recall. In G. Bower (Ed.) *The Psychology of Learning and Motivation* (Vol. 5). New York: Academic Press, 1972.

Anderson, J.R., and G.H. Bower. *Human Associative Memory*. Washington, D.C.: V.H. Vinston and Sons, 1973.

Apter, M.J. *The Computer Simulation of Behavior*. London: Hutchinson, 1970.

Bewley, W.L. *Cognitive Psychology: A Computer-Oriented Laboratory Manual*, Dartmouth College, Hanover, N.H., 1974.

Emshoff, J.R., and R.L. Sisson. *Design and Use of Computer Simulation Models*. New York: Macmillan, 1970.

Feigenbaum, E.A. The Simulation of Verbal Learning Behavior. In F.A. Feigenbaum and J. Feldman (Eds.) *Computers and Thought*. New York: McGraw-Hill, 1963.

Feigenbaum, E.A., and J. Feldman (Eds.) *Computers and Thought*. New York: McGraw-Hill, 1963.

Fox, J. The Learning of Strategies in a Simple, Two-Person Zero-Sum Game Without Saddlepoint. *Behavioral Science,*. 1972, *17*, 300-308.

Fridja, N.H. Problems of Computer Simulation. *Behavioral Science*, 1967, *12*, 59-67.

Green, B.F., Jr. The Use of Time-Shared Terminals in Psychology. *Behavior Research Methods & Instrumentation*, 1972, *4*, 51-55.

Guetzkow, H., P. Kotler, and R. Schultz. *Simulation in Social and Administrative Science: Overviews and Case Examples*. Englewood Cliffs, N.J.: Prentice-Hall, 1972.

Hintzman, D.L. Explorations with a Discrimination Net Model for Paired Associate Learning. *Journal of Mathematical Psychology*, 1968, *5*, 123-162.

Hunt, E., J. Marin, and P. Stone. *Experiments in Induction*. New York: Academic Press, 1966.

Joyner, R.C. Computer Simulation of Individual Concept Learning in the Three-Person Common Target Game. *Journal of Mathematical Psychology*, 1970, 7, 478-514.

Lehman, R.S. *Computer Modeling and Simulation: An Introduction*. Hillsdale, N.J.: Erlbaum Associates, 1976.

Neisser, U. *Cognitive Psychology*. New York: Appleton-Century-Crofts, 1967.

Selfridge, O.G. Pandemonium: A Paradigm for Learning. In D. Blake and A.M. Uttley (Eds.) *Proceedings of the Symposium on Mechanisation of Thought Processes*. London: H.M. Stationary Office, 1959.

Shank, R.C., and K.M. Colby (Eds.) *Computer Models of Thought and Language*. San Francisco: W.H. Freeman, 1973.

Uhr, L. *Pattern Recognition, Learning, and Thought*. Englewood Cliffs, N.J.: Prentice-Hall, 1973.

Wallingford, E.G. A Visual Pattern Recognizing Computer Program Based on Neurophysiological Data. *Behavioral Science*, 1972, *17*, 241-248.

Note

[1] An earlier version of this paper was presented in a symposium entitled Recent Developments in Non-Data-Analytic Applications of Computers, at the Eastern Psychological Association, Washington, D.C., 1973. The present version has benefited from contributions by James Anderson, Francis Campos, Fred Hornbeck, Stuart Rakoff, James Sakoda, and James Starr, none of whom would probably wish to claim any responsibility for its present form and content; the author expresses his appreciation to them, nonetheless.

26.
Simulation and the Possibilities of Learning: An Interpretation of the Uses of a Small Computer in Undergraduate Instruction in Economics

Ralph N. Calkins
Hanover College

Systemic Simulation

Systems analysis seeks to represent the behavior of real-world phenomena by building models. The models derive from various social sciences, administration, classical engineering, medical science, and so on. Systems analysis requires that one must have a model. A comprehension of the pure model, however, does not explain the behavior of a natural system. The model, therefore, must extend beyond the level of mere mental contemplation.

A verbal model, expressed in natural language, may be designated a logico-qualitative model. This type of model postulates logical relationships between constituent elements or parts in the real environment. Concerning those selected referents, there is limited descriptive information, sufficient only for recognition and identification. The model resembles a map that lacks a scale. The literature of economics contains many models of this variety, and many modern theories are restatements of such models.

A logico-quantitative model defines the theoretically important variables, specifies functional relationships between variables, and is able to accept hard, quantitative data for one or more parameters. The input may be hypothetical, or information taken from the environment can drive this type of model.

In this computer era, the fixed logic of logico-quantitative models is often expressed in computer language. Having been programmed to a model, a computer will accept concrete data and will output, as solutions, the desired values of other parts of a system. These solutions are simulations of some of the variables as they are constrained by the model. Whether the simulation also represents a physical system or organization is a separate question, to be answered by reference to what happened in the simulation versus what happened in the real process. Parenthetically, if the simulation of an existent situation is satisfactory, the model may be used to generate possibilities that have never occurred in the real system. The object of much operational research is to increase systemic efficiency.

Simulation has the power to display behavior and to explain that behavior by the functional relationships contained in the model, together with the appropriate exogenous constraints, if there are any on the system. In economics, simulation models are grounded in three types of theory, which are pure theory, including game theory, decision theory, and statistical theory.

Simulation for Instruction

When a problem goes on a computer, the labor is diminished and the quality of the findings is improved. That is why students should have the best computing tools available, always with the skills to use them. The object of simulation is to study what can be achieved by managerial and economic analysis. Computing is not analysis, and it is not pretended that automated processing instructs the user in modeling. The methodology of analysis is model solving and model design. Students should always approach a working program with the question: "What problem is solved by this model?" After the program has delivered the information for which it was designed, then it is asked: "What question should we ask next?" To answer the first question, the students must have sufficient theoretical understanding of the conceptual elements in the model, and they should know the algorithm followed by the analyst. The second question is also one of economic meaning. An appropriate type of interpretation of one simulation is the capability of solving related problems, if something is changed in the model or in the data.

Teaching by the assigned use of a computer takes advantage of the machine's speed and dexterity in cycling out information. Economics is rich in theories that can be computer simulated in models for which the computer is the only feasible teaching medium. A computer-based course can contain more applications than we dared hope to cover using ordinary language, analytic graphs and tables, and numerical expressions produced manually.

Computer simulations are subject to the same limitations as other intellectual models. They do not take into consideration every possible force operating on an empirical problem, for these forces are innumerable. There is also the same problem of user alienation, or resistance to unconvincing models. If the model is unstable, or generates outcomes that the user feels are improbable or inadequate, he will disregard such outcomes, and will look for more meaningful models. For those who want to view the disastrous consequences of a deliberately-induced state of user alienation, an interactive simulation of the St. Petersburg Paradox has been reported (Calkins and Voss, 1974).

Types of Models

We distinguish between microtheory, decision models, and inductive statistical models. When employed for educational purposes, macroeconomic models are evaluated like microtheory.

Microtheory. The production function is a microtheory that divides into numerous submodels. Algebraic relations are often quantified by a single hypothetical parameter. The model generates other desired values in batch mode by numerical computation. In older terminology, models that work on such principles were termed "static." Microtheory is also called abstract or pure because of its general and mathematical structure. A typical application is the study of the demand for productive factors, where total product is calculated as a function of man-days of labor. Equilibrium comes to the model when the marginal product of labor is equal to the market price for labor. This is an example of optimality in the microtheory sense. An abstract model can explore long chains of geometric-numerical logic with minimal data input, and no hard facts whatsoever. Computer analysis can take over the grueling labor of hand computation. If it is desired to see curve intersections, the computer can also perform the plotting.

The simulation of another microtheroy, the equilibrium of a market, easily justifies machine computation because the various submodels are mutually contingent. For example, the supply function of the firm, the substitution of factors, and market supply are all aspects of the same apparatus or system. Simulations have been written to view such questions as: "What happens when a production function is out of equilibrium? What is the equilibrium path?" The answer of the theorist is that it will pay some entrepreneur to shift resources into the activity that is in disequilibrium and to take the abnormal profits that are present. With each change in the prices that determine marginal product for an activity, or marginal cost of a resource, the entrepreneur will decide into which market he should go for more resources. It is the market that rules his decisions. The microtheory may assume that the decision maker conforms his behavior to the paradigm of optimality. To simulate this central concept, it is necessary only to insert different values into successive rounds of the same model. The cumulative results resemble dynamic courses of action. The simulation asserts that microdynamic processes do occur in the economic universe.

Games. Game playing requires dynamic batching, since the object of game strategy is to produce variation in the order of events which follows the first "move." The players are constrained by various requirements and rules. When these constraints are taken into account, one outcome is found to be more acceptable than any other, and the game ends. The winning play is an event within the model itself and not an event defined by the player. Thus, the concept of optimality is implicit in many games.

If the rules of a theoretical system, such as the production function, are embedded in a game, and a computer model is developed for this game, the theory will be simulated through such a model. As participants in the simulation, the players may display intelligence, initiative, and even luck. Still the system equilibrates, and the theory is vindicated. For a game model to achieve this result, it must not be static, but must allow period-to-period adjustments. In playing the role of an entrepreneur, each contestant buys and pays for factor inputs. His marginal cost is the sum of the several incremental factor costs in the production function. One model, called MARSIM, has the players taking profits along the marginal cost curve until its intersection with the price of the product. Each player secures from each round of play information about the costs and profits that have been produced by his own decisions and those of other players. Each player always moves his own position toward the collective equilibrium because he has passively adopted that target as his own goal (Calkins, 1970). As a market simulator, this game is remarkably like a pure microtheory.

Decision Models. Decision models may contain special assumptions or theorems belonging to a submodel of microstatic theory. However, they are detached from general microtheory, especially from the rule that optimality is implicit in a solution of the model. That is why the decision models deserve their name. Some objective function is evaluated—then it remains to be seen whether anybody would be willing to accept, and to pay for, that outcome.

The decision maker studies the various opportunities that lie in the economic environment, with a view to committing his resources toward any one of them. He has hard physical information. He needs a decision model to compute relations among his data. He will implement his decisions by action within a physical system. It is cheaper to solve problems by searching an information system than by attacking a physical world without data or logic. Also, by viewing the intrinsic constraints, the decision maker may find it possible to construct the physical system he wants. What the user of a decision model has in mind is the creation of a new production function that will pay off better than his present one. He is not merely a game-player, but also a systems designer.

Decision models are of diverse types. Some of the best known are models for capital budgeting, inventory control, and waiting lines. Where a firm is able to produce different products or services through different activities, it faces the problem of deciding which combination of products or services to produce. Here is the familiar and useful application of linear programming. It is of interest that the first problem in linear programming was posed and solved by the microtheorist, George Stigler. His solution was formally and nutritionally correct, but palatably unacceptable, and Stigler wrote, "No one recommends these [minimum cost] diets to anyone, let alone everyone" (DiRoccaferrera, 1964, p. 684).

Interactive simulation is a very superior tool for decision theory instruction. An interactive language allows the user to respond to the model as it feeds back to him any simulated conditions. By the real-time introduction of data, the user enters his decisions as the program progresses, and is given the opportunity to study the effects of policy.

Inductive Statistical Models. Real data are given to the statistical model. The object of the program is to develop and test selected relationships and to identify causal forces, even though such causes have not acted uniformly upon the data. The processing is an analytical search for a mathematical model that is not known at the outset. A numerical economic specification may be derived from existing market data (Anderson *et al.,* 1973). At first this procedure does not appear to fit the definition of a simulation. Nevertheless, in an orderly body of descriptive facts, there is an implicit framework or structure, consistent with the usages employed in the collection of the facts. If a mathematical function is found to generalize successfully within the data set, this curve type will give the investigator clues to explanatory relations. Besides automatic processing, the machine methods should provide visual and mathematical representations of the data and the models that imply causality.

Conclusions

Any theory can be simulated according to its own model governing the incrementation and limits of the variables. A straightforward interpretation is that the simulation isolates and amplifies selected real phenomena. That is what makes the computerized model a teaching medium. What makes it a superior medium is the convenience of replication, from elementary to complex levels, and adaptability to the types of analysis found in university economics.

References

Anderson, R., M.A. Khan, and J. Woeppel. Computer as a Teaching Aid in Economics. *Proceedings of the First Indiana University Computer Network Conference on Computer Related Curriculum Materials,* Indiana University Southeast, 1973, 38-47.

Calkins, R.N. A Computerized Model of Exchange as an Aid to Teaching Price Theory. *The Journal of Economic Education,* 1970, Vol. 1, Number 2, 97-103.

Calkins, R.N., and S.W. Voss. The Instability of Real and Simulated Service Systems: A Factor in User Alienation. *Proceedings of Annual Modeling and Simulation Conference*, University of Pittsburgh, Vol. 5, Part 1, 1974, 379.

DiRoccaferrera, G.M.F. *Operations Research Models for Business and Industry*. Cincinnati: Southwestern Publishing Co., 1964.

27.
Computer Simulation of Psychological Processes

Frederick Wm. Hornbeck
Yale University

The phrase "computer simulation" occurs in a number of places and in a variety of contexts in this volume. The meaning of the phrase varies tremendously—probably about as much as the backgrounds and interests of those who use it. The notion that there are conceptual primitives (i.e., entities that are self-defining and without ambiguity) in the cognitive realm has some appeal, but it seems that there are few, if any, in the surface structure or primary lexical units of natural languages. Words, phrases, paragraphs, and even sagas are properly understood only in their intended contexts. This observation is made primarily to preempt concern about choice of labels and to acknowledge awareness of the several meanings intended by "computer simulation" in this volume and in the world at large. Hopefully, the meaning here intended will emerge as context is developed, even if the choice of labels and of criteria for partitioning of the universe of programming efforts employed here are different from those preferred by the reader. So . . . on with the context.

The focus of this paper is on the utilization of computer simulations in the expression, explication, and verification of theory in psychology. The emphasis is—relative to most of the papers in this volume—more on how computers can and are being utilized in scientific pursuits than on pedagogical applications of computer technology. Simulation is discussed as an instrument of the scientist rather than as an instructional tool.

Nonetheless, these concerns do have ramifications for course offerings and research experience in the undergraduate and graduate curricula as well as for more mature scientists concerned with the development of new modes of theory construction and verification (e.g., McGuire, 1973). Some explicit suggestions for curriculum development and course content are presented in the final section of this paper. In the first section, some evidence—mostly casual observations—is used to construct (loosely) the argument that this kind of simulation is already important to scientific psychology *and* that it is somewhat neglected by the profession as a whole and is dealt with quite inadequately in our college and university curricula. The second section consists of a brief discussion of one source of confusion that seems to plague some of the enthusiastic advocates of simulation as well as many who are most skeptical of its potential contributions.

A Deficiency Perceived

Many major theoretical developments have already been expressed in the form of computer programs. Yet, this use of computers is well understood by but a small proportion of psychologists. Relatively few have worked or studied with the even smaller number who have taken direct advantage of this new and powerful tool. This is hardly surprising as only a tiny fraction of those who have acquired tenure *could* have been involved in such activities while students; the technology upon which it depends is too young. Even now, there are but a handful of universities (e.g., Carnegie-Mellon, Edinburgh, Harvard, MIT, and Stanford) and other research centers (e.g., Bolt, Beranek, and Newman; Stanford Research Institute, Xerox Palo Alto Research Center) that command the financial and physical resources to support serious work in the development of viable, computer-based models of perceptual, cognitive, and social processes. More importantly, the critical mass of scientific personnel for this work seems to be fairly large and capable of realization only as the result of a deliberate and considerable commitment on the part of the institution. Isolated individuals (e.g., Robert Abelson at Yale) have made considerable contributions but they are clearly the exception rather than the rule.

Some who use computers for the representation of their theories do so with greater proficiency than do others and, of course, use of this new technology provides no guarantee that the theory being expressed will be worthy of serious consideration in the marketplace of ideas. However, one must have a reasonable understanding of this aid to conceptualization itself and the epistemological considerations underlying its use to either overcome the awe induced by the technological trappings that affect some or to counter the extreme skepticism expressed by others. Before turning to a brief discussion of one of the underlying epistemological problems, let us consider some evidence that suggests the importance of this new conceptual tool and also supports the contention that too little attention has been paid to it by the profession as a whole.

Psychologists, for the most part, keep abreast of the contributions of their colleagues to the accretion of knowledge through the media of American Psychological Association (APA) journals, other specifically psychological journals and books, attendance at APA and regional meetings, and through a variety of informal communication networks that depend upon both the written and the spoken word. Psychology presents itself to the rest of the scientific community, however, much more through the aegis of the American Association for the Advancement of Science (AAAS) and similar pan-scientific organizations than through the parochial and specialized communications upon which the workaday researcher need depend. Though no defense will be provided, it may be suggested that it is primarily work able to stand rigorous criticism and of intrinsic scientific value that is apt to be presented at the annual meetings of the AAAS and other comparable convocations.

Charles Cofer organized a session on The Structure of Human Memory for the AAAS annual meeting held in New York City in January, 1975. An interesting feature of that session was the composition of the group of participants. Two of the younger speakers, Terry Winograd and Roger Schank, were trained as, and identify themselves primarily as, computer scientists. Some, such as Allen Newell and Herbert Simon, have through the years come to be associated with both computer science and psychology. Most of the others have either used computers for the development of realizations of their theoretical models or used computer metaphors in discussing their models. Anyone familiar with the memory literature will recognize more than one among them:

Cofer, David Meyer, Roger Schvaneveldt, Kevin Gilmartin, Donald Norman, Walter Kintsch, and William Estes. John R. Anderson and Richard Atkinson were scheduled to participate but were unable to do so. Estes, speaking between Winograd and Schank, suggested in his casual prefatory remarks that it was the two computer scientists whose papers bounded his that were doing the "real" work in memory research.

This is not offered as conclusive evidence on the importance of computer modeling, of course. The point is made, however, that some psychologists view the work being done in computer science as of considerable relevance and clearly see an important role for simulation in psychology. Indeed, there has been a dramatic increase in theory development in the area of human memory that is clearly traceable to the availability of the information-processing model. Even a brief examination of Minsky (1968), Norman (1970), Tulving and Donaldson (1972), and Anderson and Bower (1973) will suffice to substantiate this claim. Perusal of current and recent numbers of *Psychological Review* and the *Journal of Verbal Learning and Verbal Behavior* will reveal that the influence is not limited in appeal to those who support newer journals—such as *Cognitive Psychology*—in which information processing in general and computer simulation in particular are well represented. (Both Schank and Winograd have been featured prominently in *Cognitive Psychology*.)

Another area in which computer simulation has been employed by psychologists is that of human belief systems. Several social psychologists are now working in this area, once inhabited almost exclusively by Robert Abelson at Yale and a psychiatrist, Kenneth Colby, at Stanford. Each of them has been working with computer models of his theories for a decade or so. Each has published several articles on his work. Colby, who recently moved to UCLA, has been the more successful in terms of producing fairly large, working programs. Hence, he has gotten further along in pursuing the validation of his simulations. Some of the problems encountered in the validation process are discussed later in this paper. It is relevant to observe at this point, though, that Colby's work has been published predominantly in computer science (e.g., Colby, Weber, and Hilf, 1971; Colby, Hilf, Weber, and Kraemer, 1972) rather than in psychological journals and that an interesting dialogue

(Weizenbaum, 1974; Arbib, 1974; Colby, 1974) concerning the epistemological status of his work was initiated in the house organ of the Association for Computing Machinery (the principal professional organization for computer scientists) rather than in the *American Psychologist*—even though the belief system with which this work deals is that of a paranoid personality.

One last piece of evidence should be noted before moving on to a more direct discussion of simulation and its role in the scientific endeavor. During each of the summers of 1973 and 1974, I was privileged to be a participant in the NSF sponsored projects dealing with computer science in behavioral and social science education upon which this volume is based. On both occasions, about thirty individuals gathered to address matters of curriculum planning and course development. Each group contained about fifteen psychologists with some overlap across the summers. Other participants came from sociology, political science, economics, geography, and mathematics.

In spite of the fact that Edward Feigenbaum, one of the pioneering psychologists in computer simulation, spent a week with the group in 1973, as did Walter and Sally Sedelow, whose backgrounds are in sociology and linguistics, very little of the group's attention was addressed to the use of computers in this important and exciting mode. It is my impression that even though this neglect was in part the product of a deliberate decision, it also reflected the relative ignorance of the group as far as the use of computer simulations in theory construction and validation is concerned. Most activity centered around computer utilization in statistical analysis, on-line laboratory applications, and in various data generation and other pedagogic capacities. That the profession as a whole still lags in its appreciation of these uses of computers goes without saying, and the work carried out will certainly be helpful. It is only the absence of a serious discussion of simulation as a tool for the development and expression of theoretical models that I wish to point out. The present paper is, in part, an attempt to rectify that omission. An additional related paper in this volume is Ryan's contribution on the use of computers in the study of language. It provides a more thorough and specific course proposal of the kind that this paper is aimed at motivating, i.e., courses on the use of computers as a medium for the representation and testing of theoretical statements.

Simulation vs. Artificial Intelligence:
A Note of Caution

Discussions of dimensions along which programs labeled as "models" or "simulations" differ sometimes focus on the completeness of the program as a representation of the real object that is its referrent for a determination of how to label that particular program. The distinction of most concern in the present discussion has to do, however, with the purpose for which the program is written, i.e., the intent of the author.

The distinction between "simulation" and "artificial intelligence" is well-established in the community of scholars concerned with the production or use of computer programs that perform or seem to perform acts traditionally regarded as displaying some degree of intelligence. There is an extremely wide range of attitudes, however, as to how seriously the distinction should be taken. It is argued here that the distinction is an essential one to those who are involved in the use of simulation for genuinely scientific pursuits. Hence, the term "simulation" is reserved for reference only to those programming efforts that have as their primary purpose the realization of a theoretical model of some real phenomenon. Those programs designed to perform intelligent acts—whatever that is taken to mean—without necessarily doing so as do humans or other living organisms are referred to as artificial or machine intelligence.

Since the intention of the program's author may rightfully be regarded as an inappropriate criterion for classification, it should be pointed out that the intention of concern here does entail certain observable behaviors on the part of the author or others in the scientific community. The presence or absence of these behaviors, or at least the reasonableness of considering them with regard to the programming effort, ought to be our guide in deciding how to view particular "intelligent" programs. A simulation must be evaluated or validated with reference either to the theoretical model for which it is an intended realization or directly to that real phenomenon that is modeled. A program of the artificial or machine intelligence genre, on the other hand, if it must be evaluated at all, can be appropriately rated simply in terms of its practical characteristics of efficiency, accuracy, or even more elementarily in terms of whether or not it works at all.

Strict adherence to and insistence upon this distinction does not deny the strong similarities among particular programs generated in the two traditions. Likewise, it does not preclude the participation of various individuals in both activities. It does mean that it is essential to clear thinking about the important activities of theory construction and validation that programs that don't meet the criteria of simulation not absorb the time and energy of the scientific community—when it is engaged in the business of science.

Rather than carry on a discussion of validation requirements in the abstract, however, I will take a little time to cite some examples of the two kinds of "intelligent" programs mentioned above, for a brief discussion of the rationale and methodology of simulation, and for a cursory review of some of the activity in two areas of simulation—human belief systems and human memory.

Much of the best of the early work in both the simulation of psychological and social processes and in artificial intelligence are represented in Feingenbaum and Feldman's *Computers and Thought*. The distinction that is asserted to be so important in the present paper is made by the editors of that volume explicitly in the introduction to the second section (on simulation) and implicitly by the organization of material in the volume. Artificial intelligence efforts discussed there are typified by programs written to play chess and checkers, to prove theorems in logic and geometry, to solve symbolic integration problems in the calculus, answer natural language questions, and recognize patterns. In spite of the fact that many of these employ heuristics known to be used by humans performing the same tasks, they do not qualify as simulations because they are not fully—nor even extensively— determined by theories of human behavior but are rather designed simply to get the various tasks accomplished in whatever way possible. Part Two, dealing with the simulation of cognitive processes, however, presents programming efforts where there is an express intent to have the program embody a specific theoretical model of how humans carry out the particular act involved, e.g., general problem solving, verbal learning, concept formation, binary choice behavior, trust investment, and elementary social behavior.

Explicit data on the evaluation or validation of these models is sparse, but it is clear that the kinds of validation techniques to be discussed in this paper are relevant and essential to the role these models can play in behavioral science. The student of either artificial intelligence or simulation should look at these papers and the additional material by Turing, Armer, and Minsky that rounds out this volume. From the purely conceptual standpoint, little has been added of a metatheoretical nature in the decade or so since this volume appeared. Many of the individual papers are classics.

As already acknowledged, many different things are meant by the terms "model" and "simulation." Levine and Burke (1972) discuss three kinds of models: mathematical models of data (e.g., psychophysical laws and descriptive statistics), verbal models (theories) of behavior, and mathematical models of the verbal models. There are at least two kinds of computer models that can be added to this taxonomy. Computer programs may be required in those situations where there is a plausible mathematical model for the theory under consideration but where the mathematics are not readily carried out by non-computer methods. A second situation, leading to a different kind of computer program, is that in which the verbal model is sufficiently explicit to permit representation in a computer program but not subject to ordinary mathematical representation. These possibilities as well as others are discussed in a very good chapter on the methodology of computer simulation by Abelson (1968) in *The Handbook of Social Psychology*.

Abelson's chapter contains major sections dealing with types of simulation, the methodology of computer simulation, computer simulation of cognitive processes, and the simulation of social processes. Both of the major sections on applications (cognitive and social) contain extensive discussions of the problems of evaluation. He does not deny that substantial problems continue to plague the scientist who chooses simulation as one of his conceptual tools. Rather, he acknowledges them and suggests avenues that might be pursued in trying to overcome them. Changes in this chapter are required in the sections dealing with computer hardware and programming languages, but these are perpetually in need of updating. In addition, while his discussion of validation is one of the best available, it is inadequate in ways that should be made clear in the present paper. Otherwise, his discussion is thorough and complete.

One important contribution of Abelson's chapter with regard to the problem of validation of simulations of cognitive processes is his discussion of Turing's test. He distinguishes what seems to be the most common understanding of Turing's suggested procedures, which Abelson refers to as the "Simple Turing Test," with an alternative understanding that he calls the "Extended Turing Test." Grossly oversimplified, the task posed a judge in the simple test is that of distinguishing the input/output (I/O) protocols of the real process, e.g., a human being engaged in some sort of information processing task, from the I/O protocols produced by a computer simulation of that real process that has been "motivated" to fool the judge. In the extended test, the judge is posed the task of rating sets of I/O protocols on a specific dimension directly relevant to the simulation. In this form of the test, the sets of protocols before the judge are sometimes both derived from instances of the real processor that differ on the relevant dimension, and sometimes one is from an instance of the real processor and one is from the computer simulaton. The adequacy of the simulation with regard to the specific, relevant dimension is judged by the degree to which judges' comparisons of the simulation *vis-a-vis* an instance of the real object are indistinguishable from comparisons between two instances of the real object. Ideally, the judge does not know that a simulation is involved and so concentrates his attention solely on the theoretically relevant aspects of the protocols. This extended form of the test is intended, in addition, to be applied to a number of different dimensions along which variability is possible in the theory predicating the simulation.

Abelson further suggests that the attempt to produce new predictions from simulations has been woefully underemployed. Most validation procedures have pitted the simulation only against already established findings. Anyone interested in simulation as a method of theory explication and testing in the behavioral and social sciences should benefit from familiarity with Abelson's chapter.

Two points should be stressed at this time. First, while the importance of developing more sophisticated versions of Turing's test has been emphasized in the preceding paragraphs, it is even more important for those psychologists who add simulation to their arsenal to realize that they must retain their older, more conventional weapons as well. Second, and somewhat contradictorily, the obvious need to validate simulations using tests of I/O indistinguishability complemented by other means should not prevent the psychologist from giving serious consideration to AI models—even though they have not been validated (in our sense) by the computer scientists or others who produced them. These two points may become clearer when illuminated by the following examples.

The first point is well illustrated in the work of Abelson and Colby on the simulation of human belief systems. Even though it was Abelson who provided the important conceptual extension to Turing's proposal, he—to a much greater extent than Colby—has continued to rely primarily upon experimental verification using human subjects to test his theoretical developments (e.g., Abelson, 1975).[2]

Colby, on the other hand, has depended almost entirely (Colby, Hilf, Weber and Kraemer, 1974) upon a Turing-like indistinguishability test in evaluating his simulation of paranoid behavior. This fact is undoubtedly responsible for the interesting though somewhat unsophisticated dialogue alluded to earlier (i.e., Weizenbaum, 1974a, b; Arbib, 1974; Colby, 1974). Weizenbaum (1974a) erroneously attacks Colby's model of paranoia while his arguments are actually germane *only* to the validation procedures which Colby has reported.

Turner (1971) discusses two levels of simulation. Functional simulators possess functional or phenomenological analogy to the process being modelled. They imitate the molar acts and achievements of that process. Structural simulators, correspondingly, possess structural analogy to the imitated process. They incorporate analogs of the molecular constituents of the molar acts; they simulate the processes underlying the molar acts.

Now, while Colby's model (Colby, Weber, and Hilf, 1971) of a paranoid clearly incorporates an hypothesized set of underlying mechanisms (procedures defining the effects of verbal input upon affect and of affect upon verbal output) even the modified form of the Turing test inadequately probes the degree of analogy between these mechanisms and the causes of "paranoid" verbal behavior in the human. Colby has appropriately enough aimed at a structural simulation but his validation procedures address only the functional level. If he is seriously proposing his information-processing model as an explanation of paranoia, he should clearly pursue other validation procedures in addition to testing I/O indistinguishability. There is, in fact, a sufficient amount of psychological substance in his verbal model to allow it to be subjected to evaluation in conventional ways.

As Arbib (1974) observed in Colby's defense, Colby has never claimed more than functional analogy for his computer programming effort. Quite correctly, both have recognized demonstrated functional analogy as evidence of *sufficiency* for the simulation without claiming *necessity*. That is, if I/O indistinguishability can be demonstrated, the simulation is a member of the set of all possible mechanisms that *can* account for the observed behavior. It is not necessarily the mechanism that *does* account for it. The converse of this general proposition should also be given explicit notice: a valid structural simulation will necessarily be sufficient to produce a valid functional simulation (so Turing-like tests do, indeed, serve some purpose). Weizenbaum's (1974b) motivations are more clearly revealed when he persists in criticizing Colby's model rather than his validation procedures even after Arbib's contribution has been made. (One wonders if the exchange would have been more informative if it *had* been carried in the pages of the *American Psychologist* rather than the *Journal of the ACM*.)

As intimated earlier, these considerations of simulation and validation do constitute a two-edged sword that does indeed cut both ways. The simulation zealot who depends entirely upon tests of I/O indistinguishability faces what appear to be insurmountable problems in establishing any *more* than functional analogy between his simulation and the real process of theoretical interest. On the other hand, the theorist who foregoes the opportunity to realize his theory in the form of a computer simulation may be unable to demonstrate *even* functional analogy between his theory and the process it models. The criterion of sufficiency in scientific explanation—just because it is weaker and presumably easier to demonstrate—should perhaps be given heuristic, temporal priority over that of necessity. Simulation provides a fairly rigorous test of logical consistency and completeness among the propositions of a theory—properties frequently left undemonstrated in purely verbal statements.

Walter Kintsch (1974), while presenting an interesting and provocative theory, overlooks this point. In discussing the development of "natural" logic as a replacement for "standard" logic in contemporary theories of language and memory he states ". . . that several investigators in psychology and artificial intelligence have at least tried to make fresh starts and to construct semantic memory models with a more or less explicit disregard for standard logic. Representative examples for this kind of approach are Anderson and Bower (1973), Collins and Quillian (1971), Rumelhart, Lindsay, and Norman (1972), Quillian (1969, 1970), Schank (1972), Simmons (1972), and Winograd (1972), as well as the present work. There seems to be no way of relating these studies to a common denominator beyond saying that they are all concerned in some way or another with the development of natural logic. All of the models, *except for the present one*, are realized as computer programs, and the fact that these programs function proves their feasibility" (Kintsch, 1974, pp. 46-47, emphasis added).

While clearly recognizing successful mechanical representations as a demonstration of feasibility, he fails to use that technique or any other to establish the overall feasibility of his own theory. Inasmuch as his own model has not been demonstrated to be isomorphic with any of those for which successful machine realizations exist, there is no basis for attributing feasibility to his model. Indeed, the lack of homogeneity in the models he mentions very clearly extends to important aspects at the structural level. For instance, Kintsch and Schank both are concerned with the internal representation of knowledge. Kintsch's "base text" and Schank's "conceptualization" both have "meaning" as referent. In an historical perspective, this is a crucial similarity that sets both apart from the transformational approach in linguistics that has only recently released its strangle hold on psycholinguistics. Another noteworthy similarity is the use of a case-structure grammer (cf. Fillmore, 1968) in their work. Schank employs a well-formulated case structure in the definitions of his conceptual primitive acts. Kintsch uses a less formal one in his discussion of propositional verb frames and other predications. Beyond this, the two theories are very different.

On the whole, Kintsch's system appears to be heavily noun oriented. Not only are nouns defined by set relations but verbs may be related through the set relations associated with entities in their case structures. Schank, on the other hand, emphasizes the role of acts in his theory. Indeed, a number of important conceptual differences are thoroughly confounded in the specification of the elements of the two systems. Kintsch shuns semantic decomposition while the identification of a small set of primitive acts is central to Schank's formulation. Kintsch has retained syntactic categories from natural language analyses in discussing the propositions of base text. Schank employs a new vocabulary in which acts and picture producers (physical objects) are central constructs in his conceptualizations. Particular objects (tokens) are related to the rest of memory by occurrence lists. Both authors accept the legitimacy of the semantic-episodic distinction (Tulving, 1972) but have opposing views on the priority of the two. Schank emphasizes the importance of experience in constructing meaning: Kintsch focuses on semantic relations in the understanding of episodes.

These differences, and others as well, are far from trivial in the consideration of a sound theory of memory. Choices among them will *not* be made on the basis of their functional characteristics alone but will depend heavily upon data provided by the kind of experimentation which Kintsch reports in his volume. Nonetheless, a demonstration of completeness (as far as those processes addressed are concerned) and consistency is essential. It is *not* clear that Kintsch's verbal model could be realized as a computer program displaying those functional properties that he suggests that it has.

Antisimulationists are apt to respond "So what?" to this last observation. "Just because a computer can't be programmed to work this way doesn't mean that humans don't." Such protestation, in this and similar cases, is at best unfounded and at worst, simply antiscientific.

Entirely complete structural simulators of human cognitive

processes are, admittedly, logically unobtainable (cf. Turner, 1971, Chapter 4). Certainly, at the biological level, the degree of positive structural analogy between programs running on digital computers and human cognition will be very slight. However, it is extremely unfortunate that such arguments have been allowed to obfuscate the issues—as they have—because they are largely irrelevant. There is no single form of representation nor postulated procedure in Kintsch's model that defies realization in the very same media employed by Schank, Winograd, Collins, and all the others Kintsch cites. Indeed, Kintsch's strong insistence upon a propositional form for the representation of meaning insulates him entirely from the need for continuous or non-digital capacities. (Schank's "picture producers" are more apt to strain the limits of digital description than are the constructs suggested by any of the other theorists mentioned.)

The point here is that this *logical* question concerning degree of structural analogy is just as germane to a purely verbal theory as to a computer simulation. Yet it is seldom—indeed virtually never—addressed to those who avoid the use of machines in explicating their theories. Psychology has been too long a preparadigmatic science (Kuhn, 1962; Turner, 1971) to justify the continued consideration of theories that can't at *least* meet the test of sufficiency for the processes they seek to explain. Computer simulation provides an important—perhaps revolutionary—opportunity to begin the serious work of selective refinement and truly cumulative growth in our development of a theory for psychology.

This discussion of Kintsch's work *vis-a-vis* that of Schank and others has been included as a counterpoint in the consideration of the importance of using empirical validation techniques in addition to simulation. While successful computer implementation would clearly provide important information on the plausibility of Kintsch's model, it is no less certain that Schank's model of memory structure and language processing must do more than run on a machine to become a truly viable theory of human cognition. However, because basic AI goals do not include the requirement of structural analogy between machine and human performance, there is little reason to expect AI researchers themselves to pursue the demonstration.

Current AI endeavors, particularly in the pursuit of adequate models for the representation of knowledge, should—as Kintsch himself acknowledges—be given more than casual attention by psychologists concerned with the same problems. While not committed to establishing structural simulators, many AI researchers have explicitly, and even more implicitly, adopted the strategy of mimicking human performance.

Marvin Minsky (e.g., 1974), Schank, Winograd, and many others in the AI community are making contributions that psychologists cannot afford to ignore. Cofer's AAAS program and many similar conferences attest to the fact that there is indeed considerable communication among those in AI and psychology in those areas where there is a common ground.

Recommendations for Psychology Curricula

While it may be cliché, it is nonetheless true that the introduction of the curricular material implied by the present discussion will depend largely upon the expertise and interests of faculty. The methodological and technical skills required for a good program in computer simulation are too great to expect them to be acquired by any but those who actually expect to use them in their own substantive research. Consequently, one might realistically expect a wide range in curricular offerings among institutions—much as there has been in mathematical psychology. With that in mind, a few comments on the development of undergraduate courses relating to computer simulation are offered with no attempt made to specify norms.

The preceding section of this paper might very well provide a basis for what should, perhaps, be the most ubiquitous curricular development as far as simulation is concerned. With simulations being employed ever more frequently in perception, learning, memory, cognition, and social psychology, it is difficult to imagine an undergraduate psychology student not encountering some extensive reference to them at one point or another. These references will necessarily be included in response to developments in the various substantive areas and require no particular prompting from the computer science end. A discussion of the role of simulation addressing the need for validation and its limitations as well as its contributions should be included, however, either in the substantive courses where the contributions of simulation are presented or in separate methodological or philosophy of science courses. Abelson's (1968) chapter and Turner's (1971) book are reasonable materials around which to organize such discussions.

There is an abundance of material that might be used in a course devoted to the products of simulation efforts. Dutton and Starbuck (1971), Newell and Simon (1972), Schank and Colby (1973), Bobrow and Collins (1975), and Cofer (in press) are but a few of an ever-expanding list of contributions based heavily upon simulation efforts.

Relevant periodicals include *Artificial Intelligence, Machine Intelligence, Cognition, Cognitive Psychology,* the annual volumes of the Carnegie-Mellon symposia on cognition, and the biennial proceedings of the International Joint Conferences on Artificial Intelligence. Relevant articles appear in the *Communications of the ACM* and *ACM Computing Surveys.* The ACM Special Interest Group on Artificial Intelligence (SIGART) publishes a bimonthly newsletter.

The incorporation of the above material into the psychology curriculum presumes no computational facilities nor very much in terms of instructor preparation. Any move much beyond these minor acknowledgments of the existence of computer simulation, however, will require access to a large computer and the availability of faculty with at least some firsthand experience in simulation. Gregg (1975) recognizes simulation as one of relatively few computer applications that do require large computers by current standards. LISP is the *lingua franca* of workers in this area and this important list-processing language cannot be utilized effectively on small computers. Interesting simulations, even with highly constrained domains, tend to require large amounts of addressable storage and make heavy demands upon the central processing unit.

Fortunately, advances in communication and teleprocessing technology have dramatically attenuated the need for a researcher to be physically proximate to the computer he uses. Consequently, one can expect considerable dispersion of well-qualified personnel away from the few centers of current heavy concentration and into institutions in which they could not previously sustain their research efforts. As Gregg (1975) observes and Sher

(1974) documents, the ARPA computing network (ARPANET), in particular, has greatly expanded the availability of computing resources. In addition, and perhaps just as importantly, the network facilitates an incredibly high rate of communication throughout the community of scholars with access to it. The younger researcher can now accept a position on a campus that can not by itself begin to provide the facilities he requires *without* forgoing the use of such facilities nor giving up the necessary interaction with others working in this area. Costs will still be high but not even of the same order of magnitude as the capital outlay required to obtain adequate computer power on a stand-alone basis.

Given adequate computing resources and qualified faculty—in computer science if not in psychology—undergraduate and graduate psychology students should be offered the opportunity to acquire the skills required for developing computer simulations of their own. This entails primarily the learning of LISP or another suitable list-processing language. Because LISP and other languages constructed from it or designed after it are so pervasive, though, LISP is clearly the most useful one at the present time. Bobrow and Raphael (1974) review the development of languages for use in AI work.

With computer programming languages as with natural languages, facility is developed through use. Hence, the student should be given encouragement to work on the development of simulations of psychological processes in which he is interested. At this point, more extensive exposure to the simulation literature may be desirable if not absolutely necessary. Translation of a verbal model into a functioning computer program requires knowledge that transcends the formal specifications of the programming language. Considerable practice is required before forms that map into the constructs and structures available in the programming language or constructable from it can be discerned in the verbal theory. Considerable ingenuity may be required in reformulating poorly stated theories to make them tractable for simulation (or any logically equivalent test of consistency and completeness).

Just as only a few of the last generation of psychology students developed proficiency in the construction and utilization of mathematical models, so may one expect that few will ever utilize computer simulations effectively. Nonetheless, every well-prepared psychology major should have a basic appreciation of the technique and its epistemological status. An increasing number should be given the opportunity to fully develop the skills required to use simulation as an effective tool in the explication and verification of theoretical statements.

References

Abelson, R. Simulation of Social Behavior. In G. Lindzey and E. Aronson (Eds.), *Handbook of Social Psychology, Vol. II.* Reading, Mass.: Addison-Wesley, 1968.

Abelson, R. Script Processing in Attitude Formation and Decision-Making. Eleventh Carnegie Symposium on Cognition, *Cognition and Social Behavior*, Pittsburgh, 1975.

Anderson, J., and G. Bower. *Human Associative Memory*. Washington, D.C.: Winston, 1973.

Arbib, M. More on Computer Models of Psychopathic Behavior. *Communications of the ACM*, 1974, *17*, 543.

Bobrow, D., and A. Collins. *Representation and Understanding: Studies in Cognitive Science.* New York: Academic Press, 1975.

Bobrow, D., and B. Raphael. New Programming Languages for Artificial Intelligence Research. *ACM Computing Surveys,* 1974, *6*, 153-174.

Cofer, C. *The Structure of Human Memory*. San Francisco: Freeman, in press.

Colby, K. Ten Criticisms of PARRY. *SIGART Newsletter*, 1974, No. 48, 5-9.

Colby, K., F. Hilf, S. Weber, and H. Kraemer. Turing-like Indistinguishability Tests for the Validation of a Computer Simulation of Paranoid Processes. *Artificial Intelligence,* 1974, *3*, 199-221.

Colby, K., S. Weber, and F. Hilf. Artificial Paranoia, *Artificial Intelligence*, 1971, *2*, 1-25.

Collins, A., and M. Quillian. How to Make a Language User. In E. Tulving and W. Donaldson (Eds.), *Organization of Memory*. New York: Academic Press, 1971.

Dutton, J., and W. Starbuck. *Computer Simulation of Human Behavior*. New York: John Wiley, 1971.

Fillmore, C. The Ease for Case. In E. Bach and R. Harms (Eds.), *Universals in Linguistic Theory*. New York: Holt, Rinehart, and Winston, 1968.

Gregg, L. Computers: Large-Scale Usage in the Balance. *American Psychologist*, 1975, *30*, 199-204.

Kintsch, W. *The Representation of Meaning in Memory*. Hillsdale, N.J.: Erlbaum Associates, 1974.

Kuhn, T. *The Structure of Scientific Revolutions*. Chicago: University of Chicago Press, 1962.

Levine, G., and C. Burke. *Mathematical Model Technique for Learning Theories*. New York: Academic Press, 1972.

McGuire, W. The Yin and Yang of Progress in Social Psychology: Seven Koan. *Journal of Personality and Social Psychology*, 1973, *3*, 446-456.

Minsky, M. (Ed.) *Semantic Information Processing*. Cambridge: MIT Press, 1968.

Minsky, M. A Framework for Representing Knowledge, Massachusetts Institute of Technology Artificial Intelligence Laboratory Memo No. 306, 1974.

Newell, A., and H. Simon. *Human Problem Solving*. Englewood Cliffs, N.J.: Prentice-Hall, 1972.

Norman, D. (Ed.), *Models of Human Memory*. New York: Academic Press, 1970.

Quillian, M. The Teachable Language Comprehender. *Communications of the ACM*, 1969, *12*, 459-476.

Quillian, M. Semantic Memory. In M. Minsky (Ed.), *Semantic Information Processing*. Cambridge: MIT Press, 1970.

Rumelhart, D., P. Lindsay, and D. Norman. A Process Model for Long-Term Memory. In E. Tulving and W. Donaldson (Eds.), *Organization of Memory*. New York: Academic Press, 1972.

Schank, R. Conceptual Dependency: A Theory of Natural Language Understanding. *Cognitive Psychology*, 1972, *3*, 552-631.

Schank, R., and K. Colby. *Computer Models of Thought and Language*. San Francisco: Freeman, 1973.

Sher, M. A Case Study of Networking. *Datamation*, March 1974, 56-59.

Simmons, R. Some Semantic Structures for Representing English Meanings. In J. Carroll and R. Freedle (Eds.), *Language*

Comprehension and the Acquisition of Knowledge. Washington, D.C.: Winston, 1972.

Tulving, E. Episodic and Semantic Memory. In E. Tulving and W. Donaldson (Eds.), *Organization of Memory*. New York: Academic Press, 1972.

Tulving, E., and W. Donaldson (Eds.), *Organization of Memory*. New York: Academic Press, 1972.

Turner, M. *Realism and the Explanation of Behavior*. New York: Appleton-Century-Crofts, 1971.

Weizenbaum, J. Automating Psychotherapy. *Communications of the ACM*, 1974a, *17*, 425.

Weizenbaum, J. More on Computer Models of Psychopathic Behavior. *Communications of the ACM*, 1974b, *17*, 543.

Winograd, T. Understanding Natural Language. *Cognitive Psychology*, 1972, *3*, 1-191.

Notes

[1] This paper was begun while the author was a Workshop participant in Boulder, Colorado. It was completed while he was Visiting Fellow in Psychology at Yale University on sabbatical leave from San Diego State University. The support of both institutions is gratefully acknowledged. The author's work as a principal investigator on Navy Contract N61339-73-C-0184 provided much of the background for the ideas tentatively explored herein.

[2] The difference in procedures discussed here may be due largely to environmental influences upon the work of the two scientists involved. As far as computer simulation is concerned, Abelson has been an isolate in a traditionally experimental department of psychology. He has not had the resources required to produce models meeting even common-sensical, face-valid criteria of adequacy in terms of matching human performance. (This is *not* to say that his programming efforts have not been productive, only that they have not been sophisticated enough—particularly in terms of their ability to cope with natural language—to produce I/O protocols which could be informatively compared with human performance.) Colby, on the other hand, has been working in the

midst of one of the three or four most productive AI laboratories in the country. While it has been easy and practicable for Abelson to depend heavily upon experimentation and to complement that work with simulation, quite the opposite has been true for Colby.

The historian of science might well be interested in the effects on the work of these two of Colby's move to the UCLA Medical School and the acquisition by Yale of Roger Schank and John R. Anderson, who join Abelson in constituting the nucleus of an informal AI program that is particularly psychological in approach.

28.
CHEBO: The Checkerboard Model
of Social Interaction

James M. Sakoda
Brown University

Introduction

The purpose of the checkerboard model of social interaction is to explore the relationships among social attitudes, social interaction, and social structure. Two sets of individuals, represented by two kinds of counters, squares and crosses, are set up on a checkerboard, and each one is assigned an attitude toward members of his own group and also toward members of the other group. The basic proposition explored is that attitudes lead to a move toward those for whom an individual has positive attitudes and away from those against whom one has negative ones. Changes in positions on the board due to moves on the board are observed for a predetermined number of moves or until moves cease to be made. Because a variety of combinations of attitudes can be postulated, it is possible to use the model to explore the nature of social interaction of two groups and to study the resulting relationships among them. The model was initially developed by moving counters on a checkerboard, but was computerized in order to make the calculations and moves more precise. In this paper three examples of typical runs, covering a range of social relationships, are presented. These have been given the names Segregation, Social Climber, and Approach-Withdrawal Conflict.

The output provided in this paper can be used as a basis for discussion of the model, but it is also possible to implement the computer program, CHEBO, to allow students to study the course of other combinations of attitudes.

Use of the Model. The model can be introduced into the

classroom to enhance teaching of concepts such as social attitudes, social interaction, social structure, and social norm. These are terms frequently used in social psychology and the social sciences, but the relationships among them usually are not made explicit. The model also can be used to demonstrate how combinations of attitudes give rise to different behaviors and how this in turn results in a variety of relationships. These observations can be used as propositions, i.e., that a given set of attitudes will lead to a particular social structure. Application of these concepts to situations of interest to students should provide an opportunity for better understanding of the dynamics underlying some social situations. Still another use of the model is the discussion of the nature of models, and types of models and their function.

The Distinction Between Theoretical
Models and Simulation

The terms models and simulations are sometimes used interchangeably. The checkerboard model is a simple theoretical model in the sense that it works with a few basic concepts. Its processes and results, which correspond to social interaction among two groups, are more ideal types than representatives of any particular situation. The segregation model might be applied to the faculty party for example, at which there is frequently separation into two groups by sex. At any particular cocktail party a variety of factors can be present, and hence provide only a partial verification of the segregation prediction. The purpose of the simple theoretical model is not to predict exactly what is likely to happen in a complex real situation, but to understand the operation of a few variables in a more ideal situation, free of disturbing variables. The simplification is similar to the statement of the law of falling bodies, which assumes a perfect vacuum.

The simple theoretical model can be contrasted with the simulation of a complex real-life situation. For example, in order to evaluate data on abortion rates, one can conceive of a simulation involving many factors known to be relevant—marriage rates, age of marriage, divorce rate, birth rate, death rate, probability of miscarriage or still birth, length of gestation, length of the infertile period after birth, use of contraceptives, and effectiveness of contraceptives. To make the model as realistic as possible the best available information will be sought to put into the model as constants in order to predict the number of abortions in a particular country. Sometimes in carrying out a simulation the desire is not primarily to use basic concepts or to understand their interactions, but to make the predictions as accurate as possible. While there are many shades of models and simulations between the simple theoretical model and the complex simulation, the checkerboard model clearly falls into the range of the simple theoretical model.

Basic Theoretical Concepts

Social Attitudes. "Social attitudes" or "definition of the situation," terms coined and used extensively by W.I. Thomas (1927; Volkart, 1951), are basic concepts employed in the checkerboard model. Each participant adopts an attitude or defines the situation and then behaves in accordance with this definition. The concept of social attitude involves both a subjective and situational element—it is someone's attitude toward some thing. Because the concept of social attitude relates a particular individual to a specific situation, the process selects out pertinent perceptions and feelings from an individual which are appropriate to that situation. The term social attitude is closely related to Kurt Lewin's (1951) psychological field or life space. Lewin went further than did W.I. Thomas in the analysis of the internal structure of the psychological field and in diagramatically illustrating it. He used such concepts as field force, valence, tension and equilibrium, and paths to goals.

Difficulty of the Subjective Approach. One of the difficulties of the subjective approach is that of analyzing the interactions of two or more individuals through the concepts of attitudes or psychological field. W.I. Thomas conceived of the interaction between individual attitudes and social values to produce new attitudes and values, but he did not have a mechanism to providing for this interaction. Lewin (1951) has used separate diagrams for the husband and the wife to show differences in their understanding of the marital situation. He has also added a social objective field to portray the actual situation. This use of separate diagrams preclude portrayal of interaction within the same framework. Lewin suggested that the analysis proceed from separate life spaces to the social objective field and then back again to individual life spaces.

Development of the Checkerboard Model. The checkerboard model grew out of the writer's attempt to portray the social interaction in a relocation center during World War II (Sakoda, 1949; Thomas and Nishimoto, 1946). At one point in the analysis of the data, he drew circles and crosses to represent administrative personnel, the administrative leaders, the evacuee leaders, and evacuees. The leaders were positioned between the administrative personnel and evacuees. It occurred to the writer that social interaction might be portrayed by actually moving pieces on a board in accordance with positive and negative attitudes toward one another. He used a checkerboard and checkers and found that by assigning different combinations of attitudes and setting up rules for moving the pieces in accordance with these attitudes, it was possible to obtain a variety of patterns of relationships among the pieces. Thus, the checkerboard model was born.

The Social Field Concept. The assignment of subjective attitudes to participants in a social situation and coupling these attitudes with moves toward or away from one another provides movement which can be interpreted as social interaction. An individual, A, need not necessarily be aware that another individual, B, toward whom he has a positive attitude, also has a positive attitude toward him. A perceived the distance of this person from himself, and if B moves closer to him, he is drawn more strongly to him, since the closer the distance the stronger the effect of an attitude. The mechanism provided by the model to make subjective attitudes objectively observable is the coupling of approach and withdrawal movements. While individuals do not always exhibit behavior consistent with their attitudes, this assumption is made in the model. The process of mutually moving toward or away from one another we interpret as the process of social interaction. Such movements can result in clustering of group members, scattering of members over the board, and pairing of members from opposing groups. These patterns of relationships are interpreted as social structure. The checkerboard model allows the student to watch the process of social interaction and to analyze the resultant social structure. In some situations the pattern stabilizes quickly into an unchanging structure. In others, the structure is unstable and is subject to continual change. In both instances, one can assume that the assigned attitudes are at work.

Social Norms. In the model social norms are incorporated in the rules of the game and in the assignment of attitudes to groups. For example, individual pieces must take one step at a time and cannot leave the board or occupy a position held by another. Pieces must move in accordance with the attitudes assigned to them. Without rules the social interaction would be chaotic and nonsystematic. If individuals brought in attitudes inappropriate to the situation or left the social field in the middle of social interaction, patterns of interaction would be difficult to predict. The rules of the game have been set by the program writer and can only be changed by modifying the program. The user of the model can still change the attitudes assigned to groups to observe the effects of change in social norms. For example, a rule which forbade boys and girls from approaching more than one member of the opposite sex would result in a different pattern from one which allowed their attraction for the opposite sex to operate indiscriminately.

Rules of the Game

When the model was first created, pieces were moved by hand on a 6 x 6 board with 6 pieces in each group. Moves were made by considering the closest piece only, unless the best position to move toward or away from a piece could not be determined by considering the closest piece alone. The next closest piece was then brought into consideration in order to arrive at a best move. This approach gave the closest piece greater weight than more distant ones. It was difficult to take both positive and negative attitudes into account when playing without calculation of distances. Hence, one cycle was run with positive moves, and the next with negative moves. In making moves it was easy to make errors, and it became apparent that the use of a computer was called for.

In the latest computerized version the following features are incorporated. The board size is variable, from 2 x 2 to 12 x 12, but the standard board is 8 x 8 in size. The number of pieces in each group can be varied from 1 to 12. The standard number is six

Squares and six Crosses. Moves are determined by calculating distances from a piece to every other piece, taking into account the distance, the valence, which could be varied by intensity, and by a distance weight to provide varying weights for distant pieces. Moves, instead of being made in a set order, are randomized within groups to provide more flexibility. To avoid ending of a game by pieces being trapped in a corner or along the edge, a jump over one square is allowed if a move cannot be found without making a jump. The starting positions are usually random ones. Provision is made to read in initial positions on the board, making it possible to carry on a game with predetermined starting positions or to carry on interaction with a new set of attitudes. Another option which has been added is the provision of equal or unequal speed of movement. Speed is interpreted as power so that the effects of differences in power can now be investigated. The following rules describe the present operation of the checkerboard model, CHEBO:

1. An 8 x 8 checkerboard represents the field of social interaction. The rows are numbered from 1-8 from left to right. Each of the 64 cells is identified by its row number followed by its column number. Thus, a piece in Row 3 and Column 5 will have the coordinates 03, 05.

2. Two sets of six pieces each are used in the standard play and they are referred to as Squares and Crosses. The two sets represent two groups and pieces members of groups. Members within groups are assigned the same attitudes but are identified by numbers, 1 to 6. The number in each group can be varied from 1 to 12.

3. In the standard play the starting positions on the board are determined by a random process. This produces a social structure in which groups are scattered throughout the board. The random assignment leaves an opportunity for pieces to move on the board to satisfy their needs. Provision is made for specification of a starting random number, which enables the user to repeat plays with the same random number or to select a different one. Starting positions can be read in, if desired, thus making it possible to start from a desired social structure or to incorporate change into a play by stopping it, and starting a new play by starting from the same positions with a changed set of attitudes.

4. Each Square or Cross is assigned a positive, neutral, or

negative valence or value, represented by +1, 0 or -1. There are two sets of such values, one toward members of one's own group and another toward members of the other group. These represent attitudes toward members of one's own or the opposing group. There are therefore four attitudes which can be assigned in any particular game and are usually listed in the following order:

00: Square's attitude toward its own members.

OX: Square's attitude toward members of the other group.

XX: Cross's attitude toward its own member.

XO: Cross's attitude toward members of the other group.

Each group can be assigned nine different combinations of attitudes. In all there are 45 different combinations of attitudes, when both groups are assigned attitudes for play. Nine of these are symmetric, i.e., both groups are given the same set of attitudes so that the two groups cannot be distinguished by their attitudes. For example, boys and girls are given the same set of attitude and either Squares or Crosses can be considered to be boys. The remaining combinations are asymmetric, and therefore there is a need to identify each as Squares or Crosses, e.g., social workers and lost souls.

The intensity of attitudes can be varied by specifying the valence with an integer, e.g., +2, -4, etc. The difference in intensity of attitudes only applies to the relative weight of a group's attitude toward its own members or toward the other group. Since the calculation of the best move is carried independently for Squares and Crosses, assigning weights of +1, -1 to Squares and +4, -4 to Crosses will not show appreciable differences in the choice of best moves.

5. Members of each group make their moves in a random order. Groups alternate in making moves: the first Square, the first Cross, the second Square, the second Cross, etc. A cycle consists of a round of one turn each for all pieces.

6. Normally each piece takes one step on each move, unless it finds it advantageous not to move, or it has neutral attitudes both to its own and to the other group. A step can be up, down, or to the side; or to one of the diagonal cells. That is, pieces can move plus or minus one position along both the row and column coordinates. In order to overcome a tendency of a cohesive group

not to move after it is solidified, pieces that are unable to move are allowed to search a distance of two squares in both the row and column coordinates to find the most advantageous position. This, therefore, allows a jump over any position to which a move was previously possible.

7. In determining the choice of move by a piece, i, the inverse of the distance to all other pieces, j, is calculated. This distance is based on the sum of squares of the distance along the X and Y coordinates. For example, the squared distance between the ith and jth pieces would be given by:

$$D_{ij}^2 = (X_i - X_j)^2 + (Y_i - Y_j)^2$$

This distance is weighted in two ways. First, the wth root of this distance is taken (w is a positive integer, such as 2, 4, 6). Secondly, the inverse of this is weighted by the valence of the attitude. These calculations are then summed for all pieces. The formula for the calculation of weighted distance that provides an index of the desirability of a move is given by:

$$F_i = \sum_{k=1}^{4} \sum_{j=1}^{n} \frac{V_k}{D_{ij}^{1/w}}$$

The summation is over n Squares or Crosses and over the 4 attitude combinations—00, 0X, XX, X0. The squaring of distances give large weights to close pieces and small weights to distant ones. Increasing w from 2 to 4 or larger has the effect of increasing the weights of distant pieces on F relative to the closer ones. The standard moves have been made with the distance weight of w at 4. If F is minus, negative valence prevails over positive one, after taking into account the distance and distance weight. In determining the best move for Piece i, the position associated with the highest positive or lowest negative F is selected.

8. When the speed factor is set to 0, the two groups move one square in any direction, except when a move cannot be made. In that case they are allowed a jump over one square. When the speed factor is set to 1, the Crosses alone will be allowed to search a field of two squares in any direction for a best move. The Crosses are

able to move faster in a desired direction than will the Squares. Added speed is interpreted as increased power.

9. The play can continue for as many cycles as the player specifies. For some attitude combinations a stable relationship is reached and no further moves occur. It is possible for the player to specify the number of no-move cycles, after which the play is terminated even though the maximum number of cycles has been completed. This number of no-move cycles can be set at one, two, or three. The reason for setting it at two or more is that on rare occasion the random arrangement of order of play can cause a move even after a cycle of no moves.

10. After each cycle the position of each piece is shown in a printout of the board. It is possible to suppress this intermediate printout if only the final position at the end of play is desired. It is also possible to request a listing of the moves made by each piece during each cycle to study individual moves more closely.

11. The main objectives of the play is to observe the nature of the interactions, given the initially-assigned attitudes, i.e., to watch the process of social interaction. Another is to observe the pattern of pieces, interpreted as social structure, in the process of formation and in its final form. The following descriptive measures are calculated and printed out at the end of a run:

a. Number of cycles run. The more stable an interaction pattern, the fewer the number of cycles. b. For each group the mean X and Y coordinates, $\overline{X}$ and $\overline{Y}$, indicating the positions of the group centroids. c. The distance between the centroids of the two groups. This is one measure of the social distance between the two groups. d. For each group the index of dispersion, which is calculated as:

$$\text{Disp} = \sqrt{\frac{\Sigma (X_i - \overline{X})^2 + \Sigma (\overline{Y}_i - \overline{Y})^2}{N}}$$

This is a measure of the extent to which a group lacks solidarity. e. There is need for a measure of clustering. In a "Couples" situation, for example, the two centroids are close together in the center of the board and the dispersions within groups are equally large. But there are no measures to show the extent to which Squares and Crosses are clustered together in pairs.

Implementation of CHEBO

Implementation of the computer program, CHEBO, adds another dimension to an understanding of models. It allows a student to make use of the program to run other combinations of attitudes and conditions not presented here. It also provides an opportunity for a student to look at the program to see its structure. CHEBO is written in a straightforward manner, but nonetheless it has, for example, a random number generator which is useful in most models. It also gathers statistics as well as providing printed output of the steps of each run. Some students may also be inspired to write a model of their own, either modifying CHEBO or starting from scratch. CHEBO, as it is presently written, uses card input and printer output and is written for batch processing. A student once wrote a graphics terminal version of the checkerboard model, but it has not been put to general use because of the scarcity of graphical terminals. A more feasible project is the implementation of the program on a typewriter terminal with a video screen display. This will allow students an opportunity to explore different combinations of inputs and examine changes in social patterns immediately. Provision for offline output will take care of the need for hard-copy output.

Description of the Program. CHEBO is written in Basic FORTRAN IV, except for the use of DATA statements, and consists of about 863 source cards. It consists of a main program and some nine subroutines. The program is written for batch processing, with input from cards and output on a printer. NRD, the device number for the card reader, is set to 5 and NPR for the printer to 6, and these are located at the beginning of the main program. They can be changed as needed for other device numbers. The program reads instruction cards, one for each run, and carries out all calculations step by step and prints out position of pieces on the board. This printout is centered on a page and suitable for display. For more economical use of output paper the output routine can be rewritten to provide for several printouts on the same page.

The program is quite general, permitting the user to specify all of the parameters necessary to implement almost any conceivable model. Among the input parameters are: Size of board, number of

Squares and Crosses, number of cycles, the power to jump, attitudes of "pieces" toward each other, distance weight, title, and identifier of run. The starting positions for Squares and Crosses are also specifiable by input cards or may be selected by a random-number procedure in the program.

Illustrative Runs

One of the uses of the checkerboard model is to assign combinations of attitudes, observe the interactional process and the final social structure, and then apply these to typical social situations that they seem to illustrate. On the basis of such observations one can predict that, given certain combinations of attitudes, certain relationships will hold. It is also possible to reverse the process of inference and observe a final social structure in a real situation and predict that the underlying social structure to achieve it may have been the one provided in one of the typical runs of the checkerboard model. At least there is a clear statement of propositions: given a particular combination of attitudes one can expect attractions and withdrawals to lead to typical interactional patterns and social structures.

Segregation. The segregation situation, shown in Figure 1, combines for both Squares and Crosses, a positive attitude toward members of one's own group and a negative attitude toward members of the opposing group. With this combination, both groups move into opposing corners, forming widely separated groups, which are each cohesive. In a faculty party where men and women tend to separate out into two groups in different rooms one can speculate that there are negative attitudes toward the opposite sex as well as positive ones toward one's own sex. One explanation is that at faculty parties the main activity is conversation, and members of both sexes want to avoid becoming caught in a conversation of the opposite sex and seek conversation with members of one's own sex. Racial residential segregation can be assumed to involve both an attempt to avoid members of the opposing group as well as approach toward members of one's own group.

Social Climber. The Social Climber situation, shown in Figure 2, is a pursuit situation with the Squares (social climbers) pursuing the Crosses (an elite group). The Crosses are given additional

Figure 1

Segregation

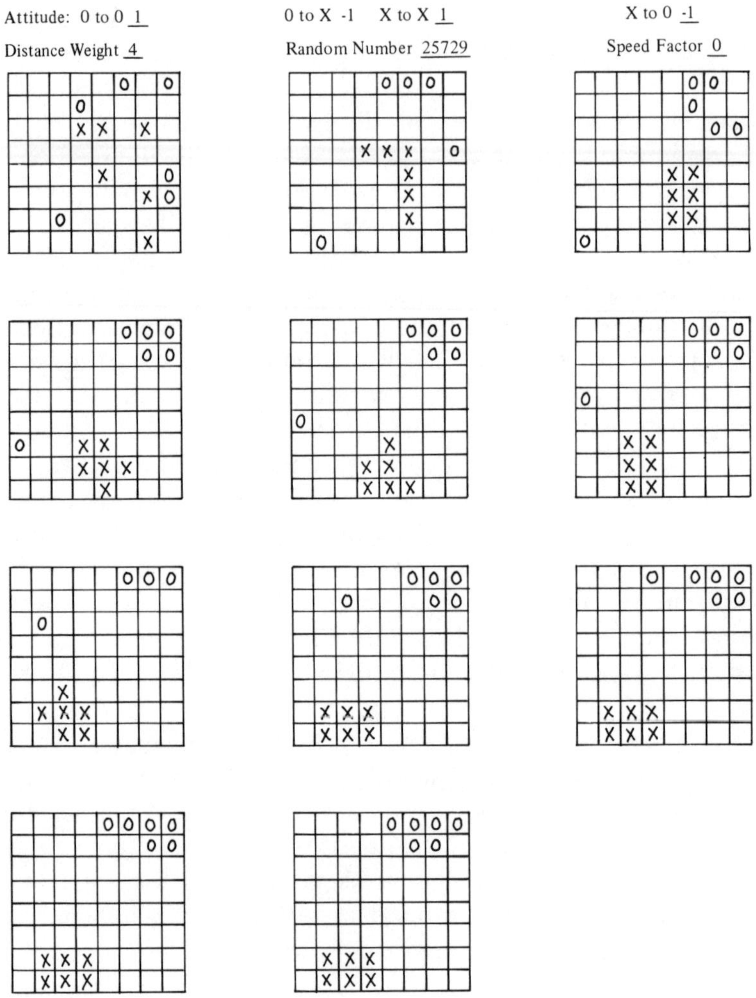

Attitude: 0 to 0 <u>1</u>   0 to X -1   X to X <u>1</u>   X to 0 <u>-1</u>

Distance Weight <u>4</u>   Random Number <u>25729</u>   Speed Factor <u>0</u>

power to permit them to move somewhat faster than the Squares. The Squares have negative attitudes toward one another, thus are generally spread out to catch the Crosses. The Crosses have positive ties with one another, and hence are slowed down in their attempt to escape from the Squares. The Crosses, when completely surrounded by Squares, cannot remain in the same location. They need to break out and move to a new location. In the process of breaking away, their solidarity is likely to be broken, and attempts are made to reestablish it. This unstable process continues without end. Only every other cycle is shown here. This situation is reminiscent of residential succession, in which the elite group moves out farther and farther into the suburb and then into less accessible exurbia as other groups move in on them. Fads and fashion also exhibit this unstable pattern of change in order to avoid association with the pursuing lower class group. To avoid pursuit and the need to move, the elite group needs to put up barriers that will discourage pursuit.

Approach-Withdrawal Conflict. Lewin portrayed three types of conflict situations—approach-approach, withdrawal-withdrawal, and approach-withdrawal. In Figure 3, the approach-withdrawal conflict situation is set up by arranging pairs of Squares and Crosses in each corner and four Squares in the center. The conflict is caused by a strong negative attitude on the part of Squares to get away from each other and a positive attitude to approach a Cross. The four Squares in the center start out by moving away from one another toward the corners, but as they approach the corners they find it necessary to avoid close contact with the Square already at each corner. If it is possible for a Square to attach itself to a Cross without contacting the Square, it does so. Otherwise, it keeps a distance of one space away from both the Square and Cross. This is obviously a compromise equilibrium situation. The approach-approach and withdrawal-withdrawal conflict situation can be created by having Crosses at opposing corners with neutral attitudes and Squares in the center of the board with neutral attitudes toward themselves and either positive or negative attitudes toward Crosses.

Figure 2

Social Climber

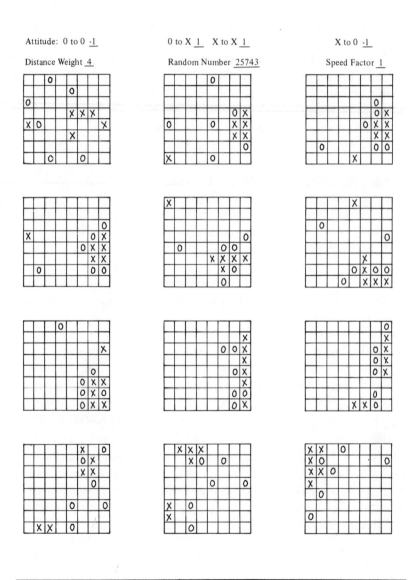

Figure 3

Approach-Withdrawal Conflict

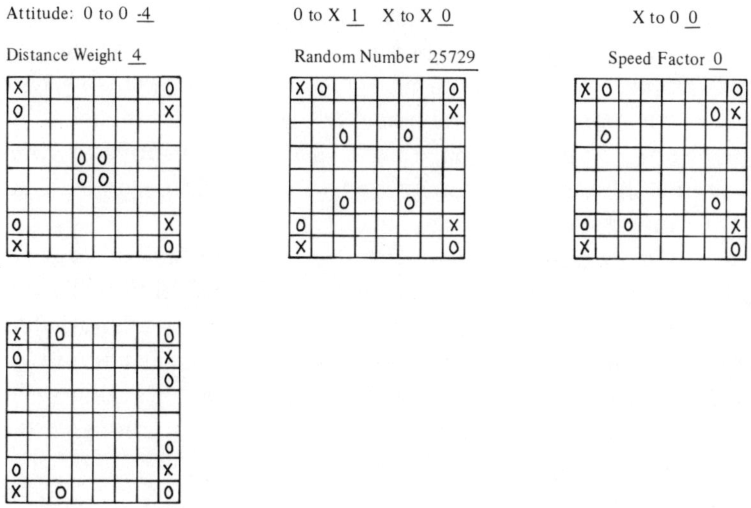

Attitude: 0 to 0 _-4_   0 to X _1_   X to X _0_   X to 0 _0_

Distance Weight _4_   Random Number _25729_   Speed Factor _0_

Propositions. It is difficult to find propositions to teach in the social sciences. The checkerboard model offers some propositions in the form:

Combination of attitudes → Social Interaction → Social Structure. Using these propositions it is possible to predict the social structure or from observation of the social structure one can infer the underlying combination of attitudes.

Power of Influence. An important concept in social psychology is the notion of power of influence—the ability to change another person's behavior. A proposition that arises from the checkerboard model is that the more positive B's attitude toward A the greater is A's power over B. The closer B gets to A the greater the influence A will have in determining B's next move.

Discussion

The checkerboard model and illustrative runs can be used in a variety of ways. They can be applied to particular situations of interest to a class or they can be used to clarify theoretical concepts. A few of the possible topics are listed here with brief comments.

Group as a System of Roles. Pairs of roles, such as lovers, husbands-wives, social worker-lost souls, leader-follower, can be observed in any illustrative run. An important feature of roles is that they are interdependent—one role is dependent on the other. For example, a leader is no longer a leader if he loses his followers. Some of the roles are symmetrical and interchangeable, e.g., both Squares and Crosses can be assumed to represent boys or girls. In the model the same role is assigned to each member in a group so that the members are interchangeable.

Roles in Different Situations. Part of the simplicity of the model is achieved by limiting the nature of the situation. The same individual can participate in different situations, using different sets of attitudes. Different situations can conceivably interact through conflicts imposed on an individual participating in both situations. But these interactions between situations are not examined here.

References

Lewin, K. *Field Theory in Social Science.* New York: Harper and Brothers, 1951.

Sakoda, J.M. *Minidoka: An Analysis of Changing Patterns of Social Interaction*, Doctoral Dissertation, University of California, Berkeley, 1949.

Sakoda, J.M. The Checkerboard Model of Social Interaction. *Journal of Mathematical Sociology*, 1971, *1*, 119-132.

Thomas, D.S. and R.S. Nishimoto. *The Spoilage.* Berkeley: University of California Press, 1946.

Thomas, W.I. *The Polish Peasant in Europe and America.* New York: Alfred A. Knopf, 1927.

Volkart, E.H. (Ed.). *Social Behavior and Personality.* New York: Social Science Research Council, 1951.

Notes

[1] This article is based partially on a previous description of the checkerboard model by Sakoda (1971). The program, written by

William J. Sakoda, was modified to introduce increased power for Crosses. New runs were made and the discussion rewritten to emphasize use of the model for class use. The development of the checkerboard model was partially supported by National Institutes of Mental Health Grant MN-08177-05, Computer Utilization for Behavioral Sciences.

29.
Interactive Causal Modeling in the Social Sciences

James G. Anderson
Purdue University

Social Theory Construction

Causal models are increasingly being used to draw causal inferences from nonexperimental data (Anderson, 1973; Blalock, 1971; Costner, 1974; Duncan, 1975; Goldberger and Duncan, 1973). Nevertheless, a hiatus exists between social theory and empirical research in the social sciences (Blumer, 1955). This gap results, in large part, from the lack of articulation among the verbal languages used to state social theories, the operational languages that specify how concepts are to be measured, and the mathematical languages that permit the empirical verification of the theory (Blalock, 1964). Recent works by Blalock (1969), Glaser and Strauss (1967) and Stinchcombe (1968) address this problem and attempt to explicate the process by which social scientists may effectively formulate verbal theories in terms of more rigorous mathematical models that can be empirically verified.

Students in the social sciences are not generally exposed to this causal modeling approach to formal theory construction in standard methods or theory courses. One attempt to introduce students to the general logic of causal analysis, albeit using much simpler statistical tools, is the IMPRESS system at Dartmouth College. This system comprises an integrated software package consisting of a heterogeneous data bank of social survey data and a set of statistical routines (Cline and Meyers, 1970; Davis, 1971). It permits students to analyze archival data through a conversation with the computer at a teletype terminal, largely in English.

Analyses are performed for the student and the results are displayed at the terminal. Anderson (1971) and Anderson and Coover (1972) review several similar interactive instructional systems. This approach has been extended to path analysis (i.e., causal models consisting of a set of recursive linear equations) by Nygreen (1971) at Princeton University. His interactive path analysis program permits the student or researcher to construct a path model at a terminal by specifying the paths between variables that make up the structure of the model and by entering the intercorrelation matrix for his own data.

The present paper generalizes this causal modeling approach to theory construction involving models containing reciprocal causation and feedback loops among the variables. Such models involving feedback are of a great deal of interest to students in the engineering sciences (de Neufville and Stafford, 1971) and are becoming increasingly important to social scientists (Anderson, 1973; Duncan, Haller and Portes, 1968; Mason and Halter, 1968; Nolle, 1973).

The first part of the paper develops an algorithm that allows social scientists to construct such models from empirical data. The second part of the paper demonstrates the implementation of this model building program on a time sharing computer system. Such an approach permits instructors to teach students how to construct, modify and reconstruct complex causal models from real data such as the one developed here for demonstration purposes.

Causal Modeling:
An Algorithmic Approach

The first step in the construction of a causal model involves a diagram that depicts the hypothesized relationships among a set of variables. This usually takes the form of a path diagram such as the one depicted in Figure 1.

A number of conventions are followed in drawing path diagrams (Duncan, 1966; Land, 1969). A hypothetical causal relation between two variables included in the model is depicted by a unidirectional arrow drawn from one variable to another variable which it affects. Relations between two variables that are not causal are represented by a two-headed arrow connecting them.

Figure 1

Causal Model of Achievement Motivation

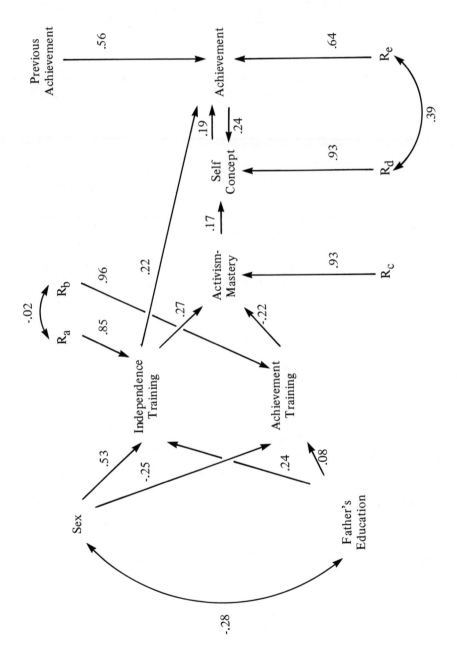

Standardized regression coefficients (i.e., path coefficients) are written alongside of the unidirectional arrows. Zero-order correlation coefficients are written alongside of the two-headed arrows. An unmeasured variable is introduced with a literal subscript to account for variation in the variable that it is linked to which cannot be accounted for by the model.

The model can be written as a set of linear equations, of the general form $Y_i = B_i + B_{i1} X_1 + \ldots + B_{ik} X_k + e$, where the range of i and k depend on the specific model. In certain portions of the model, the values of X_j are in fact defined by other equations in the set, e.g., $X_j = Y_n$. Such a situation is called recursion (feedback).

Recursive models or models that involve only one-way causation and no feedback loops can be estimated by applying ordinary least squares (OLS) procedures to each equation in turn. Paths depicted in the original model with nonsignificant regression parameters can be deleted from the path diagram and from the corresponding equation. The equation can then be rerun and new estimates of the coefficients of the remaining variables generated.

Equations that involve reciprocal causation or feedback cannot be estimated using OLS. If OLS is used to estimate the regression coefficients, these estimates will be biased and inconsistent (Johnston, 1963). For equations involving recursion, two-stage least squares (TSLS) can be used to estimate the regression coefficients if the equation is identified or over-identified. Identification of the equations in this model involves specifying that certain variables do not appear in the equation. In essence, this assumes that the regression coefficient for that variable is zero. Fisher (1966) provides a means of determining whether or not each equation is identified. An equation is identified if a number of variables equal to one less than the total number of equations is excluded from that equation.

Data may be input at the terminal or called from an internal storage device. In order to facilitate the programming, two data arrays are created. One consists of all predetermined variables (i.e., exogenous and lagged endogenous variables). The second data matrix contains the endogenous or jointly determined variables.

First, a vector containing the observed values of the endogenous variable on the left side of the equation is created, i.e., the vector of Y_i observations. Next, a matrix containing the variables that appear on the right side of the equation is created.

Two additional vectors are created; one containing the regression parameters to be estimated; one containing the differences between the observed values of Y_i and the predicted values, $\hat{Y}_i$.

The orders of these matrices (i.e., the numbers of rows, columns, elements) depend on the specific equations being evaluated and the properties of the model. Solution of the regression equations to produce the regression coefficients and multiple correlations is achieved by standard multiple regression calculations provided by common statistical computer program packages. Applying a standard test of significance for a given regression coefficient determines whether the variable involved should be retained in the equation or in the model.

When a model contains recursive or feedback elements the regression solutions are slightly more complicated. The parameters of the equations involving such recursive elements can be estimated by two-stage least-squares procedures.

Interactive Causal Modeling

The major feature of an interactive causal modeling approach is the almost immediate feedback that the student receives from the computer. After specification of his causal model and entry of his data, the computer performs the computations and displays the results almost immediately. The student is then able to postulate an alternative causal model, or he can modify his first model based on the outcome of his initial effort. The computations are then performed and results of the new analysis displayed in a matter of seconds.

This approach allows a student to learn basic correlation and regression techniques; their extension into multiple regression, path analysis, and simultaneous equation models; and approach to an inductive sociological theory. Induction in this instance involves drawing theoretical conclusions from empirical data. The example that is illustrated below has been used in a methods course to teach students how to construct simultaneous equation models. It could also be used in a social psychology course to inductively develop a theory of achievement motivation.

The program is written in the BASIC language. In the run that is illustrated here the data are stored in advance on a disc under the file name ACH. This is advisable when data files are large and cannot easily be entered at the terminal. Students are provided with a codebook that describes how each variable was defined and measured and how they are stored on the disc.

Students are required first to formulate a theoretical model of achievement motivation such as the one shown in Figure 1. This requires a careful reading of selected literature on achievement motivation (Evans and Anderson, 1973; McClelland *et al.*, 1953; Rosen *et al.*, 1969).

The run reported below is for the hypothetical causal structure depicted in Figure 1. The questions posed by the computer are in capital letters while the student's responses are in lower case letters.

INTERACTIVE CAUSAL MODELING
DO YOU WISH TO ENTER THE DATA? no
WHAT IS THE FILE NAME OF YOUR DATA? ach
IS YOUR EQUATION RECURSIVE? yes
WHAT IS THE COLUMN NUMBER OF THE ENDOGENOUS VARI-
    ABLE ON THE LEFT SIDE OF YOUR EQUATION? 3
WHAT ARE THE COLUMN NUMBERS OF THE ENDOGENOUS AND
    EXOGENOUS VARIABLES ON THE RIGHT SIDE OF YOUR
    EQUATION? 1, 2

STANDARDIZED AND UNSTANDARDIZED REGRESSION COEFFICIENTS AND STANDARD ERRORS

VARIABLE NUMBER	STANDARDIZED REGRESSION COEFFICIENT	UNSTANDARDIZED REGRESSION COEFFICIENT	STANDARD ERROR
0		3.83	.65
1	.53	2.75	.70
2	.24	.37	.20

MULTIPLE CORRELATION COEFFICIENT

$R = .52$

RESIDUAL PATH COEFFICIENT

.69

DO YOU WISH TO RERUN THIS EQUATION? no
DO YOU WISH TO FIT ANOTHER EQUATION? yes
IS YOUR EQUATION RECURSIVE? no
IS YOUR EQUATION IDENTIFIED? ARE VARIABLES EQUAL TO ONE LESS THAN THE TOTAL NUMBER OF EQUATIONS EXCLUDED FROM THE EQUATION? yes
WHAT IS THE COLUMN NUMBER OF THE ENDOGENOUS VARIABLE ON THE LEFT SIDE OF YOUR EQUATION? 8
WHAT ARE THE COLUMN NUMBERS OF THE ENDOGENOUS VARIABLES ON THE RIGHT SIDE OF YOUR EQUATION? 3, 6
WHAT ARE THE COLUMN NUMBERS OF ALL EXOGENOUS AND LAGGED ENDOGENOUS VARIABLES IN THE COMPLETE SET OF EQUATIONS? 1, 2, 7
WHAT ARE THE COLUMN NUMBERS OF THE EXOGENOUS AND LAGGED ENDOGENOUS VARIABLES ON THE RIGHT SIDE OF YOUR EQUATION? 7

STANDARDIZED AND UNSTANDARDIZED REGRESSION COEFFICIENTS AND STANDARD ERRORS

VARIABLE NUMBER	STANDARDIZED REGRESSION COEFFICIENT	UNSTANDARDIZED REGRESSION COEFFICIENT	STANDARD ERROR
3	.22	.95	.45
6	.19	6.09	4.95
0		11.74	7.29
7	.56	.57	.16

MULTIPLE CORRELATION COEFFICIENT

R = .58

RESIDUAL PATH COEFFICIENT

.48

DO YOU WISH TO FIT ANOTHER EQUATION? yes

The program continues in this fashion until the parameters of all five equations are estimated. The student would then answer no to the question above. He is then asked if he wants to see the reduced form of the equation.

DO YOU WISH TO SEE THE REDUCED FORM OF YOUR MODEL? yes

HOW MANY ENDOGENOUS VARIABLES ARE THERE IN YOUR COMPLETE MODEL? 5
HOW MANY EXOGENOUS AND LAGGED ENDOGENOUS VARIABLES ARE THERE IN YOUR COMPLETE MODEL? 3
ENTER IN NUMERICAL ORDER THE COLUMN NUMBERS OF ALL OF THE ENDOGENOUS VARIABLES IN YOUR COMPLETE MODEL. 3, 4, 5, 6, 8
ENTER IN NUMERICAL ORDER THE ESTIMATED COEFFICIENTS OF YOUR ENDOGENOUS VARIABLES AN EQUATION AT A TIME. ENTER A -1 FOR THE COEFFICIENT THAT APPEARS ON THE LEFT SIDE OF THE EQUATION AND A 0 FOR THE COEFFICIENT OF ANY ENDOGENOUS VARIABLE THAT DOES NOT APPEAR IN THE EQUATION. -1, 0, 0, 0, 0, 0, -1, 0, 0, 0, .08, -.17, -1, 0, 0, 0, 0, .21, -1, .03, .44, 0, 0, 6.09, -1
ENTER IN NUMERICAL ORDER THE COLUMN NUMBERS OF ALL OF THE EXOGENOUS AND LAGGED ENDOGENOUS VARIABLES IN YOUR COMPLETE MODEL. 1, 2, 7
ENTER IN NUMERICAL ORDER THE ESTIMATED COEFFICIENTS OF YOUR CONSTANT TERM, EXOGENOUS AND LAGGED ENDO-GENOUS VARIABLES AN EQUATION AT A TIME. ENTER A 0 FOR THE COEFFICIENT OF ANY EXOGENOUS OR LAGGED ENDOGENOUS VARIABLE THAT DOES NOT APPEAR IN THE EQUATION. 3.83, 2.75, .37, 0, .09, -.49, .04, 0, -.63, 0, 0, 0, -1.16, 0, 0, 0, 11.74, 0, 0, .57

THE COEFFICIENTS FOR THE REDUCED
FORM EQUATIONS

ENDOGENOUS VARIABLE NUMBER	EXOGENOUS AND LAGGED ENDOGENOUS VARIABLE NUMBER			
	0	1	2	7
3	3.83	2.75	.37	0
4	.09	-.49	.04	0
5	-.35	.30	.02	0
6	-1.05	.11	.01	.02
8	7.05	1.92	.23	.67

DO YOU WISH TO MODIFY YOUR MODEL? no
END INTERACTIVE CAUSAL MODELING

Once the run is completed the numerical values of the path coefficients shown in Figure 1 can be added to the path diagram. The original theoretical model that was formulated can now be examined in light of the empirical evidence.

Conclusion

The approach to formal theory construction developed here permits the student to develop and empirically examine his theoretical model in a step-wise fashion. The rapid feedback of the interactive system makes it possible for him to test alternative hypotheses or to modify his model on the basis of the results of a previous step in his analysis.

The algorithm and the interactive program that have been developed here provide the student with opportunities to analyze research data and to construct social theories in much the same fashion as the professional social scientist. Successively complex multivariate models can be constructed and analyzed in a relatively short period of time.

References

Anderson, J.G. Causal Models and Social Indicators. *American Sociological Review*, 1973, *38*, 285-301.

Anderson, R.E. A Survey of Application Software for Social Data Analysis Instruction. In *Proceedings of a Conference on Computers in the Undergraduate Curricula*, Darthmouth College, Hanover, New Hampshire, 1971.

Anderson, R.E., and E.R. Coover. Wrapping Up the Package: Critical Thoughts on Applications Software for Social Data Analysis. *Computers and the Humanities*, 1972, *7*, 81-95.

Blalock, H.M., Jr. *Causal Inferences in Nonexperimental Research*. Chapel Hill: University of North Carolina, 1964.

Blalock, H.M., Jr. *Theory Construction*. Englewood Cliffs, N.J.: Prentice Hall, 1969.

Blalock, H.M., Jr. *Causal Models in the Social Sciences*. Chicago: Aldine, 1971.

Blumer, H. What Is Wrong with Social Theory? *American Sociological Review*, 1955, *19*, 3-10.

Cline, H.H., and O. Meyers. Problem-Solving Computer Systems for Instruction in Sociology. *American Sociologist*, 1970, 365-370.

Costner, H.L. (Ed.), *Sociological Methodology 1973-1974*. San Francisco: Jossey-Bass, 1974.

Davis, J.A. Using the IMPRESS System to Teach Sociology. In

Proceedings of the Second Annual Conference on Computers in the Undergraduate Curricula, Dartmouth College, Hanover, New Hampshire, 1971.

de Nuefville, R., and J.H. Stafford. *Systems Analysis for Engineers and Managers*. New York: McGraw Hiil, 1971.

Duncan, O.D. Path Analysis: Sociological Examples. *American Journal of Sociology*, 1966, *72*, 1-16.

Duncan, O.D. *Introduction to Structural Equation Models*. New York: Academic Press, 1975.

Duncan, O.D., A.O. Haller, and A. Portes. Peer Influences on Aspirations: A Reinterpretation. *American Journal of Sociology*, 1968, *74*, 119-137.

Duncan, O.D., A.O. Haller, and A. Portes. Duncan's Corrections of Published Text of Peer Influences on Aspirations: A Reinterpretation. *American Journal of Sociology*, 1970, *75*, 1042-1046.

Evans, F.B., and J.G. Anderson. The Psychocultural Origins of Achievement and Achievement Motivation: The Mexican-American Family. *Sociology of Education*, 1973, *46*, 396-416.

Fisher, F.M. *The Identification Problem in Econometrics*. New York: McGraw Hill, 1966.

Glaser, B.G., and A.L. Strauss. *The Discovery of Grounded Theory*. Chicago, Illinois: Aldine, 1967.

Goldberger, A.S., and O.D. Duncan. *Structural Equation Models*. New York: Seminar Press, 1973.

Johnston, J. *Econometric Methods*. New York: McGraw Hill, 1963.

Land, K.C. Principles of Path Analysis. In E.F. Borgatta (Ed.), *Sociological Methodology 1969*. San Francisco: Jossey Bass, 1969.

Mason, R., and R.N. Halter. The Application of a System of Simultaneous Equations to an Innovation Diffusion Model. *Social Forces*, 1968, *47*, 182-195.

McClelland, D.C., J.W. Atkinson, R.A. Clark, and E.L. Lowell. *The Achievement Motive*. New York: Appleton-Century-Crofts, 1953.

Nolle, D.B. Alternative Path Analytic Models of Student-Teacher Influence: The Implications of Different Strokes for Different Folks. *Sociology of Education*, 1973, *46*, 417-426.

Nygreen, G.T. Interactive Path Analysis. *The American Sociologist*, 1971, *6*, 37-43.

Rosen, B.C., H.J. Crockett, and C.Z. Nunn. *Achievement in American Society*. Cambridge: Schenkman, 1969.

Stinchcombe, A.L. *Constructing Social Theories*. New York: Harcourt, Brace, and World, 1968.

Theil, H. *Principles of Econometrics*. New York: John Wiley, 1971.

30.
Computer Based Instruction in Sociology: A Computer Simulation Approach

James G. Anderson
Purdue University

Computer Based Instruction

Anderson (1974a) has observed that computer simulation as an instructional approach has been slow to diffuse in the social science curriculum. Moreover, most applications are still confined to the teaching of statistics and research methods. A recent survey of sociology instructors by CONDUIT under an NSF grant dramatically illustrates this point (Anderson, 1974b). Out of 383 sociology courses that utilized the computer for instructional purposes in any fashion, 63 percent were research methods or statistics courses; an additional 13 courses (3%) were computer methods courses.

In the case of methods and statistics courses, computer programs have been developed to simulate samples drawn from populations with known parameters and to demonstrate basic theorems of probability and statistics (Appelbaum and Guthrie, 1970; Garrett, 1970; Lohnes and Cooley, 1968; Wikoff, 1970). Also, simulation has been used to generate data for courses in experimental design (Lehman, 1972; Main and Head, 1971). Computer simulation exercises have also been used to teach population dynamics in demography courses (van de Walle and Knodel, 1970).

Lehman (1973) has pointed to a promising growth in the area of computer modeling of psychological processes and the impact that it has begun to have on classroom instruction in the field of psychology. Models of learning phenomena developed by Hintzman (1968) and Anderson (1972) are beginning to be used in the teaching of learning courses. Some courses in perception include computer models developed by Selfridge (1959) and Wallingford (1972), while models developed by Siegel and Wolf (1969), Joyner (1970), and Green (1972) have been incorporated into courses in social psychology.

Computer Simulation in the Sociology
Curriculum: An Example

The present paper demonstrates how a computer simulation model can be developed and utilized to organize classroom discussion in a social psychology course. The model that is developed here involves small-group behavior.

The model building process involves the following steps (Blalock, 1969). First, a formal model is developed from verbal theories contained in the literature. Theoretical propositions are used to systematically link concepts or variables. A causal diagram such as the one depicted in Figure 1 is constructed. Unidirectional arrows indicate the hypothesized direction of causality. Variables linked by two arrows running in opposite directions involve reciprocal causation. A circular arrow connecting a variable with itself indicates that the value of the variable at a point in time is affected by its value at an earlier point in time.

Festinger (1950) has stated a number of propositions about communication processes in small groups. He hypothesizes that the group process involving pressure to achieve uniformity involves six variables. These are: the amount of group pressure on members to communicate, $P(t)$; the perceived discrepency in opinion among group members, $D(t)$; the degree of relevance of the issue to the group's functioning, R; the cohesiveness of the group, $C(t)$; the amount of group pressure to achieve uniformity, $U(t)$; and the willingness of group members to change their opinions, $L(t)$. R, the relevance of the particular issue to the group's functioning, is considered to be constant for the group, while all other variables are considered to change over time.

Figure 1 depicts the hypothetical model. The model postulates instantaneous feedback occurring from perceived discrepancy of opinion, $D(t)$, to pressure on members to communicate, $P(t)$; also from group cohesiveness, $C(t)$, to pressure to achieve uniformity, $U(t)$. Any change in the level of discrepency or cohesiveness brings

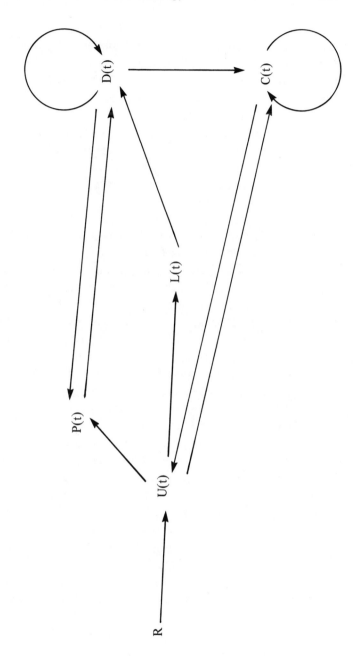

Figure 1

Course Diagram of Group Pressures Toward Uniformity

about an immediate adjustment in the amount of pressure on members to communicate or to achieve uniformity, respectively. Levels of discrepency of opinion, D(t), and group cohesiveness, C(t), change more slowly over time. These levels are affected by their own previous levels as well as by the levels of other variables that appear in the model.

The second step involves the translation of the causal diagram into a mathematical model. For example, the model depicted in Figure 1 can be represented by the following set of equations:

(1) $P(t) = 0.5\ D(t) + 0.5\ U(t)$

(2) $U(t) = 0.5\ R + 0.5\ C(t)$

(3) $L(t) = U(t)$

(4) $D(t + \Delta t) = D(t) + \Delta t\ D(t)\ (g(P(t)) + h(L(t)))$

(5) $C(t + \Delta t) = C(t) + \Delta t\ C(t)\ (v(D(t)) + w(U(t)))$

Next, the coefficients that appear in the equations need to be estimated. This can be accomplished by considering the behavior of the system at an equilibrium point where the rates of change of discrepency are zero. All of the variables involved in the model are considered to be in standard form and consequently are dimensionless.

The system was considered to be in equilibrium when the values of all six variables were one. Consequently, the coefficients for D(t) and U(t) in equation (1) would have to be 0.5, assuming that these two variables have an equal additive effect on P(t), pressure to communicate. A similar line of reasoning results in values of 0.5 for the two coefficients in equation (2). The coefficient for U(t), pressure to achieve uniformity, in equation (3) then has to be one in order to ensure that L(t), readiness to change, will also equal one under equilibrium conditions.

If the rate of change of D(t) in equation (4) is to be zero at equilibrium, the two functions g(P(t)) and h(L(t)), have to assume values of zero when P(t) and L(t) assume values of one, respectively. The values of these two functions were arrived at by reasoning that when either pressure to communicate or the readiness of group members to change were low (i.e., P(t) = 0 or L(t) = 0), the rate of increase in discrepency, D(t), would be high; whereas, high values of these variables (i.e., P(t) = 3 or L(t) = 3) would result in a correspondingly high rate of change in discrepency, but in a negative direction. The same functions were used to describe the effects of D(t) and U(t) on the rate of change of group cohesiveness, C(t). When these two variables assumed values of one, the rate of change in C(t) had to be zero. Again, low values of either variable cause a large positive increase in cohesiveness while high values result in a high rate of change but in a negative direction.

The fourth step involves actually simulating the group process. The technique used to simulate the behavior of the system as characterized by the five equations and to trace the time paths of the variables is that of systems dynamics (Forrester, 1968). The computational sequence involves first specifying the coefficients of the terms appearing in the equations and the four functions, g(P(t)), h(L(t)), v(D(t)), and w(U(t)). Next, R, the relevance of the issue to the group's functioning, is set to a constant value and the initial levels of D(t), the perceived discrepency among group members, and C(t), the cohesiveness of the group, are set. Equation (2) is then used to calculate U(t), the pressure to achieve uniformity. Once this value has been calculated, equations (1) and (3) are used to calculate P(t), the pressure on members to communicate, and L(t), the group's readiness to change, respectively. Finally, equations (4) and (5) in conjunction with the step functions specified earlier are used to calculate new values of D(t + Δ t) and C(t + Δ T), the values of discrepency and cohesiveness for the next period. Once a run is completed, values of the coefficients can be altered or the initial levels of discrepency, cohesiveness or relevance can be changed and another run made and compared with the earlier one.

Using the model developed here, the behavior of the group was simulated for 40 time periods. The horizontal axis represents time while the vertical axis represents values of the variables ranging from 0 to 8. Time paths for discrepency, D(t), cohesiveness, C(t), pressure to achieve uniformity, U(t), and pressure to communicate, P(t), are plotted. Neither L(t), readiness to change, nor R, relevance, were plotted, since the time path of the former variable is identical with that of U(t), and the latter variable is a constant for a particular run.

In the results of the first simulation run, initial values of relevance, R, and discrepency, D(t), were one. Group cohesiveness, C(t), was initially high (i.e., C(t) = 1.5) for this run. The results indicate that as the group functions, the pressure on group members to achieve uniformity, U(t), increases rapidly. This results in greater pressure to communicate, P(t). As a result, there is a rapid decrease in the amount of discrepency of opinion, D(t), among members of the group.

The findings of several studies can be used to validate the results of this run. Back's (1951, p. 16) experimental study of the effects of cohesiveness on group behavior found that over two-thirds of the individuals who were members of high cohesive groups reported that their partners tried to influence them, whereas, less than one-half of the members of low cohesive groups reported similar pressure. Apparently pressure to achieve uniformity, U(t), does indeed increase markedly with cohesiveness, C(t), as predicted.

Back's finding that self-ratings of resistance to influence showed a slight decrease in the high cohesive groups also confirms another of the model's predictions. Equation (3) indicates that group members readiness to change, L(t), is directly proportional to pressure to achieve uniformity, U(t), which is related to cohesiveness, C(t), through equation (2). Thus, the model predicts that an increase in cohesiveness, C(t), will indirectly result in an increase in the readiness of group members to change their opinions, L(t).

A high level of cohesiveness, C(t), also results in a significant decrease in the discrepancy of opinion among group members, D(t), as predicted. Again, this result is confirmed by Back's experiment. Back (1951, p. 18) concludes that "... there is a definite increase in change toward features of the partner's stories when cohesiveness increases." He concludes that the mechanism by which this occurs is essentially the one hypothesized by this model when he states that "... as we expected, the greater pressure towards uniformity in the high cohesive groups results in the possibility that some members can be influenced quite strongly."

Simon and Guetzkow (1955, pp. 144-145) present data from a study by Festinger, Schachter, and Back (1950) that can also be used to validate the model. They investigated the operation of group standards in two housing projects. Cohesiveness, C(t), was defined as the tendency of residents of a court to associate with one another. Discrepency in opinion regarding a tenants' organization was used as a measure of discrepency, D(t). Simon and Gutzkow reason that over time the system will reach equilibrium. Courts that were initially high in discrepency will ultimately be low in cohesiveness and those initially low in discrepency will ultimately be highly cohesive. They present a plot of the data from the original study to support their contention (Simon and Guetzkow, 1955, p. 67).

A computer simulation run was designed to test this hypothesis. Discrepency, D(t), was initially set at a high level (i.e., D(t) = 1.5) while relevance, R, and cohesiveness, C(t), were initially set to one. As discrepency, D(t), begins to rise there is at first increased pressure to communicate, P(t). At the same time, cohesiveness, C(t), decreases, resulting in less pressure to achieve uniformity, U(t). This ultimately causes pressure to communicate, P(t), to level off. As the system stabilizes, saturation occurs as Simon and Guetzkow predicted. When discrepency, D(t), reaches very high levels, cohesiveness, C(t), levels off at a low level and further increases in discrepency no longer affect cohesiveness.

Conclusion

This paper has provided an example of how computer simulation can be used as an instructional approach in sociology. The simulation model constructed here in order to examine the process by which groups generate pressures toward uniformity has led to a number of major insights into this dynamic process. The model suggests that group cohesiveness and the relevance of the issue to the groups' functioning produce pressures toward uniformity. Such pressures result in increased pressure to communicate and an increased readiness on the part of group members to change their opinions. Through this process, discrepency in opinions is reduced resulting in increased group cohesiveness.

The model developed here has been used to demonstrate how computer simulation can contribute to the teaching of social theory. Formulating a social theory as a computer model requires the student to synthesize the pertinent social science literature; to generate a causal model that explicitly states his hypotheses concerning the relationships among the variables; to translate his verbal model into a mathematical model; to estimate the parameters of this model; and to examine the logical consequences of his hypotheses about the social process under investigation.

References

Anderson, J.R. FRAN: A Simulation Model of Free Recall. In G.H. Bower (Ed), *The Psychology of Learning and Motivation, Vol. 5*. New York: Academic Press, 1972.

Anderson, R.E. Computer Based Instructional Units in the Social Sciences: A "State of the Art" Report. Unpublished manuscript, University of Minnesota, Minneapolis, 1974a.

Anderson, R.E. A Survey of Computer Use in Sociology Instruction. Unpublished manuscript, University of Minnesota, Minneapolis, 1974b.

Appelbaum, M.E., and D. Guthrie. Use of Computers in Undergraduate Statistics Instruction. In *Conference on Computers in the Undergraduate Curricula, 1970*, Center for Conferences and Institutes, University of Iowa, Iowa City, 1970.

Back, K.W. Influence Through Social Communication. *Journal of Abnormal and Social Psychology*, 1951, *46*, 9-23.

Blalock, H.M., Jr. *Theory Construction*. Englewood Cliffs, N.J.: Prentice Hall, 1969.

Festinger, L. Informal Social Communication. *Psychological Review*, 1950, *57*, 271-282.

Festinger, L., S. Schachter, and K. Back. *Social Pressure in Informal Groups*. New York: Harper, 1950.

Forrester, J.W. *Principles of Systems*. Cambridge, Mass.: Wright-Allen Press, 1968.

Garrett, H.G. SAMDS: A Program to Generate Empirical Sampling Distributions of the Mean. In *Conference on Computers in the Undergraduate Curricula 1970*, Center for Conferences and Institutes, University of Iowa, Iowa City, 1970.

Green, B.F., Jr. The Use of Time-Shared Terminals in Psychology. *Behavior Research Methods & Instrumentation*, 1972, *4*, 51-55.

Hintzman, D.L. Explorations with a Discrimination Net Model for Paired Associate Learning. *Journal of Mathematical Psychology*, 1968, *7*, 478-514.

Joyner, R.C. Computer Simulation of Individual Concept Learning in the Three-Person Common Target Game. *Journal of Mathematical Psychology*, 1970, *7*, 478-514.

Lehman, R.S. The Use of the Unknown in Teaching Statistics. Paper presented at the Annual Meeting of the Eastern Psychological Association, Boston, Massachusetts, 1972.

Lehman, R.S. Computer Models in the Classroom. Paper presented at the Annual Meeting of the Eastern Psychological Association, Washington, D.C., 1973.

Lohnes, P.R., and W.W. Cooley. *Introduction to Statistical Procedures with Computer Exercises.* New York: John Wiley, 1968.

Main, D., and C. Head. Computer Simulations in the Elementary Psychology Laboratory. In *Conference on Computers in the Undergraduate Curricula 1971,* University Press of New England, Hanover, New Hampshire, 1971.

Selfridge, O.G. Pandemonium: A Paradigm for Learning. *The Mechanization of Thought Processes.* London: H.M. Stationery Office, 1959.

Siegel, A.I., and J.J. Wolf. *Man-Machine Simulation Models.* New York: John Wiley, 1969.

Simon, H.A., and H. Guetzkow. A Model of Short- and Long-Run Mechanisms Involved in Pressures Toward Uniformity in Groups. *Psychological Bulletin,* 1955, *62,* 56-68.

van de Walle, E., and J. Knodel. Teaching Population Dynamics with a Simulation Exercise. *Demography,* 1970, 7, 433-448.

Wallingford, E.G. A Visual Pattern Recognizing Computer Program Based on Neurophysiological Data. *Behavioral Science,* 1972, *17,* 241-248.

Wikoff, R.L. Using the Computer in Basic Statistics Courses. In *Conference on Computers in the Undergraduate Curricula 1970,* Center for Conferences and Institutes, University of Iowa, Iowa City, 1970.

31.
Computer Simulation of Human Intelligence and Analysis of Natural Language

Ellen Bouchard Ryan
University of Notre Dame

Patrick J. Ryan
Indiana University at South Bend

Introduction

This paper describes a course intended to introduce the advanced undergraduate as well as the graduate student to computer applications that go beyond the computation of numerical quantities, the task for which the computer is best known. Although the content is perhaps of most interest to psychology majors, the typical class would include students from a variety of disciplines, such as computer science, mathematics, modern languages, English, business, and social sciences. In general, some programming knowledge is assumed, although there will be a wide variation in the degree and quality of the students' programming experiences.

The purposes of this course are two: (1) to provide an understanding of the methods and goals of computer simulations of thinking processes and of computer analysis of language; and (2) to teach the computer programming skills basic to these applications. These course goals are intentionally intertwined, as we feel that it is impossible to comprehend discussions in the literature concerning computer models of language and thought without working with simple programs illustrating the various approaches. Furthermore, it makes sense to learn programming techniques in the context of their applications to theoretical and practical problems.

A number of learning vehicles can be utilized in this course. First of all, students must become familiar with the literature, by reading the text (for example, Apter's *Computer Simulation of*

Behavior) as well as selected articles from journals and other reference books. Flow charts are perhaps the best way to communicate to the students the basic idea of many of the computer models described in the readings. Second, students can read and run a number of practice programs illustrating both programming techniques and applications to content areas. Third, students should become involved actively by writing short programs and revising prepared programs to expand their capabilities. Finally, the development of a major program on a topic selected during conferences between student and professor should enable the student to integrate and apply much of what he has learned in the course (with regard to both technique and content). Class presentation of these term projects would further broaden the scope of the course and enhance the active learning of the students.

Content

The introduction to the course involves an overview of computer applications that go beyond computations with numeric data. Programming skills are taught throughout the course, with the heaviest emphasis necessarily in the beginning. Following are (1) a course outline, and (2) some illustrative suggestions for short programs and term projects.

Outline of Course
I.   Introduction
    A.   Non-Numeric uses of the computer
    B.   Programming in PL/I (especially manipulation of alphameric data and list processing
II. Models of thinking processes
    A.   Learning
    B.   Pattern recognition
    C.   Concept formation
    D.   Problem solving
    E.   Other topics (e.g., game playing, theorem proving)
III. Natural language processing
    A.   Computational linguistics
    B.   Grammatical analysis
IV. Semantic information processing

    A.   Question-answering systems

    B.   Applications to computer-assisted-instruction

Some Suggestions for Short Programs
and Term Projects

1. Write an interactive program to collect data from subjects in a verbal learning study and then create a subroutine to simulate the learning which occurs and another to simulate the subject's responding.

2. Write a program to collect and summarize data from a subject in a simple concept formation task (using either the selective or receptive paradigm). Then, substitute subroutines simulating a subject for each section of the program requesting a response of the subject. Of particular interest would be contrasting simulations based on all-or-none hypothesis-testing approach versus an optimal successive-elimination approach.

3. Design a program that will simulate a person's rule learning behavior for an artificial language. The subject is presented with strings, labeled as grammatical or ungrammatical, and his task is to anticipate the categorization of successive strings.

4. Write a program to evaluate poker hands (e.g., two-of-a-kind, three-of-a-kind, full house, etc.) and then simulate a poker match by dealing two or three players' hands, evaluating them, setting up betting strategies, and recording the amount of money of each player after each round.

5. Write a program to play bridge. Begin with very automatic straightforward rules for bidding and playing. After the program is working, gradually add strategies to improve the abilities of the players.

6. Simulate a tennis match between two players given input concerning their relative abilities to serve easy or hard shots, to return easy or hard shots, and to return a shot with an easy or hard shot.

7. Write a program that can solve at least some number sequence problems found on IQ tests and programming aptitude tests. Incorporate a simulation that provides a rank order of difficulty similar to that experienced by human problem solving.

8. Given a dictionary, including phrases as well as words, tag each occurrence of an entry in a text with the associated meaning and calculate frequencies of occurrence.

9. Write a program to pluralize English nouns.

10. Given a set of simple grammatical rules and a dictionary with grammatically-tagged words, generate a set of random "grammatical sentences." Furthermore, use whatever inconsistencies exist in the output to revise the set of rules or the dictionary.

11. Design a computer-assisted instruction system to teach sentence translation to a first-year foreign-language student. The system randomly presents sentences in the native or the second language. The student types in a translation sentence or requests vocabulary information. If the translation is correct, the system presents a new sentence problem. After an incorrect response, the part of the response that is correct is repeated with dashes representing information still to be supplied by the student. Appropriate drill (periodic repetition of sentences which cause difficulty) is provided.

12. Design a computer-assisted instruction system for vocabulary and spelling that will provide definitions to a fifth-grade child and check his one-word answer for semantic appropriateness and for spelling. If the spelling is slightly incorrect, the system should present the correct word with only the correct letters and dashes replacing the others. After the child inputs another attempt, the system continues on to the next problem after providing the correct answer if the pupil is wrong again.

Discussion of Content

The principles underlying the use of computer programs to simulate man's thinking processes form the foundation for consideration of actual simulations. Although reading summaries of many models helps to provide the student with a general idea of the state of the art, a few representative programs are selected for detailed presentations, including such aids as flow charts describing the basic operations and programs illustrating the required programming techniques. Since learning and memory, concept formation (including pattern recognition), and problem solving are the major topics in the psychology of thinking, at least one programmed model in each of these areas should be examined. Attempts are made to detect and discuss similarities in the approaches employed to simulate the different processes, since the ultimate goal is a single program that can perform all intelligent activities.

As the ability to communicate and think with language is often considered the key distinguishing characteristic of human intelligence, computer simulation of human behavior eventually must include the comprehension and production of natural language. Techniques for the segmentation of a text into words and sentences and for the analysis of grammatical structures are discussed, followed by a review of applications in computational linguistics (e.g., studies of the statistical properties of texts), theoretical linguistics (e.g., concordances), and machine translation.

Semantic information processing systems are programs designed to answer natural-language questions concerning a stored data base. These systems must combine routines for simulating human intelligence with routines for processing natural language. The extent to which these two tasks become intertwined in some of the more successful models is of particular importance.

Programming Techniques

PL/I has been selected as the optimal programming language to employ in this course. This widely-available language, which can be used both interactively and in batch-processing, includes a large number of special features for easy handling of alphameric data as well as the capability for list processing.

As far as string manipulation is concerned, PL/I allows the programmer to read in alphameric (character) information, to concatenate character variables, to manipulate specific substrings of character variables, and to output such variables conveniently.

More importantly, list processing operations can be performed with PL/I. List processing involves the computer storage and accessing of information according to the logical relationships within the data, rather than according to some prearranged structure. This capability is essential in many nonnumeric applications, such as simulation of intelligent processes, understanding of natural language, and question-answering systems.

Conclusion

We have attempted to present briefly a prototype for courses that combine the study of computer models of intelligent processes with the learning of advanced programming skills. It is hoped that the preceding comments will strike the imaginations of some readers and lead them to develop their own courses, using as guides our course outline and list of programming projects.

In addition, the list of references at the end of this paper provide valuable information for the course designer.

A Selected Reading List

I. General Texts for Reference

A. *Programming and Data Structures*

Gear, C.W. *Introduction to Computer Science* (Chapter 7). Chicago: S.R.A., 1973.

Knuth, D.E. *The Art of Computer Programming, Vol. I. Fundamental Algorithms.* Reading, Mass.: Addison-Wesley, 1968.

Lawson, H.W., Jr. PL/I List Processing. *Communications of the ACM*, 1967, *10* (6), 358-367.

Ryan, E.B., P.J. Ryan, and N. Catrambone. *A Manual for List-Processing in PL/I*, University of Notre Dame, 1975. (Copies available from the authors).

B. *Content*

Apter, M. *The Computer Simulation of Behavior.* New York: Harper & Row, 1971.

Apter, M.J., and G. Westby (Eds.), *The Computer in Psychology.* New York: John Wiley, 1973.

Scientific American. *Computers and Computation.* San Francisco: W.H. Freeman, 1971.

Feigenbaum, E.A., and J. Feldman (Eds.), *Computers and Thought.* New York: McGraw-Hill, 1963.

Hunt, E.B. *Artificial Intelligence.* New York: Academic Press, 1975.

Minsky, M. (Ed.), *Semantic Information Processing.* Cambridge: MIT Press, 1968.

Reitman, W.R. *Cognition and Thought: An Information Processing Approach.* New York: John Wiley, 1965.

Schank, R., and R. Colby (Eds.), *Computer Models of Language and Thought.* San Francisco: W.H. Freeman, 1973.

Simon, H.A., and L. Siklossy (Eds.), *Representation and*

Meaning: Experiments with Information Processing Systems. Englewood Cliffs, N.J.: Prentice-Hall, 1972.

II. *Thinking Processes*

Abelson, R.P. Simulation of Social Behavior. In G. Lindzey and E. Aronson (Eds.), *The Handbook of Social Psychology, Vol. 2.* Reading, Mass.: Addison-Wesley, 1968.

Bourne, L., R. Ekstrand, and R. Dominowski. *The Psychology of Thinking.* Englewood Cliffs, N.J.: Prentice-Hall, 1973.

Green, B.F. Computer Models of Psychological Processes. In B.F. Green (Ed.), *Digital Computers in Research.* New York: McGraw-Hill, 1963.

Hintzman, D.L. Exploration with a Discrimination Net Model for Paired-Associate Learning. *Journal of Math. Psych.*, 1968, *5*, 123-162.

Newell, A., and H.A. Simon. Computers in Psychology. In R.D. Luce, R. Bush, and E. Galanter (Eds.), *Handbook of Mathematical Psychology, Vol. 1.* New York: John Wiley, 1963.

Pollio, H. *The Psychology of Symbolic Activity.* Reading, Mass.: Addison-Wesley, 1974.

Simon, H. Simulation of Human Thinking. In M. Greenberger (Ed.), *Computers and the World of the Future.* Cambridge, Mass.: MIT Press, 1967.

III. *Natural Language Processing*

Borko, H. (Ed.), *Automated Language Processing: The State of the Art.* New York: John Wiley, 1967.

Friedman, J. A Computer System for Transformational Grammer. *Communications of the ACM*, 1969, *12*, 341-348.

Garvin, P. (Ed.), *Natural Language and the Computer.* New York: McGraw-Hill, 1963.

Hays, D.G. (Ed.), *Readings in Automated Language Processing.* New York: American Elsevier, 1966.

IBM. *Literary Data Processing: Conference Proceedings*, 1964.

Kucera, H., and W.N. Francis. *Computational Analysis of Present-Day American English.* Providence, R.I.: Brown University Press, 1967.

Siklossy, L., and H.A. Simon. Some Semantic Methods for

Language Processing. In H.A. Simon and L. Siklossy (Eds.), *Representation and Meaning: Experiments with Information Processing Systems.* Englewood Cliffs, N.J.: Prentice-Hall, 1972.

Thorne, J.P., P. Bratley, and H. Dewar. The Syntactic Analysis of English by Machines. In D. Michie (Ed.), *Machine Intelligence 3.* Edinburgh: Edinburgh University Press, 1968.

IV. *Semantic Information Processing*

Becker, J.D. A Model for the Encoding of Experimental Information. In Schank and Colby, see above.

Bobrow, D.G. Natural Language Input for a Computer Problem-Solving System. In Minsky, see above.

Green, B.F., *et al.* Baseball: An Automatic Question Answer. In Feigenbaum and Feldman, see above.

Harrison, G. The Computer in the Psychology of Language. In Apter and Westby, see above.

Lindsay, R.K. Inferential Memory as the Basis of Machines Which Understand Natural Language. In Feigenbaum and Feldman, see above.

Quillian, M.R. Semantic Memory. In Minsky, see above.

Simmons, R.F. Semantic Networks: Their Computation and Use for Understanding English-Sentences. In Schank and Colby, see above.

Weizenbaum, J. Contextual Understanding by Computers. *Communications of the ACM*, 1967, *10*, 474-480.

Winograd, T. *Understanding Natural Language.* Academic Press, New York, 1973.

Winograd, T. A Procedural Model of Language Understanding. In Schank and Colby, see above.

V. *Relevant Journals*
Artificial Intelligence
Behavior Research Methods & Instrumentation
Behavioral Science
Communications of the Association for Computing Machinery
Computer Studies in Humanities and Verbal Behavior
Computers and Automation
Computers and Humanities

Computers and Information Systems' Information Processing Journal
Educational Technology
Information and Control
Journal of the Association for Computing Machinery
Journal of Computational Linguistics
Mechanical Translation and Computational Linguistics
Pattern Recognition

PART VI
Bibliographies

32.
Computers in Science Fiction:
A Brief Annotated Bibliography
for the Social and Behavioral Scientist

Norman E. Sondak

Worcester Polytechnic Institute

Vernon Sondak

Boston University

A successful writer of science fiction once suggested the proper method for him was to select an illogical situation and follow it to a logical conclusion. Just as conventional literature has given the social and behavioral scientist scholar a deeper insight into the working of the mind, and interpersonal relationships between individuals and social orders, so science fiction can give the undergraduate student a more intimate and personal example of what the instructor is trying to bring across. Certain classics of history like *Frankenstein, The Strange Case of Dr. Jeckle and Mr. Hyde*, or even *Gulliver's Travels* if written today might reasonably be classified as "sci-fi." George Orwell's *1984* certainly fits into the general category. For this paper, certain limiting constraints are placed on the broad medium of science-fiction. We are concerned with those stories in which an intelligent machine or device, a computer, robot, or even android, plays a central or important role. The coverage is also limited to those books or anthologies currently available, preferably in paper back form. The authors have exercised editorial discretion in preparing this brief bibliography and apologize for any omissions of readers' pet stories or texts. Please notify us of these so we can either defend or improve ourselves.

Bibliography

Anthony, P. *Macroscope*. Avon Books, New York, 1969.
Preprogrammed instruction is broadcast on the "macroband," to support galaxy-wide cultures.

Anthony, P. *The Ring*. Ace Books, New York, 1968.
A computer must provide conscience in cases where the human one fails.

Asimov, I. *I, Robot*. Doubleday, New York, 1950.
A collection of stories about positronic robots. They set the theme of many science fiction stories to follow. The robots are programmed with Three Laws that determine their behavior.

Asimov, I. *The Caves of Steel*. Doubleday, New York, 1956.
A journey to the future where people live underground in "Caves of Steel," and robots are so perfectly humanoid as to be indistinguishable from men.

Asimov, I. *The Naked Sun*. Doubleday, New York, 1956.
After all Earthlings have moved underground, one man and a robot must solve a murder on another planet—under the naked sun—that only a robot could have committed.

Asimov, I. *Earth is Room Enough*. Doubleday, 1957.
Multivac, the super-computer of the future, is so advanced it requires men who do nothing but think up questions to ask it. When Multivac begins analyzing jokes, it comes up with some startling conclusions about the origins and purposes of humans.

Bradbury, R. "April, 2005: Usher II." In *The Martian Chronicles*, Bantam Books, New York, 1972.
Robot doubles of invited guests, and unwanted visitors, are tortured in an exact model of Edgar Allan Poe's horror-filled "House of Usher," in an age where fiction is illegal. But who is the human and who is the robot?

Clarke, A. *2001: A Space Oddysey*. New American Library, New York, 1968.
This is about the famous HAL computer that sacrifices human life to complete its mission.

Clarke, A. *Nine Billion Names of God*. New American Library, New York, 1974.
The title story is about a computer enumerating all of God's names and thereby ending the world.

Conklin, G. (Ed.), *Science Fiction Thinking Machines*. Vanguard, New York, 1954.
Stories about robots, computers and androids.

Crichton, M. *Andromeda Strain*. Dell, New York, 1969.
A sloppily designed though very expensive computer system

fails twice, once by not indicating an important message and once by not highlighting a minimal growth environment. Human insight and courage, not the computer, save the world from a terrible micro-organism.

Crichton, M. *Terminal Man*. Bantam, 1972.

An arrogant scientist does not foresee the limits of a computer attached to the human brain.

Dickson, G.R. "Computers Don't Argue." In *Analog*, LXXVI, September 1965.

An unyielding computer starts with a book club billing mistake, and winds up sentencing the innocent victim of its error to death, with the reprieve sent back by the computer because it wasn't properly prepared.

Gerrold, D. *When Harlie Was One*. Ballantine Books, New York, 1973.

A computer designed with built-in emotions becomes power hungry and creates its own God.

Greenberg, M. (Ed.), *The Robot and the Man*. Gnome Press, 1953.

Heinlein, R. *The Moon is a Harsh Mistress*. Putnam, New York, 1966.

A computer technician uses a giant computer to lead a revolution on the moon.

Herbert, F. *Dune*. Ace Books, New York, 1965.

Computers are proscribed by religious order, and human "Mentats" take their place.

Jones, D.F. *Colossus*. Putnam, New York, 1966.

The two most powerful war computers in history join forces, ending all war by ending all human freedom.

Jones, R.F. "Rat Race." In *Analog*, LXXVII, April 1966.

Computers are able to provide for every human desire and want, but people also have a need to create.

Knight, D. *Orbit 14*. Harper and Row, 1974.

Contains "Tin Soldier" by Joan Vinge, where a human computer stands between the love of a half-human bartender and a whole female spacewoman, until she too becomes less than human.

McCafferey, A. *The Ship Who Sang*. Ballantine Books, New York, 1969.

Should a crippled human child die, or should its mind be linked to a computer and used in a spaceship?

Moskowitz, S. (Ed.), *The Coming of the Robots.* Macmillan, New York, 1966.

Silverberg, R. (Ed.), *Science Fiction Hall of Fame, Vol. 1.* Doubleday, New York, 1970.

Contains "The Quest for Saint Aquin," by Anthony Boucher, about the search for the robot saint, and "Hellen O'Lay," by Lester Del Ray, where a user falls in love with his robot servant.

Van Vogt, A.E. *The Weapon Shops of Isher.* Ace Books, New York, 1951.

A giant, and illegal, super-organization uses computers to keep track of the world's government, and to make sure people get what they deserve.

Vonnegut, K., Jr. *Welcome to the Monkey House.* Delacorte, New York, 1968.

Contains "EPICAC," the story of a poetically inclined computer that falls in love with its female programmer.

Vonnegut, K., Jr. *Player Piano.* Delacorte, New York, 1971.

A leading scientist revolts against technology run wild.

"Star Trek"

No treatment of modern science fiction would be complete without some reference to "Star Trek," the television series that altered the country's exposure to science-fiction permanently. Now, many of the original scripts have been adapted by James K. Blish into short stories, and published by Bantam Books. Many of these stories revolve around computers. Here are some examples:

"A Taste of Armageddon" in *Star Trek 2,* adapted from the script by Robert Hamner and Gene L. Coon. A planet where war is fought entirely by computer, no weapons, no damage, just death, until Captain Kirk forces the leaders to see war as it really is.

"The Changeling" in *Star Trek 7,* adapted from the script by John Meredyth Lucas. An ancient space probe from Earth is reprogrammed by contact with "The Other," so that its new mission is to sterilize all biological life forms, including the crew of the Enterprise. Kirk uses the computer's own inescapable logic to force it to destroy itself. Another good example of several stories where logic is turned against the computer is "Return to the Archons" in *Star Trek 9*, adapted from Boris Sobelman's script, where Kirk and Spock destroy a computer that has sought to provide men with happiness by destroying their souls.

"The Ultimate Computer" in *Star Trek 9*, adapted from the script by D.C. Fontana and Laurence N. Wolfe. A computer is imprinted with human "engrams," and replaces Captain Kirk as commander of the Enterprise. But the computer retains the failings of the human who "programmed" it, and must be destroyed.

All in all, Kirk and Co. did an awful lot of damage to some very expensive hardware throughout the galaxy. Of course, the U.S.S. Enterprise had some very sophisticated computers on board, but their main function seems to have been to "crash" at moments of dire emergency. Still, *Star Trek* contains many valuable insights into the future of computers—and men.

Other Sources

For those who wish to pursue the subject further, the following general sources may be useful.

Ascher, M. The Computer as Seen Through Science Fiction. *Harvard Business Review*, 1963, *41*, pp. 40-45.

Briney, R.E. and D. Wood. *Science Fiction Bibliographies.* Chicago: Advent Publishers, Inc., 1972.

Fidell, E. *Short Story Index.* Supplement 1964-1968, New York: The H.W. Wilson Company, 1969. Subject: Automata, pp. 29-30; electronic computers, p. 149.

Hall, H. *SFBRI, Science Fiction Book Review Index.* Texas, 3608 Meadow Oaks Lane, Texas 77801, 1970.

Kelly, L. *Themes in Science Fictions.* McGraw-Hill, 1972.

Siemon, F. *Science Fiction Story Index.* Chicago: American Library Association, 1971.

Note

[1] The authors wish to acknowledge the suggestions of Anne W. Laffan, Stanley I. Goldfarb, and Daniel E. Bailey in compiling this bibliography.

33.
A Bibliography on Social Science Computing

Ronald E. Anderson
University of Minnesota

ABELSON R P   BERNSTEIN A
A COMPUTER SIMULATION MODEL OF COMMUNITY REFERENDUM
CONTROVERSIES.
PUBLIC OPINION QUARTERLY 27(SPRING 1963), 93-122

ABELSON R P   CARROLL D.
COMPUTER SIMULATION OF INDIVIDUAL BELIEF SYSTEMS.
AMERICAN BEHAVIORAL SCIENTIST, MAY 1965, 24-30

ABELSON R P
COMPUTER SIMULATION OF PERSONALITY.
PP 227-298 IN S TOMPKINS AND S MESSICK (EDS), COMPUTER
SIMULATION OF HOT COGNITION. NEW YORK, WILEY, 1963

ABELSON R P
SIMULATION OF SOCIAL BEHAVIOR.
PP 274-356 IN G LINDZEY AND E ARONSON (EDS), THE HANDBOOK OF
SOCIAL PSYCHOLOGY, VOLUME II. READING, MASS, ADDISON-
WESLEY, 1968

ABT C   GORDON M
REPORT ON PROJECT TEMPER.
PAPER PRESENTED AT THE INSTITUTE ON COMPUTERS AND THE POLICY
MAKING COMMUNITY, UNIVERSITY OF CALIFORNIA, LAWRENCE
RADIATION LABORATORY, APRIL 1966

ADELMAN IRMA
ECONOMIC SYSTEMS SIMULATION.
PP 268-273 IN INTERNATIONAL ENCYCLOPEDIA OF THE SOCIAL
SCIENCES (2ND EDITION), VOL 14. MACMILLAN AND THE FREE
PRESS, 1968

AIKEN JOHN O   MILLWARD RICHARD B
SOME COMMENTS ON CONNECTING A SMALL ON-LINE COMPUTER TO A
LARGE DATA PROCESSING MACHINE.
BEHAVIOR RESEARCH METHODS AND INSTRUMENTATION, 4,
2(MARCH 1972), 99-100

ALKER HAYWARD R JR
COMPUTER SIMULATIONS, CONCEPTUAL FRAMEWORKS AND COALITION
BEHAVIOR.
YALE UNIVERSITY AND CENTER FOR ADVANCED STUDY IN THE
BEHAVIORAL SCIENCES, SEPTEMBER 1967

ALKER HAYWARD R JR   BRUNNER RONALD D
SIMULATION OF INTERNATIONAL CONFLICT—A COMPARISON OF
THREE APPROACHES.
INTERNATIONAL STUDIES QUARTERLY, SPRING 1969, 70-110

ALLEN MAX
A CONCEPT ATTAINMENT PROGRAM THAT SIMULATES A SIMULTANEOUS
SCANNING STRATEGY.
BEHAVIORAL SCIENCE 7(APRIL 1962), 247-249

AMERICAN BEHAVIORAL SCIENTIST
10, 3(NOVEMBER 1966), 1-36.
12, 6(JULY-AUGUST 1969), 1-49

AMES RICHARD G
COMPUTER PROGRAMMING PHILOSOPHY IN A SOCIOLOGY DEPARTMENT—
THEORY AND APPLICATION.
BEHAVIOR SCIENCE 8(JULY 1963), 257-258

ANDERBERG MICHAEL
CLUSTER ANALYSIS FOR APPLICATIONS.
NEW YORK, ACADEMIC PRESS, 1973

ANDERSON R E
DIFFUSION OF COMPUTER UTILIZATION AMONG SOCIOLOGY
INSTRUCTORS.
COMPUTERS AND THE HUMANITIES 10(1976), 201-207.

ANDERSON R E
BIBLIOGRAPHY ON SOCIAL SCIENCE COMPUTING.
COMPUTING REVIEWS 15, 7(JULY 1974), 247-261

ANDERSON R E   ET AL.
MINNESOTA INTERACTIVE STATISTICAL SYSTEM.
BEHAVIOR RESEARCH METHODS AND INSTRUMENTATION 6, 2
(MARCH 1974), 194-200

ANDERSON RONALD E
A SURVEY OF APPLICATION SOFTWARE FOR SOCIAL DATA ANALYSIS
INSTRUCTION.
PP 135-141 IN PROCEEDINGS OF A CONFERENCE ON COMPUTERS IN
THE UNDERGRADUATE CURRICULA, DARTMOUTH COLLEGE, JUNE 1971

ANDERSON RONALD E
GUIDELINES FOR A SOCIAL SCIENCE COMPUTING CURRICULUM.
PP 223-225 IN PROCEEDINGS OF THE ACM ANNUAL CONFERENCE,
CHICAGO, AUGUST 1971

ANDERSON RONALD E   COOVER EDWIN R
WRAPPING THE PACKAGE—CRITICAL THOUGHTS ON APPLICATIONS

SOFTWARE FOR SOCIAL DATA ANALYSIS
COMPUTERS AND THE HUMANITIES, 7, 2(NOVEMBER 1972), 81-95

ANDERSON RONALD E   GROSS JONATHAN
MINI-COMPUTERS IN A SOCIAL SCIENCE INSTRUCTIONAL CONTEXT.
PROCEEDINGS OF THE ACM ANNUAL CONFERENCE, 1972, 952-963

ANDERSON RONALD E   MCTAVISH DONALD G
SOCIOLOGY, COMPUTERS AND MASS UNDERGRADUATE EDUCATION.
PP 8.35-8.39 IN PROCEEDINGS OF A CONFERENCE ON COMPUTERS IN
THE UNDERGRADUATE CURRICULA, UNIVERSITY OF IOWA, IOWA CITY,
IA, 1970.

APTER MICHAEL J
THE COMPUTER SIMULATION OF BEHAVIOR.
NEW YORK, HARPER AND ROW, 1971

ARMER PAUL
COMPUTER APPLICATIONS IN GOVERNMENT.
PP 123-239 IN IRENE TAVISS (ED), THE COMPUTER IMPACT.
ENGLEWOOD CLIFFS, N J, PRENTICE-HALL, 1970

ARMINGTON JOHN C
USING LAB-8 FOR EXPERIMENTS WITH THE HUMAN VISUAL SYSTEM.
BEHAVIOR RESEARCH METHODS AND INSTRUMENTATION, 4,
2(MARCH 1972), 61-63

ARMOR DAVID J
DEVELOPMENTS IN DATA ANALYSIS SYSTEMS FOR THE SOCIAL
SCIENCES.
SOCIAL SCIENCE INFORMATION 3(JUNE 1970), 145-156

BAILEY DANIEL E
THE COMPUTER LABORATORY FOR INSTRUCTION IN PSYCHOLOGICAL
RESEARCH.
BEHAVIOR RESEARCH METHODS AND INSTRUMENTATION, 4,
2(MARCH 1972), 95-96

BAILEY DANIEL E   POLSON PETER G
REAL-TIME COMPUTING IN PSYCHOLOGY AT THE UNIVERSITY OF
COLORADO.
AMERICAN PSYCHOLOGIST, 30, 3(MARCH 1975), 212

BAKER FRANK B
THE INTERNAL ORGANIZATION OF COMPUTER MODELS OF COGNITIVE
BEHAVIOR.
BEHAVIORAL SCIENCE 12(MARCH 1967), 156-161

BALL GOEFFREY H   HALL DAVID J
A CLUSTERING TECHNIQUE FOR SUMMARIZING MULTIVARIATE DATA.
BEHAVIORAL SCIENCE 12(MARCH 1967), 153-155.

BALZER ROBERT M
A MATHEMATICAL MODEL FOR PERFORMING A COMPLEX TASK IN A
CARD GAME.
BEHAVIORAL SCIENCE 11(MAY 1966), 219-228

BARNETT MICHAEL P
SNAP—A PROGRAMMING LANGUAGE FOR THE HUMANITIES.
COMPUTERS AND THE HUMANITIES 4(MARCH 1970), 225-240

BARTHOLOMEW JOHN   JOHNSTON JUDITH   KONSTAM AARON H
A SERIOUS GAME AS AN INTRODUCTION TO URBAN PLANNING.
PROCEEDINGS OF THE CONFERENCE ON COMPUTERS IN
UNDERGRADUATE CURRICULA, 1972, 495-504

BARTON RICHARD
A GENERALIZED RESPONSIVENESS (ELASTICITY) FUNCTION FOR
SIMULATIONS.
BEHAVIORAL SCIENCE 12(JULY 1968), 337-343

BARTON RICHARD F
INCORPORATING QUALITATIVE JUDGMENTS INTO MAN-COMPUTER
SIMULATIONS.
SIMULATION AND GAMES 3, (JUNE 1972), 79-88

BAUER RAYMOND A
SOCIAL PLANNING.
PP 145-152 IN IRENE TAVISS (ED), THE COMPUTER IMPACT.
ENGLEWOOD CLIFFS, N J, PRENTICE-HALL, 1970

BAUER R A   BUZZEL R P
MATING BEHAVIOR SCIENCE AND SIMULATION.
HARVARD BUSINESS REVIEW, SEPTEMBER-OCTOBER 1964, 116-124

BEAN JEFFREY   KIDD STEPHEN   ET AL.
THE BEAST—A USER ORIENTED PROCEDURAL LANGUAGE FOR SOCIAL
SCIENCE RESEARCH.
THE BROOKINGS INSTITUTION, WASHINGTON D C, 1968

BEAZLEY WILLIAM   SWANSON JAMES M   ALLAN JOHN J III
AN INTERACTIVE, INTERDISCIPLINARY ON-LINE GRAPHICS
SYSTEM FOR PRESENTING AND MANIPULATING DIRECTED GRAPHS.
BEHAVIOR RESEARCH METHODS AND INSTRUMENTATION 6, 2(MARCH
1974), 213-218.

BECK CARL   MCKECKNIE JOHN T
OPEN-ENDED DATA FILES—A FORMAT FOR RAGGED DATA FILES.
SOCIAL SCIENCE INFORMATION VI, 5(OCTOBER 1967), 129-131

BELL CHARLES G
THE JOYS AND SORROWS OF SECONDARY DATA USE.
PP 52-60 IN R L BISCO (ED), DATA BASES, COMPUTERS AND THE
SOCIAL SCIENCES. NEW YORK, WILEY, 1970

BELLMAN RICHARD   ET AL.
SIMULATION OF THE INITIAL PSYCHIATRIC INTERVIEW.
BEHAVIORAL SCIENCE 11(SEPTEMBER 1966), 389-399

BENISHAY H
BIRTHS AND DEATHS OF PROJECTS.
BEHAVIORAL SCIENCE 16, 2(MARCH 1971), 169-173

BERGER EDWARD   BOULAY HARVEY   ZISK BETTY
   SIMULATION AND THE CITY—A CRITICAL OVERVIEW.
   SIMULATION AND GAMES 1, 4(DECEMBER 1970), 411-428

BERKHOUT JAN   ET AL.
   AUTOMATIC COMPUTATION OF EVOKED HEART-RATE AND PULSE
   VOLUME RESPONSES TO VERBAL STIMULI.
   BEHAVIORAL SCIENCE 14(SEPTEMBER 1969), 393-403

BESHERS J M
   BIRTH PROJECTIONS WITH COHORT MODELS.
   DEMOGRAPHY 2(1965), 593-599

BESHERS J M
   COMPUTER METHODS IN THE ANALYSIS OF LARGE SCALE SOCIAL
   SYSTEMS.
   CAMBRIDGE, MASS, HARVARD PRESS, 1965

BESHERS J M
   COMPUTER MODELS OF SOCIAL PROCESSES—THE CASE OF MIGRATION.
   PAPER PRESENTED AT THE MEETINGS OF THE POPULATION
   ASSOCIATION OF AMERICA, APRIL 1967

BISCO RALPH L
   DATA BASES, COMPUTERS AND THE SOCIAL SCIENCES.
   NEW YORK, WILEY, 1970

BISCO RALPH L
   SOCIAL SCIENCE DATA ARCHIVES—PROGRESS AND PROSPECTS.
   SOCIAL SCIENCE INFORMATION VI, 1(FEBRUARY 1967), 39-74

BLACKMORE W R
   SOME COMMENTS ON COMPUTER SIMULATION OF A MODEL OF
   NEUROTIC DEFENSE PROCESSES
   BEHAVIORAL SCIENCE 17(MARCH 1972), 229-231.

BOBROW DAVIS B
   CHANGING SOCIAL SCIENCE AND CHANGING SOCIETY—IMPLICATIONS
   FOR SOCIAL SCIENCE COMPUTING CURRICULA.
   PP 211-213 IN PROCEEDINGS OF THE ACM ANNUAL CONFERENCE,
   CHICAGO, AUGUST 1971

BOBROW DAVIS B
   INTERNATIONAL INTERACTIONS—SURVEYS AND COMPUTERS.
   PP 81-110 IN D B BOBROW AND J L SCHWARTZ (EDS), COMPUTERS
   AND THE POLICY-MAKING COMMUNITY. ENGLEWOOD CLIFFS, N J,
   PRENTICE-HALL, 1968

BOBROW DAVIS B
   INTERNATIONAL INDICATORS.
   PAPER PRESENTED AT ANNUAL MEETING OF THE AMERICAN
   POLITICAL SCIENCE ASSOCIATION, SEPTEMBER 1969

BOBROW DAVIS B
ORGANIZATIONS OF AMERICAN NATIONAL SECURITY OPINIONS.
PUBLIC OPINION QUARTERLY 33(1969), 223-239

BOBROW DAVIS B
COMPUTERS AND A NORMATIVE MODEL OF THE POLICY PROCESS.
PAPER PRESENTED AT 1969 MEETING OF THE AMERICAN
ASSOCIATION FOR THE ADVANCEMENT OF SCIENCE, DECEMBER 1970

BOBROW DAVIS B   SCHWARTZ JUDAH L
COMPUTERS AND THE POLICY-MAKING COMMUNITY.
ENGLEWOOD CLIFFS, N J, PRENTICE-HALL, 1963

BORDEN GEORGE A   WATTS JAMES J
A COMPUTERIZED LANGUAGE ANALYSIS SYSTEM.
COMPUTERS AND THE HUMANITIES 5, 3(JANUARY 1971), 129-142

BOGULSAW ROBERT   DAVIS ROBERT
SOCIAL PROCESS MODELING—A COMPARISON OF A LIVE AND
COMPUTERIZED SIMULATION.
BEHAVIORAL SCIENCE 14(1969), 3, 197-203

BOGUSLAW ROBERT   DAVIS R H   ET AL.
A SIMULATION VEHICLE FOR STUDYING NATIONAL POLICY
FORMATION IN A LESS ARMED WORLD.
BEHAVIORAL SCIENCE 11(1966), 43-61

BORKO H
COMPUTER APPLICATIONS IN THE BEHAVIORAL SCIENCES.
ENGLEWOOD CLIFFS, N J, PRENTICE-HALL, 1962

BORKO H
COMPUTER SIMULATIONS OF NEUROPHYSIOLOGICAL AND SOCIAL
SCIENCES.
BEHAVIORAL SCIENCE 7(JULY 1962), 407-411

BORKOWSKI CASIMIR
SOME PRINCIPLES AND TECHNIQUES OF AUTOMATIC ASSIGNMENT
OF WORDS AND WORD STRINGS IN TEXTS TO SPECIAL PURPOSE
SUBLANGUAGES.
PP 515-522 IN G GERBNER ET AL. (EDS), THE ANALYSIS OF
COMMUNICATION CONTENT. NEW YORK, WILEY, 1969

BOUDON R
REFLEXIONS SUR LA LOGIQUE DES MODELES SIMULES.
EUROPEAN JOURNAL OF SOCIOLOGY 6(MAY 1965), 3-20

BOWEN BRUCE D   DAVIS WAYNE K
VOTER—A SOCIAL SCIENCE DATA ANALYSIS PROGRAM
PROCEEDINGS OF THE 1972 CONFERENCE ON COMPUTERS IN
UNDERGRADUATE CURRICULA, 1972, 463-466

BOWER JOSEPH L
SYSTEMS ANALYSIS FOR SOCIAL DECISIONS.
COMPUTERS AND AUTOMATION 19, 3(MARCH 1970), 38-42.

BOWLES E A (ED)
COMPUTERS IN HUMANISTIC RESEARCH.
ENGLEWOOD CLIFFS, N J, PRENTICE-HALL, 1967

BOWMAN RAYMOND T
THE IDEA OF A FEDERAL STATISTICAL DATA CENTER—ITS
PURPOSES AND STRUCTURE.
PP 63-69 IN R L BISCO (ED), DATA BASES, COMPUTERS, AND THE
SOCIAL SCIENCES. NEW YORK, WILEY, 1970

BRACKETT JAMES W
SOME COMPUTER APPLICATIONS TO POPULATION PROJECTIONS AND
DEMOGRAPHIC ANALYSIS.
PP 94-102 IN J M BESHERS (ED), COMPUTER METHODS IN THE
ANALYSIS OF LARGE-SCALE SOCIAL SYSTEMS. CAMBRIDGE, MASS,
MIT PRESS, 1968

BRADDOCK FRED
THE INFORMATICS MARK IV FILE MANAGEMENT.
PP 158-172 IN R L BISCO (ED), DATA BASES, COMPUTERS, AND
THE SOCIAL SCIENCES. NEW YORK, WILEY, 1970

BRATEN STEIN
A SIMULATION STUDY OF PERSONAL AND MASS COMMUNICATION.
IAG QUARTERLY 1, 2(MAY 1968), 7-28

BRETON RAYMOND
OUTPUT NORMS AND PRODUCTIVE BEHAVIOR IN NONCOOPERATIVE
WORK GROUPS.
SIMULATION AND GAMES 2, 1(MARCH 1971), 45-72

BRIER ALAN   ROBINSON IAN
COMPUTERS AND THE SOCIAL SCIENCES.
NEW YORK, COLUMBIA UNIVERSITY PRESS, 1974

BRIGHTMAN H J   ET AL.
A SIMULATION MODEL OF INDIVIDUAL BEHAVIOR IN A WORK GROUP.
CENTER FOR BUSINESS AND ECONOMIC RESEARCH, SCHOOL OF
BUSINESS ADMINISTRATION, UNIVERSITY OF MASS, AMHERST, MASS,
SEPTEMBER 1969

BROWNING RUFUS P
HYPOTHESES ABOUT POLITICAL RECRUITMENT—A PARTIALLY DATA-
BASED COMPUTER SIMULATION.
PP 303-326 IN W. COPLIN (ED), SIMULATION IN THE STUDY OF
POLITICS. CHICAGO, MARKHAM PUBLISHING, 1969

BROWNING RUFUS P
QUALITY OF COLLECTIVE DECISIONS, SOME THEORY AND COMPUTER
SIMULATION.
UNPUBLISHED PAPER, MICHIGAN STATE UNIVERSITY, EAST LANSING,
MICHIGAN, JUNE 1968

BROWNING RUFUS P
COMPUTER SIMULATION OF POLITICAL BARGAINING.
COOPERATION/CONFLICT RESEARCH GROUP, MICHIGAN STATE
UNIVERSITY, NOVEMBER 1969

BUHLER ROALD
P-STAT—AN EVOLVING USER-ORIENTED LANGUAGE FOR STATISTICAL
ANALYSIS OF SOCIAL SCIENCE DATA.
COMPUTER CENTER, PRINCETON UNIVERSITY, 1968

BURGESS PHILIP M
COMPUTERS AND THE PROBLEM-SOLVER STATE.
PP 220-223 OF PROCEEDINGS OF THE ACM ANNUAL CONFERENCE,
CHICAGO, AUGUST 1971

BURGESS PHILIP M   ROBINSON J A
ALLIANCES AND THE THEORY OF COLLECTIVE ACTION—A
SIMULATION OF COALITION PROCESSES.
MIDWEST JOURNAL OF POLITICAL SCIENCE 13, 2(MAY 1970), 194-218

BURTON MICHAEL L
COMPUTER APPLICATIONS IN CULTURAL ANTHROPOLOGY.
COMPUTERS AND THE HUMANITIES, 5, 1(SEPTEMBER 1970), 47-52

CANGELOSI VINCENT   MARCH JAMES G
AN EXPERIMENT IN MODEL BUILDING.
BEHAVIORAL SCIENCE 11(JANUARY 1966), 71-74

CARLSON ARTHUR R
CONCEPT FREQUENCY IN POLITICAL TEXT—AN APPLICATION OF A
TOTAL INDEXING METHOD OF AUTOMATED CONTENT ANALYSIS.
BEHAVIORAL SCIENCE 12(JANUARY 1967), 68-71

CARROLL TOM W
SINDI 2 SIMULATION OF INNOVATION DIFFUSION IN A RURAL
COMMUNITY OF BRAZIL.
MICHIGAN STATE UNIVERSITY, MAY 1969

CARROLL TOM W
SYSTEMS ANALYSIS, COMPUTER SIMULATION AND SURVEY RESEARCH—
APPLICATIONS TO SOCIAL RESEARCH IN DEVELOPING COUNTRIES.
MICHIGAN STATE UNIVERSITY, JANUARY 1968

CARROLL TOM W   HANNEMAN GERHARD J
TWO MODELS OF INNOVATION DIFFUSION.
AN ABSTRACT PREPARED FOR THE SECOND CONFERENCE ON
APPLICATION OF SIMULATION, DECEMBER 2-4, 1968, NEW YORK,
MICHIGAN STATE UNIVERSITY, OCTOBER 1968

CASTELLAN N JOHN JR
THE MODERN MINICOMPUTER IN LABORATORY AUTOMATION.
AMERICAN PSYCHOLOGIST, 30, 3(MARCH 1975), 205

CASTLEMAN PAUL A
DATA MANAGEMENT TECHNIQUES FOR THE SOCIAL SCIENCES.
PP 139-157 IN RL BISCO (ED), DATA BASES, COMPUTERS AND THE
SOCIAL SCIENCES. NEW YORK, WILEY, 1970

CATEWELL RAYMOND B   FOSTER MERLIN J
THE TOTOPLOT PROGRAM FOR MULTIPLE, SINGLE-PLANE, VISUALLY
GUIDED ROTATION.
BEHAVIORAL SCIENCE 8(APRIL 1963), 156-164

CHAMBERLAIN RICHARD L
COMPUTER GRAPHICS AND TIME SERIES ANALYSIS.
PP 20-26 IN PROCEEDINGS OF THE COMPUTER SCIENCE AND
STATISTICS EIGHTH ANNUAL SYMPOSIUM ON THE INTERFACE
HEALTH SCIENCES COMPUTING FACILITY, UNIV OF CALIFORNIA
LOS ANGELES, 1975

CHAPMAN ROBERT L
ALL COMPUTER VS. MAN-COMPUTER SYSTEMS IN THE SIMULATION OF
GROUP PROCESSES.
PAPER PRESENTED AT 1961 CONVENTION OF THE AMERICAN
PSYCHOLOGICAL ASSOCIATION, NEW YORK, 1961

CHAPMAN ROBERT M   CHAPMAN JOHN A
THE GENERAL AUTOMATION 18/30 AS A SYSTEM FOR THE GENERAL
ANALYSIS AND ACQUISITION OF DATA IN PHYSIOLOGICAL
PSYCHOLOGY.
BEHAVIOR RESEARCH METHODS AND INSTRUMENTATION, 4,
2(MARCH 1972), 77-80

CHAVCHANIDZE V
INDUCTION OF PSYCHOINTELLECTUAL ACTIVITY IN LONG-TERM
FORECASTING AND PLANNING OF RESEARCH.
TECHNOLOGICAL FORECASTING 1(FALL 1969), 129-139

CHENHALL ROBERT G
THE ARCHAEOLOGICAL DATA BANK—A PROGRESS REPORT.
COMPUTERS AND THE HUMANITIES 5, 3(JANUARY 1971), 159-169

CHENHALL ROBERT G
THE IMPACT OF COMPUTERS ON ARCHAEOLOGICAL THEORY.
COMPUTERS AND THE HUMANITIES 1(SEPTEMBER 1968), 15-24

CHENHALL R G
COMPUTERS IN ANTHROPOLOGY AND ARCHEOLOGY
IBM CORP, WHITE PLAINS, NY, 1971

CHERRYHOLMES C H   SHAPIRO M J
REPRESENTATIVES AND ROLL CALLS, A COMPUTER SIMULATION
OF VOTING IN THE EIGHTY-EIGHTH CONGRESS.
INDIANAPOLIS, BOBBS-MERRILL, 1969

CHU KONG   SPEAKS TERRY   WALL JOHN
ET AL.
POPULATION POLICY SIMULATIONS PERFORMED WITH AN ECONOMETRIC
MODEL OF TAIWAN.
SIMULATION AND GAMES 3 (SEPTEMBER 1972), 291-307.

CIOFALO VINCENT B   TEDFORD ROBERT H   ET AL.
THE USE OF A DIGITAL COMPUTER FOR CONTROL OF BEHAVIORAL
RESEARCH IN ANIMALS.
BEHAVIORAL SCIENCE 13(MAY 1968), 252-256

CLARKSON GEOFFREY
DECISION MAKING IN SMALL GROUPS—A SIMULATION STUDY.
BEHAVIORAL SCIENCE 13, 4(JULY 1968), 288-305

CLARKSON G P   SIMON H A
SIMULATION OF INDIVIDUAL AND GROUP BEHAVIOR.
AMERICAN ECONOMIC REVIEW 50(1960), 920-932

CLEMA JOE   KIRKHAM JOHN
CONSIM (CONFLICT SIMULATOR)—RISK, COST, AND BENEFIT IN
POLITICAL SIMULATIONS.
PP 226-235 IN PROCEEDINGS OF THE ACM ANNUAL CONFERENCE,
CHICAGO, AUGUST 1971

CLEMENS W C JR
A PROPOSITIONAL ANALYSIS OF THE INTERNATIONAL RELATIONS
THEORY IN TEMPER—A COMPUTER SIMULATION OF COLD WAR
CONFLICT.
PP 59-101 IN W COPLIN (ED), SIMULATION IN THE STUDY OF
POLITICS. CHICAGO, MARKHAM, 1968

CLINE HUGH F
COMPUTER INSTRUCTION FOR SCHOLARS IN THE HUMANITIES.
COMPUTERS AND THE HUMANITIES 3(SEPTEMBER 1968), 31-40

CLINE HUGH F
SOCIAL SCIENCE COMPUTING—1967-1972
JOINT COMPUTER CONFERENCE 40(Spring 1972), 868-874.

CLINE HUGH F   MEYERS EDMUND D JR
PROBLEM-SOLVING COMPUTER SYSTEMS FOR INSTRUCTION IN
SOCIOLOGY.
THE AMERICAN SOCIOLOGIST 5(NOVEMBER 1970), 365-370

CLYDE DEAN J   ET AL.
MULTIVARIATE STATISTICAL PROGRAMS.
BIOMETRIC LABORATORY, UNIVERSITY OF MIAMI, CORAL GABLES,
FLORIDA, 1966

COALE A J   HOOVER E M
POPULATION GROWTH AND ECONOMIC DEVELOPMENT IN LOW-INCOME
COUNTRIES.
PRINCETON, N J, PRINCETON UNIVERSITY PRESS, 1958

COE RODNEY M
CONFLICT, INTERFERENCE AND AGGRESSION—COMPUTER SIMULATION
OF A SOCIAL PROCESS.
BEHAVIORAL SCIENCE 9, 2(APRIL 1964), 186-197

COLBY KENNETH
COMPUTER SIMULATION OF CHANGE IN PERSONAL BELIEF SYSTEMS.
BEHAVIORAL SCIENCE 12(MAY 1967), 248-253

COLBY KENNETH
COMPUTER SIMULATION OF A NEUROTIC PROCESS.
PP 165-179 IN S TOMKINS AND S MESSICK (EDS), COMPUTER
SIMULATION OF PERSONALITY. NEW YORK, WILEY, 1963

COLEMAN JAMES S
ANALYSIS OF SOCIAL STRUCTURES AND SIMULATION OF SOCIAL
PROCESSES WITH ELECTRONIC COMPUTERS.
PP 61-69 IN H GUETZKOW (ED), SIMULATION IN SOCIAL SCIENCE—
READINGS. ENGLEWOOD CLIFFS, N J, PRENTICE-HALL, 1962

COLEMAN JAMES S
IN DEFENSE OF GAMES.
AMERICAN BEHAVIORAL SCIENTIST 10(OCTOBER 1966), 3-4

COLEMAN JAMES S
INTRODUCTION TO MATHEMATICAL SOCIOLOGY.
NEW YORK, FREE PRESS, 1964

COLEMAN JAMES S
MATHEMATICAL MODELS AND COMPUTER SIMULATION.
PP 1027-1062 IN R E L FARIS (ED), HANDBOOK OF MODERN
SOCIOLOGY. CHICAGO, RAND-MCNALLY, 1964

COLEMAN JAMES S
THE USE OF ELECTRONIC COMPUTERS IN THE STUDY OF SOCIAL
ORGANIZATION.
EUROPEAN JOURNAL OF SOCIOLOGY 6(MAY 1965), 89-107

COLEMAN JAMES S   ET AL.
MEDICAL INNOVATION.
INDIANAPOLIS, BOBBS-MERRILL, 1966

COOLEY WILLIAM W   LOHNES PAUL
MULTIVARIATE PROCEDURES FOR THE BEHAVIORAL SCIENCES.
NEW YORK, WILEY, 1962

COOLEY WILLIAM W   LOHNES PAUL
MULTIVARIATE DATA ANALYSIS.
NEW YORK, WILEY, 1971

COOMBS S   FRIED M   ET AL.
AN APPROACH TO ELECTION SIMULATION THROUGH MODULAR SYSTEMS.
PP 286-299 IN W COPLIN (ED), SIMULATION IN THE STUDY OF
POLITICS. CHICAGO, MARKHAM PUBLISHING, 1968

COOPERBAND ALVIN S
THE USE OF A COMPUTER IN CONDUCTING PSYCHOLOGICAL
EXPERIMENTS.
BEHAVIORAL SCIENCE 11(JULY 1966), 307-311

COOPERBAND ALVIN S   MOORE WILLIAM H JR   MEEKER ROBERT J
SHURE GERALD H
TRACE-III—AN IMPLICIT PROGRAMMING SYSTEM FOR INDUCTIVE
DATA ANALYSIS.
PP 127-138 IN PROCEEDINGS OF THE ACM ANNUAL CONFERENCE,
CHICAGO, AUGUST 1971

COPLIN WILLIAM D
APPROACHES TO THE SOCIAL SCIENCES THROUGH MAN-COMPUTER
SIMULATIONS.
SIMULATION AND GAMES 1, 4(DECEMBER 1970), 391-410

COPLIN WILLIAM
SIMULATION IN THE STUDY OF POLITICS.
CHICAGO, MARKHAM PUBLISHING CO, 1969

COPLIN WILLIAM D   OLEARY MICHAEL K
EDUCATIONAL USES OF PRINCE.
PROCEEDINGS OF THE 1972 CONFERENCE ON COMPUTERS IN
UNDERGRADUATE CURRICULA, 1972, 459-462

COUCH ARTHUR S
THE DATA-TEXT SYSTEM—A COMPUTER LANGUAGE FOR SOCIAL
SCIENCE RESEARCH.
HARVARD UNIVERSITY, DEPARTMENT OF SOCIAL RELATIONS,
CAMBRIDGE, MASS, 1967

COULT A D   RANDOLPH R R
COMPUTER METHODS FOR ANALYZING GENEALOGICAL SPACE.
AMERICAN ANTHROPOLOGIST 67(1965), 21-29

COUNCIL OF SOCIAL SCIENCE DATA ARCHIVES
SOCIAL SCIENCE DATA ARCHIVES IN THE UNITED STATES.
COUNCIL OF SOCIAL SCIENCE DATA ARCHIVES, 1967.

CRECINE JOHN P
A DYNAMIC MODEL OF URBAN STRUCTURE.
RAND CORPORATION, 1967.

CRECINE JOHN P
GOVERNMENTAL PROBLEM SOLVING—A COMPUTER SIMULATION OF
MUNICIPAL BUDGETING.
CHICAGO, RAND-MCNALLY, 1969

CRECINE JOHN P
SPATIAL LOCATION DECISIONS AND URBAN STRUCTURE—A TIME
ORIENTED MODEL.
INSTITUTE OF PUBLIC POLICY STUDIES DISCUSSION, UNIVERSITY
OF MICHIGAN, PAPER NUMBER 4, 1969

CROMER ARTHUR
TEACHING RESEARCH THEORY AND APPLICATION THROUGH ON-LINE
SIMULATION.
BEHAVIOR RESEARCH METHODS AND INSTRUMENTATION 6, 2(MARCH
1974), 126-127.

CROMER ARTHUR O   THURMOND JOHN B
TOWARD THE OPTIMAL USE OF COMPUTER SIMULATIONS IN
TEACHING SCIENTIFIC RESEARCH STRATEGY.
PROCEEDINGS OF THE CONFERENCE ON COMPUTERS IN UNDERGRADUATE
CURRICULA, 1972, 493-494

CUTLER STEPHEN J   BLAGG DAVID V
COMPUTER APPLICATIONS IN THE UNDERGRADUATE SOCIOLOGY
CURRICULUM AT OBERLIN COLLEGE.

PP 371-378 IN PROCEEDINGS OF A CONFERENCE ON COMPUTERS IN
THE UNDERGRADUATE CURRICULA, DARTMOUTH COLLEGE, JUNE 1971

DAVENPORT JOHN W   BENSON ROBERT   HAGQUIST WILLIAM W
ET AL.
COMPUTERIZED ANIMAL INTELLIGENCE TESTING.
BEHAVIOR RESEARCH METHODS AND INSTRUMENTATION, 4,
2(MARCH 1972), 67-70

DAVIS JAMES A
USING THE IMPRESS SYSTEM TO TEACH SOCIOLOGY.
PP 382-388 IN PROCEEDINGS OF A CONFERENCE ON COMPUTERS IN
THE UNDERGRADUATE CURRICULA, DARTHMOUTH COLLEGE, JUNE 1971

DAVIS JAMES A   STERNICK JOANNA H
THE IMPRESS PRIMER.
HANOVER, N H, PROJECT IMPRESS, FEBRUARY 1971 (2ND PRINTING)

DAVIS R H
ARMS CONTROL SIMULATION—THE SEARCH FOR AN ACCEPTABLE
METHOD.
JOURNAL OF ARMS CONTROL 1(OCTOBER 1963), 684-696

DAVISSON WILLIAM I
INFORMATION PROCESSING—APPLICATIONS IN THE SOCIAL AND
BEHAVIORAL SCIENCES.
NEW YORK, APPLETON-CENTURY-CROFTS, 1970

DENK JOSEPH R
POISSON—A DAUGHTER OF DARTMOUTHS IMPRESS HAS BEEN BORN IN
THE ENVIRONMENT OF IBM TIME-SHARING.
PROCEEDING OF THE CONFERENCE ON COMPUTERS
IN UNDERGRADUATE CURRICULA, 1972, 483-488

DENNETT DANIEL C
MACHINE TRACES AND PROTOCOL STATEMENTS.
BEHAVIORAL SCIENCE 13(MARCH 1968), 155-161

DEUTCH KARL W
THE IMPACT OF COMPLEX DATA BASES ON THE SOCIAL SCIENCES.
PP 19-41 IN R L BISCO (ED), DATA BASES, COMPUTERS AND THE
SOCIAL SCIENCES. NEW YORK, WILEY, 1970

DEUTSCHMANN R J
A MACHINE SIMULATION OF ATTITUDE CHANGE IN A POLARIZED
COMMUNITY.
UNPUBLISHED PAPER, PROGRAMA INTERAMERICANA DE INFORMACION
POPULAR, SAN JOSE, COSTA RICA, 1962

DEUTSCHMANN R J
A MACHINE SIMULATION OF INFORMATION DIFFUSION IN A SMALL
COMMUNITY.
UNPUBLISHED PAPER, PROGRAMA INTERAMERICANA DE INFORMACION
POPULAR, SAN JOSE, COSTA RICA, 1962

DEUTSCHMANN R J
    A MODEL FOR MACHINE SIMULATION OF INFORMATION AND ATTITUDE
    FLOW.
    UNPUBLISHED PAPER, PROGRAMA INTERAMERICANA DE INFORMACION
    POPULAR, SAN JOSE, COSTA RICA, 1962

DEYOUNG GERRIT E   TEPAS DONALD I   CLEMMER EDWARD I
    TEACHING MAXI-AND MINICOMPUTER PROGRAMMING AT THE SAME
    TIME—IS THERE AN ADVANTAGE.
    BEHAVIOR RESEARCH METHODS AND INSTRUMENTATION 6, 2(MARCH
    1974), 233-234

DINGMANN HARVEY F   ET AL.
    A COMPARISON BETWEEN TWO ANALYTIC ROTATIONAL SOLUTIONS WHERE
    THE NUMBER OF FACTORS IS INDETERMINATE.
    BEHAVIORAL SCIENCE 9(JANUARY 1964), 76-79

DIXON W J
    BMD—BIOMEDICAL COMPUTER PROGRAMS.
    BERKELEY AND LOS ANGELES, UNIVERSITY OF CALIFORNIA PRESS,
    1967

DOLLAR C M   ACCOLA W V
    MAKING IT IN THE GHETTO—A COMPUTER SIMULATION.
    PP 185-194 IN PROCEEDINGS OF THE CONFERENCE ON
    COMPUTERS IN THE UNDERGRADUATE CURRICULA, 1975

DRABEK THOMAS E   HAAS EUGENE H
    LABORATORY SIMULATION OF A POLICE COMMUNICATION SYSTEM UNDER
    STRESS—PRELIMINARY FINDINGS.
    UNIVERSITY OF DENVER AND OHIO STATE UNIVERSITY, AUGUST-
    SEPTEMBER 1966

DRUCKMAN DANIEL
    UNDERSTANDING THE OPERATION OF COMPLEX SOCIAL SYSTEMS.
    SIMULATION AND GAMES 11, (JUNE 1971), 173-195

DUBOIS N DANDREA
    A DOCUMENT LINKAGE PROGRAM FOR DIGITAL COMPUTERS.
    BEHAVIORAL SCIENCE 10(JULY 1965), 312-318

DUNN-RANKIN PETER
    HIERARCHIAL TRIANGULAR CLUSTERING.
    BEHAVIORAL SCIENCE 17, (NOVEMBER 1972), 553-557

DUNPHY DEXTER C   ET AL.
    THE GENERAL INQUIRER—FURTHER DEVELOPMENTS IN A COMPUTER
    SYSTEM FOR CONTENT ANALYSIS OF VERBAL DATA IN THE SOCIAL
    SCIENCES.
    BEHAVIORAL SCIENCE 10(OCTOBER 1965), 468-480

DURRETT H J JR
    A MULTIPROGRAM APPROACH TO REAL-TIME EXPERIMENTATION.
    BEHAVIOR RESEARCH METHODS—INSTRUMENTATION 6, 2(MARCH
    1974), 259-261

DUTTON JOHN M   STARBUCK WILLIAM H
COMPUTER SIMULATION OF HUMAN BEHAVIOR.
NEW YORK, WILEY, 1971

EIDUSON BERNICE T   BROOKS SAMUEL H   ET AL.
A GENERALIZED PSYCHIATRIC INFORMATION-PROCESSING SYSTEM.
BEHAVIORAL SCIENCE 11(MARCH 1966), 133-142

EIDUSON BERNICE T   BROOKS SAMUEL H   ET AL.
RECENT DEVELOPMENTS IN THE PSYCHIATRIC CASE HISTORY EVENT
SYSTEM.
BEHAVIORAL SCIENCE 12 (MAY 1967), 254-267

EINBORN HILLEL J
ALCHEMY IN THE BEHAVIORAL SCIENCES.
PUBLIC OPINION QUARTERLY, (FALL 1972), 367-378

ELLEN PAUL   DELOACHE HERBERT C   BONDS JOSEPH
TIME-SHARED CONTROL OF A VARIETY OF PSYCHOLOGICAL
LABORATORIES USING THE IBM 1800 DATA ACQUISITION AND
CONTROL COMPUTER.
BEHAVIOR RESEARCH METHODS AND INSTRUMENTATION, 4,
2(MARCH 1972), 81-84

ELWOOD DAVID L
TEST RETEST RELIABILITY AND COST ANALYSIS OF AUTOMATED
AND FACE TO FACE INTELLIGENCE TESTING.
INTERNATIONAL JOURNAL OF MAN-MACHINE STUDIES 4,
(JANUARY 1972), 1-22
(REVIEWED IN COMPUTER REVIEWS, DECEMBER 1972, 24, 186)

ERICKSON M L   JACOBSEN R B
ON COMPUTER APPLICATIONS AND STATISTICS IN
SOCIOLOGY—TOWARD THE PASSING AWAY OF AN
ANTIQUATED TECHNOLOGY.
TEACHING SOCIOLOGY 1, 1(OCTOBER 1973), 84-102

ETTLINGER G
TRAINING MONKEYS BY LINC-8 COMPUTER.
CORTEX 6, (DECEMBER 1970), 410-416
(REVIEWED IN COMPUTER REVIEWS, AUGUST 1972, 23, 608)

EVANS GEORGE W II   ET AL.
SIMULATION USING DIGITAL COMPUTERS.
ENGLEWOOD CLIFFS, N J, PRENTICE-HALL, 1967

EVANS SELBY
VARGUS 7—COMPUTED PATTERNS FROM MARKOV PROCESSES.
BEHAVIORAL SCIENCE 12(JULY 1967), 323-328

FANG IRVING E
BY COMPUTER—FLESCH'S READING EASE SCORE AND A SYLLABLE
COUNTER.
BEHAVIORAL SCIENCE 13(MAY 1968), 249-251

FARR GRANT   EIK ROBERT K
COMPUTER SIMULATION OF INTERPERSONAL CHOICE.

UNPUBLISHED PAPER, UNIVERSITY OF WASHINGTON, DEPARTMENT OF
SOCIOLOGY, 1970

FAY WILLIAM T
GRID COORDINATE GEOGRAPHICAL IDENTIFICATION.
PP 211-219 IN R L BISCO (ED), DATA BASES, COMPUTERS, AND THE
SOCIAL SCIENCES. NEW YORK, WILEY, 1970

FEIGE EDGAR L   WATTS HAROLD W
PROTECTION OF PRIVACY THROUGH MICRO-AGGREGATION.
PP 261-272 IN R L BISCO (ED), DATA BASES, COMPUTER, AND THE
SOCIAL SCIENCES. NEW YORK, WILEY, 1970

FEIGENBAUM EDWARD
AN EXPERIMENTAL COURSE IN SIMULATION OF COGNITIVE PROCESSES.
BEHAVIORAL SCIENCE 7(APRIL 1962), 244.

FEIGENBAUM EDWARD   SIMON HERBERT A
PERFORMANCE OF A READING TASK BY AN ELEMENTARY PERCEIVING
AND MEMORIZING PROGRAM.
BEHAVIORAL SCIENCE 8(JANUARY 1963), 72-74

FEIN LOUIS
A PROPOSAL FOR A SCIENTIFIC COMPUTER-ORIENTED PROJECT ON
WORLD PEACE RESEARCH.
BACKGROUND 7, 2(AUGUST 1963), 2-13.

FEIN LOUIS
THE STRUCTURE AND CHARACTER OF USEFUL INFORMATION-PROCESSING
SIMULATION, SYNNOETIC SYSTEMS.
PP 277-282 IN PROCEEDINGS—FALL JOINT COMPUTER CONFERENCE,
PALO ALTO, CALIFORNIA, 1965

FIELD CRAIG
ABOUT COMPUTERS.
BOSTON, WINTHROP PRESS, 1973

FINDLER N V   MCKINZLE W R
ON A COMPUTER PROGRAM THAT GENERATES AND QUERIES KINSHIP
STRUCTURES.
BEHAVIORAL SCIENCE 14(JULY 1969), 334-340

FINDLER N V   MCKINZLE W R
RESEARCH NOTE STORY OF THE DOCTOR, THE MISSIONARY AND THE
COMPUTER SCIENTIST.
AMERICAN BEHAVIORAL SCIENCE 12, 6(JULY-AUGUST 1969)

FINDLER NICHOLAS V   MCKINZLE, W.R.
THE STORY OF THE DOCTOR, THE MISSIONARY AND THE COMPUTER
SCIENTIST—COMPUTER SIMULATION OF A DEMOGRAPHICAL AND
KINSHIP MODEL.
INTERNATIONAL JOURNAL OF COMPARATIVE SOCIOLOGY 11, (JUNE 1970),
166-170

FINNEY JOSEPH C
METHODOLOGICAL PROBLEMS IN PROGRAMMED COMPOSITION OF
PSYCHOLOGICAL TEST REPORTS.
BEHAVIORAL SCIENCE 12(MARCH 1967), 142-152

FISEK M H
SEDAD—THE SEQUENTIAL DATA DESCRIPTION.
UNPUBLISHED PAPER, STANFORD UNIVERSITY, DEPARTMENT OF
SOCIOLOGY, 1968

FITZHUGH ROBERT J
LABORATORY CONTROL WITH A MEDIUM SCALE TIME-SHARING
SYSTEM.
BEHAVIOR RESEARCH METHODS AND INSTRUMENTATION 6, 2(MARCH
1974), 131-138

FITZHUGH ROBERT J   GLASER ROBERT
A GENERAL-PURPOSE COMPUTER SYSTEM FOR A RESEARCH AND
DEVELOPMENT CENTER.
AMERICAN PSYCHOLOGIST, 30, 3(MARCH 1975), 219

FRANCIS IVOR   HEIBERGER RICHARD M
THE EVALUATION OF STATISTICAL PROGRAM PACKAGES—THE
BEGINNING.
PP 106-109 IN PROCEEDINGS OF THE COMPUTER SCIENCE AND
STATISTICS EIGHTH ANNUAL SYMPOSIUM ON THE INTERFACE
HEALTH SCIENCES COMPUTING FACILITY, UNIV OF CALIFORNIA
LOS ANGELES, 1975

FRANCIS IVOR   VALLIANT RICHARD
THE NOVICE WITH A STATISTICAL PACKAGE—PERFORMANCE
WITHOUT COMPETENCE.
PP 110-114 IN PROCEEDINGS OF THE COMPUTER SCIENCE AND
STATISTICS EIGHTH ANNUAL SYMPOSIUM ON THE INTERFACE
HEALTH SCIENCES COMPUTING FACILITY, UNIV OF CALIFORNIA
LOS ANGELES, 1975

FRANCIS J ET AL.
COMPUTER-BASED INSTRUCTION IN THE SOCIAL SCIENCES AND
EXPERIMENTAL COURSE IN RESEARCH.
PP 8.30-8.34 IN PROCEEDINGS OF A CONFERENCE ON COMPUTERS IN
THE UNDERGRADUATE CURRICULA, UNIVERSITY OF IOWA, IOWA CITY,
1970

FREEMAN LINTON C
A COMPUTER CONTROLLED EXPERIMENT ON RECENCY IN PROBABILITY
LEARNING.
BEHAVIORAL SCIENCE 16, 2(MARCH 1971), 174-179

FREEMAN LINTON C
THE USE OF SIMPLIFIED PROGRAMMING SYSTEMS IN IBN 650 DATA
PROCESSING.
BEHAVIORAL SCIENCE 7(JANUARY 1962), 117-119

FREEMAN LINTON C
MATHEMATICAL MODELS AND COMPUTER SIMULATION.
UNIVERSITY OF PITTSBURGH, 1969

FREEMAN LINTON   SUNSHINE MORRIS
  PATTERNS OF RESIDENTIAL SEGREGATION.
  CAMBRIDGE, MASS, SCHENKMAN PUBLISHING, 1970

FRITJA NICE H
  PROBLEMS OF COMPUTER SIMULATION.
  BEHAVIORAL SCIENCE 12(1967), 59-67

FRUMKES DANIEL   NELSON CAMPBELL
  INTERACTIVE MANAGEMENT AND ANALYSIS OF NONRECTANGULAR
  DATA MATRICES.
  PP 41-48 IN PROCEEDINGS OF THE COMPUTER SCIENCE AND
  STATISTICS EIGHTH ANNUAL SYMPOSIUM ON THE INTERFACE
  HEALTH SCIENCES COMPUTING FACILITY, UNIV OF CALIFORNIA
  LOS ANGELES, 1975

FORSHEE JERRY C
  DESIGN AND ORGANIZATION IN A COMPUTERIZED PSYCHOLOGY
  LABORATORY.
  BEHAVIOR RESEARCH METHODS AND INSTRUMENTATION 6, 2(MARCH
  1974), 146-148

FOWLER RAYMOND D   MARLOWE GUY H JR
  A COMPUTER PROGRAM FOR PERSONALITY ANALYSIS.
  BEHAVIORAL SCIENCE 13(SEPTEMBER 1968), 413-416.

GARDIN J C
  THE RECONSTRUCTION OF AN ECONOMIC NETWORK OF THE SECOND
  MILLENIUM.
  PP 378-391 IN D HYMES (ED), THE USE OF COMPUTERS IN
  ANTHROPOLOGY. THE HAGUE, NETHERLANDS, MOUTON, 1965

GARSIDE, DANIEL B
  HOMANS HUMAN EXCHANGE SIMULATOR.
  CO-OPERATIVE VENTURE IN COLLEGE CURRICULUM DEVELOPMENT,
  ILLINOIS INSTITUTE OF TECHNOLOGY, CHICAGO, ILL, 1970

GEARHART BURTON C   LIITSCHWAGER JOHN
  LEGISLATIVE DISTRICTING BY COMPUTER.
  BEHAVIORAL SCIENCE 14(SEPTEMBER 1969), 404-417

GERBNER GEORGE   ET AL.
  THE ANALYSIS OF COMMUNICATION CONTENT.
  NEW YORK, WILEY, 1969

GIANNITRAPANI D   RAST VILLARD T   SHULHAFER BURTON J
  MULTIPLE CHANNEL DIRECT DIGITAL RECORDING OF EEG DATA.
  BEHAVIORAL SCIENCE 16, 3(MAY 1971), 239-243

GILBERT J P   HAMMEL E A
  COMPUTER SIMULATION AND ANALYSIS OF PROBLEMS IN KINSHIP
  AND SOCIAL STRUCTURE.
  AMERICAN ANTHROPOLOGIST 68(FEBRUARY 1966), 71-93

GILBERT J P HAMMEL E A
COMPUTER SIMULATION OF PROBLEMS IN KINSHIP AND SOCIAL
STRUCTURES.
PP 513-531 IN D HYMES (ED), THE USE OF COMPUTERS IN
ANTHROPOLOGY. THE HAGUE, NETHERLANDS, MOUTON, 1965

GILLMAN CLIFFORD B   LAPIN DAVID J   BUCKLEY PAUL B
HIERARCHICALLY DISTRIBUTED PROCESSING FOR PSYCHOLOGY.
BEHAVIOR RESEARCH METHODS AND INSTRUMENTATION 6, 2(MARCH
1974), 149-154

GIPS JAMES   PFEFFERBAUM ADOLF   BUCHSBAUM MONTE
ERL—A LANGUAGE FOR IMPLEMENTING EVOKED RESPONSE AND
PSYCHO-PHYSIOLOGICAL EXPERIMENTS.
BEHAVIOR RESEARCH METHODS AND INSTRUMENTATION 3,
(JULY 1971), 199-201

GOODMAN LEO A
A SHORT COMPUTER PROGRAM FOR THE ANALYSIS OF TRANSACTION
FLOWS.
BEHAVIORAL SCIENCE 9(APRIL 1964), 176-185

GORDEN MORTON
BURDENS FOR THE DESIGNER OF A COMPUTER SIMULATION OF
INTERNATIONAL RELATIONS.
PP 222-245 IN D B BOBROW AND J L SCHWARTZ (EDS), COMPUTERS
AND THE POLICY-MAKING COMMUNITY. ENGLEWOOD CLIFFS, N J,
PRENTICE-HALL, 1968

GOODE FRANK M
TRAINING MATHEMATICAL PSYCHOLOGY STUDENTS IN THE USE OF A
LABORAOTRY COMPUTER.
BEHAVIOR RESEARCH METHODS AND INSTRUMENTATION 4,
2 (MARCH 1972), 96-97

GRAETZ ROBERT E
RESEARCH UTILIZATION OF PATIENT DATA FILES IN CLINICAL DRUG
STUDIES.
BEHAVIORAL SCIENCE 10(JULY 1965), 320-322

GREEN B F JR
DIGITAL COMPUTERS IN RESEARCH.
NEW YORK, MCGRAW-HILL, 1963

GREEN B F JR
INTELLIGENCE AND COMPUTER SIMULATION.
TRANSACTIONS OF THE NEW YORK ACADEMY OF SCIENCES 2, 27, 1
(NOVEMBER 1964), 55-63

GREEN B F JR
INTRODUCTION—CURRENT TRENDS IN PROBLEM SOLVING.
IN B KLEIMUNTZ (ED), PROBLEM SOLVING. NEW YORK, WILEY, 1966

GREEN B F JR
THE COMPUTER CONQUEST OF PSYCHOLOGY.
PSYCHOLOGY TODAY, 1967, 56-61

GREEN B F JR
THE COMPUTER REVOLUTION IN PSYCHOMETRICS.
PSYCHOMETRIKA 31, 4(DECEMBER 1966), 437-445

GREEN B F JR
THE USE OF TIME-SHARED TERMINALS IN PSYCHOLOGY.
BEHAVIOR RESEARCH METHODS AND INSTRUMENTATION 4,
2(MARCH 1972), 51-55

GREENBERGER MARTIN
SIMULATION AND A HOUSE-HEATING PROBLEM.
BEHAVIORAL SCIENCE 11(MARCH 1966), 143-147

GREGG LEE W
COMPUTERS—LARGE-SCALE USAGE IN THE BALANCE.
AMERICAN PSYCHOLOGIST, 30, 3(MARCH 1975), 199-204

GREGG LEE W   SIMON H A
PROCESS MODELS AND STOCHASTIC THEORIES OF SIMPLE CONCEPT
FORMATION.
JOURNAL OF MATHEMATICAL PSYCHOLOGY 4(1967), 246-276

GROVES PATRICIA H
A COMPUTER SIMULATION OF INTERACTION IN DECISION MAKING.
BEHAVIORAL SCIENCE 15(MAY 1970), 277-285.

GULLAHORN J T   GULLAHORN J E
A COMPUTER MODEL OF ELEMENTARY SOCIAL BEHAVIOR.
PP 375-386 IN E FEIGENBAUM AND J FELDMAN (EDS), COMPUTERS
AND THOUGHT. NEW YORK, MCGRAW HILL, 1963

GULLAHORN J T   GULLAHORN J E
A COMPUTER SIMULATION MODEL OF SOCIAL BEHAVIOR AND STEPS
TOWARD ITS EMPIRICAL VALIDATION.
MICHIGAN STATE UNIVERSITY, OCTOBER 1965

GULLAHORN J T   GULLAHORN J E
A NON-RANDOM WALK IN THE ODYSSEY OF A COMPUTER MODEL.
IN M INBAR AND S S STOLL (EDS), SOCIAL SCIENCE SIMULATIONS.
NEW YORK, FREE PRESS, 1970

GULLAHORN J T   GULLAHORN J E
APPROACHES TO TESTING THEORIES OF ORGANIZATION DESIGN.
MICHIGAN STATE UNIVERSITY, JANUARY 1964

GULLAHORN J T   GULLAHORN J E
A COMPUTER MODEL OF ELEMENTARY SOCIAL BEHAVIOR.
BEHAVIORAL SCIENCE 8(1963), 354-362

GULLAHORN J T   GULLAHORN J E
COMPUTER SIMULATION OF HUMAN INTERACTION IN SMALL GROUPS.
PROCEEDINGS—SPRING JOINT COMPUTER CONFERENCE, MICHIGAN
STATE UNIVERSITY, COMPUTER INSTITUTE FOR SOCIAL SCIENCE
RESEARCH, DEPARTMENT OF SOCIOLOGY AND ANTHROPOLOGY, 1964

GULLAHORN J T   GULLAHORN J E
COMPUTER SIMULATION OF ROLE CONFLICT RESOLUTION.
IN W A STARBUCK AND J M DUTTON (EDS), COMPUTER SIMULATION
IN HUMAN BEHAVIOR. NEW YORK, WILEY, 1970

GULLAHORN J E   GULLAHORN J T
SIMULATION AND SOCIAL SYSTEM THEORY—THE STATE OF THE
UNION.
SIMULATION AND GAMES 1, 1(MARCH 1970), 19-42

GULLAHORN J T   GULLAHORN J E
SOCIAL AND CULTURAL SYSTEM SIMULATIONS.
MICHIGAN STATE UNIVERSITY, AUGUST 1969

GULLAHORN J T   GULLAHORN J E
SOME COMPUTER APPLICATIONS IN SOCIAL SCIENCE.
AMERICAN SOCIOLOGICAL REVIEW 30(1965), 353-365

GULLAHORN J T   GULLAHORN J E
THE COMPUTER AS A TOOL FOR THEORY DEVELOPMENT.
PP 427-444 IN D HYMES (ED), THE USE OF COMPUTERS IN
ANTHROPOLOGY. THE HAGUE, NETHERLANDS, MOUTON, 1965

GUTHRIE DONALD
DANGERS IN INTERACTIVE STATISTICAL SYSTEMS.
PP 8-10 IN PROCEEDINGS OF THE COMPUTER SCIENCE AND
STATISTICS EIGHTH ANNUAL SYMPOSIUM ON THE INTERFACE
HEALTH SCIENCES COMPUTING FACILITY, UNIV OF CALIFORNIA
LOS ANGELES, 1975

GUTHRIE HAROLD W   ET AL.
MICROANALYTIC SIMULATION OF HOUSEHOLD BEHAVIOR.
ANNALS OF ECONOMIC AND SOCIAL MEASUREMENT 1, (APRIL 1972),
141-169

GYR JOHN   ET AL.
COMPUTER SIMULATION OF A MODEL OF COGNITIVE ORGANIZATION.
BEHAVIORAL SCIENCE 7(JANUARY 1962), 111-116

HAGERSTRAND T
INNOVATION DIFFUSION AS A SPATIAL PROCESS.
TRANSLATED BY ALAN PRED. CHICAGO, UNIVERSITY OF CHICAGO
PRESS, 1968

HAGERSTRAND T
QUANTITATIVE TECHNIQUES FOR ANALYSIS OF THE SPREAD OF
INFORMATION AND TECHNOLOGY.
PP 244-280 IN C A ANDERSON AND M J BOWMAN (EDS), EDUCATION
AND ECONOMIC DEVELOPMENT. CHICAGO, ALDINE, 1965

HAGERSTRAND T
A MONTE CARLO APPROACH TO DIFFUSION.
EUROPEAN JOURNAL OF SOCIOLOGY 6(MAY 1965), 43-67

HALLENBECK CHARLES ESWELCH ROBERT B
GENERALIZING THE PROBLEM OF DEFINITION STEP ON THE COMPUTER
SIMULATION OF FACTORIAL EXPERIMENTS.
BEHAVIOR RESEARCH METHODS AND INSTRUMENTATION 6, 2(MARCH
1974), 111-121

HALLEY F S
PROGRAMS FOR USE IN TEACHING RESEARCH METHODS FOR
SMALL COMPUTERS.
TEACHING SOCIOLOGY 2, 2(APRIL 1975), 218-221

HALLWORTH HERBERT
THE USE OF COMPUTERS BY PSYCHOLOGISTS IN BRITAIN.
BEHAVIORAL SCIENCE 9(APRIL 1964), 172-175

HALPERIN SILAS LISSITZ ROBERT W
STATISTICAL PROPERTIES OF MARKOV CHAINS—A COMPUTER
PROGRAM.
BEHAVIORAL SCIENCE 16, 3(MAY 1971), 244-247

HANNA J
INFORMATION—THEORETIC TECHNIQUES FOR EVALUATING SIMULATION
MODELS.
IN W A STARBUCK AND J M DUTTON (EDS), COMPUTER SIMULATION
IN HUMAN BEHAVIOR. NEW YORK, WILEY, 1970

HANSON R C MCPHEE W N
A SIMULATION MODEL OF URBANIZATION PROCESSES.
PAPER PRESENTED AT THE AMERICAN SOCIOLOGICAL ASSOCIATION
MEETING, SAN FRANCISCO, 1967

HANSON ROBERT C SIMMONS OZZIE G
THE ROLE PATH—A CONCEPT AND PROCEDURE FOR STUDYING
MIGRATION TO URBAN COMMUNITIES.
UNIVERSITY OF COLORADO, 1966

HARE A PAUL
SIMULATING GROUP DECISIONS.
SIMULATION AND GAMES 1, 4(DECEMBER 1970), 361-376

HARE PAUL A SCHEIBLECHNER H
COMPUTER SIMULATION OF SMALL GROUP DECISIONS—MODEL THREE.
BEHAVIORAL SCIENCE 16, 4(JULY 1971), 399-403

HARF JAMES E
A STUDENT HANDBOOK OF EMPIRICAL EVIDENCE—THE UTILIZATION
OF CAPE DATA IN UNDERGRADUATE EDUCATION.
PROCEEDINGS OF THE CONFERENCE ON COMPUTERS IN THE UNDER-
GRADUATE CURRICULA, 1972, 467-476

HARKINS P B ISENHOUR T L JURS P C
INTRODUCTION TO COMPUTER PROGRAMMING FOR THE SOCIAL
SCIENCES.
BOSTON, ALLYN AND BACON, INC, 1973

HARPER D H
THE COMPUTER SIMULATION OF A SOCIOLOGICAL SURVEY.
IN CALCUL ET FORMULISATION DANS LES SCIENCES DE L'HOMME.
PARIS, FRANCE, EDITIONS DE CENTRE NATIONAL DE LA RESCHER CHE
SCIENTIFIQUE, 1968

HARPER DEAN
THE COMPUTER SIMULATION OF SOCIOLOGICAL SURVEYS.
BEHAVIORAL SCIENCE 17, (SEPTEMBER 1972), 471-480

HARTMAN JOHN J
ANNOTATED BIBLIOGRAPHY ON SIMULATION IN THE SOCIAL SCIENCES.
IOWA STATE UNIVERSITY, 1966

HARTMAN JOHN J   WALSH JAMES A
COMPUTER SIMULATION—CASE FOR INCREASED RIGOR.
IOWA STATE UNIVERSITY, 1968

HARTMAN JOHN J   WALSH JAMES A
SIMULATION OF NEWSPAPER READERSHIP—AN EXPLORATION IN
COMPUTER ANALYSIS OF SOCIAL DATA.
SOCIAL SCIENCE QUARTERLY 49(MARCH 1969), 840-852

HARWAY NORMAN   IKER HOWARD P
COMPUTER ANALYSIS OF CONTENT IN PSYCHOTHERAPY.
PSYCHOLOGICAL REPORTS 14(1964), 720-722

HARWAY NORMAN I   IKER HOWARD P
CONTENT ANALYSIS AND PSYCHOTHERAPY.
PSYCHOTHERAPY—THEORY, RESEARCH AND PRACTICE 6, 2(SPRING
1969), 97-104

HAUER HERBERT
AN IPL 5 PROBLEM FOR FORMAL INTEGRATION USING TABLES.
BEHAVIORAL SCIENCE 7(APRIL 1962), 252-255

HAWTHORNE G B JR
DIGITAL SIMULATION AND MODELLING.
DATAMATION 10(OCTOBER 1964), 25-29

HAYES-ROTH FREDER   LONGABAUGH RICHARD
REACT—A TOOL FOR THE ANALYSIS OF COMPLEX TRANSITIONAL
BEHAVIOR MATRICES.
BEHAVIORAL SCIENCE 17, (JULY 1972), 384-394

HEMMENS GEORGE C
ANALYSIS AND SIMULATION OF URBAN ACTIVITY PATTERNS OF CITY
AND REGIONAL PLANNING.
UNIVERSITY OF NORTH CAROLINA AT CHAPEL HILL, SEPTEMBER 1968

HESS SIDNEY W
ONE MAN, ONE VOTE AND COUNTY POLITICAL INTEGRITY—
APPORTION TO SATISFY BOTH.
JURIMETRICS JOURNAL 11, (MARCH 1971), 123-141

HILSENRATH JOSEPH   ET AL.
OMNITAB—A COMPUTER PROGRAM FOR STATISTICAL AND NUMERICAL
ANALYSIS.
NATIONAL BUREAU OF STANDARDS HANDBOOK 101, U S DEPARTMENT OF
COMMERCE, 1968

HOFFMAN THOMAS R
PROGRAMMED HEURISTICS AND THE CONCEPT OF PAR IN BUSINESS
GAMES.
BEHAVIORAL SCIENCE 10(APRIL 1965), 169-172

HOGGE JAMES H
PROGRAMMING THE STATISTICAL LIBRARY.
PHILADELPHIA, AUERBACH, 1972

HOLDER HAROLD D   EHLING WILLIAM P
CONSTRUCTION AND SIMULATION OF AN INFORMATION-DECISION
MODEL.
JOURNAL OF COMMUNICATIONS 4(DECEMBER 1967), 302-315

HOLLAN JAMES D   OSTEEN ROBERT E
PROJECT X—A PL
DIGRAPHS.
BEHAVIOR RESEARCH METHODS AND INSTRUMENTATION, 7, 2(MARCH
1975), 105-106

HOLSTI OLE R
AN ADAPTION OF THE GENERAL INQUIRER FOR THE SYSTEMATIC
ANALYSIS OF POLITICAL DOCUMENTS.
BEHAVIORAL SCIENCE 10(OCTOBER 1965), 382-387

HOLSTI OLE R
COMPUTER CONTENT ANALYSIS FOR MEASURING ATTITUDES—THE
ASSESSMENT OF QUALITIES AND PERFORMANCE.
COMPUTER STUDIES IN THE HUMANITIES AND VERBAL BEHAVIOR
1, 4(DECEMBER 1968), 200-216

HOLSTI OLE R
CONTENT ANALYSIS FOR THE SOCIAL SCIENCES AND HUMANITIES.
READING, MASS, ADDISON-WESLEY, 1969

HOLSTI OLE
CONTENT ANALYSIS IN POLITICAL RESEARCH.
PP 111-153 IN D B BOBROW AND J L SCHWARTZ (EDS), COMPUTERS
AND THE POLICY-MAKING COMMUNITY. ENGLEWOOD CLIFFS, N J,
PRENTICE-HALL, 1968

HOLT CHARLES C
A SYSTEM OF INFORMATION CENTERS FOR RESEARCH AND DECISION
MAKING.
AMERICAN ECONOMIC REVIEW 50, 2(MAY 1970), 140-165

HOROVITZ MARK W
RECOG, A COMPUTER PROGRAM FOR THE AUTOMATIC SCANNING OF
BUBBLE CHAMBER PHOTOGRAPHS.
BEHAVIORAL SCIENCE 7(APRIL 1962), 256-257

HORWOOD EDGAR M
GRID COORDINATE GEOGRAPHICAL IDENTIFICATION SYSTEMS.
PP 220-237 IN RALPH J BISCO (ED), DATA BASES, COMPUTERS AND
THE SOCIAL SCIENCES. NEW YORK, WILEY, 1970

HOWERTON ROBERT J
INFORMATION RETRIEVAL AND COMPUTERS.
PP 71-80 IN D B BOBROW AND J L SCHWARTZ (EDS), COMPUTERS
AND THE POLICY-MAKING COMMUNITY. ENGLEWOOD CLIFFS, N J,
PRENTICE-HALL, 1968

HUBBELL C
AN INPUT-OUTPUT APPROACH TO CLIQUE IDENTIFICATION.
SOCIOMETRY 28(DECEMBER 1964), 809-818

HUESMANN L ROWELL
COMPUTER SCIENCE FOR SOCIAL SCIENCE STUDENTS AT YALE.
PP 8.1-8.4 IN PROCEEDINGS OF A CONFERENCE ON COMPUTERS IN
THE UNDERGRADUATE CURRICULA, UNIVERSITY OF IOWA, IOWA CITY,
1970

HURLEY JOHN R   CATTELL RAYMOND B
THE PROCUSTES PROGRAM—PRODUCING DIRECT ROTATION TO TEST A
HYPOTHESIZED FACTOR STRUCTURE.
BEHAVIORAL SCIENCE 7(APRIL 1962), 258-261

HYMES DELL (ED)
THE USE OF COMPUTERS IN ANTHROPOLOGY.
THE HAGUE, NETHERLANDS, MOUTON, 1965

IKER HOWARD P   HARWAY NORMAN I
A COMPUTER APPROACH TOWARDS THE ANALYSIS OF CONTENT.
BEHAVIORAL SCIENCE 10(APRIL 1965), 173-181

IKER HOWARD P   HARWAY NORMAN I
A COMPUTER SYSTEMS APPROACH TOWARD THE RECOGNITION AND
ANALYSIS OF CONTENT.
PP 381-406 IN G GERBNER ET AL. (EDS), THE ANALYSIS OF
COMMUNICATION CONTENT. NEW YORK, WILEY, 1969

INBAR MICHAEL   STOLL CLARICE
SIMULATION AND GAMING IN SOCIAL SCIENCE.
NEW YORK, FREE PRESS, 1972

JANDA K
DATA PROCESSING APPLICATIONS TO POLITICAL RESEARCH.
EVANSTON, ILL, NORTHWESTERN UNIVERSITY PRESS, 1965

JANDA K
SOME COMPUTER APPLICATIONS IN POLITICAL SCIENCE.
COMPUTERS AND THE HUMANITIES 2(SEPTEMBER 1967), 12-16

JANDA K
INFORMATION RETRIEVAL APPLICATIONS TO POLITICAL SCIENCE.
INDIANAPOLIS, BOBBS-MERRILL, 1968

JANDA K
DATA PROCESSING APPLICATIONS TO POLITICAL RESEARCH. (2ND ED)
EVANSTON, ILL, NORTHWESTERN UNIVERSITY PRESS, 1969

JANDA K
A MICROFILM AND COMPUTER SYSTEM FOR ANALYZING COMPARATIVE
POLITICS LITERATURE.
PP 407-436 IN G GERBNER ET AL. (EDS), THE ANALYSIS OF
COMMUNICATION CONTENT. NEW YORK, WILEY, 1969

JANDA K   KLECKA W (EDS)
USERS GUIDE TO THE INTERSOCIETAL INFORMATION CENTER.
EVANSTON, ILL, CENTER FOR INTERSOCIETAL STUDIES, NORTHWESTERN
UNIVERSITY, 1970

JANDA K   TETZLAFF W H
TRIAL—A COMPUTER TECHNIQUE FOR RETRIEVING INFORMATION FROM
ABSTRACTS TO LITERATURE.
BEHAVIORAL SCIENCE 11(NOVEMBER 1966), 480-486

JANSEN B DOUGLASS
A SYSTEM FOR CONTENT ANALYSIS BY COMPUTER OF INTERNATIONAL
COMUUNICATIONS FOR SELECTED CATEGORIES OF ACTION.
THE AMERICAN BEHAVIORAL SCIENTIST, MARCH 1966, 28-32

JENSEMA CARL
A REVIEW OF A ROTATION TO OBTAIN MAXIMUM SIMILARITY AND
SIMPLE STRUCTURE AMONG FACTOR PATTERNS.
BEHAVIORAL SCIENCE 17, (MARCH 1972), 235-240

JOHNSON DOUGLAS F   MIHAL WILLIAM L
THE COMPUTERIZED STATESMAN—FURTHER EXPLORATIONS INTO THE
ESCALATION OF CONFLICT.
PP 156-168 IN PROCEEDINGS OF THE ACM ANNUAL CONFERENCE,
CHICAGO, AUGUST 1971

JOHNSON EDWARD S
THE COMPUTER AS EXPERIMENTER.
BEHAVIORAL SCIENCE 12(NOVEMBER 1967), 484-489

JOHNSON EDWARD S   BAKER ROBERT F
THE COMPUTER AS EXPERIMENTER—NEW RESULTS.
BEHAVIORAL SCIENCE, 18, 5(SEPTEMBER 1973), 377-386

JOHNSON JAMES H   WILLIAMS THOMAS A
THE USE OF ON-LINE COMPUTER TECHNOLOGY IN A MENTAL
HEALTH ADMITTING SYSTEM.
AMERICAN PSYCHOLOGIST, 30, 3(MARCH 1975), 388

JOHNSON RICHARD R
INSTRUCTIONAL SIMULATION—THE INTERFACE WITH THE
STUDENT.
BEHAVIOR RESEARCH METHODS AND INSTRUMENTATION 6, 2(MARCH
1974), 128-130

JOHNSON RICHARD R
DATACALL—A COMPUTER-BASED SIMULATION GAME FOR TEACHING
STRATEGY IN SCIENTIFIC RESEARCH.
PP 419-423 IN PROCEEDINGS OF A CONFERENCE ON COMPUTERS IN
THE UNDERGRADUATE CURRICULA, DARTMOUTH COLLEGE, JUNE 1971

JONES KENNETH J
PROBLEMS OF GROUPING INDIVIDUALS AND THE METHOD OF MODALITY.
BEHAVIORAL SCIENCE 13(NOVEMBER 1968), 496-511

JONES KENNETH J
THE MULTIVARIATE STATISTICAL ANALYZER.
BEHAVIORAL SCIENCE 10(1965), 326-327

JONES T L
A COMPUTER MODEL OF SIMPLE FORMS OF LEARNING IN INFANTS.
JOINT COMPUTER CONFERENCE 40, (SPRING 1971), 885-895

JOYNER ROBERT C   GREEN CHRISTOPHER
DEMONSTRATION OF COMPUTER-AUGMENTED GROUP PROBLEM SOLVING.
BEHAVIORAL SCIENCE 15, 5(SEPTEMBER 1970), 452-462

KADNOFF L P   ET AL.
A CITY GROWS BEFORE YOUR EYES.
COMPUTER DECISIONS 1(1969), 16-23

KAHNE MERTON J   ET AL.
SLIDES—A DICTIONARY SYSTEM FOR COMPUTER CONTROLLED STUDY
OF GRAPHIC OR PICTORIAL DISPLAYS.
BEHAVIORAL SCIENCE 14(SEPTEMBER 1969), 418-428

KAM ALAN C H   WALL CHARLES F
DYNA—DYNAMIC STORAGE ALLOCATION IN FORTRAN FOR THE
IBM/360 OPERATING SYSTEM.
BEHAVIORAL SCIENCE 17, (SEPTEMBER 1972), 481-484

KAMIL ALAN C   SACKS ROBERT A
THE LEHIGH VALLEY INTERACT—AN OPERANT RESEARCH COMPUTER
SYSTEM FOR THE NONCOMPUTER JOCKY.
BEHAVIOR RESEARCH METHODS AND INSTRUMENTATION 4,
2(MARCH 1972), 64-66

KARLSSON G
SOCIAL MECHANISMS—STUDIES IN SOCIOLOGICAL THEORY.
NEW YORK, FREE PRESS, 1958

KATZENMEYER CONRAD   ET AL.
ESTIMATION OF GENETIC PARAMETERS BY COMPUTER.
BEHAVIORAL SCIENCE 14(MARCH 1969), 160-163

KELLY EDWARD   STONE PHILIP
COMPUTER RECOGNITION OF ENGLISH WORD SENSES.
AMSTERDAM, NETHERLANDS, NORTH-HOLLAND
PUBLISHING COMPANY, 1975

KERSHNER THOMAS P
COMPUTER APPLICATIONS FOR SOCIAL SCIENTISTS.
PROCEEDINGS OF THE CONFERENCE ON COMPUTERS IN UNDERGRADUATE
CURRICULA, 1972, 489-492

KEYFITZ NATHAN   TYREE ANDREA
COMPUTERIZATION OF THE BRANCHING PROCESS.
BEHAVIORAL SCIENCE 12(JULY 1967), 629-336.

KEYFITZ NATHAN   MURPHY EMUND M
HOW MUCH DEMOGRAPHIC RETURN CAN A SINGLE PROGRAM EXTRACT.
PP 67-73 IN JAMES M BESHERS (ED), COMPUTER METHODS IN THE
ANALYSIS OF LARGE-SCALE SOCIAL SYSTEMS. CAMBRIDGE, MASS,
MIT PRESS, 1968

KEYFITZ NATHAN
MACHINE COMPUTATION AND THE WORKING DEMOGRAPHER.
PP 74-93 IN JAMES M BESHERS (ED), COMPUTER METHODS IN THE
ANALYSIS OF LARGE-SCALE SOCIAL SYSTEMS. CAMBRIDGE, MASS,
MIT PRESS, 1968

KENNEDY J M   NEWCOMBE J B   ET AL.
LIST-PROCESSING METHODS FOR ORGANIZING FILES OF LINKED
RECORDS.
PP 45-50 IN JAMES M BESHERS (ED), COMPUTER METHODS IN THE
ANALYSIS OF LARGE-SCALE SOCIAL SYSTEMS. CAMBRIDGE, MASS,
MIT PRESS, 1968

KING GERALD A   ANDERSON RONALD E
COMPUTER AND SOCIAL SCIENTIST IN INTERACTION.
PP 332-343 IN J FOLTA AND DECK (EDS), A SOCIOLOGICAL
FRAMEWORK FOR PATIENT CARE. NEW YORK, WILEY, 1966

KING JOHN F
TIME-SHARED CONTROL SYSTEMS—PROMISES AND PROBLEMS.
AMERICAN PSYCHOLOGIST, 30, 3(MARCH 1975), 226

KISSLER GERALD R
EVALUATION OF COMPUTER-BASED LABORATORY SIMULATION MODELS
TO TEACH SCIENTIFIC RESEARCH STRATEGIES.
BEHAVIOR RESEARCH METHODS AND INSTRUMENTATION 6, 2(MARCH
1974), 124-126

KLAIR DAVID
A COMPUTER SIMULATION OF THE PARADOX OF VOTING.
AMERICAN POLITICAL SCIENCE REVIEW 60, 2(JUNE 1966) 384-390

KLEIN S   ET AL.
MONTE CARLO SIMULATION OF LANGUAGE CHANGE IN TIKOPIA AND
MAORI.
UNIVERSITY OF WISCONSIN, COMPUTER SCIENCES DEPARTMENT,
TECHNICAL REPORT 62(JUNE 1969).

KLEINMUNTZ BENJAMIN
THE COMPUTER AS CLINICIAN.
AMERICAN PSYCHOLOGIST, 30, 3(MARCH 1975), 379

KLEINMUNTZ B
A PORTRAIT OF THE COMPUTER AS A YOUNG CLINICIAN.
BEHAVIORAL SCIENCE 8(APRIL 1963), 154-155

KLEINMUNTZ B   MCLEAN ROBERT S
DIAGNOSTIC INTERVIEWING BY DIGITAL COMPUTER.
BEHAVIORAL SCIENCE 13(JANUARY 1968), 76-80

KLINE F GERALD
VOTER ATTITUDES AND BEHAVIOR IN COMPUTER SIMULATION—AN
INTRODUCTORY OVERVIEW.
UNIVERSITY OF MINNESOTA, SCHOOL OF JOURNALISM AND MASS
COMMUNICATIONS, 1970

KNIGHT JOHN   ET AL.
AN EXPERIMENT CONTROL COMPUTER SYSTEM TIME SHARED BY
SEVERAL LABORATORIES.
BEHAVIOR RESEARCH METHODS AND INSTRUMENTATION 6, 2(MARCH
1974), 143-145

KNOTT G D   ET AL.
A TABLE-MAKING LANGUAGE.
PROCEEDINGS OF THE IEE 54, 12(DECEMBER 1966), 1779-1787

KORNBERG, ALLAN   ET AL.
SOCIALIZING POLITICAL PARTY OFFICIALS—A SIMULATION
EXPERIMENT.
SIMULATION AND GAMES 3, (JUNE 1972), 379-406

KRAMER J F
A COMPUTER SIMULATION OF AUDIENCE EXPOSURE IN A MASS MEDIA
SYSTEM—THE UNITED NATIONS INFORMATION CAMPAIGN IN
CINCINNATI, 1947-1948.
MIT, DEPARTMENT OF POLITICAL SCIENCE, 1969

KRANZ PETER
WHAT DO PEOPLE DO ALL DAY.
BEHAVIORAL SCIENCE 15(MAY 1970), 286-291

KREIDER GLEN D   SIM FRANCIS M
INSTANT TURNAROUND IN INSTRUCTIONAL COMPUTING—SOME
EXAMPLES FROM THE SOCIAL SCIENCES AT THE PENNSYLVANIA STATE
UNIVERSITY.
PP 8.16-8.32 IN PROCEEDINGS OF A CONFERENCE ON COMPUTERS IN
THE UNDERGRADUATE CURRICULA, UNIVERSITY OF IOWA, IOWA CITY,
IA, 1970

KRUEGEL D   PEASE J
USE OF THE GENERAL SOCIAL SURVEY DATA AND CROSS-
TABULATING PROGRAMS IN TEACHING DATA ANALYSIS.
HIGH SCHOOL BEHAVIORAL SCIENCE 3, 1(FALL 1975), 30-33

KRULEE GILBERT K   ET AL.
   NATURAL LANGUAGE INPUTS FOR A PROBLEM-SOLVING SYSTEM.
   BEHAVIORAL SCIENCE 9(JULY 1964), 281-287

KRUSKAL J B
   EXTREMELY PORTABLE RANDOM NUMBER GENERATOR.
   COMMUNICATIONS OF THE ACM 12, 2(FEBRUARY 1969)

KUNSTADTER P
   COMPUTER SIMULATION OF PREFERENTIAL MARRIAGE SYSTEMS.
   PP 520-521 IN D HYMES (ED), THE USE OF COMPUTERS IN
   ANTHROPOLOGY. THE HAGUE, NETHERLANDS, MOUTON, 1965

KINSTADTER P   ET AL.
   DEMOGRAPHIC VARIABILITY AND PREFERENTIAL MARRIAGE
   PATTERNS. AMERICAN JOURNAL OF PHYSICAL ANTHROPOLOGY 21
   (DECEMBER 1963), 511-519

LANGEVIN R A   OWENS M F
   COMPUTER ANALYSIS OF THE NUCLEAR TEST BAN TREATY.
   SCIENCE 146(NOVEMBER 1964)

LANKFORD PHILIP M
   SPATIAL MODEL BUILDING IN THE SOCIAL SCIENCES.
   PROCEEDINGS OF THE 1972 CONFERENCE ON COMPUTERS IN
   UNDERGRADUATE CURRICULA, 1972, 285-290

LASKA RICHARD M
   THE WORLD MODEL CONTROVERSY—WILL MANKIND SURVIVE.
   COMPUTER DECISIONS 4, (APRIL 1971), 24-27

LAZER S C
   TOWARD A FORMULIZATION OF DEMOGRAPHIC TRANSITION THEORY.
   MICHIGAN STATE UNIVERSITY, DEPARTMENT OF SOCIOLOGY, 1969

LEE HANS E
   TOWARDS RESPONSIBLE USE OF COMPUTERS BY SOCIAL SCIENTISTS.
   PP 213-216 IN PROCEEDINGS OF THE ACM ANNUAL CONFERENCE,
   CHICAGO, AUGUST 1971

LEH ROBERT G
   THE INCORPORATION OF QUANTITATIVE METHODOLOGY IN POLITICAL
   SCIENCE UNDERGRADUATE PROGRAMS.
   8.45-8.50 IN PROCEEDINGS OF A CONFERENCE ON COMPUTERS IN
   THE UNDERGRADUATE CURRICULA, UNIVERSITY OF IOWA, IOWA CITY,
   IA, 1970

LEHMAN RICHARD S   ET AL.
   COMPUTER AIDS IN TEACHING STATISTICS AND METHODOLOGY.
   BEHAVIOR RESEARCH METHODS AND INSTRUMENTATION, 7, 2(MARCH
   1975), 93-102

LEHMAN RICHARD S   BAILEY DANIEL E
   DIGITAL COMPUTING—FORTRAN IV AND ITS APPLICATIONS IN
   BEHAVIORAL SCIENCE.
   NEW YORK, WILEY, 1968

LEVIN M
DISPLAYING SOCIOMETRIC STRUCTURES.
SIMULATION AND GAMES 7(SEPTEMBER 1976) 295-310

LEVIN MARTIN L
A SIMULATION MODEL OF THE FLOW OF INFLUENCE IN SOCIAL
SYSTEMS.
SIMULATION AND GAMES 1, 3(SEPTEMBER 1970), 305-318

LEVIN MARTIN L
SIMULATION OF SOCIAL PROCESSES.
PUBLIC OPINION QUARTERLY 26(FALL 1962), 483-484

LEVONIAN EDWARD   COMREY ANDREW L
FACTORAL STABILITY AS A FUNCTION OF THE NUMBER OF
ORTHOGONALLY-ROTATED FACTORS.
BEHAVIORAL SCIENCE 11(SEPTEMBER 1966), 400-404

LICKLIDER ROY E
SIMULATION AND THE PRIVATE NUCLEAR STRATEGIST.
SIMULATION AND GAMES, (JUNE 1971), 163-172

LINGOES JAMES C
INFORMATION PROCESSING IN PSYCHOLOGICAL RESEARCH.
BEHAVIORAL SCIENCE 7(JULY 1962), 412-417

LOEHLIN JOHN C
INTERPERSONAL EXPERIMENTS WITH A COMPUTER MODEL OF
PERSONALITY.
JOURNAL OF PERSONALITY AND SOCIAL PSYCHOLOGY 2(1965), 580-
584

LOEHLIN JOHN C
COMPUTER MODELS OF PERSONALITY.
NEW YORK, RANDOM HOUSE, 1968

LOVINGOOD P E JR   COWEN DAVID J
THE USE OF COMPUTERS IN GEOGRAPHIC INSTRUCTION AS A MEANS
FOR STIMULATING INTEREST IN STATISTICAL METHODS.
PROCEEDINGS OF THE 1972 CONFERENCE ON COMPUTERS IN
UNDERGRADUATE CURRICULA, 1972, 299-304

LOWRY IRA S
SEVEN MODELS OF URBAN DEVELOPMENT.
RAND CORPORATION, 1967

LOWRY ROY E L
FEDERAL INFORMATION SYSTEMS—SOME CURRENT DEVELOPMENTS.
PP 70-80 IN R L BISCO (ED), DATA BASES, COMPUTERS AND THE
SOCIAL SCIENCES. NEW YORK, WILEY, 1970

LUCAS NANCY C   ET AL.
AN EXPERIMENT IN LEARNING BEHAVIOR USING COMPUTER-ASSISTED
INSTRUCTION.
BEHAVIORAL SCIENCE 15, 5(SEPTEMBER 1970), 447-451

MACHOVER, C
COMPUTER GRAPHICS IN THE UNITED STATES.
COMPUTER GRAPHICS, 1969, 61-83

MACKINNON WILLIAM   MACKINNON MARY K
THE DECISIONAL DESIGN AND CYCLIC COMPUTATION OF SPAN.
BEHAVIORAL SCIENCE 14(MAY 1969), 244-247

MACRE JOHN   SMOKER PAUL
A VIETNAM SIMULATION—A REPORT ON THE CANADIAN ENGLISH
JOINT PROJECT.
JOURNAL OF PEACE RESEARCH 1(1967), 1-25

MAIN DANA B   HEAD SABIN
COMPUTER SIMULATIONS IN THE ELEMENTARY PSYCHOLOGY
LABORATORY.
PP 424-428 IN PROCEEDINGS OF A CONFERENCE ON COMPUTERS IN
THE UNDERGRADUATE CURRICULA, DARTMOUTH COLLEGE, JUNE 1971

MANSER MARILYN E   NAYLOR THOMAS H   WERTZ KENNETH L
EFFECTS OF ALTERNATIVE POLICIES FOR ALLOCATING FEDERAL AID
FOR EDUCATION TO THE STATES.
SIMULATION AND GAMES 1, 2(JUNE 1970), 135-154

MARBLE D F   NYSTUEN J D
AN APPROACH TO THE DIRECT MEASUREMENT OF COMMUNITY MEAN
INFORMATION FIELDS.
PAPERS, REGIONAL SCIENCE ASSOCIATION 11(1963), 99-109

MARKS GREGORY A
DESIGN OF A STATISTICAL SYSTEM FOR A NETWORK ENVIRONMENT.
PP 11-19 IN PROCEEDINGS OF THE COMPUTER SCIENCE AND
STATISTICS EIGHTH ANNUAL SYMPOSIUM ON THE INTERFACE
HEALTH SCIENCES COMPUTING FACILITY, UNIV OF CALIFORNIA
LOS ANGELES, 1975

MARON M E
PROBABILITY AND THE LIBRARY PROBLEM.
BEHAVIORAL SCIENCE 8(JULY 1963), 250-256

MARSCHAK JACOB
OPTIMAL SYMBOL-PROCESSING—A PROBLEM IN INDIVIDUAL AND
SOCIAL ECONOMICS.
BEHAVIORAL SCIENCE 16, (MAY 1971), 202-217

MARTON THEODORE   HELM CARL E
THE ASSESSMENT OF HUMAN PERFORMANCE FOR THE ANALYSIS OF
SPACE MISSIONS.
BEHAVIORAL SCIENCE 12(NOVEMBER 1967), 490-497

MCCRACKEN MICHAEL C
A COMPUTER SYSTEM FOR ECONOMETRIC RESEARCH.
SOCIAL SCIENCE INFORMATION VOL VI 5(OCTOBER 1967), 151-158

MCCRACKEN M C   SONNEN CARL A
A SYSTEM FOR LARGE ECONOMETRIC MODELS.
PROCEEDINGS OF THE ACM ANNUAL CONFERENCE, 1972, 964-974

MCFARLANE PAUL T
SIMULATION GAMES AS SOCIAL PSYCHOLOGICAL RESEARCH SITES.
SIMULATION AND GAMES 11, (JUNE 1971), 149-161

MCGINNIS ROBERT
A STOCHASTIC MODEL OF SOCIAL MOBILITY.
AMERICAN SOCIOLOGICAL REVIEW 33, 5(OCTOBER 1968), 712-722

MCGOVERN P J
COMPUTER CONVERSATION COMPARED WITH HUMAN CONVERSATION.
COMPUTERS AND AUTOMATION 9(1960), 6-11

MCINTOSH STUART   GRIFFEL DAVID
THE CURRENT ADMIS SYSTEM FOR NON-TEXTUAL DATA.
CAMBRIDGE, MASS, CENTER FOR INTERNATIONAL STUDIES, 1967

MCKENNEY JAMES L
COMPUTER BASED MODELS AS ADAPTIVE COMMUNICATORS BETWEEN
DIFFERENT COGNITIVE STYLES.
PP 279-300, IN CHARLES KRIEBEL, RICHARD VAN HORN AND
TIMOTHY HEAMES (EDS), MANAGEMENT INFORMATION SYSTEMS—
PROGRESS AND PERSPECTIVE, PITTSBURGH, PA, CARNEGIE-MELLON
UNIV, 1971

MCLEAN ROBERT S
MICROCOMPUTERS FOR EXPERIMENTAL PSYCHOLOGY.
BEHAVIOR RESEARCH METHODS AND INSTRUMENTATION 6, 2(MARCH
1974), 155-158

MCLEOD JOHN
SIMULATION.
NEW YORK, MCGRAW-HILL, 1968

MCPHEE W N
FORMAL THEORIES OF MASS BEHAVIOR.
NEW YORK, FREE PRESS, 1963

MCPHEE W N
NOTE ON A CAMPAIGN SIMULATOR.
PUBLIC OPINION QUARTERLY 25(JULY 1961), 184-193

MCPHEE W N   SMITH R B
A MODEL FOR ANALYZING VOTING SYSTEMS.
IN W N MCPHEE AND W A GLASER (EDS), PUBLIC OPINION AND
CONGRESSIONAL ELECTION. NEW YORK, FREE PRESS, 1962

MCWHINNEY WILLIAM H
SIMULATING THE COMMUNICATION NETWORK EXPERIMENTS.
BEHAVIORAL SCIENCE 9(JANUARY 1964), 80-83

MEEKER ROBERT J   SHURE GERALD H   COOPERBAND ALVIN S
AN IMPLEMENTATION SYSTEM FOR DESIGNING COMPUTER-BASED
EXPERIMENTS.
PP 169-178 IN PROCEEDINGS OF THE ACM ANNUAL CONFERENCE,
CHICAGO, AUGUST 1971

MEIER RICHARD   DUKE RICHARD
GAMING-SIMULATION FOR URBAN PLANNING.
JOURNAL OF THE AMERICAN INSTITUTE OF PLANNERS, JANUARY 1968,
3-16

MEIER RICHARD L   BLAKELOCK EDWIN H
SIMULATION OF ECOLOGICAL RELATIONSHIPS.
BEHAVIORAL SCIENCE 9(JANUARY 1964), 67-75

MENDELSSOHN R C
THE SYSTEM FOR INTEGRATED STORAGE RETRIEVAL AND REDUCTION OF
ECONOMIC DATA OF THE BUREAU OF LABOR STATISTICS.
SOCIAL SCIENCE INFORMATION VOL VI 4(AUGUST 1967), 197-206

MESSICK DAVID M   RAPOPORT AMNON
COMPUTER-CONTROLLED EXPERIMENTS IN PSYCHOLOGY.
BEHAVIORAL SCIENCE 10(OCTOBER 1964), 378-381

MEYERS EDMUND D JR
TIME SHARING COMPUTATION IN THE SOCIAL SCIENCES.
ENGLEWOOD CLIFFS, N J, PRENTICE-HALL, 1973

MEYERS EDMUND D JR
INTERACTIVE SYSTEMS AND SOCIAL SCIENCE RESEARCH AND
INSTRUCTION.
COMPUTERS AND DATA PROCESSING 9(1971), 3, 151-171

MEYERS EDMUND D JR
PROJECT IMPRESS—TIMESHARING IN THE SOCIAL SCIENCES.
PP 673-680 IN PROCEEDINGS OF THE SPRING JOINT COMPUTER
CONFERENCE, 1969

MEYERS EDMUND D
WE DONT KNOW WHAT WE ARE DOING.
PP 159-170 IN PROCEEDINGS OF A CONFERENCE ON COMPUTERS IN
THE UNDERGRADUATE CURRICULA, DARTMOUTH COLLEGE, JUNE 1971

MILLENSON J R
A PROGRAMMING LANGUAGE FOR ON-LINE CONTROL OF PSYCHOLOGICAL
EXPERIMENTS.
BEHAVIORAL SCIENCE 16, 3(MAY 1971), 248-256

MILLER CURTIS R   CASSADY J MICHAEL   ET AL.
A GENERAL PURPOSE SET OF STATISTICAL PROGRAMS FOR SMALLER
COMPUTERS WITH AN EMPHASIS ON DATA MANIPULATION.
BEHAVIORAL SCIENCE 14(NOVEMBER 1969), 508-512

MILLER JAMES R
DATANAL—AN INTERPRETIVE LANGUAGE FOR ON-LINE ANALYSIS OF
EMPIRICAL DATA.
SLOAN SCHOOL WORKING PAPER, 1967, 275-267

MILLER JAMES R
ON-LINE ANALYSIS FOR SOCIAL SCIENTISTS.
SOCIAL SCIENCE INFORMATION 7, 2(1968), 171-191

MILLER JAMES R   HAIRE MASON
MANPLAN—A MICRO-SIMULATOR FOR MANPOWER PLANNING.
BEHAVIORAL SCIENCE 15, 6(NOVEMBER 1970), 524-531

MILLER M CLINTON
COMPUTATIONAL PROCEDURE FOR FACTORIAL EXPERIMENTS.
BEHAVIORAL SCIENCE 11(MARCH 1966), 148-152

MILLER ROGER F
COMPUTERS AND PRIVACY—WHAT PRICE ANALYTIC POWER.
PP 706-716 IN PROCEEDINGS OF THE ACM ANNUAL CONFERENCE,
CHICAGO, AUGUST 1971

MILLER ROGER F   DAVID MARTIN
SIMULATION IN A TAX MODEL.
PP 236-244 IN PROCEEDINGS OF THE ACM ANNUAL CONFERENCE,
CHICAGO, AUGUST 1971

MILSTEIN JEFFREY S   BOBROW DAVIS B
AN EDUCATIONAL EXPERIMENT.
PP 315-346 IN D B BOBROW AND J L SCHWARTZ (EDS), COMPUTERS
AND THE POLICY-MAKING COMMUNITY. ENGLEWOOD CLIFFS, N J,
PRENTICE-HALL, 1968

MILSTEIN JEFFREY S   MITCHELL W C
DYNAMICS OF THE VIETNAM CONFLICT—A QUANTITATIVE ANALYSIS
AND PREDICTIVE COMPUTER SIMULATION.
PP 163-213 IN W IZARD (ED), VIETNAM—ISSUES AND
ALTERNATIVES. CAMBRIDGE, MASS, 1969

MINTON GEORGE
INSPECTION AND CORRECTION ERROR IN DATA PROCESSING.
AMERICAN STATISTICAL ASSOCIATION JOURNAL,
(DECEMBER 1969), 1256-1275

MOSER ULRICH   ET AL.
COMPUTER SIMULATION OF A MODEL OF NEUROTIC DEFENSE
PROCESSES.
BEHAVIORAL SCIENCE 15(MARCH 1970), 194-202

MOSER ULRICH   VON ZEPPELIN ILKA   SCHNEIDER WERNER
    REPLY TO W R BLACKMORE—SOME COMMENTS ON COMPUTER
    SIMULATION OF A MODEL OF NEUROTIC DEFENSE PROCESSES.
    BEHAVIORAL SCIENCE 17, (MARCH 1972), 232-234

MULLER MERVIN E
    STATISTICS AND COMPUTERS IN RELATION TO LARGE DATA BASES.
    IN MILTON AND NELDER (EDS), STATISTICAL COMPUTATION. NEW
    YORK, ACADEMIC PRESS, 1969

MURDOCK BENNET B   DUFTY PHILIP O   OKADA RONALD
    USING THE PDP-12 IN VERBAL LEARNING AND SHORT TERM
    MEMORY RESEARCH.
    BEHAVIOR RESEARCH METHODS AND INSTRUMENTATION 4,
    2(MARCH 1972), 70-71

MURPHY GEORGE G S
    HISTORICAL INVESTIGATION AND AUTOMATIC DATA PROCESSING
    EQUIPMENT.
    COMPUTERS AND THE HUMANITIES 3(SEPTEMBER 1968), 1-14

NADDOR ELIEZER
    GOMOKU PLAYED BY COMPUTERS.
    BEHAVIORAL SCIENCE 14(JANUARY 1969), 71-73

NAMBOODIRI N K   CARTER L F   BLALOCK H M JR
    APPLIED MULTIVARIATE ANALYSIS AND EXPERIMENTAL
    DESIGNS.
    NEW YORK, MCGRAW-HILL, 1975

NAYLOR, THOMAS H
    COMPUTER SIMULATION EXPERIMENTS WITH MODELS OF ECONOMIC
    SYSTEMS
    NEW YORK, WILEY, 1971

NAYLOR T J   ET AL.
    COMPUTER SIMULATION TECHNIQUES.
    NEW YORK, WILEY, 1966

NEWELL A   ROBERTSON G
    SOME ISSUES IN PROGRAMMING MULTI-MINI-PROCESSORS.
    BEHAVIOR RESEARCH METHODS AND INSTRUMENTATION, 7, 2(MARCH
    1975), 75-86

NIE NORMAN H   ET AL.
    STATISTICAL PACKAGE FOR THE SOCIAL SCIENCES.
    NEW YORK, SECOND EDITION, MCGRAW-HILL, 1975

NIE NORMAN H   ET AL.
    STATISTICAL PACKAGE FOR THE SOCIAL SCIENCES.
    NEW YORK, MCGRAW-HILL, 1970

NOEL R C   JACKSON T
AN INFORMATION MANAGEMENT SYSTEM FOR SOCIAL GAMING.
JOINT COMPUTER CONFERENCE 40, (SPRING 1972), 897-905

OKANE JAMES M
THE APPLICATION OF EMPIRICAL AND COMPUTER TECHNIQUES TO
UNDERGRADUATE SOCIOLOGY RESEARCH COURSES.
PP 8.40-8.44 IN PROCEEDINGS ON A CONFERENCE ON COMPUTERS IN
THE UNDERGRADUATE CURRICULA, UNIVERSITY OF IOWA, IOWA CITY,
IA, 1970

ORCUTT GUY H
DATA NEEDS FOR COMPUTER SIMULATION OF LARGE-SCALE SOCIAL
SYSTEMS.
PP 230-239 IN JAMES M BESHERS (ED), COMPUTER METHODS IN THE
ANALYSIS OF LARGE-SCALE SOCIAL SYSTEMS. CAMBRIDGE, MASS,
MIT PRESS, 1968

ORCUTT GUY H   ET AL.
MICRO-ANALYSIS OF SOCIO-ECONOMIC SYSTEMS—A SIMULATION
STUDY.
NEW YORK, HARPER, 1961

ORCUTT JAMES D   ANDERSON RONALD E
HUMAN-COMPUTER RELATIONSHIPS—INTERACTION AND ATTITUDES.
BEHAVIOR RESEARCH METHODS—INSTRUMENTATION 6, 2(MARCH
1974), 219-222

OWEN GUILLERMO
GAME THEORY.
PHILADELPHIA, W B SAUNDERS, 1968

OZKAPTAN HALIM   GETTING ROBERT
COMPUTER SIMULATION OF MAN-INTEGRATED SYSTEMS.
BEHAVIORAL SCIENCE 8(JULY 1963), 259-265

PAULIK G J   GREENOUGH J W JR
MANAGEMENT ANALYSIS FOR A SALMON RESOURCE SYSTEM.
PP 215-252 IN KENNETH WATT (ED), SYSTEMS ANALYSIS IN
ECOLOGY. NEW YORK, AMERICAN PRESS, 1966

PEARCE, K I
COMPUTER SIMULATION AS AN AID TO THE PLANNING OF
PSYCHIATRIC SERVICES.
CANADIAN PSYCHIATRIC ASSOCIATION JOURNAL 12(1967), 219-
221

PFALTZ JOHN L
MANIPULATION AND DISPLAY OF GEOGRAPHICALLY DISTRIBUTED DATA.
SOCIAL SCIENCE INFORMATION VOL VI, 4(AUGUST 1967), 217-222

PIRRO ELLEN B
UTILIZATION OF CONTENT ANALYSIS AS A METHODOLOGY FOR

POLITICAL SCIENCE ANALYSIS—SOME ILLUSTRATIONS FROM AFRICAN
POLITICS.
PAPER PRESENTED AT THE AMERICAN POLITICAL SCIENCE
ASSOCIATION CONVENTION, SEPTEMBER 1969

PIRRO ELLEN B   CLEVELAND EDWARD
CHANGES IN CONTEXT IN COMMUNICATION AND SMALL GROUP
DECISION-MAKING—SIMULATIONS OF INTERNATION POLITICS.
UNIVERSITY OF MINNESOTA, MINNEAPOLIS, MINN, 1970

POLIT ANDRES C
A SOFTWARE ENVIRONMENT FOR PROBLEM-ORIENTED SYSTEMS.
BEHAVIOR RESEARCH METHODS AND INSTRUMENTATION 6, 2(MARCH
1974), 267-280

POLSON PETER G   CAMPBELL GARY
EXTENDED SCAT.
BEHAVIORAL SCIENCE 17, (NOVEMBER 1972), 558-565

POOL I DE SOLA
COMPUTER SIMULATIONS OF TOTAL SOCIETIES.
PP 45-65 IN S KLAUSNER (ED), THE STUDY OF TOTAL SOCIETIES.
NEW YORK, DOUBLEDAY ANCHOR, 1967

POOL I DE SOLA
BEHAVIORAL TECHNOLOGY.
PP 87-96 IN TOWARD THE YEAR 2018. NEW YORK, COWLES
EDUCATION CORP, 1968

POOL I DE SOLA   ET AL.
CANDIDATES, ISSUES, AND STRATEGIES—A COMPUTER SIMULATION
OF THE 1960 PRESIDENTIAL ELECTION.
CAMBRIDGE, MASS, MIT PRESS, 1964

POOL I DE SOLA   ET AL.
ON THE DESIGN OF COMPUTER-BASED INFORMATION SYSTEM.
SOCIAL SCIENCE INFORMATION 8(1970), 5, 69-118

POOL I DE SOLA   KESSLER A
THE KAISER, THE TSAR, AND THE COMPUTER—INFORMATION
PROCESSING IN A CRISIS.
AMERICAN BEHAVIORAL SCIENTIST 8(MAY 1965), 31-38

POPKINS S L
A MODEL OF A COMMUNICATION SYSTEM.
AMERICAN BEHAVIORAL SCIENTIST 8(MAY 1965), 8-11

PRESS LAURENCE I   ET AL.
AN INTERACTIVE TECHNIQUE FOR THE ANALYSIS OF MULTIVARIATE
DATA.
BEHAVIORAL SCIENCE 14(1969), 364-370

PSATHAS GEORGE
ANALYZING DYADIC INTERACTION.

PP 437-458 IN GEORGE GERBNER ET AL. (EDS), THE ANALYSIS OF COMMUNICATION CONTENT. NEW YORK, WILEY, 1969

PYLYSHYN ZENON W
FINDSIT—A COMPUTER PROGRAM FOR LANGUAGE RESEARCH.
BEHAVIORAL SCIENCE 14(MAY 1969), 248-251

QUINLAN JOHN R   HUNT EARL B
THE FORTRAN DEDUCTIVE SYSTEM.
BEHAVIORAL SCIENCE 14(JANUARY 1969), 74-79

QUILLIAN M ROSS
WORD CONCEPTS—A THEORY AND SIMULATION OF SOME BASIC SEMANTIC CAPABILITIES.
BEHAVIORAL SCIENCE 12(SEPTEMBER 1967), 410-430

RAHMI MORTEZA AMIR   EULENBERG JOHN BRYSON
A COMPUTER TERMINAL WITH SYNTHETIC SPEECH OUTPUT.
BEHAVIOR RESEARCH METHODS AND INSTRUMENTATION 6, 2(MARCH 1974), 255-258

RAINIO K
A STOCHASTIC THEORY OF SOCIAL CONTACTS—A LABORATORY STUDY AND APPLICATION TO SOCIOMETRY.
TRANSACTIONS OF THE WESTERMARCK SOCIETY, VOL 8. COPENHAGEN, MUNKSGAARD, 1962

RANINIO K
SOCIAL INTERACTION AS A STOCHASTIC LEARNING PROCESS.
EUROPEAN JOURNAL OF SOCIOLOGY (1965), 68-88

RAINIO K
A STUDY OF SOCIOMETRIC GROUP STRUCTURE.
VOL 1 IN J BERGER ET AL., SOCIOLOGICAL THEORIES IN PROGRESS.
BOSTON, HOUGHTON MIFFLIN, 1966

RANDOLPH R   COULT A
A COMPUTER ANALYSIS OF BEDOUIN MARRIAGE.
SOUTHWESTERN JOURNAL OF ANTHROPOLOGY 24(SPRING 1968), 83-99

RAPOPORT AMNON   KAHAN JAMES P
COMPUTER CONTROLLED RESEARCH ON BARGAINING AND COALITION FORMATION.
BEHAVIOR RESEARCH METHODS AND INSTRUMENTATION 6, 2(MARCH 1974), 87-93

RASER JOHN R
SIMULATION AND SOCIETY—AN EXPLORATION OF SCIENTIFIC GAMING.
BOSTON, ALLYN AND BACON, 1969

RASKIN JEFFREY F
PROGRAMMING LANGUAGES FOR THE HUMANITIES.
COMPUTERS AND THE HUMANITIES 5, 3(JANUARY 1971), 155-158

RATTENBURY JUDITH   PELLETIER PAULA
DATA PROCESSING IN THE SOCIAL SCIENCES WITH OSIRIS.

ANN ARBOR, MICHIGAN, SURVEY RESEARCH CENTER OF THE
INSTITUTE FOR SOCIAL RESEARCH, UNIVERSITY OF MICHIGAN, 1974

RAY PAUL H   ET AL.
  GAMING-SIMULATIONS FOR TRANSMITTING CONCEPTS OF URBAN
  DEVELOPMENT.
  PAPER PRESENTED AT THE SUMMER MEETINGS OF THE AMERICAN
  SOCIOLOGICAL ASSOCIATION, 1966
RAY WILLIAM
  LOGIC FOR A RANDOMIZATION TEST.
  BEHAVIORAL SCIENCE 11(SEPTEMBER 1966), 405-406

REDDY R   ET AL.
  COMPUTER GRAPHICS IN RESEARCH—SOME STATE-OF-THE-ART
  SYSTEMS.
  AMERICAN PSYCHOLOGIST, 30, 3(MARCH 1975), 239

REISMAN SOREL
  DOMINOES—A COMPUTER SIMULATION OF COGNITIVE PROCESSES.
  SIMULATION AND GAMES 3, (JUNE 1972), 155-164

REISS DAVID   SHERIFF W H JR
  A COMPUTER-AUTOMATED PROCEDURE FOR TESTING SOME EXPERIENCES
  OF FAMILY MEMBERSHIP.
  BEHAVIORAL SCIENCE 15, 5(SEPTEMBER 1970), 431-443

REITMAN WALTER R   ET AL.
  ARGUS—AN INFORMATION—PROCESSING MODEL OF THINKING.
  BEHAVIORAL SCIENCE 9(JULY 1964), 270-280

RESTLE FRANK   SHAFFER W O
  MONITORING EXPERIMENTAL RESULTS.
  BEHAVIOR RESEARCH METHODS—INSTRUMENTATION 6, 2(MARCH
  1974), 262-266

REYNOLDS JAMES H   ET AL.
  AN INTRODUCTORY COMPUTING COURSE FOR UNDERGRADUATES IN THE
  SOCIAL SCIENCES AND HUMANITIES.
  PP 8.5-8.15 IN PROCEEDINGS OF A CONFERENCE ON COMPUTERS IN
  THE UNDERGRADUATE CURRICULA, UNIVERSITY OF IOWA, IOWA CITY,
  IA, 1970

RICHARDSON J T   FRANKEL R S   RANKIN W L
  GAUSTAD G R
  COMPUTERS IN THE SOCIAL AND BEHAVIORAL SCIENCES.
  THE AMERICAN SOCIOLOGIST 6, 2(MAY 1971), 143-152

ROBERTSON GARY N   GEOFFREY C   FERNALD E
  MYERS JOHN G
  DECISION MAKING AND LEARNING—A SIMULATED MARKETING
  MANAGER.
  BEHAVIORAL SCIENCE 15, 4(JULY 1971), 370-379

ROBY T B   BUDROSE C R
  PATTERN RECOGNITION IN GROUPS—LABORATORY AND SIMULATION
  STUDIES.

JOURNAL OF PERSONALITY AND SOCIAL PSYCHOLOGY 2(1965), 5, 648-653

RODEWALD H KEITH
PDP-8/LVE SYSTEM IN AN UNDERGRADUATE ENVIRONMENT.
BEHAVIOR RESEARCH METHOD AND INSTRUMENTATION 4, 2(MARCH 1972), 73-76

ROEMER RICHARD A
SOME INTERACTIVE COMPUTER APPLICATIONS IN A PHYSIOLOGICAL PSYCHOLOGY LABORATORY.
AMERICAN PSYCHOLOGIST, 30, 3(MARCH 1975), 295

ROGERS E M   SVENNING L
MODERNIZATION AMONG PEASANTS.
NEW YORK, HOLT, RINEHART AND WINSTON, 1969

ROISTACHER RICHARD C
ON-LINE COMPUTER TEXT PROCESSING—A TUTORIAL.
BEHAVIOR RESEARCH METHODS AND INSTRUMENTATION 6, 2(MARCH 1974), 159-166

ROME B   ROME S
LEVIATHAN—AN EXPERIMENTAL STUDY OF LARGE ORGANIZATIONS WITH THE AID OF COMPUTERS.
PP 257-310 IN R BOWERS (ED), STUDIES ON BEHAVIORS IN ORGANIZATIONS. ATHENS, GA, UNIVERSITY OF GEORGIA PRESS, 1966

ROOS LESLIE L JR
URBANIZATION AND MODERNIZATION—SOME COMPUTER-BASED EXPERIMENTS.
BEHAVIORAL SCIENCE 15, 4(JULY 1970), 350-358

ROSENTHAL HOWARD
ELECTION SIMULATION.
EUROPEAN JOURNAL OF SOCIOLOGY 6(1965), 21-42

ROSENTHAL HOWARD
VOTING AND COALITION MODELS IN ELECTION SIMULATIONS.
PP 237-285 IN W COPLIN (ED), SIMULATION IN THE STUDY OF POLITICS. CHICAGO, MARKHAM, 1968

ROTHAM STANLEY
PROTECTING PRIVACY—PROS AND CONS.
PP 255-260 IN RALPH L BISCO (ED), DATA BASES, COMPUTERS, AND THE SOCIAL SCIENCES. NEW YORK, WILEY, 1970

RUGGLES NANCY   RUGGLES RICHARD
DATA FILES FOR A GENERALIZED ECONOMIC INFORMATION SYSTEM,
SOCIAL SCIENCE INFORMATION VOL VI, 4(AUGUST 1967), 187-196

RUMMEL RUDOLPH
INTERNATIONAL PATTERN AND NATIONAL PROFILE DELINEATION.
PP 154-202 IN D B BOBROW AND J L SCHWARTZ (EDS), COMPUTERS
AND THE POLICY-MAKING COMMUNITY. ENGLEWOOD CLIFFS, N J,
PRENTICE-HALL, 1968

RYWICK THOMAS
INCREASING STUDENT INTEREST BY THE USE OF INTERACTIVE
COMPUTER SIMULATIONS.
BEHAVIOR RESEARCH METHODS AND INSTRUMENTATION, 7, 2(MARCH
1975), 103-104

SADOWSKY G
POTENTIAL FUTURE DEVELOPMENTS IN SOCIAL SCIENCE COMPUTING.
JOINT COMPUTER CONFERENCE 40, (SPRING 1972), 875-883

SAKODA JAMES M
THE CHECKERBOARD MODEL OF SOCIAL INTERACTION.
JOURNAL OF MATHEMATICAL SOCIOLOGY 2(1971)

SAKODA JAMES M
DYSTAL MANUAL (DYNAMIC STORAGE ALLOCATION LANGUAGE IN
FORTRAN).
BEHAVIORAL SCIENCE 10(APRIL 1965), 182-183

SAKODA JAMES M
A GENERAL COMPUTER LANGUAGE FOR THE SOCIAL SCIENCES.
PP 31-36 IN JAMES M BESHERS (ED), COMPUTER METHODS IN THE
ANALYSIS OF LARGE-SCALE SOCIAL SYSTEMS. CAMBRIDGE, MASS,
MIT PRESS, 1968

SANDUSKY ARTHUR   CAMPOS FRANCIS   LIVINGSTON JAMES
LOVEJOY ELIJAH P   MESSICK DAVID M
INSTRUCTION IN STATISTICS—A REPORT ON THE COMPUTER
LABORATORY FOR ANALYSIS OF DATA IN PSYCHOLOGY.
PP 429-436 IN PROCEEDINGS OF A CONFERENCE ON COMPUTERS IN
THE UNDERGRADUATE CURRICULA, DARTMOUTH COLLEGE, JUNE 1971

SAWYER JACK   SCHECHTER HOWARD
COMPUTER, PRIVACY AND THE NATIONAL DATA CENTER—THE
RESPONSIBILITY OF SOCIAL SCIENTISTS.
AMERICAN PSYCHOLOGIST 23(1968), 810-818

SHECHTER MORDECHAI
ON THE USE OF COMPUTER SIMULATION FOR RESEARCH.
SIMULATION AND GAMES 2, 1(MARCH 1971), 73-88

SCHEUCH ERWIN K   ET AL.
EXPERIMENTS IN RETRIEVAL FROM SURVEY RESEARCH QUESTIONNAIRES
BY MAN AND MACHINE.
SOCIAL SCIENCE INFORMATION VOL VI, 2/3(APRIL, JUNE), 137-167

SCHOLZ KARL W   HALFF HENRY
A DECENTRALIZED COMPUTER NETWORK FOR SUPERVISION OF

MULTIPLE PSYCHOLOGICAL LABORATORIES.
BEHAVIOR RESEARCH METHODS AND INSTRUMENTATION 6, 2(MARCH 1974), 139-142

SCHULZ JAMES H
COMPARATIVE ANALYSIS OF SOCIAL SECURITY SYSTEMS.
ANNALS OF ECONOMIC AND SOCIAL MEASUREMENT 1, (APRIL 1972), 109-127

SCHULTZ RANDALL L   SULLIVAN EDWARD M
DEVELOPMENTS IN SIMULATION IN SOCIAL AND ADMINISTRATIVE SCIENCE.
INDIANA UNIVERSITY AND NORTHWESTERN UNIVERSITY, MARCH 1970

SEDELOW SALLY Y   SEDELOW W A JR
CATEGORIES AND PROCEDURES FOR CONTENT ANALYSIS IN THE HUMANITIES.
PP 487-500 IN GEORGE GERBNER ET AL. (EDS), THE ANALYSIS OF COMMUNICATION CONTENT. NEW YORK, WILEY, 1969

SELFRIDGE OLIVER G
SOCIAL RESPONSIBILITY AND COMPUTERS.
PP 213-218 IN JAMES M BESHERS (ED), COMPUTER METHODS IN THE ANALYSIS OF LARGE-SCALE SOCIAL SYSTEMS. CAMBRIDGE, MASS, MIT PRESS, 1968

SERVICE JOLAYNE
ADAPTING A BATCH-ORIENTED STATISTICAL ANALYSIS SYSTEM TO INTERACTIVE USE—THE CASE OF SAS.
PP 73-76 IN PROCEEDINGS OF THE COMPUTER SCIENCE AND STATISTICS EIGHTH ANNUAL SYMPOSIUM ON THE INTERFACE HEALTH SCIENCES COMPUTING FACILITY, UNIV OF CALIFORNIA LOS ANGELES, 1975

SHANKS J MERRILL
THE QUALITY OF ELECTORAL CHANGE—1952-1964.
PAPER PRESENTED AT THE AMERICAN POLITICAL SCIENCE ASSOCIATION MEETINGS, NEW YORK, 1969

SHEPHERD M J   WILLMONT A J
CLUSTER ANALYSIS ON THE ATLAS COMPUTER.
COMPUTER JOURNAL 11, 1(MAY 1968), 57-62

SHERIDAN THOMAS B
TECHNOLOGY FOR GROUP DIALOGUE AND SOCIAL CHOICE.
AFIPS JOINT COMPUTER CONFERENCE, (FALL 1971), 327-335

SHORTER EDWARD
THE HISTORIAN AND THE COMPUTER.
ENGLEWOOD CLIFFS, N J, PRENTICE-HALL, 1971

SHUBIK GERRIT WOLF   LOCKHART SCOTT
AN ARTIFICIAL PLAYER FOR A BUSINESS MARKET GAME.
SIMULATION AND GAMES 2, 1(MARCH 1971), 27-44

SHUBIK MARTIN   BREWER GARRY
  METHODOLOGICAL ADVANCES IN GAMING—THE ONE-PERSON,
  COMPUTER INTERACTIVE, QUASI-RIGID RULE GAME.
  SIMULATION AND GAMES 3, (JUNE 1972), 329-348

SHURE GERALD H   MEEKER ROBERT J
  LABORATORY EXPERIMENTATION AT THE CENTER FOR
  COMPUTER-BASED STUDIES.
  BEHAVIOR RESEARCH METHODS AND INSTRUMENTATION 6, 2(MARCH
  1974), 241-247

SHURE GERALD H   MEEKER ROBERT J
  A COMPUTER-BASED EXPERIMENTAL LABORATORY.
  ADMINISTRATIVE SCIENCE QUARTERLY 14(JUNE 1969), 286-293

SIDOWSKI JOSEPH B
  INSTRUMENTATION AND COMPUTER TECHNOLOGY—APPLICATIONS AND
  INFLUENCES IN MODERN PSYCHOLOGY.
  AMERICAN PSYCHOLOGIST, 30, 3(MARCH 1975), 191-198

SIDOWSKI JOSEPH B
  MINICOMPUTERS.
  BEHAVIORAL RESEARCH METHODS AND INSTRUMENTATION 2,6
  (NOVEMBER 1970) 267-289

SIM F M   ROSEN L S   KREIDER G D
  INSTANT TURNAROUND AND CONVERSATIONAL COMPUTING AS
  INSTRUCTIONAL TOOLS IN THE SOCIAL SCIENCES.
  PP 142-151 IN PROCEEDINGS OF A CONFERENCE ON COMPUTERS
  IN THE UNDERGRADUATE CURRICULA, DARTMOUTH COLLEGE
  AUGUST 1971

SIM FRANCIS M   ROSEN LAURENCE S   KREIDER GLEN D
  INSTANT TURNAROUND AND CONVERSATIONAL COMPUTING AS
  INSTRUCTIONAL TOOLS IN THE SOCIAL SCIENCES.
  PP 142-151 IN PROCEEDINGS OF A CONFERENCE ON COMPUTERS IN
  THE UNDERGRADUATE CURRICULA, DARTMOUTH COLLEGE, AUGUST 1971

SIMMONS ROBERT F   ET AL.
  TOWARD THE SYNTHESIS OF HUMAN LANGUAGE BEHAVIOR.
  BEHAVIORAL SCIENCE 7(JULY 1962), 402-406

SMITH ROBERT B
  PRESIDENTIAL DECISION-MAKING DURING THE CUBAN MISSILE
  CRISIS—A COMPUTER SIMULATION.
  SIMULATION AND GAMES 1, 2(JUNE 1970), 173-201

SMITH ROBERT B
  SIMULATION MODELS FOR ACCOUNTING SCHEMES.
  AMERICAN BEHAVIORAL SCIENTIST 12, 6(JULY-AUGUST 1969), 21-30

SMITH ROBERT B
  EXAMINATION BY COMPUTER.
  BEHAVIORAL SCIENCE 8(JANUARY 1963), 76-78

SMOKER P
INTERNATIONAL PROCESSES SIMULATION—MAN-COMPUTER MODEL.
NORTHWESTERN UNIVERSITY, EVANSTON, ILL, 1968

SONQUIST JOHN A
MULTIVARIATE MODEL BUILDING.
ANN ARBOR, MICH, BRAUN AND BRUMFIELD, 1970

SONQUIST JOHN A
STIMULATING THE RESEARCH ANALYST.
SOCIAL SCIENCE INFORMATION VOL VI, 4(AUGUST 1967), 207-215

SONQUIST JOHN A
WHY DO WE TEACH WHAT WE TEACH ABOUT COMPUTING.
PP 216-220 IN PROCEEDINGS OF THE ACM ANNUAL CONFERENCE,
CHICAGO, AUGUST 1971

SORKIN ALLEN   ET AL.
AN IBM 7090 FORTRAN PROGRAM FOR 1-THROUGH 4-WAY ANALYSIS.
BEHAVIORAL SCIENCE 10(OCTOBER 1965), 377

SPARKS DAVID L
PROPOSED USAGE OF A SMALL COMPUTER IN AN UNDERGRADUATE
PSYCHOLOGICAL LABORATORY.
PP 8.51-8.54 IN PROCEEDINGS OF A CONFERENCE ON COMPUTERS IN
THE UNDERGRADUATE CURRICULA, UNIVERSITY OF IOWA, IOWA CITY,
1970

SPARKS DAVID L
USE OF A SMALL COMPUTER IN AN UNDERGRADUATE PSYCHOLOGICAL
LABORATORY—A PROGRESS REPORT.
PP 417-418 IN PROCEEDINGS OF A CONFERENCE ON COMPUTERS IN
THE UNDERGRADUATE CURRICULA, DARTMOUTH COLLEGE, JUNE 1971

SPEAR TERRY L   OVERGARD DENNIS   CHRISTIAN THOMAS W
THE CLIPR DISPLAY TERMINAL EXPERIMENT SYSTEM.
BEHAVIORAL RESEARCH METHODS AND INSTRUMENTATION, 7, 2(MARCH
1975), 107-112

SPILERMAN SEYMOUR
STRUCTURAL ANALYSIS AND THE GENERATION OF SOCIOGRAMS.
BEHAVIORAL SCIENCE 11(JULY 1966), 312-318

SPOLSKY BERNARD
SOME PROBLEMS OF COMPUTER-BASED INSTRUCTION.
BEHAVIORAL SCIENCE 11(NOVEMBER 1966), 487-496

STANFIELD J DAVID   CLARK JAMES A   ET AL.
COMPUTER SIMULATION OF INNOVATION DIFFUSION—AN
ILLUSTRATION FROM A LATIN AMERICAN VILLAGE.
UNPUBLISHED PAPER, MICHIGAN STATE UNIVERSITY, DEPARTMENT OF
COMMUNICATIONS, SEPTEMBER 1965

STANG DAVID J   O'CONNELL EDWARD J
THE COMPUTER AS EXPERIMENTER IN SOCIAL PSYCHOLOGICAL
RESEARCH.

BEHAVIOR RESEARCH METHODS AND INSTRUMENTATION 6, 2(MARCH 1974), 223-234

STANNON STAN   HENSCHKE CLAUDIA
STAT-PAK—A BIOSTATISTICAL PROGRAMMING PACKAGE.
COMMUNICATIONS OF THE ACM 10(FEBRUARY 1967), 123-125

STARKWEATHER J A   DECKER J BARRY
COMPUTER ANALYSIS OF INTERVIEW CONTENT.
PSYCHOLOGICAL REPORTS 15(1964), 875-882

STARKWEATHER J A
OVERVIEW—COMPUTER-AIDED APPROACHES TO CONTENT ANALYSIS.
PP 339-342 IN GEORGE GERBNER ET AL. (EDS), THE ANALYSIS OF
COMMUNICATION CONTENT. NEW YORK, WILEY, 1969

STARKWEATHER J A
PILOT—A SYSTEM FOR PROGRAMMED INQUIRY, LEARNING, OR
TEACHING.
PP 501-514 IN GEORGE GERBNER ET AL. (EDS), THE ANALYSIS OF
COMMUNICATION CONTENT. NEW YORK, WILEY, 1969

STEINBERG JOSEPH
SOME ASPECTS OF STATISTICAL DATA LINKAGE.
PP 238-252 IN RALPH L BISCO (ED), DATA BASES, COMPUTERS AND
THE SOCIAL SCIENCES. NEW YORK, WILEY, 1970

STERLING T D   POLLACK S V
INTRODUCTION TO STATISTICAL DATA PROCESSING.
ENGLEWOOD CLIFFS, N J, PRENTICE-HALL, 1968

STERLING THEODOR D   ET AL.
ROBOT DATA SCREENING—A UBIQUITOUS AUTOMATIC SEARCH
TECHNIQUE.
PP 319-333 in R C MILTON AND J A NELDER (EDS), STATISTICAL
COMPUTATION. NEW YORK, ACADEMIC PRESS, 1969

STONE PHILIP J
USERS MANUAL FOR THE GENERAL INQUIRER.
CAMBRIDGE, MASS, MIT PRESS, 1968

STONE PHILIP J
CONFRONTATION OF ISSUES—EXCERPTS FROM THE DISCUSSION
SESSION AT THE CONFERENCE.
PP 523-538 IN GEORGE GERBNER ET AL. (EDS), THE ANALYSIS OF
COMMUNICATION CONTENT. NEW YORK, WILEY, 1969

STONE PHILIP J   ET AL.
THE GENERAL INQUIRER—A COMPUTER APPROACH TO CONTENT
ANALYSIS.
CAMBRIDGE, MASS, MIT PRESS, 1966

STONE PHILIP J   ET AL.
THE GENERAL INQUIRER—A COMPUTER SYSTEM FOR CONTENT
ANALYSIS AND RETRIEVAL BASED ON THE SENTENCE AS A UNIT OF
INFORMATION.
BEHAVIORAL SCIENCE 7(OCTOBER 1962), 484-497

STOUT ROBERT L
MODELING AND THE MICHIGAN EXPERIMENTAL SIMULATION
SUPERVISOR—AN OVERVIEW AND SOME PROSPECTS.
BEHAVIOR RESEARCH METHODS AND INSTRUMENTATION 6, 2(MARCH
1974), 121-123

STROEBEL CHARLES F
COMPUTER DERIVED GLOBAL JUDGMENTS IN PSYCHIATRY.
PP 36-42 IN PROCEEDINGS OF THE ANNUAL MEETING OF THE
AMERICAN PSYCHIATRIC ASSOCIATION, 1969

SUSSMAN MARVIN B   HAUG MARIE R
HUMAN AND MECHANICAL ERROR—AN UNKNOWN QUANTITY IN
RESEARCH.
THE AMERICAN BEHAVIORAL SCIENTIST, NOVEMBER-DECEMBER 1967,
55-56

SWIERENGA ROBERT P
CLIO AND COMPUTERS—A SURVEY OF COMPUTERIZED RESEARCH IN
HISTORY.
COMPUTERS AND THE HUMANITIES 5, 1(SEPTEMBER 1970), 1-22

TAEBER CONRAD
NEW METHODS FOR DISSEMINATING CENSUS RESULTS.
PP 223-229 IN JAMES M BESHERS (ED), COMPUTER METHODS IN THE
ANALYSIS OF LARGE-SCALE SOCIAL SYSTEMS. CAMBRIDGE, MASS,
MIT PRESS, 1968

TAVISS IRENE
THE COMPUTER IMPACT.
ENGLEWOOD CLIFFS, N J, PRENTICE-HALL, 1970

TAYLOR RICHARD L
COGLAB—A COMPUTER SYSTEM DESIGNED FOR HUMAN RESEARCH.
BEHAVIOR RESEARCH METHODS AND INSTRUMENTATION 4,
2(MARCH 1972), 94-95

TEPAS DONALD I
COMPUTER ANALYSIS OF THE ELECTROENCEPHALOGRAM—EVOKING,
PROMOTING, AND PROVOKING.
BEHAVIOR RESEARCH METHODS AND INSTRUMENTATION 6, 2(MARCH
1974), 95-110

THIELE T N   ET AL.
A DIGITAL CARD-PLAYING PROGRAM.
BEHAVIORAL SCIENCE 8(OCTOBER 1963), 362-367

THORESON JAMES   LIITSCHWAGER JOHN
LEGISLATIVE DISTRICTING BY COMPUTER SIMULATION.
BEHAVIORAL SCIENCE 12(MAY 1967), 237-247

TIEDEMANN C E   VANDOREN C S
THE DIFFUSION OF HYBRID SEED CORN IN IOWA—A SPATIAL
SIMULATION MODEL.
MICHIGAN STATE UNIVERSITY, INSTITUTE FOR COMMUNITY
DEVELOPMENT AND SERVICES, TECHNICAL BULLETIN B-44, 1964

TOBLER WALDO R
COMPUTER USE IN GEOGRAPHY.
BEHAVIORAL SCIENCE 12(JANUARY 1967), 57-58

TRYON R C   BAILEY D E
THE BC-TRY COMPUTER SYSTEM OF CLUSTER AND FACTOR
ANALYSIS.
MULTIVARIATE BEHAVIORAL RESEARCH 1(1966), 95-111

TRYON RC   BAILEY D E
THE BC-TRY COMPUTER SYSTEM OF CLUSTER AND FACTOR ANALYSIS.
MULTIVARIATE BEHAVIORAL RESEARCH 1(1966), 95-111

TULLAR WILLIAM L   CASCIO WAYNE F
COMMUNITY RECREATION PLANNING BY COMPUTER SIMULATION—GOLF
IN GPSS.
PP 245-252 IN PROCEEDINGS OF THE ACM ANNUAL CONFERENCE,
CHICAGO, AUGUST 1971

TURSKY BERNARD   SHAPIRO DAVID   ET AL.
AUTOMATIC DATA PROCESSING IN PSYCHOPHYSIOLOGY—A SYSTEM IN
OPERATION.
BEHAVIORAL SCIENCE 11(JANUARY 1966), 64-70

UMPLEBY STUART
THE TEACHING COMPUTER AS A GAMING LABORATORY.
SIMULATION AND GAMES 2, 1(MARCH 1971), 5-26

UNESCO
UNESCO COMPUTERIZED DATA RETRIEVAL SYSTEM FOR DOCUMENTATION
IN THE SOCIAL AND HUMAN SCIENCES.
UNESCO REPORTS AND PAPERS IN THE SOCIAL SCIENCES, NO 27

U S DEPARTMENT OF COMMERCE
NTIS SUMSTST CATALOG—SUMMARY STATISTICAL DATA FILES ON
MAGNETIC TAPE PUBLICLY AVAILABLE FROM THE DEPARTMENT OF
COMMERCE.
NATIONAL TECHNICAL INFORMATION SERVICE NUMBER COM-72-90042

UTTAL WILLIAM R
AN AUTOCORRELATION THEORY OF VISUAL FORM DETECTION—A
COMPUTER EXPERIMENT AND A COMPUTER MODEL.
BEHAVIOR RESEARCH METHODS AND INSTRUMENTATION, 7, 2(MARCH
1975), 87-91

UTTAL WILLIAM R
MISUSE, ABUSE, OVERUSE AND UNUSE OF ON-LINE COMPUTER
FACILITIES BY PSYCHOLOGISTS.
BEHAVIOR RESEARCH METHODS AND INSTRUMENTATION 4,
2(MARCH 1972), 55-60

UTTAL WILLIAM R
REAL-TIME COMPUTERS, TECHNIQUE AND APPLICATIONS IN THE
PSYCHOLOGICAL SCIENCES.
NEW YORK, HARPER AND ROW, 1967

VANDENBERG S G   GREEN BERT F   ET AL.
A SURVEY OF COMPUTER USAGE IN DEPARTMENTS OF PSYCHOLOGY AND
SOCIOLOGY.
BEHAVIORAL SCIENCE 7(JANUARY 1962), 108-110

VANDENBERG S G
TEACHING BEHAVIORAL SCIENTIST HOW TO USE THEIR BRAINS.
BEHAVIORAL SCIENCE 8(JULY 1963), 247-249

VANDEPORTAELA DAN   STIFF RONALD
THE CREATION AND DIFFUSION OF INNOVATIVE USES OF THE
COMPUTER IN SOCIOLOGY EDUCATION.
PROCEEDINGS OF THE CONFERENCE ON COMPUTERS IN
UNDERGRADUATE CURRICULA, 1972, 477-482

VAN GELDER G A   MUNSINGER RON
HARDWARE AND SOFTWARE CONSIDERATIONS IN USING A LINC-8
COMPUTER IN A BEHAVIORAL TOXICOLOGY LABORATORY.
BEHAVIOR RESEARCH METHODS AND INSTRUMENTATION 4,
2(MARCH 1972), 101-102

VAN GELDER PETER
CRT DISPLAYS IN THE EXPERIMENTAL PSYCHOLOGY LABORATORY.
BEHAVIOR RESEARCH METHODS AND INSTRUMENTATION 4,
2(MARCH 1972), 102-103

VARGUS BRIAN C   WHITE DOUGLAS
AN ATTEMPT TO UTILIZE COMPUTERS IN URBAN AFFAIRS EDUCATION.
PP 365-370 IN PROCEEDINGS OF A CONFERENCE ON COMPUTERS IN
THE UNDERGRADUATE CURRICULA, DARTMOUTH COLLEGE, JUNE 1971

VELDMAN DONALD J   ET AL.
COMPUTER SCORING OF SENTENCE COMPLETION DATA.
BEHAVIORAL SCIENCE 14(NOVEMBER 1969), 501-507

VELDMAN DONALD J
FORTRAN PROGRAMMING FOR THE BEHAVIORAL SCIENCES.
NEW YORK, HOLT, RINEHART AND WINSTON, 1967

VELLEMAN PAUL
PROJECT IMPRESS, SEVERAL PERSPECTIVES—INTERACTIVE
COMPUTING AND DATA ANALYSIS.
BEHAVIOR RESEARCH METHODS AND INSTRUMENTATION 6, 2(MARCH
1974), 248-254

VERTINSKY ILAN   ET AL.
FAMILY PLANNING COMPUTER SIMULATION—THE COSTA RICA
POPULATION CONTROL MODEL.
SIMULATION AND GAMES 3, (JUNE 1972), 123-145

WAKSMAN ABRAHAM
THE INTERFACE PROBLEM IN INTERACTIVE SYSTEMS.
BEHAVIOR RESEARCH METHODS AND INSTRUMENTATION 6, 2(MARCH
1974), 235-236

WALLINGFORD E G JR
A VISUAL PATTERN RECOGNIZING COMPUTER BASED ON
NEUROPHYSIOLOGICAL DATA.
BEHAVIORAL SCIENCE 17, (MARCH 1972), 241-248

WATT KENNETH
SYSTEMS ANALYSIS IN ECOLOGY.
NEW YORK, ACADEMIC PRESS, 1966

WEIL ROMAN L JR
THE N-PERSON PRISONER'S DILEMMA—SOME THEORY AND A
COMPUTER-ORIENTED APPROACH.
BEHAVIORAL SCIENCE 11(MAY 1966), 227-233

WELDON ROGER J
A GENERAL PURPOSE PROGRAM FOR THE ANALYSIS OF VARIANCE.
BEHAVIORAL SCIENCE 10(OCTOBER 1965), 481-486

WELSH W A
THE TRIAL SYSTEM—INFORMATION RETRIEVAL IN POLITICAL
SCIENCE.
AMERICAN SCIENTIST 10(JANUARY 1967), 11-24

WERNER RONALD   WERNER JOAN T
BIBLIOGRAPHY OF SIMULATIONS SOCIAL SYSTEMS AND EDUCATION.
WESTERN BEHAVIORAL SCIENCES INSTITUTE, LA JOLLA, CAL,
JANUARY 1969

WESTIN ALAN
INFORMATION SYSTEMS AND POLITICAL DECISION-MAKING.
PP 130-144 IN I TAVISS (ED), THE COMPUTER IMPACT. ENGLEWOOD
CLIFFS, N J, PRENTICE-HALL, 1970

WHITE BENJAMIN W
COMPUTER APPLICATIONS TO PSYCHOLOGICAL RESEARCH—STUDIES IN
PERCEPTION.
BEHAVIORAL SCIENCE 7 (JULY 1962), 396-401

WHITE DOUGLAS R
SOCIETAL RESEARCH ARCHIVES SYSTEM—RETRIEVAL, QUALITY
CONTROL AND ANALYSIS OF COMPARATIVE DATA.
SOCIAL SCIENCE INFORMATION, 7, 3(1968), 79-94.

PART VII
The Bottom Line

34.
Why Correct Programs Give Wrong Answers

Richard V. Andree
University of Oklahoma

Have you ever obtained a wrong answer from a computer? It *is* possible for a correctly working computer, using a valid program based on a mathematically correct technique, to produce invalid answers: a correlation coefficient of 2.76, or a product of positive numbers that is negative, or different values for $Z1 = X*(A + B)$ and $Z2 = (X*A + X*B)$.

Nothing need be wrong with the computer, nor with the program, to produce such wild results. Of course, it is wise to check your programming and your mathematical algorithm first, since these are the most frequent places for errors to hide. Modern computer hardware is so reliable that undetected machine errors are rare, but errors in programs and/or in mathematical analysis are frequent. Still, it is possible for perfectly valid programs using proved techniques to give erroneous results on properly functioning computers.

Statisticians and mathematicians use different number systems to create their algorithms than computers use to run them. This is the crux of the problem.

Know Thy Enemy

Statistics and applied mathematics use number systems called fields. The rational field, the real field, and the field of complex numbers are tools used to devise the mathematical techniques for solving today's applied problems. The actual postulates for a "mathematical field" (or a "ring" or a "group" or an "integral domain") are of more interest to mathematicians than to behavioral and/or social scientists. However, if a scientist who uses mathematics or statistics, in his research, wishes to use a computer, he may run afoul of a little publicized but vitally important conflict. Almost all statistical and mathematical analysis is based on number systems that satisfy the field postulates. However, computer number systems do NOT meet these requirements. It is not surprising that computers sometimes produce rather unexpected results. Correlation coefficients greater than one, sums of squares that are negative, and the mathematically invalid conclusion that B + X = B has many thousands of perfectly valid computer solutions in addition to the expected X = 0 solution of mathematics. The fact that 1/3 + 2/3 does not equal one on most computers does not upset us as much as the observation that for large values of X, $\sqrt{X + 10} - \sqrt{X}$ is *zero* on the computer, whereas it is clearly not zero for any real value X. As computer knowledgeability increases, one often marvels that computer results are as close to correct as they are. The reasons are deeply hidden, and are not our currect project, which is to ferret out some of the gremlins that cause perfectly valid computer programs to produce radically incorrect results when used by mathematically unsophisticated users.

Consider a simple FORTRAN program to produce a sum of squares of a set of integer (whole number) data. On most computers (excepting CDC 6000's and 7000's) FORTRAN integer arithmetic is both faster (more efficient) and more accurate than floating-point arithmetic, so integer arithmetic will be used. Let us compute

$$\text{NSUM} = 14 + 28 + 56 + 112 + 224 \ldots + 7{\cdot}2^{35} = \sum_{N=1}^{35} (7{\cdot}2^N)$$

The value of NSUM is a positive whole number.

[High school algebra calls this SUM a geometric progression with a = 14, r = 2, N = 35 and

$$\text{NSUM} = \frac{a(1\text{-}r^n)}{1\text{-}r} = \frac{14{\cdot}(1\text{-}2^{35})}{1\text{-}2} = 14(2^{35}\text{-}1)$$

but we shall use the computer instead.]

```
      NSUM = 0
      K = 7
      DO 9 L = 1,35
          K = K * 2
          NSUM = NSUM + K
9         CONTINUE
      WRITE (6,10)NSUM
10    FORMAT(1X, 'NSUM = ',I14)
      STOP
      END

      $EXEC
```

NSUM =   -14

However, the program produces the result NSUM = -14. (This result is obtained using WATFIV and also FORTRAN level G on an IBM 370/158. Most computers produce similar obviously fallacious results.)

Let us modify the program slightly to print out intermediate results by inserting instructions 7, 8 as shown below.

```
      NSUM = 0
      K = 7
      DO 9 L = 1,35
          K = K * 2
          NSUM = NSUM + K
7     WRITE(6,8)L,K,NSUM
8     FORMAT(1X,3I15)
9     CONTINUE
      WRITE(6,10)NSUM
10    FORMAT(X, 'NSUM = ',I14)
      STOP
      END
```

The output now is.

L	7×2^L	$\sum\limits_{N=1}^{L} 7 \times 2^N$
1	14	14
2	28	42
3	56	98
4	112	210

5	224	434
6	448	882
7	896	1778
8	1792	3570
9	3584	7154
10	7168	14322
11	14336	28658
12	28672	57330
13	57344	114674
14	114688	229362
15	229376	458738
16	458752	917490
17	917504	1834994
18	1835008	3670002
19	3670416	7340018
20	7340032	14680050
21	14680064	29360114
22	29360128	59720242
23	58720256	117440498
24	117440512	234881010
25	234881024	469762034
26	469762048	939524082
27	939524096	1879048178
28	1879048192	-536870926
29	-536870912	-1073741838
30	-1073741824	2147483634
31	-2147483648	-14
32	0	-14
33	0	-14
34	0	-14
35	0	-14

NSUM =   -14

Clearly, something unexpected has occured here.

Note that when $L = 29$, then $7 \cdot 2^L$ is negative, which is nonsense. Even before this, when $L = 28$, the value of NSUM was negative, which is also nonsense in ordinary mathematics. To examine what has really happened, we need to study a bit more about how computers really work.

The computer uses a 0-1 *binary* number system in which 7 is represented as

$$000 \ldots 000111_2 = 0+0+0+ \ldots +0+1 \cdot 2^2 +1 \cdot 2+1 = 4+2+1 = 7_{10}$$

Thus, 14 is represented as

$$000 \ldots 001110_2 = 1 \cdot 2^3 + 1 \cdot 2^2 + 1 \cdot 2 + 0 = 8 + 4 + 2 = 14_{10}$$

and 28 is represented as

$$000 \ldots 011100_2 = 1 \cdot 2^4 + 1 \cdot 2^3 + 1 \cdot 2^2 + 0 \cdot 2 + 0 = 16 + * + 4 = 28_{10}$$

In this system, the high order (left most) bit is a *sign* bit, and not really part of the number. 0 represents +; 1 represents -. Each multiplication by 2 pushes the three ones another unit to the left. Eventually, the three ones march across the entire number to become $011100 \ldots 0$ which is a large positive number, as it should be.

The next multiplication by 2 produced $111000 \ldots 0$, which one might expect to represent an even larger positive number, as it should. However, the first (high order, left most) bit is the *sign* bit and hence, while

$$011100 \ldots 0 = +11100 \ldots 0_2 = +1879048192_{10}$$

$$11100 \ldots 0 = -11000 \ldots 0_2 = -536870912_{10}$$

This is an explanation of what has happened. The next three numbers obtained are

$1100 \ldots 0 =$ a large negative number
$10000 \ldots 0 =$ the largest possible negative number
$00000 \ldots 0 =$ zero

Similar, but more complicated manipulations also explain why the value of NSUM became negative. $1000 \ldots 0$ is *not* a negative zero, as one might expect, but the "largest" possible negative number instead, due to the way in which the computer does "twos-complement" or "ones-complement" arithmetic.

Mathematicians are familiar with such systems, and often employ them in advanced theory. They are studied in courses of modern abstract algebra and in number theory. The basic idea is simple and is familiar to all. It is known as *modular arithmetic*.

Computer Integer Arithmetic

Computer integer arithmetic has peculiarities that need to be recognized. The so-called "integer arithmetic" system used by most computers, is actually what mathematicians call a *modular system*, under +, -, and * (but not under ÷), and is NOT an integer system. To understand this, consider the arithmetic of the clock.

Two hours after 11:30, it is 1:30, thus 11:30 + 2 hours = 1:30, not 13:30 on 12-hour clocks.

The usual computer integer arithmetic would number the clock hours as 1,2,3,4,5,-6,-5,-4,-3,-2,-1,0 instead of 1,2,3,4,5,6,7,8,9,10,11,12.

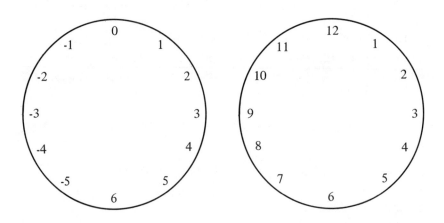

Clock numbered as computer
integer arithmetic.
Modulo 12 system.

Usual clock.
Modulo 12 system.

Thus, 4 + 3 = -5 in this system. Computer integer arithmetic uses a modulus much larger than 12—often it uses 2^{16} = 65536 in which case values range between -32768 and +32767. Some hardware uses 2^{32} = 4294967296, in which case the values range between -2147483648 and +2147483647.

In the latter case there may seem to be small likelihood of overflow into the negative portion of the number system. However, this is exactly what happened on the above $\Sigma 7 \cdot 2^k$ problem. It *can* happen on any system and is likely to occur in obtaining a "sum of squares," for example. This can lead to puzzled users if one is not aware of the possibility.

Another simple example is obtained in computing IN = K * L * M with K = M = 1024, L = 2048.

```
C    WRONG SIGN PROBLEM
     K = 1024
     L = 2048
     M = 1024
     IN - K*L*M
     WRITE (6, 6)K, L, M, IN
     STOP
6    FORMAT (1X, 3I6, 5X, I12)
     END
```

The output is:

$$1024 \qquad 2048 \qquad 1024 \qquad -2147483648$$

where the negative value is correct in a mod 2^{32} system, but not in the system of integers that the user often believes he is using.

Another pecularity of computer integer arithmetic in which it differs not only from ordinary arithmetic but also from the mathematicians' modular arithmetic, is the way in which division is carried out. Computer arithmetic forms 4/5 as a decimal 0.8, and then *drops* the decimal portion, thus

$$4/5 = 0 \qquad \text{while} \qquad 8/3 = 2 \qquad \text{and} \qquad 9/5 = 1.$$

In a modulo 12 system, however, the mathematician would see 9/5 as the solution of the equation $5 * X \equiv 9$ mod 12 and would obtain $X \equiv 9 \equiv -3$ modulo 12 as the solution. If that went by a bit too fast for comfort, don't let it bother you. The critical point is that the computer integer system is *not* the regular whole number system and it is not the mathematical system known as "modular system" or "congruence," either. Although it follows those rules for addition, subtraction, and multiplication, the rule for division is different. If you really want more details, see *Selections from Modern Abstract Algebra* by Andree (Holt, 1971).

Thus, we see the so-called "computer integer" system has some rather strange properties in addition to the easily explainable discrepancies illustrated by $7/2 = 3$ and $2/3 = 0$.

Computer floating-point arithmetic (often called REAL by computer manufacturers) may seem a reasonable solution. "Who needs to worry about a little speed anyway?" say you. Unfortunately, floating-point arithmetic raises more problems than it solves, as we shall see. The reasonable reader may well say, "What should we use then?" The answer is, "You have little choice other than to use the tools you have available—computer integer arithmetic and floating-point arithmetic." They are the only tools available!

It is vital to recognize the limitations and shortcomings of using inappropriate tools. It is possible to open a can of paint with scissors or to pound nails with a crescent wrench or to remove nuts with a pair of pliers, but one should anticipate possible difficulties from misusing tools. However, if they are the only tools available, use them, you must. A realist does not expect as satisfactory results as if he used suitable tools and is alert to possible mishaps. This same caution must be yours.

Floating-Point Arithmetic
(So-Called Computer REAL Numbers)

Let us examine a few points on which the rational numbers of mathematics and statistics differ from the computer floating-point numbers and see how to avoid some obvious pitfalls before examining the floating-point numbers in greater detail.

Fuzzy Zeros

In ordinary algebra either $A = 0$ or $A \neq 0$, but this is not a clear distinction in floating-point systems. $7 + A = 7$ implies $A = 0$ and no other value of A satisfies the equation $7 + A = 0$, in the algebra of rational numbers. However, on a computer there exist literally hundreds of thousands of different values of A such that $7 + A = 7$. $A = 4.731 \times 10^{-11}$ is one such example. On most computers, so is any other A such that $|A| < 10^{-9}$. This distinction is of interest to all computer users as well as to mathematicians, since the question of whether or not a given value is actually zero or merely close to zero is vital in determining whether or not a system of equations has a solution. It is critical in factor analysis and statistics as well as in linear programming and in problems involving systems of equations. The simplest case is the equation A·X = B. If A ≠ 0, a unique solution exists and can be found easily but if A = 0, then if B ≠ 0, no solution exists; while if B = 0, then every value of X is a valid solution of the equation 0·X = 0. However, in computer mathematics, the fundamental question of "When is a computed value of A or B equal to zero?" is *not* easily determined. The zeroes are "fuzzy" to say the least. On the computer there exist values of A ≠ 0 and B such that no computer x satisfies Ax = B. There are others in which one or more computer values of x exist such that Ax = B, but x = B/A (on the computer) is *not* one of these solutions. There also exist values of A ≠ 0 and B such that Ax = B has many valid computer solutions. Computer mathematics is not as simple as manufacturers would have you believe.

Catastrophic Subtraction

On computing standard deviation (i.e., square root of the variance), it is usual to use one of the following formulae:

$$SD = \frac{1}{N} \Sigma(x_i - \bar{x})^2 \qquad\qquad SD = \frac{1}{N} \Sigma(x^2) - N\bar{x}^2$$

In either case a subtraction is included. In a floating-point number system, subtraction of two numbers of almost equal size often results in a catastrophic loss of most of the accuracy present in the original numbers. Similar problems come up in other statistical and non-statistical computations as the following simple example shows.

Write a computer program to compute

$$Y = \sqrt{x + 1} - \sqrt{x} \text{ for large values of } x.$$

Note that for any positive value of x it follows that $\sqrt{x + 1} > \sqrt{x}$, and hence $F(x) = \sqrt{x + 1} - \sqrt{x}$ is *greater than zero*. We now write a program to evaluate $Y = \sqrt{x + 1} - \sqrt{x}$ for large values of x. The neophyte is apt to write:

```
        READ(2,9) X
  9     FORMAT(F    )
        Y=SQRT(X + 1.0) - SQRT(X)
        WRITE(3,8) X,Y
  8     FORMAT(1X, F   , F   )
```

with suitable FORMAT statements in the FORTRAN version. If you input a large value of X, say X = 7.2E10 the computer will either produce 0 as the answer (obviously incorrect) or it will print out a string of digits which are also (not as obviously) incorrect for that value of Y. The trouble is we are subtracting two floating-point numbers of nearly the same size. Whenever this occurs, loss of accuracy is almost guaranteed.

A = .123456789

> Nine significant digits of accuracy in each

B = .123456787

A - B = 000000002 = .2E-8   only *one* significant digit of accuracy left after subtraction, but the computer writes this as .200000000 E-8

In the case of $Y = \sqrt{x+1} - \sqrt{x}$, a very simple algebraic trick permits us to avoid the pitfalls of subtracting two numbers of close to the same size. We *rationalize* the *numerator* (*not* the denominator, as you did in your high school algebra class) multiplying by a "well chosen 1", namely

$$1 = \frac{\sqrt{x+1} + \sqrt{x}}{\sqrt{x+1} + \sqrt{x}}$$

producing:

$$F(x) = \sqrt{x+1} - \sqrt{x} = (\sqrt{x+1} - \sqrt{x}) \frac{(\sqrt{x+1} + \sqrt{x})}{(\sqrt{x+1} + \sqrt{x})} =$$

$$\frac{\sqrt{x+1}\sqrt{x+1} + \sqrt{x+1}\sqrt{x} - \sqrt{x}\sqrt{x+1} - \sqrt{x}\sqrt{x}}{\sqrt{X+1} + \sqrt{x}}$$

$$= \frac{x+1-x}{\sqrt{x+1} + \sqrt{x}} = \frac{1}{\sqrt{x+1} + \sqrt{x}}$$

which has no subtraction left in it at all.

The latter expression is algebraically equivalent to the original function, but involves an addition and a division which cause little difficulty rather than the catastrophic subtraction.

If, in the programs given above, the steps

$$Y = SQRT(X + 1.0) - SQRT(X)$$

is replaced by

$$Y = 1.0/(SQRT(X + 1.0) + SQRT(X))$$

the resulting programs will run and produce very close approximations of the true value of Y. The original programs do not produce even one digit of accuracy for large X.

The technique of "rationalizing the numerator" is used in evaluating limits in calculus. Actually, a competent programmer soon learns through experience to automatically use the various techniques learned for evaluating limits to avoid numerical folly in computer computation. This becomes standard operating procedure.

Let us consider a simpler example to pinpoint the difficulties of catastrophic subtraction.

Example. If W, R, and S are each accurate to 10 significant decimal digits, then how much accuracy will *you* expect in the computed value of

$$Z = W * (R - S)?$$

Let us consider an example (not the worst possible example by any means)

$$W = \underline{4444444444}. \pm .5$$
$$R = 1234567898. \pm .5$$
$$S = 1234567897. \pm .5$$

So each of W, R, S is accurate to 10 significant digits and is in error by no more than ½ unit in the eleventh digit. This is better accuracy than most computers produce in standard precision, and more accuracy than most scientists (even Nobel prize winners) attain. The computed result will be $Z = W * (R - S) = 4444444444$ $* (1234567898. - 1234567897.) = 4,444,444,444.$ which looks accurate to 10 significant digits. However:

> The *biggest* possible true value of Z will be when
> true R = 1234567898.5
> true S = 1234567896.5
> in which case
> biggest possible true $Z = W * (R - S) = W * (2) = 8,888,888,889$
>
> The *smallest* possible true value of Z will be when
> true R = 1234567897.5
> true S = 1234567897.5
> in which case
> smallest possible true $Z = W * (R - S) = W * (0) = 0.$

Thus, although the computed value is 4,444,444,444. the actual true value could be anywhere between zero and over 8.8 billion. What do you think would happen to a bridge if the true value of the stress that could be safely placed on a given member was 4286.4 pounds, but the engineer based his design on a computed strength of over four billion pounds as a safe load? The same collapse can occur in any statistical or theoretical research result in behavioral science, but the rubble is not as public. Don't let it happen to you.

In ordinary algebra it is true that $W * (C + D) = W * C + W * D$ (the distributive property). However, floating-point arithmetic does *not* always have this property, sometimes $W * (C + D) = W * C + W * D$, but sometimes $W * (C + D) \neq W * C + W * D$.

Sums of Many Terms

Many problems in statistics involve the summing of sets of numbers. This seems an innocent, simple, routine task on which to use the power of a computer.

We have already noted the distributive properties do not necessarily hold in computer arithmetic. It is also true that the associative properties cannot be guaranteed. That is, $(A + B) + C$ and $A + (B + C)$ need not be equal, nor is $A * (B * C)$ necessarily the same as $(A * B) * C$. The usual reaction is, "Well, they are almost equal, and that is good enough," or "These things only happen to other people, but not to me." This is a nice comforting feeling, like the belief in a fairy godmother. Experienced programmers have a much more cynical attitude. They say, "If it can happen, it will; and if it cannot, it is apt to happen anyway." Such cynicism is the result of experience.

We are discussing difficulties caused mainly by the way in which the computer does arithmetic—basically this is because all computers have finite word lengths—you cannot represent 1/3 or even 1/10 exactly on a binary computer. When you approximate it, the *little error* on the end will eventually creep up and hit you if you compute long enough. Experienced programmers realize that different results may be obtained when one computes 30! as 30*29*28*27 ... *3*2 or as 2*3*48 ... *28*29*30. Indeed,

$$\text{FACT } 1 = 30*29*28*27 \text{ ... } *3*2 = 265252859 \times 10^{24}$$

$$\text{FACT } 2 = 2*3 \text{ ... } *27*28*29*30 = 265252860 \times 10^{24}$$

Should be equal, but actually differ by 10^{24}, and 10^{24} *is not small*.

This may be a bit hard to demonstrate on some systems, because they contain a "round on output" routine which only prints 6 digits of the accuracy present in the computer.

Order becomes even more important in summation operations. Let us assume your computer keeps 8-decimal digits in standard precision. [It actually computes in binary or hexidecimal or some such system, but it is easier to think in the familiar decimal system.] Our 8-digit precision computer will then add 10000 and .00025 as follows:

```
      10000.000              8 significant digits
+        .00025000000        8 significant digits
      ─────────────────
      10000.000·25000000
```

```
retained by      ·      truncated by
computer         ·      computer &
                 ·        discarded
                 ·
```

Thus, 10000. + .00025 = 10000, sheer nonsense! But, then that's what the computer says, ... so.

Furthermore, the sum $10000.0 + 0.00025 + 0.00025 + 0.00025 + 0.00025$ will be incorrectly computed to be 10000.000.

Whereas, the sum $0.00025 + 0.00025 + 0.00025 + 10000.000$ will be accurately computed as 10000.001. The difference between the two totals here is small, but the general case may be more violent, as we shall see. Consider the common statistical problem of summing a collection of numbers. The two sums below should produce the same result, since the same numbers are added, in reversed order. On most computers the two sums are *not* identical (try it and see).

$$SUM1 = \frac{1}{10^5} + \frac{1}{99999} + \frac{1}{99998} + \ldots + \frac{1}{3} + \frac{1}{2} + 1 = 12.0421400 = \sum_{i=1}^{10^5} \frac{1}{100001-i}$$

and

$$SUM2 = 1 + \frac{1}{2} + \frac{1}{3} + \frac{1}{4} + \ldots + \frac{1}{99999} + \frac{1}{10^5} = 12.07092 = \sum_{i=1}^{10^5} \frac{1}{i}$$

This is because the smaller terms may, if added together first, form a term large enough to affect the total. On the other hand, if each small term is added to a larger cumulative sum, it is simply rounded out of existence. Only the first eight or nine significant digits are retained by the computer.

Also it is more accurate to sum

$$W = \sum_{N=2}^{1000} \frac{1}{(1002-N)^2-1} = \frac{1}{(1000)^2-1} \frac{1}{(999)^2-1} \frac{1}{(998)^2-1} \cdots \frac{1}{3^2-1} \frac{1}{2^2-1}$$
$$= 0.7489998$$

than it is to sum

$$K = \sum_{N=2}^{1000} \frac{1}{N^2-1} = \frac{1}{2^2-1} \frac{1}{3^2-1} \frac{1}{1000^2-1} = 0.7489714$$

Try it and see.

The length of the series needed to show the difference depends upon the system used, but it is always present and often serious.

However, even more accuracy can be obtained by applying a bit of mathematical know-how. Write

$$\sum_{n=2}^{1000} \frac{1}{n^2 - 1} \quad \text{as} \quad \sum_{n=2}^{1000} \left(\frac{\frac{1}{2}}{n-1} - \frac{\frac{1}{2}}{n+1} \right)$$

Note that

$$\sum_{n=2}^{1000} \frac{1}{n^2 - 1} = \sum_{n=2}^{1000} \left(\frac{\frac{1}{2}}{n-1} - \frac{\frac{1}{2}}{n+1} \right)$$

$$= \frac{1}{2} \sum_{n=2}^{1000} \frac{1}{n-1} - \frac{1}{2} \sum_{n=2}^{1000} \frac{1}{n+1}$$

$$= \left[\frac{1}{2}(1 + \frac{1}{2}) + \frac{1}{2} \sum_{n=4}^{1000} \frac{1}{n-1} \right] - \left[\frac{1}{2} \sum_{n=2}^{998} \frac{1}{n+1} + \frac{1}{2} \left(\frac{1}{1000} + \frac{1}{1001} \right) \right]$$

[by removing two terms from each Σ]

We now make the substitution K = n + 2 in the second Σ

$$\frac{1}{2} + \frac{1}{4} - \frac{1}{2000} - \frac{1}{2002} + \frac{1}{2} \sum_{n=4}^{1000} \frac{1}{n-1} - \frac{1}{2} \sum_{K=4}^{1000} \frac{1}{K-1}$$

The last two series add out, leaving:

$$= \frac{1}{2} + \frac{1}{4} - \frac{1}{2000} - \frac{1}{2002}$$

$$= 0.5 + 0.25 - 0.0005 - 0.0004995004995...$$

$$= 0.75 - 0.0009995004995...$$

$$= 0.7490004995004^+$$

Thus, we can produce a result as exact as needed by using high school mathematics and common sense. Such ingenious devices are common "tricks of the trade" in any programmer's life. Without them, brute force is seldom effective for long.

We examine one more problem that arises in using computers on large summation problems. We examine the infinite series:

$$\Sigma \frac{1}{n} = 1 + \frac{1}{2} + \frac{1}{3} + \frac{1}{4} + \frac{1}{5} + \frac{1}{6} + \frac{1}{7} + \frac{1}{8} + \frac{1}{9} + \frac{1}{10} + \frac{1}{11} + \frac{1}{12} + ... + \frac{1}{n} + ...$$

This is a classic example of a series whose terms keep getting smaller (approach zero) as N increases, but whose SUM of the first N terms increases without bound as N increases. (See any calculus text.)

A very simple computer program can produce interesting results. We sum the series and print the sum after each set of 1,000,000 terms have been added. The program is designed to terminate after 10 lines of output, but the reader may well wish to terminate it sooner as he watches the output.

A possible program is:

```
 10  N = 0.0
 20  S = 0.0
 30  FOR K = 1 TO 10
 40  FOR L = 1 TO 1000000
 50  N = N + 1
 60  S = S + 1 N
 70  NEXT L
 80  PRINT N    S
 90  NEXT K
100  END
```

Whether or not this program runs at all on your computer depends in part on the word size. The point is that the series $\Sigma \frac{1}{n}$ which is known to *diverge* seems to *converge* when you run it on the computer. If you ran a program to compute $\sum\limits_{n=1}^{\infty} \frac{1}{n}$ and it produced consistent results that suggested convergence, wouldn't you be tempted to accept the answer, if you didn't already know that actually $\sum \frac{1}{n}$ diverged (gets larger than any preassigned bound as n increases)?

Output:

1000000	13.97111
2000000	14.01743
3000000	14.01743
4000000	14.01743
5000000	14.01743

The Distribution of Floating-Point Numbers

The real numbers of mathematics form a continuous, dense set, like the points on a line.

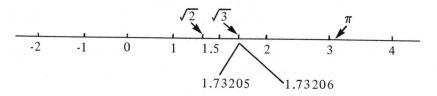

The word "dense" means between any two numbers, there is another number that also belongs to the set. This means between any two numbers there are actually infinitely many numbers in the set.

Actually, the real numbers are more than dense, they are also continuous. If you have studied calculus, you know the meaning of this word. If not, let us postpone its full meaning until you have. The rational numbers are a subset of the real numbers—namely, those real numbers of the form a/b where a and b are integers with b $\neq$ 0. There are many fewer rational numbers than there are real numbers, but even so, the rational numbers still form a dense, but not a continuous, set. (What does "dense" mean?) Before you continue, name three real numbers other than $\sqrt{2}$ and π which are *not* included in the set of rational numbers.

The floating-point numbers that computers use (often referred to as real numbers by computer companies) do not even form a dense set, let alone a continuous set. Furthermore, the set of floating-point numbers is only finite. The really critical point is that floating-point numbers are not uniformly distributed on the number line.

Let us examine this in more detail. Floating-point numbers are a finite subset of the rational numbers and hence, automatically not dense in any region, however small. It follows that given any floating-point number (except the largest one), there will be a "next larger floating-point number."

Consider a floating-point number lying between 0 and 1 inclusive, say: $1.00000 * 10^{-38}$.

For ease in understanding, we have assumed here that computers carry six significant *decimal* digits of accuracy. Actually, the numbers inside the computer are stored as binary numbers of between 12 and 60 bits depending upon the computer. One bit in each case is reserved for the sign of the number. These binary bits correspond to somewhere between 5 and 7 significant decimal digits for standard precision, or between 9 and 12 decimal digits of accuracy for extended precision. Although most computers work in some modified binary system, we use the decimal notation in our explanation. The theory is valid in any case.

In this case, the adjacent floating-point number (i.e., next larger floating-point number) would be: $1.00001 * 10^{-38}$ and the difference (distance) between these two consecutive floating-point numbers is:

$$.00001 * 10^{-38} = 10^{-43} = 0.\underbrace{00000000000000000000000000...000001}_{\text{42 zeros}}$$

which is rather small.

On the other hand, consider two large adjacent floating-point numbers, say

$$1.00000 * 10^{+38}$$

$$1.00001 * 10^{+38}$$

In this case, the difference (distance) between these two consecutive floating-point numbers is

$$.00001 * 10^{+38} = 10^{+33} = 1\underset{\text{33 zeros}}{\underline{00000000000000000000...000000000.}}$$

which is a huge number in almost anyone's language. (It is larger than the world GNP multiplied by our total national debt in mills, for example—or larger than the number of grains of sand in all the oceans, lakes, beaches and deserts in the world.)

The critical thing to note is the floating-point numbers are not uniformly spaced.

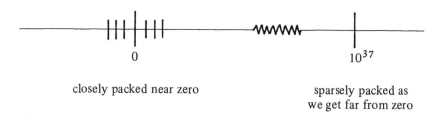

closely packed near zero   sparsely packed as
we get far from zero

This means the difference between two large floating-point numbers cannot be computed very accurately by direct subtraction. Much nonsense that has been written concerning numerical analysis and computer related mathematics can be avoided by simply understanding this one fact. I repeat, not only is the set of floating-point numbers not dense, they are finite in number. Furthermore, floating-point numbers are not distributed uniformly along the number axis.

The $\sqrt{x+1} - \sqrt{x}$ problem is an example of what happens. Either both $X + 1$ and X are mapped onto the same point of the floating-point system, or they are mapped on different adjacent points that are actually very far apart (say 10^{33} units apart instead of 1 unit apart).

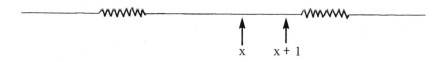

The difficulty in the W*(R-S) problem is different in nature. The basic nature of inexact arithmetic is involved here and no matter whether done by computer, desk calculator, or pencil and paper if two approximate values that are close to the same size are subtracted, accuracy goes down the drain, no matter how much accuracy was in the original data.

No cure for these problems seems to be in sight. The only way to avoid the difficulty is to *avoid subtraction* whenever possible.

35.
Effective vs. Efficient Computing

Richard V. Andree
University of Oklahoma

There are some very simple, basic considerations of good programming practice that need to be taught, and can be presented with little effort or strain. Mainly, they involve common sense and an appreciation of how a computer computes.

An *effective* computer program is one that produces the desired results at a cost (your effort plus computer time) you are willing to pay. Such a program may or may not also be *efficient*. Many programmers feel that if a program produces the result the user desires, at a price he is willing to pay, there is no reason to bother with making the program efficient as well as *effective*. In many cases they are correct, but in others they err seriously. The primary question is one of economics and common sense. Fortunately, it is rather simple to write more efficient programs.

The Principle of Mutual Superiority:

"Anything you programmed, I can program better",

"Anything I programmed, you can program better";

and its corollary:

"Anything I programmed, I can program better,"

are probably true, but are not always applicable. Many "one-time-only" jobs using less than $10.00 in computing time are not worth reprogramming—especially if a modicum of programming good sense was used in writing the original code.

I propose the following two tests to determine whether or not a program is worth rewriting:

1. If the program will use a *total* of less than $10.00 worth of computing time in a month, it is probably not worth rewriting.

2. If a computer programmer cannot materially improve a program by investing *ten times the monthly running time* of the program in an effort to improve it, then it is probably efficient enough.

This means if a program with a 60-second monthly run time cannot be materially improved by 10 minutes of extra effort, it is classified as efficient, providing it is effective (produces desired results at a palatable cost). An elaborate tape-search and data massaging program (or a payroll) that uses 45 minutes of CPU time would not be rated as efficient unless a competent programmer was unable to improve it with 7.5 hours effort. This is realistic in today's economy and is well worth teaching students who will eventually seek employment. Employers do not take programming efficiency as lightly as do many academicians. If your students are to be employable, you must teach them the value of efficient as well as effective programming. Little saving can be realized on "one-time-only" programs using less than 5 minutes of CPU time. However, valuable savings can be made on much shorter programs that are run frequently. (An Oklahoma engineering firm estimates that one of my students saved $800.00 a month ($9,600.00 a year) by cutting 1/1000 *second* off a frequently-used hyperbolic function routine.)

Neither you nor your students need be experts to write reasonably efficient programs. A few common sense rules can make a big difference in run time on your programs. Won't you at least consider them—for your students' benefit, if not your own? The differences between inefficient and efficient programs are simple to teach and even easier to employ. If you are interested either in improving the employability of your students or in increasing their respect for your knowledge, half a dozen common sense principles will do the job. Here are some suggestions for FORTRAN. Most apply to BASIC, too.

1. *Don't compute (or read) a value more than once. If you will need it again, store it.*

Example 1.1

In a program to compute mean = $\bar{x} = \dfrac{1}{N} \Sigma\, x_i$

and standard deviation = $\sqrt{\dfrac{\Sigma (x_i - \bar{x})^2}{N}}$

Don't compute $\bar{x}$ first and then compute SD, instead use the equivalent formula

$$SD = \sqrt{\dfrac{\Sigma (x_i)^2 - \bar{x}^2}{N}}$$

and compute both Σx_i and $\Sigma (x_i)^2$ in the same fetch of the x_i.

Example 1.2

If you need to compute

$Y = 7(e^x)^4 + 5(e^x)^3 - 8(e^x)^2$,

don't use $Y = 7.*EXP(x)**4. + 5.*EXP(x)**3. - 8.*EXP(x)**2.$

Use $E = EXP(x)$

$Y = ((7.*E+5.)*E-8.)*E*E$

instead and save three ways. [Hey—what three ways is he talking about? I see the $E = EXP(x)$ and the use of nested parentheses to cut down on multiplications, but what is the third savings?]

2. Use the faster forms when feasible.

Examples

$A + A$ is faster than $2.0*A$ which is faster than $2*A$.
$.2*B$ is faster than $B/5.0$. (Avoid division if convenient.)
$C*C*C*C$ is faster than $C**4$ which is much faster than $C**4.0$.
$SQRT(x)$ is faster than $x**.5$.
$1.23456E12$ is faster than $1.23456*10**23$.
The "shell sort" is much faster than the usual "bubble sort" (Knuth).

3. *Use subscripted variables with caution.*

Subscripted variables are a blessing when needed, but an extravagance when not essential. It often requires more time and more arithmetic to locate a subscripted variable than to do the computation after you get it. The difference becomes more pronounced if double or triple subscripted variables are used.

Example 3.1

Don't use a subscripted variable inside a DO-loop if the subscript is not changing. In finding the row-sums of a matrix, for example:

```
      DO   12  I = 1,500
            S(I)  = 0.0
      DO   10  J = 1,600
10    S(I) = S(I) + B(I,J)
12    CONTINUE
```

is better accomplished as:

```
      DO   12  I = 1,500
            V = 0.0
      DO   10  J = 1,600
10    V = V + B(I,J)
12    S(I) = V
```

or much better yet as:

```
      DO   12  I = 1,500
            V = 0.0
      DO   10  J = 1,596,5
10    V = V + B(I,J) + B(I,J+1) + B(I,J+2) + B(I,J+3) + B(J+4)
12    S(I) = V
```

since the latter program requires only 1/5 as much expensive loop-opening and loop-closing activity.

4. *DO-loops (FOR–NEXT loops in BASIC).*

DO-loops are easy to improve.

If your program uses more than one DO-loop with the same limits, see if you can eliminate the extra DO-loops. Closing and opening loops is costly.

You can also reduce the number of times through a DO-loop by repeating instructions and incrementing in larger steps.

Replace

```
    S = 0.0
    DO 3 K = 1,1500
3   S = S + X(K)
```

by

```
    S = 0.0
    DO 3 K = 1,500,3
3   S = S + X(K) + X(K + 1) + X(K + 2)
```

If your program contains long and/or nested DO-loops use smaller limits on your debugging runs.

Use

```
    DO   12   K = 1,3
    DO   10   L = 1,2
```

rather than

```
    DO   12   K = 1,300
    DO   10   L = 1,200
```

and then change it when debugging is complete. You can run 10,000 low-limit double loops (above) for the cost of running one high-limit double loop. Don't be so egocentric as to think your programs will run the first time. This is a sign of a rank amateur.

Bury the most frequently executed DO loop, deep in a nested set. It saves initialization costs.

Remember if A is a DIMENSIONed variable,

```
    READ(  )A
    WRITE(  )A
```

are faster than the implied DO-loops

```
READ(   ) (A(I)  I = 1  200)
WRITE(   ) (A(I)  I = 1  200)
```

which are faster than actual written out DO-loops.

5. *Don't use DOUBLE PRECISION if single precision will do.*

It is often possible to carry out one small critical part of a computation in double precision and the rest in single precision to achieve higher accuracy without vast increase in cost (Forsythe and Moler, 1967). This is true, for example, in solving large systems of linear equations—a common occurrence in many applications.

Note that this does not apply to IBM 1130 "extended precision" which is actually faster than their standard precision (but takes more core storage to run).

6. *Your program should check the data for reasonableness.*

This is particularly vital if data are from a data bank. Don't let "sex 5" slip by if you are using 0 and 1 as sex indicators. Don't let a man work 170 hours in one week. Be suspicious if he works more than 50 hours. Put in "warning zones" when the data boundary is fuzzy. Don't let your program accept garbage, or else accept garbage output.

7. *Avoid mixed arithmetic expressions.*

Most programmers recognize that A = 5/7 will give A = 0.0 and avoid such slips, but the same programmer may blythly use B = 4 * X - 3*M/(Z+2) without realizing the compiler must convert each of the integer values and the integer variable M into floating-point form to accomplish the desired arithmetic. It is more efficient as well as effective to avoid unexpected 5/7 type blunders by writing

```
FM = M
B = 4.0*X - 3.0*FM/(Z+2.0)
```

Don't mix computer integer and computer real arithmetic on the right side of an equals sign.

Let us now examine ways some of these suggestions can be applied in a simple program.

Problem

Determine all of the three-digit whole numbers (positive integers) for which the sum of the cubes of the digits of the number equal the number.

Since $1^3 + 5^3 + 3^3 = 1 + 125 + 27 = 153$ we know such numbers do exist.

Inefficient First Attempt at Solution

The following program, written in BASIC, produced the results indicated.

Let H, T and U represent the hundreds, tens and units digits. The original number is $N = 100*H + 10*T + U$ and the sum of the cubes of the digits is $S = H↑3 + T↑3 + U↑3$.

The program uses a "brute force" technique in which we simply try all possible three-digit numbers to see if $N = 100*H + 10*T + U$ and $S = H↑3 + T↑3 + U↑3$ are equal and print out those N that do satisfy the given condition. We let H take on the values from 1 to 9 while T and U take on values from 0 to 9. (Why?) The values HTU advance much as a car odometer would in going from 100 to 999 with tests occuring at each value.

```
10   REM FIRST TRIAL AT SUM OF CUBES OF DIGITS = NUMBER
20   FOR H = 1 TO 9
30      FOR T = 0 TO 9
40         FOR U = 0 TO 9
50            LET N = 100*H + 10*T + U
60            LET S = H↑3 + T↑3 + U↑3
70            IF S <> N THEN 80
75            PRINT N;
80         NEXT U
90      NEXT T
100  NEXT H
110  PRINT "   END OF DIGIT↑3 PROBLEM   FIRST TRIAL."
120  END
```

The reader should study the above program with care and be sure it will perform as desired before continuing.

The actual output from the program is:

RUN

153   370   371   407   END OF DIGIT↑3 PROBLEM   FIRST TRIAL.
END OF PROGRAM

The time elapsed in executing this program on the WANG 3300 was 3 minutes and 8 seconds (with only one terminal in operation). On a NOVA it took 40 seconds. On an IBM 370 using ITF, 11.7 seconds of CPU time was used, but no answers were obtained.

Try it on your computer. If you don't get any numbers out (you know that 153 is a solution) insert the following instruction:

65   PRINT N S

and look at the output. Many computers use EXP(3.*LOG(W)) for W↑3 or W**3 even though the exponent is integral. Some round on output and hence, print (N;S) = 153; 153) even though internally the N ?=? S fails since internally S = 152.99999999999 or some such. This is the time to investigate your own computer's arithmetic pecularities.

We can remove this bug by using

$$S = H*H*H + T*T*T + U*U*U$$

which is both more efficient (faster) and more effective (more apt to produce correct answers).

If you are only running the program once, this would not be an intolerable amount of time to spend, but the given program does violate several cardinal principles of efficient programming. Perhaps the most serious violation is of suggestion #1:

NEVER RECOMPUTE VALUES IF YOU CAN
FEASIBLY AVOID DOING SO.

The given program computes

$$N = H^3 + T^3 + U^3$$

each time it goes through the inside (FOR U = 0 to 9 ... NEXT U) loop for a total of 3x2x900 = 5400 time-consuming multiplications and 1800 additions. If each digit is cubed directly after the FOR loop for that digit, it would cut this down from 5400 multiplications to 18 + 180 + 1800 = 1998 multiplications and the same 1800 additions (which take much less time than multiplications do). *This saving of 3402 multiplications is the difference between a complete hack programmer and a respectable amateur.*

We can also save some time by using H*H*H rather than the slower H↑3 instruction. The following program will do this. An output identification statement has also been added.

```
10   REM FASTER VERSION OF SUM OF CUBES OF DIGITS =
     NUMBER
15   PRINT "THE THREE DIGIT INTEGERS N FOR WHICH
     THE SUM OF THE CUBES OF"
16   PRINT "THE DIGITS OF N IS EQUAL TO N ARE   "
20   FOR H = 1 TO 9
25     LET H3 = H*H*H*
26     LET H1 = 100*H
30     FOR T = 0 TO 9
35       LET T3 = T*T*T
36       LET T1 = 10*T
40       FOR U = 0 TO 9
50         LET N = H1 + T1 + U
60         LET S = H3 + T3 + U*U*U
70         IF S <> N THEN 80
75         PRINT N;
80       NEXT U
90     NEXT T
100  NEXT H
110  PRINT "    END OF SECOND VERSION OF DIGIT↑3 PROBLEM."
120  END
```

Output:

THE THREE DIGIT INTEGERS N FOR WHICH THE SUM OF THE CUBES OF THE DIGITS OF N IS EQUAL TO N ARE

       153   370   371   407
END OF SECOND VERSION OF DIGIT↑3 PROBLEM.

The WANG time used in this revised version is 0 minutes and 47 seconds as compared with 188 seconds for the original program. (NOVA time is about 8 or 9 seconds and the IBM 370 under ITF is about the same as NOVA). This may seem a small savings in seconds, but a savings of 75% of the computing time is very worthwhile, especially when it was so simply achieved. It is quite possible to further reduce the computing time on this problem, but since it is to be run only once, we may have achieved sufficient efficiency to be effective.

You should encourage your students to think about the efficient use of a computer if they plan to use one. The use of human intelligence as a computer-saving device is what makes one programmer worth three times as much as another with the same experience. If you can save only ten minutes per working day on a computer worth $600 an hour, you have saved between $2000 and $3000 per month. No wonder employers are willing to pay an extra $1000 per month to a really able programmer over and above what they will pay an ordinary programmer. Which will your students be?

References

Forsythe, G.E., and C.B. Moler. *Computer Solution of Linear Algebraic Systems*. Englewood Cliffs, N.J.: Prentice Hall, 1967.

Knuth, D.E. *The Art of Computer Programming, Vol. 2*. Reading, Mass.: Addison-Wesley, 1969.